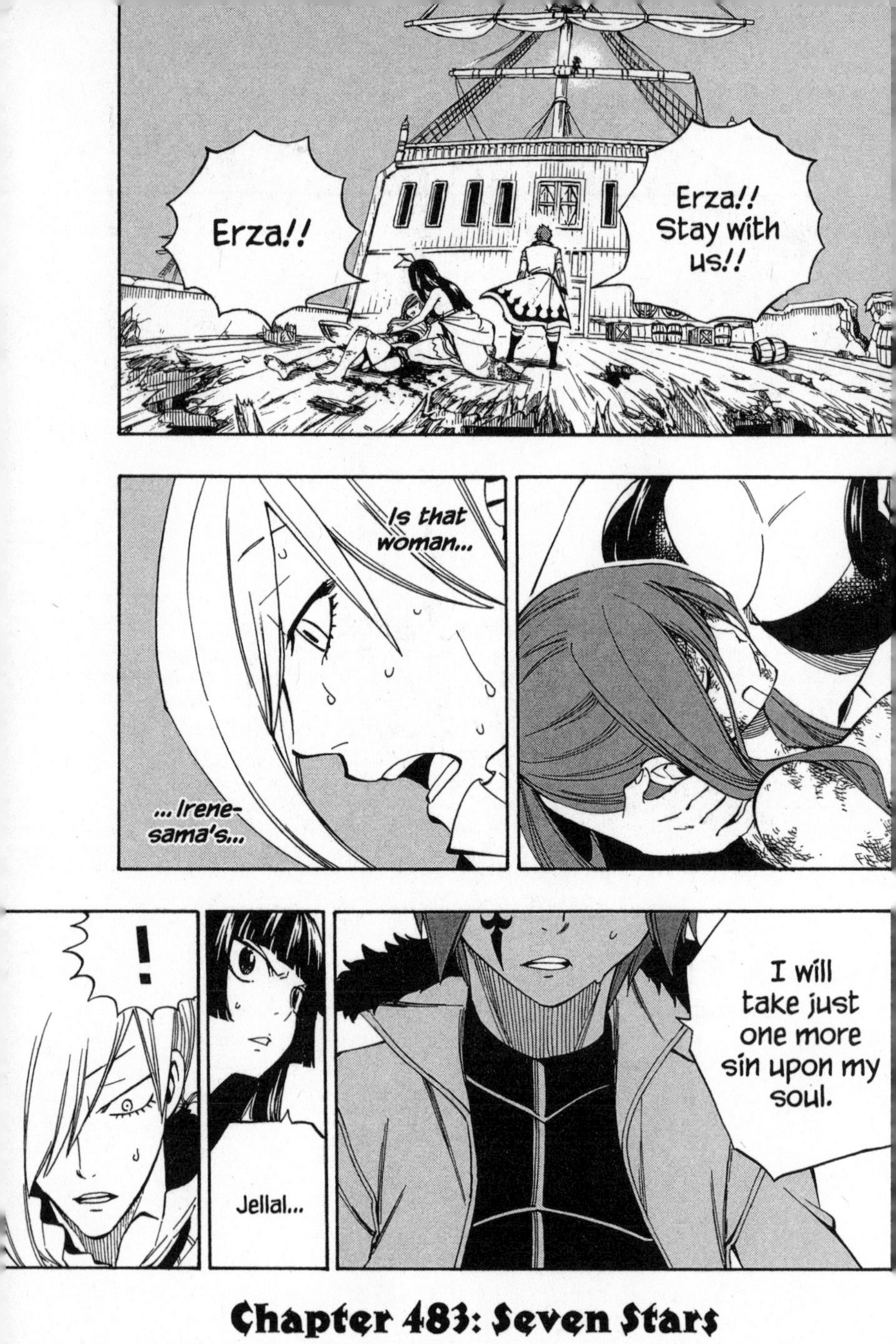
Erza!! Stay with us!!
Erza!!
Is that woman...
...Irene-sama's...
I will take just one more sin upon my soul.
Jellal...
!

Chapter 483: Seven Stars

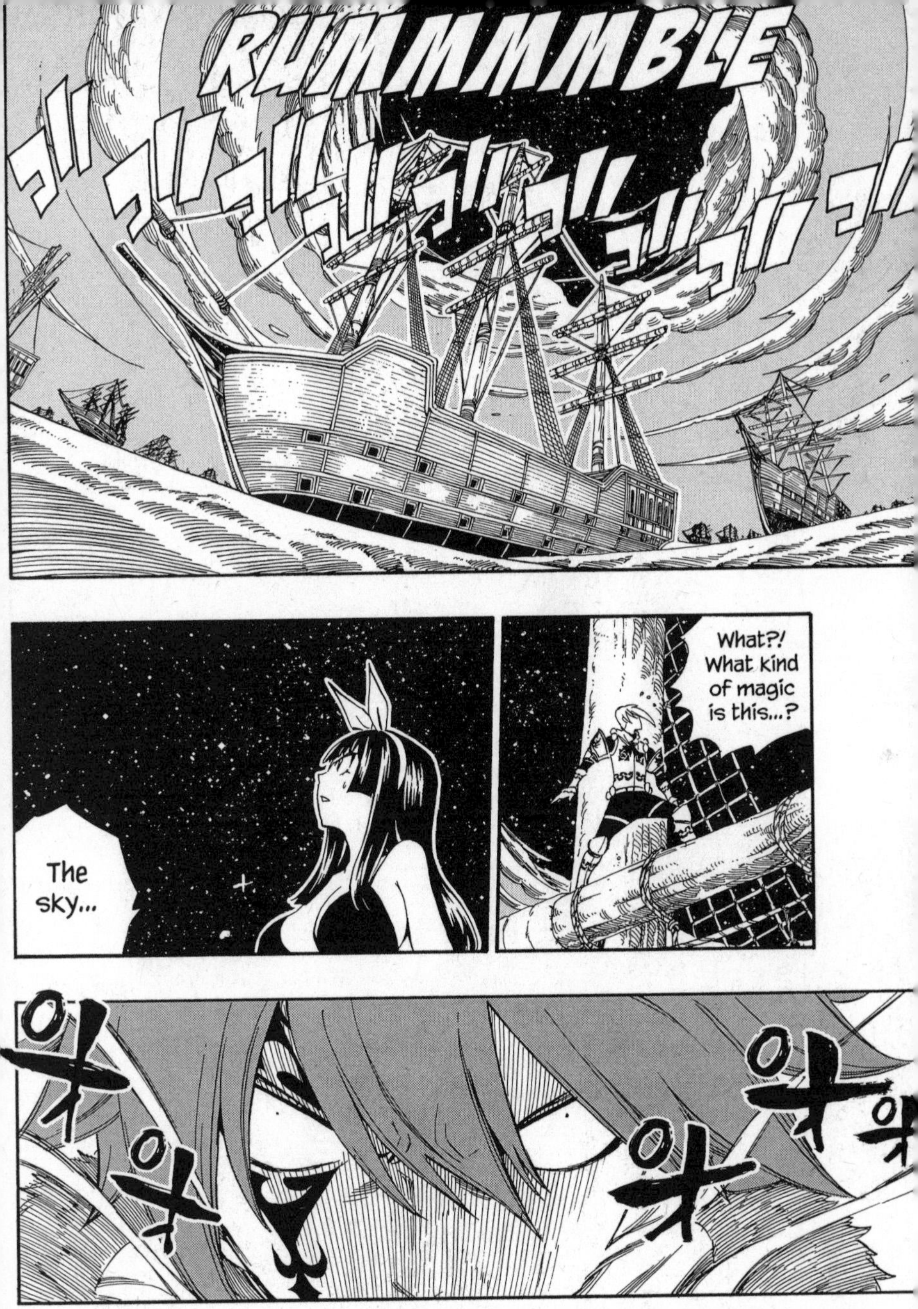
RUMMMMMBLE
What?! What kind of magic is this...?
The sky...

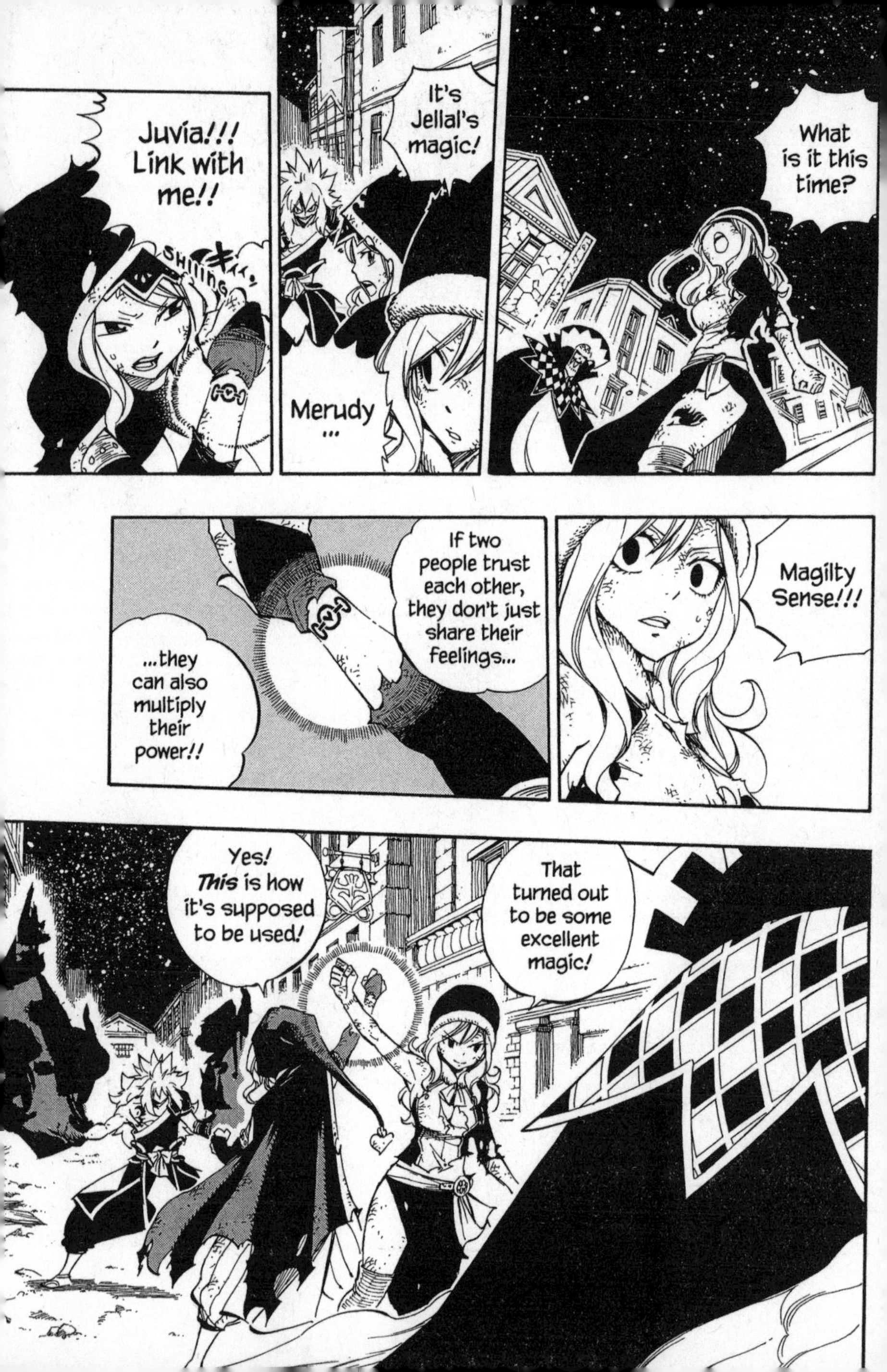
What is it this time?
It's Jellal's magic!
Merudy ...
Juvia!!! Link with me!!
SHIIING
Magilty Sense!!!
If two people trust each other, they don't just share their feelings...
...they can also multiply their power!!
That turned out to be some excellent magic!
Yes! *This* is how it's supposed to be used!

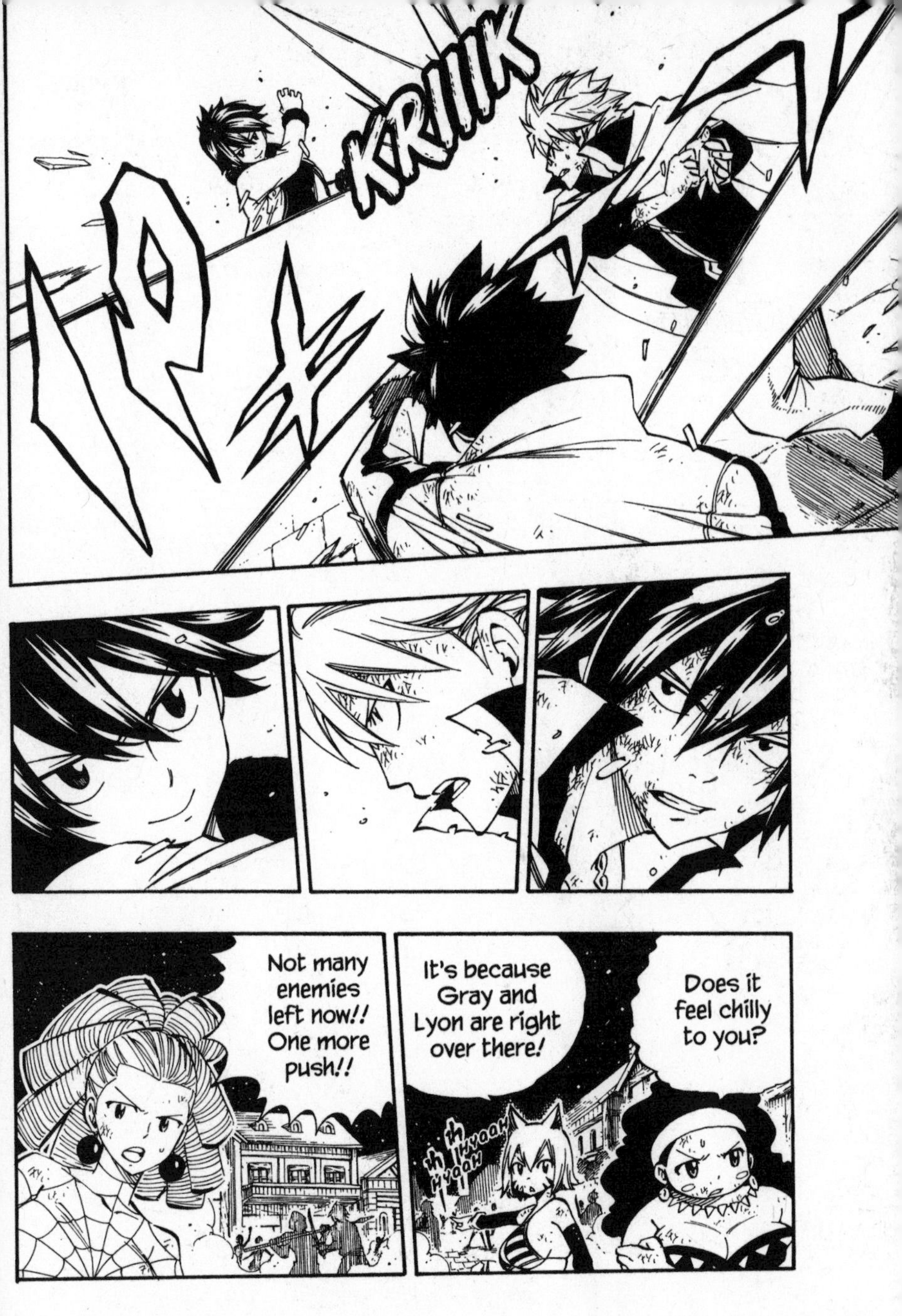
KRIIIK
Does it feel chilly to you?
It's because Gray and Lyon are right over there!
Not many enemies left now!! One more push!!

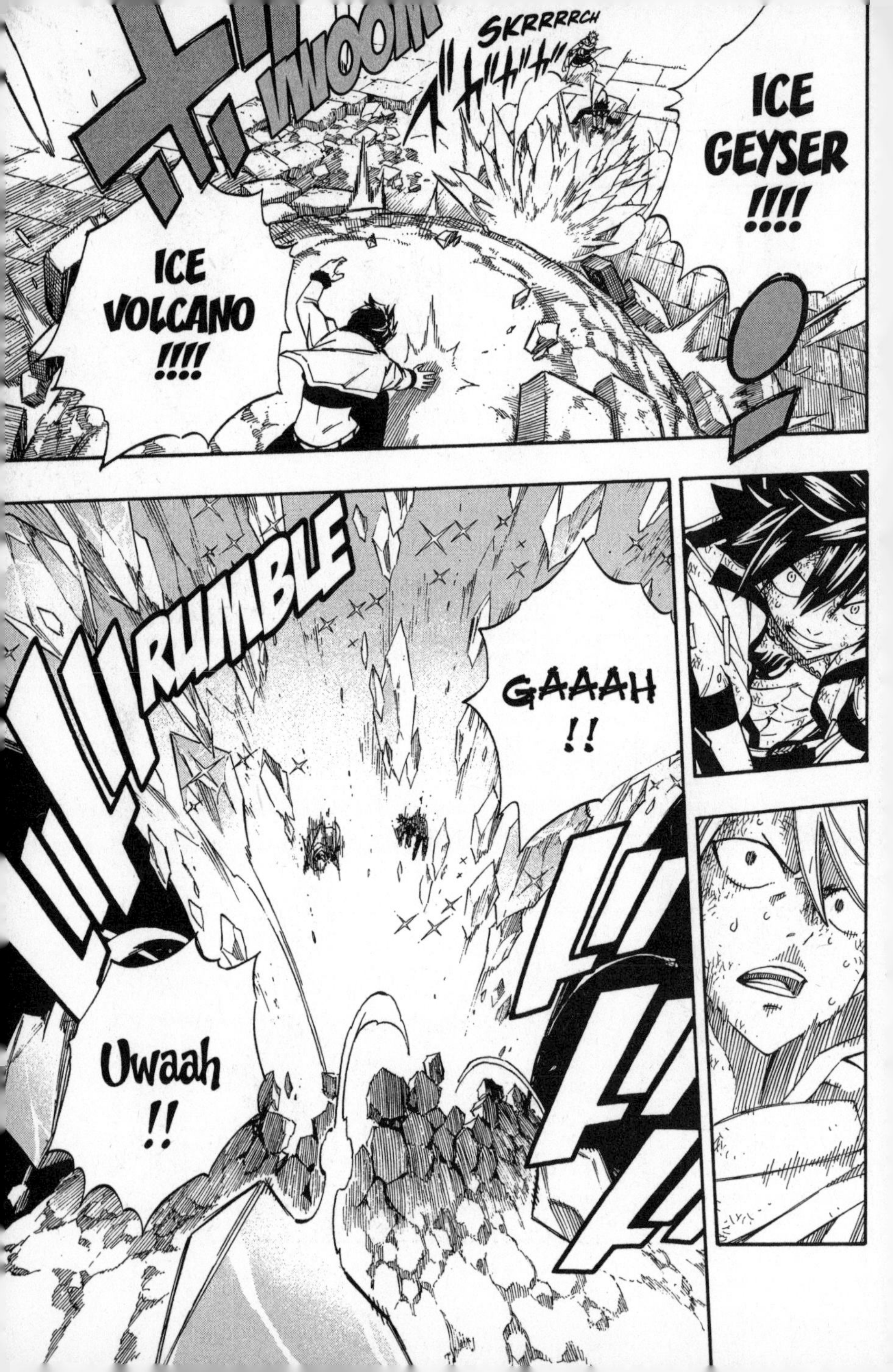
ICE GEYSER!!!!
SKRRRRCH
VWOOM
ICE VOLCANO!!!!
GAAAH!!
RUMBLE
Uwaah!!

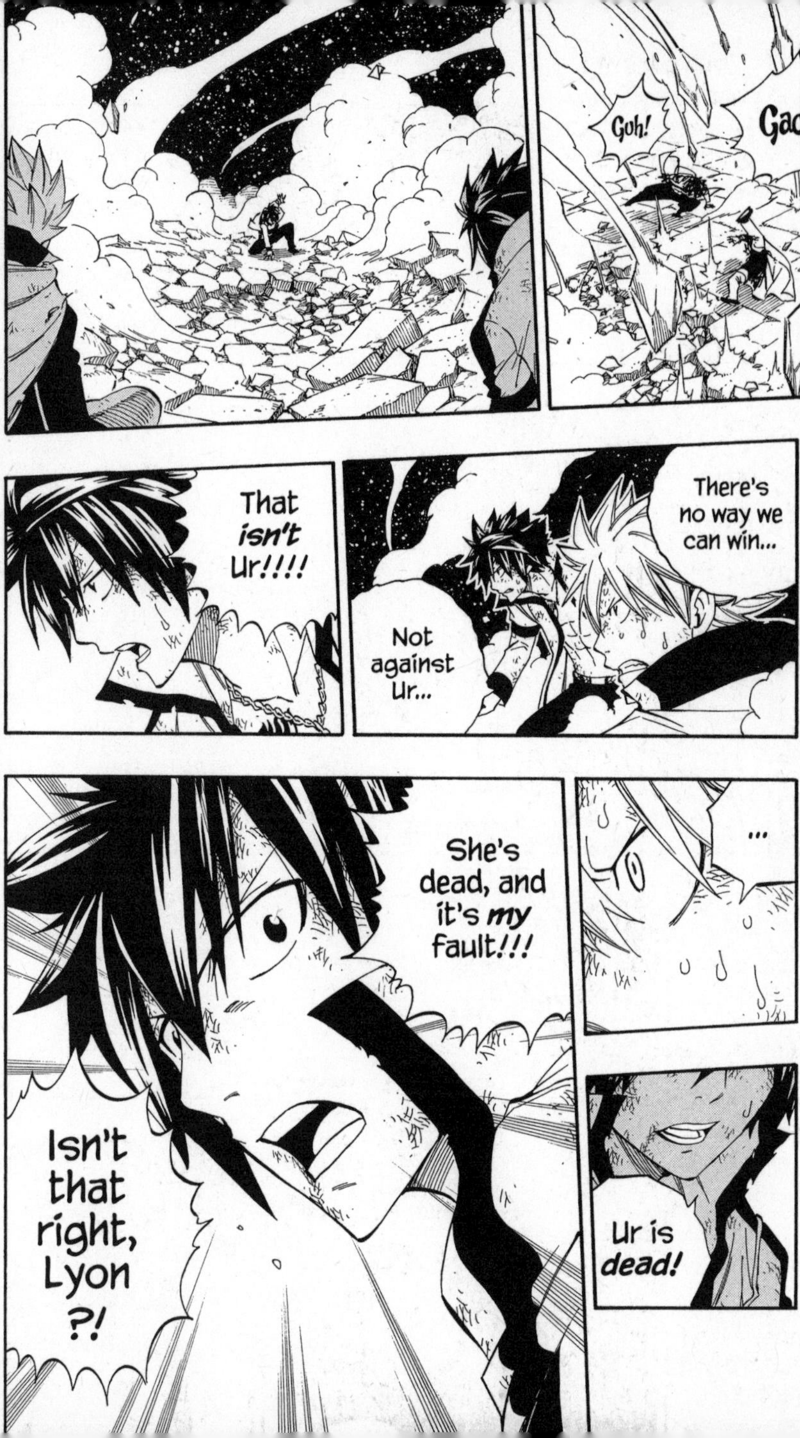
Gack!
Goh!
There's no way we can win...
Not against Ur...
That isn't Ur!!!!
...
Ur is dead!
She's dead, and it's my fault!!!
Isn't that right, Lyon ?!

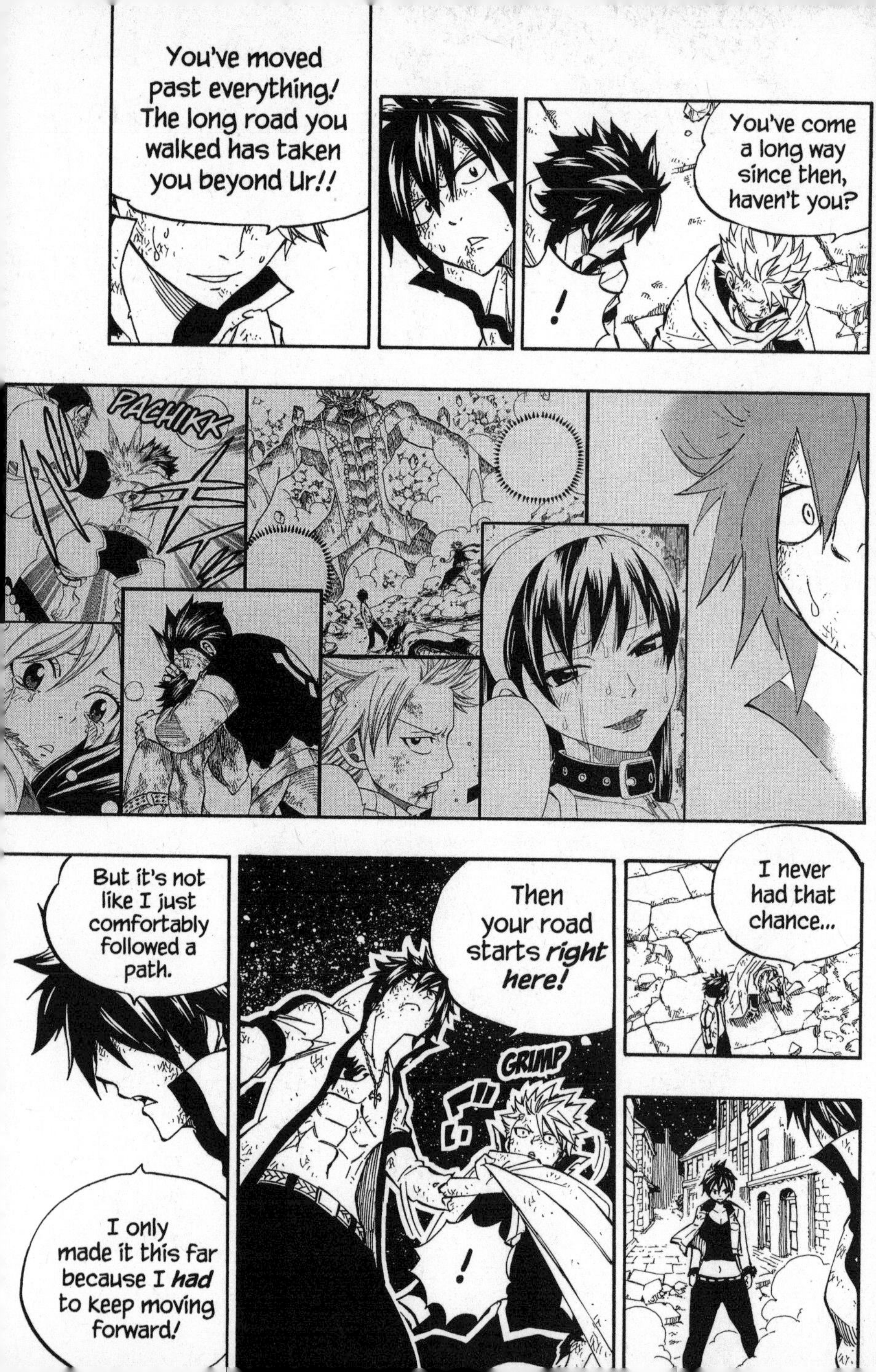
You've come a long way since then, haven't you?
!
You've moved past everything! The long road you walked has taken you beyond Ur!!
PACHIKK
I never had that chance...
Then your road starts *right here!*
GRIMP
!!
!
But it's not like I just comfortably followed a path.
I only made it this far because I *had* to keep moving forward!

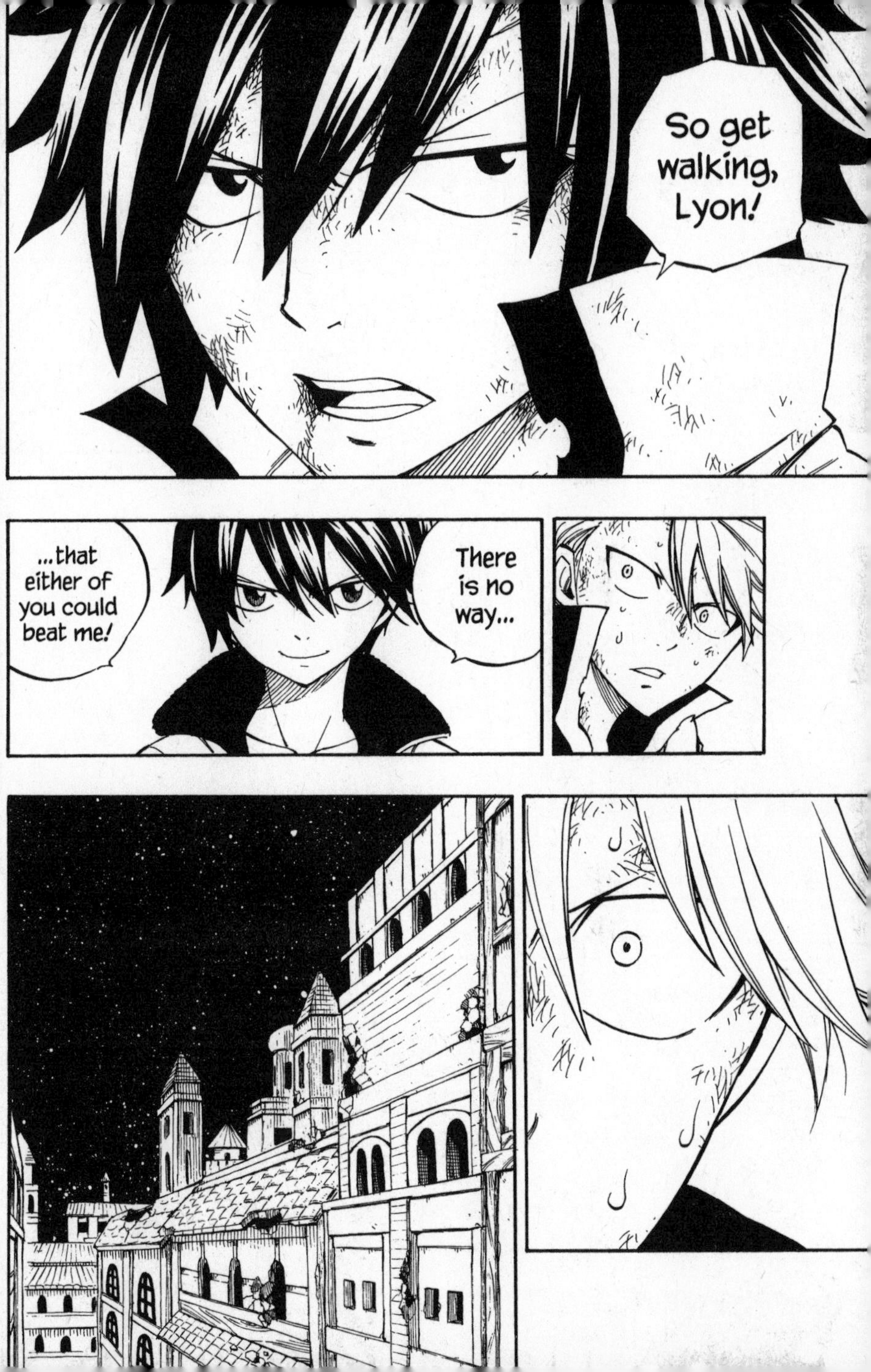
So get walking, Lyon!
There is no way...
...that either of you could beat me!

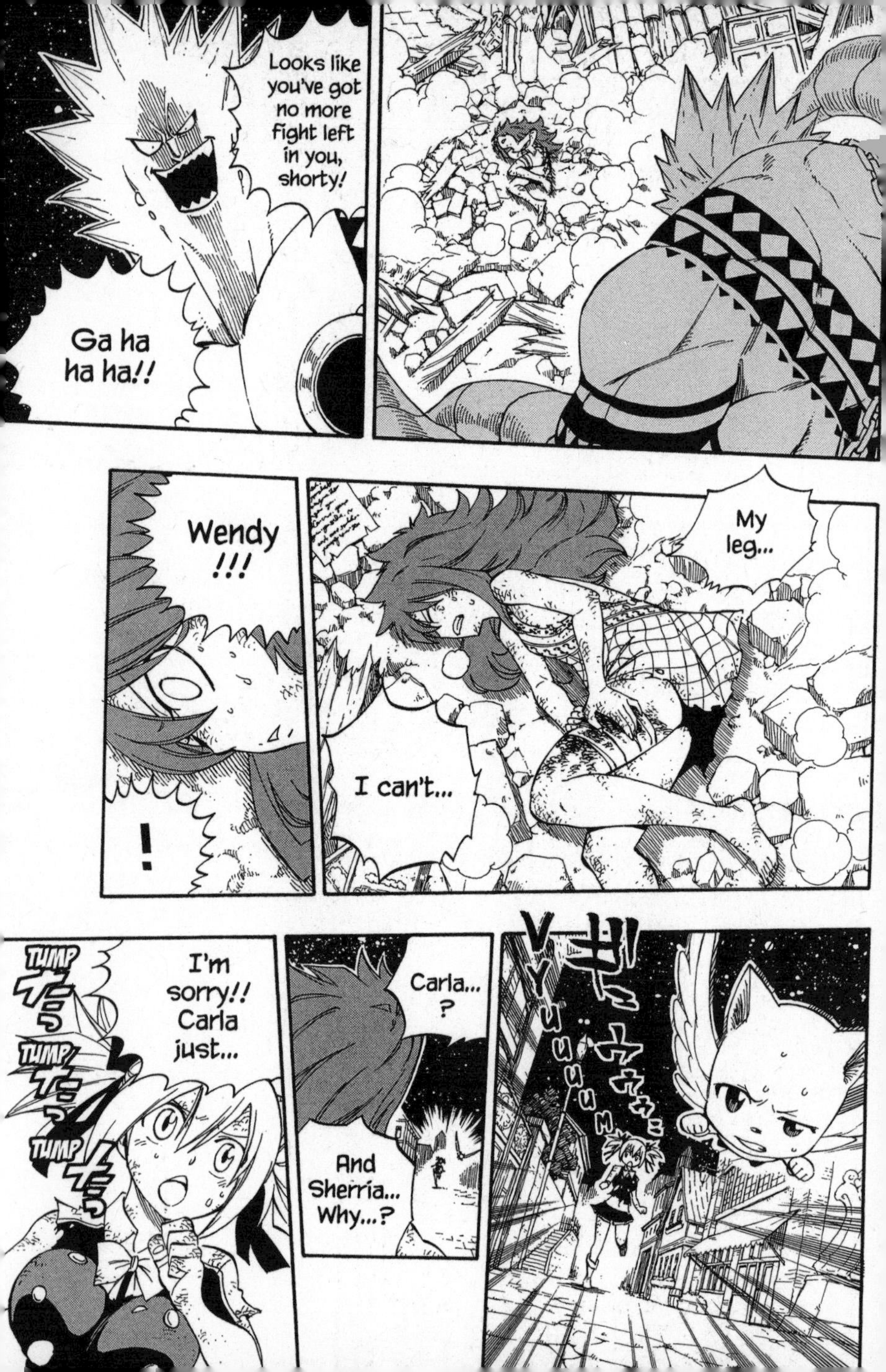
Looks like you've got no more fight left in you, shorty!
Ga ha ha ha!!
My leg...
I can't...
Wendy !!!
!
VVuuuuuUM
Carla...?
And Sherria... Why...?
I'm sorry!! Carla just...
TUMP
TUMP
TUMP

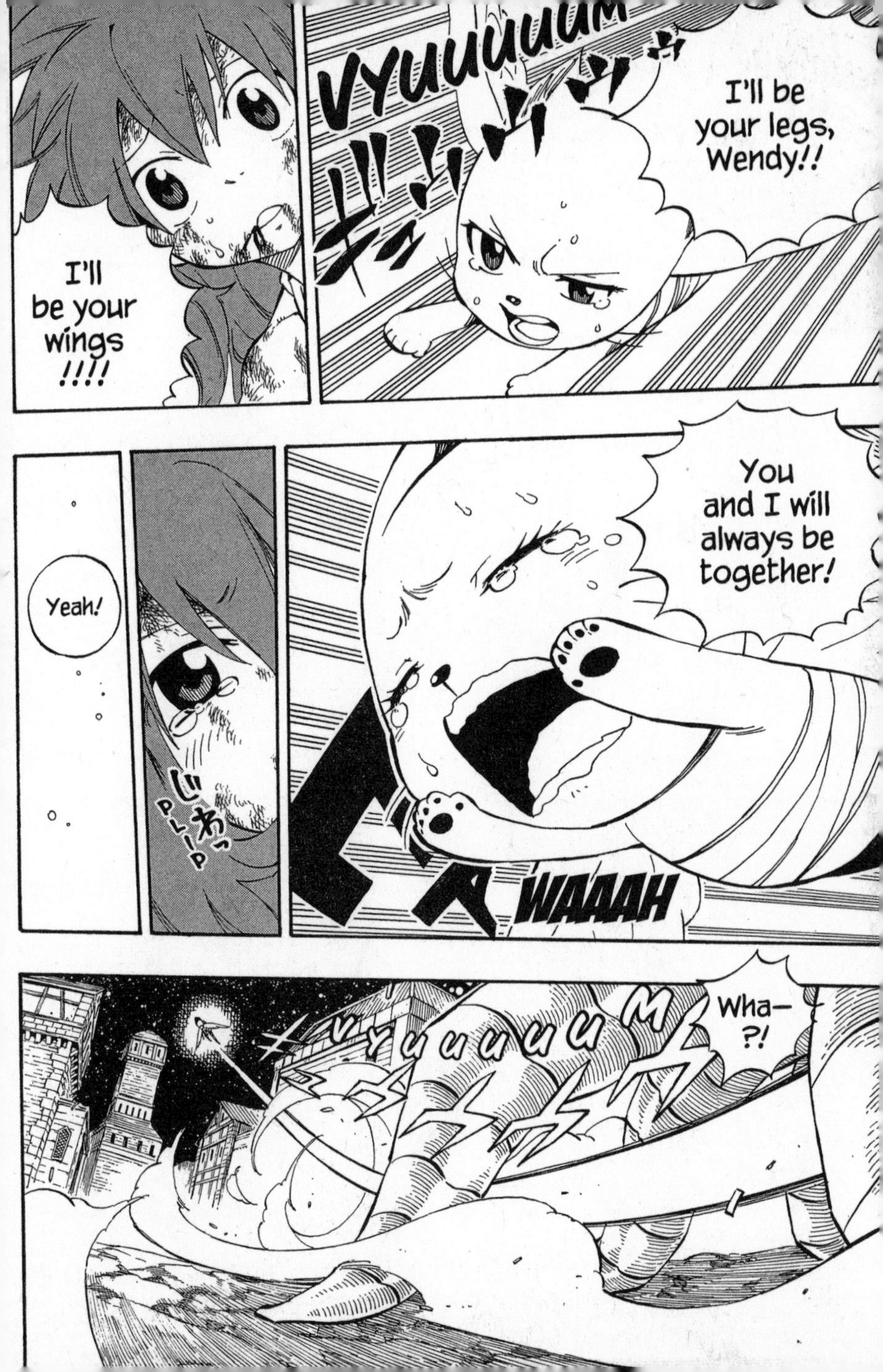
VYUUUUUUM
I'll be your legs, Wendy!!
I'll be your wings !!!!
You and I will always be together!
WAAAH
PLIP
Yeah!
Wha— ?!
VYUUUUUUM

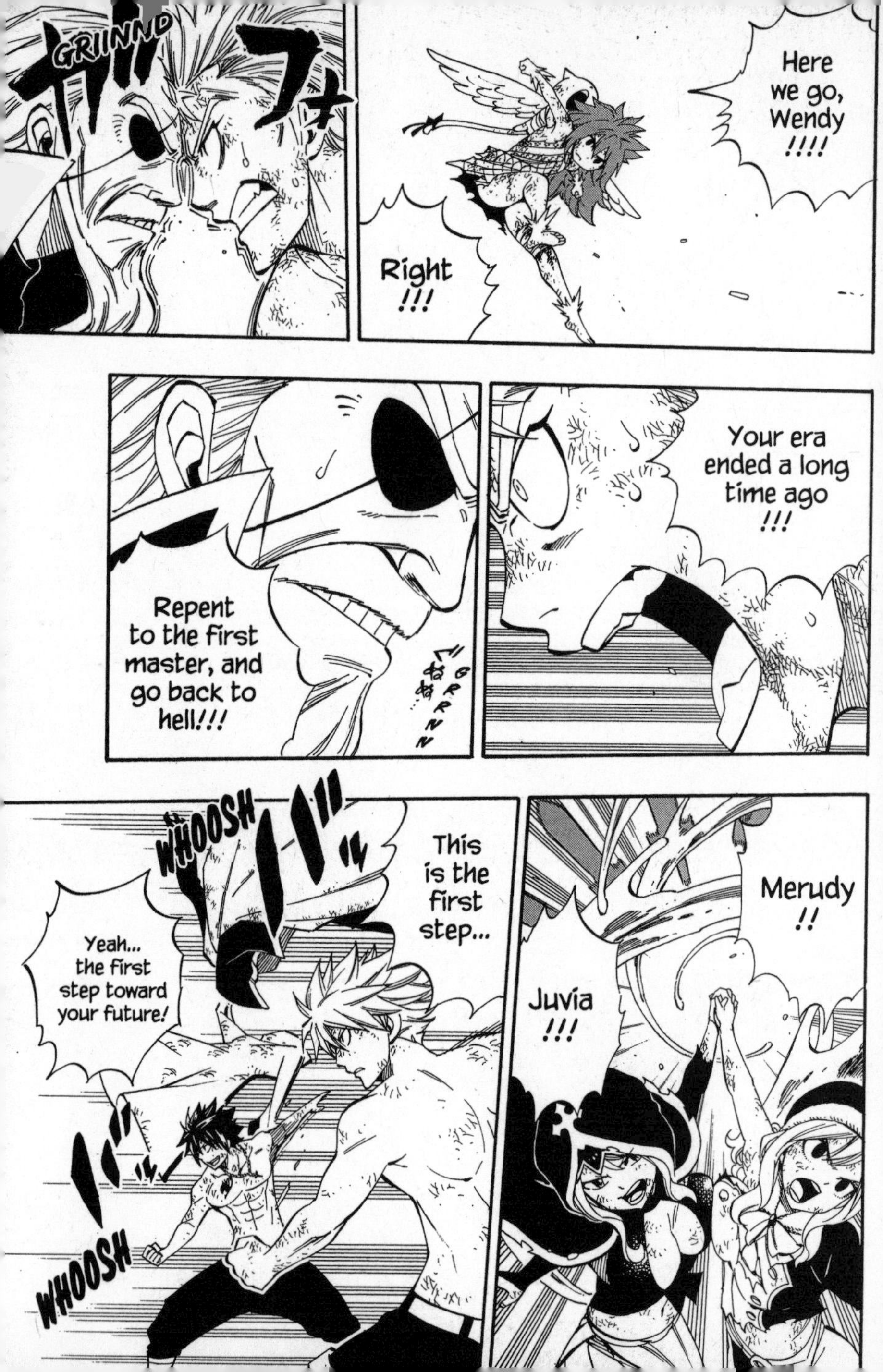
Here we go, Wendy!!!!
Right!!!
GRIINND
Your era ended a long time ago!!!
Repent to the first master, and go back to hell!!!
GRRNN
Merudy!!
Juvia!!!
WHOOSH
This is the first step...
Yeah... the first step toward your future!
WHOOSH

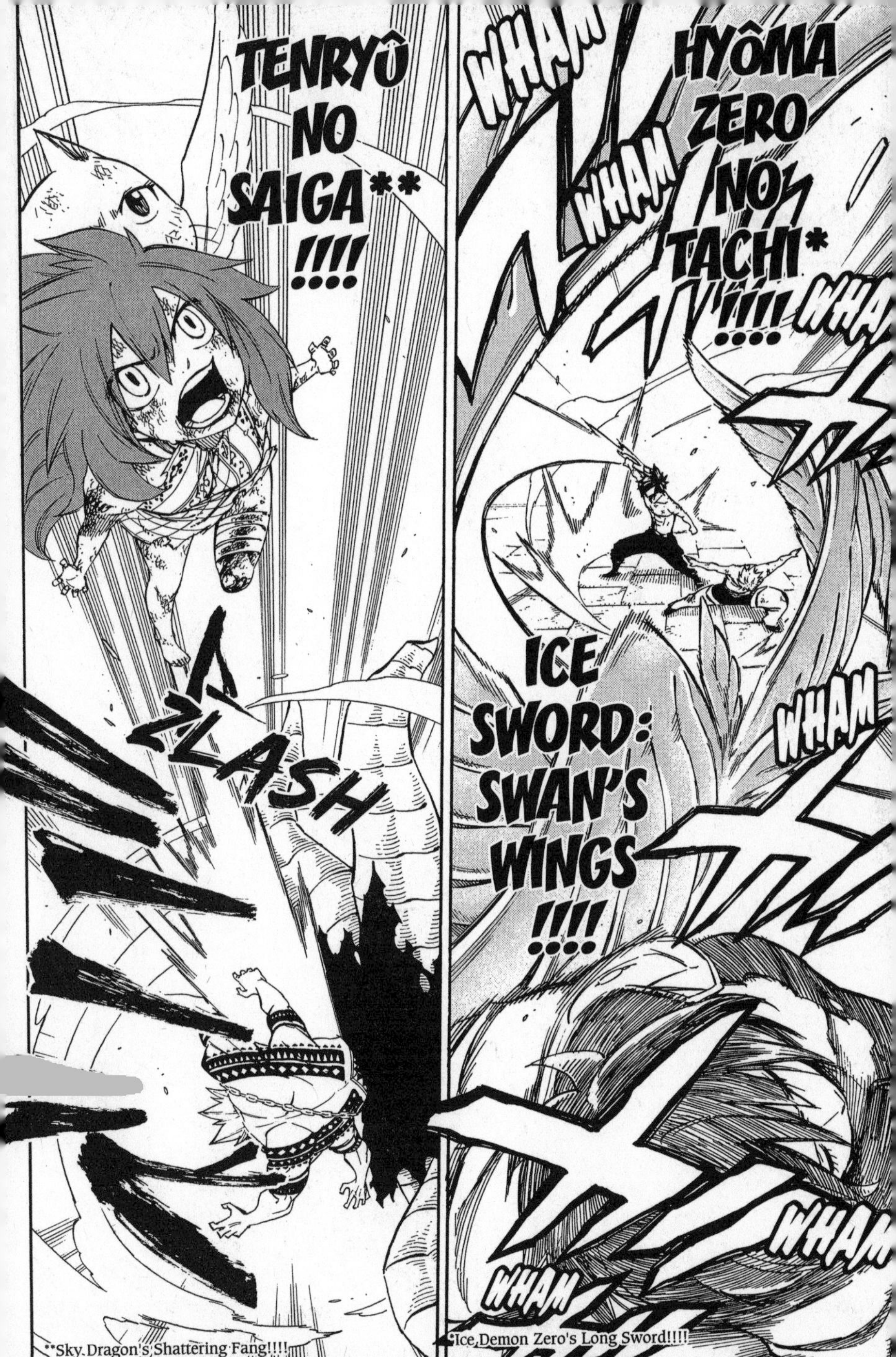
WHAM
HYÔMA ZERO NO TACHI* !!!!
WHAM
WHAM
WHAM
ICE SWORD: SWAN'S WINGS !!!!
WHAM
WHAM
TENRYÛ NO SAIGA** !!!!
ZLASH

*Ice Demon Zero's Long Sword!!!!

**Sky Dragon's Shattering Fang!!!!

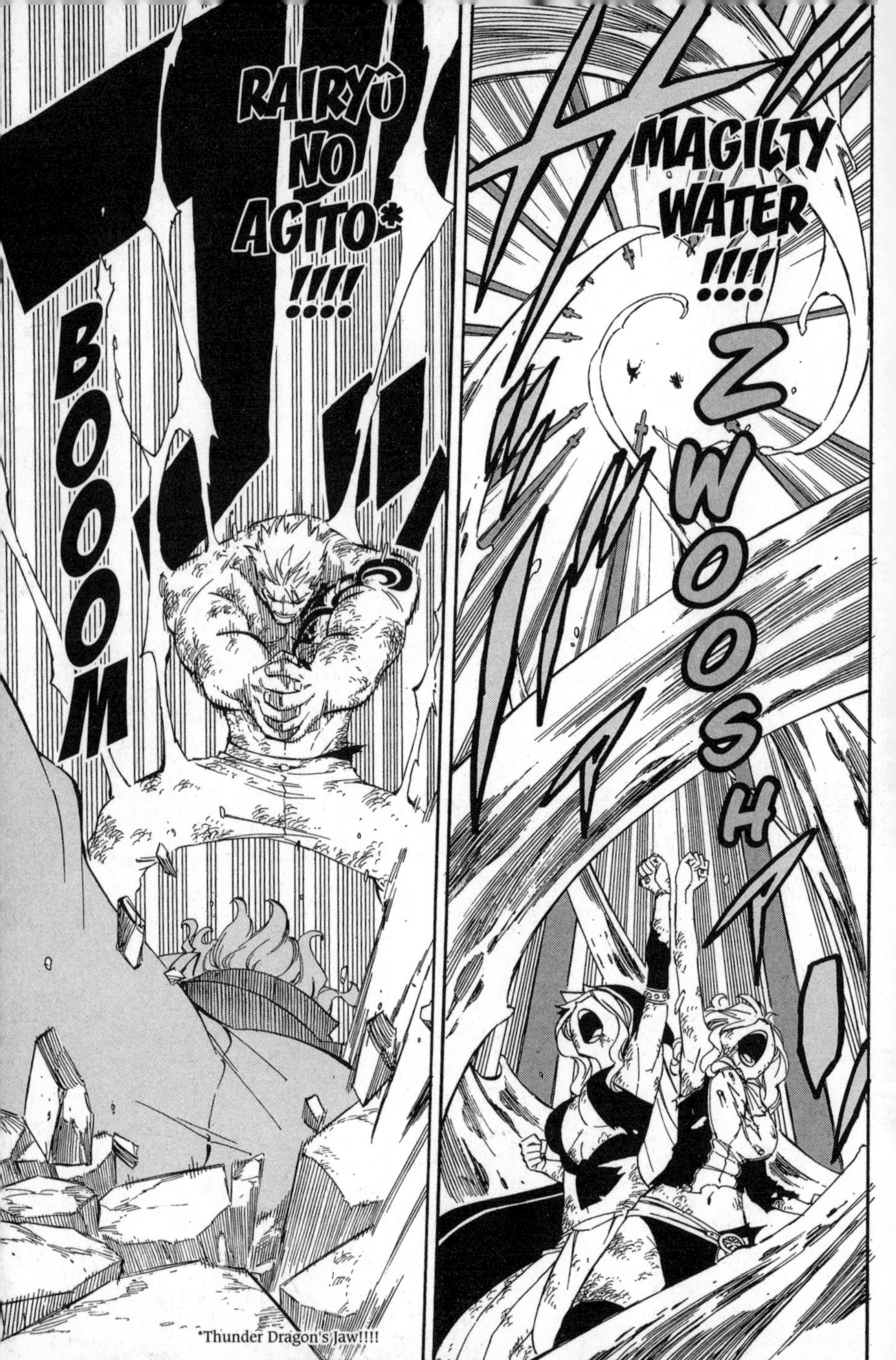
MAGILTY WATER !!!!
ZWOOSH
RAIRYÛ NO AGITO* !!!!
BOOOOM
*Thunder Dragon's Jaw!!!!

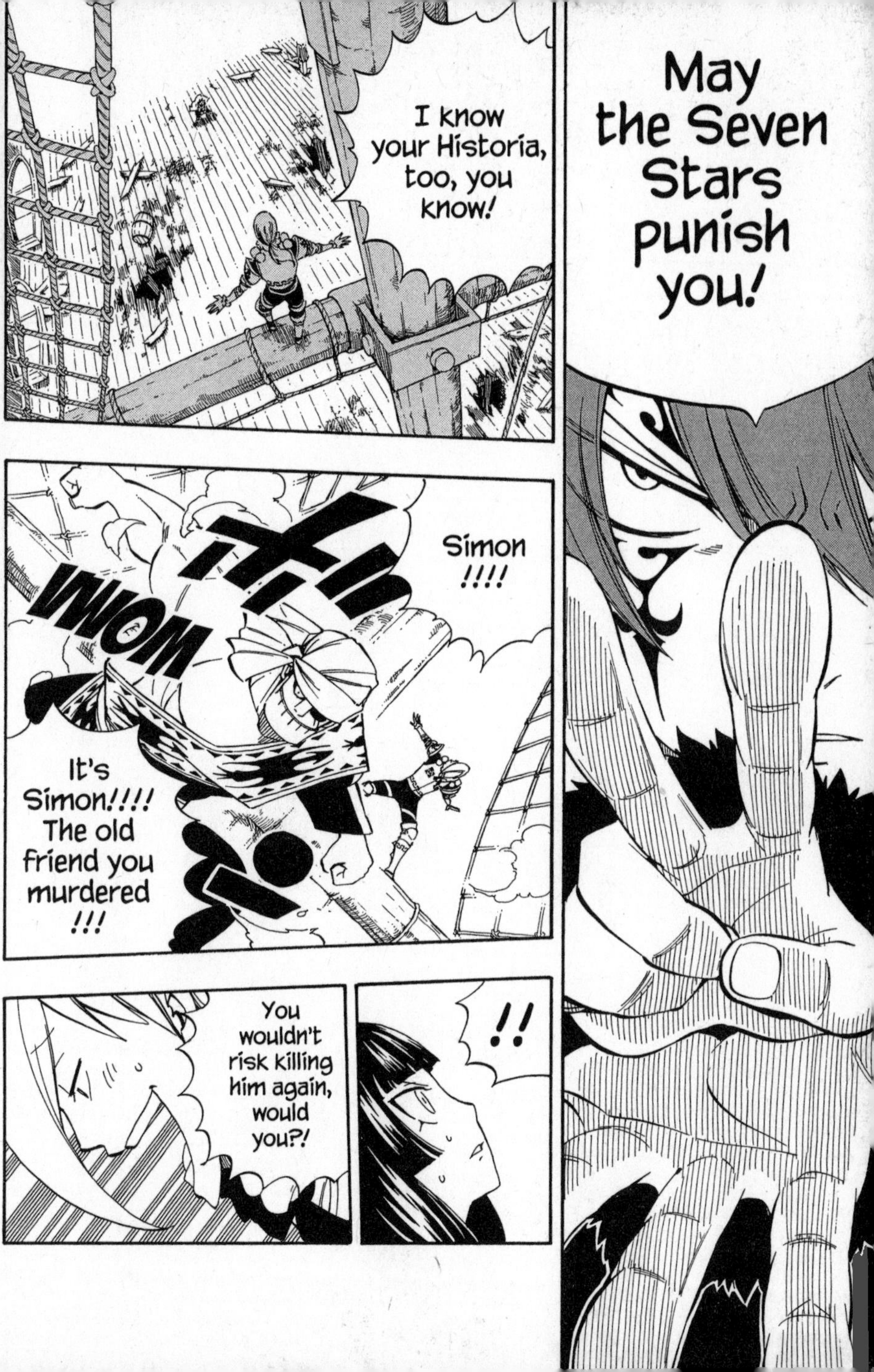
May the Seven Stars punish you!
I know your Historia, too, you know!
Simon !!!!
It's Simon!!!! The old friend you murdered !!!
!!
You wouldn't risk killing him again, would you?!

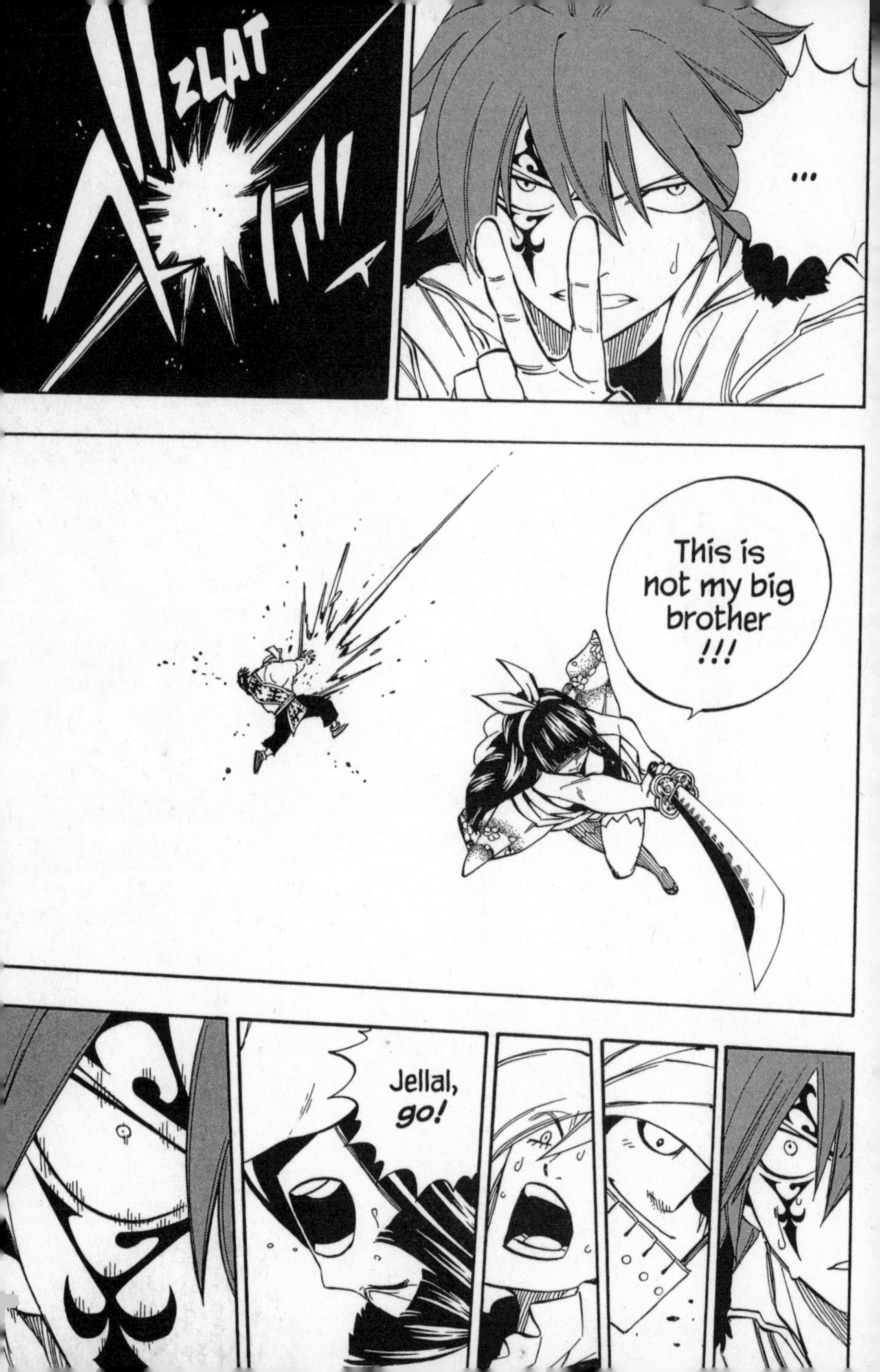
...
ZLAT
This is not my big brother!!!
Jellal, go!

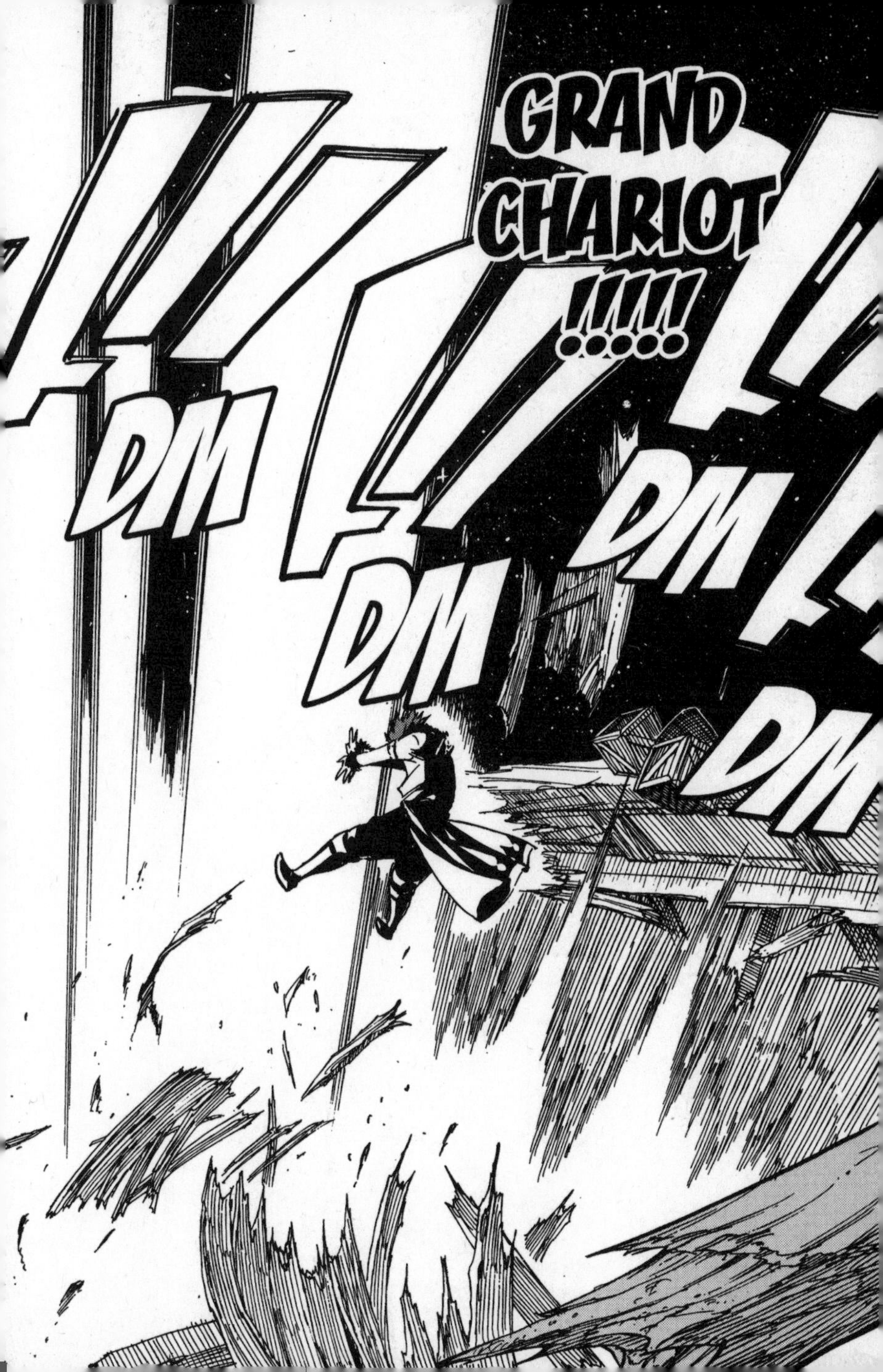
GRAND CHARIOT!!!!!
DM
DM
DM
DM

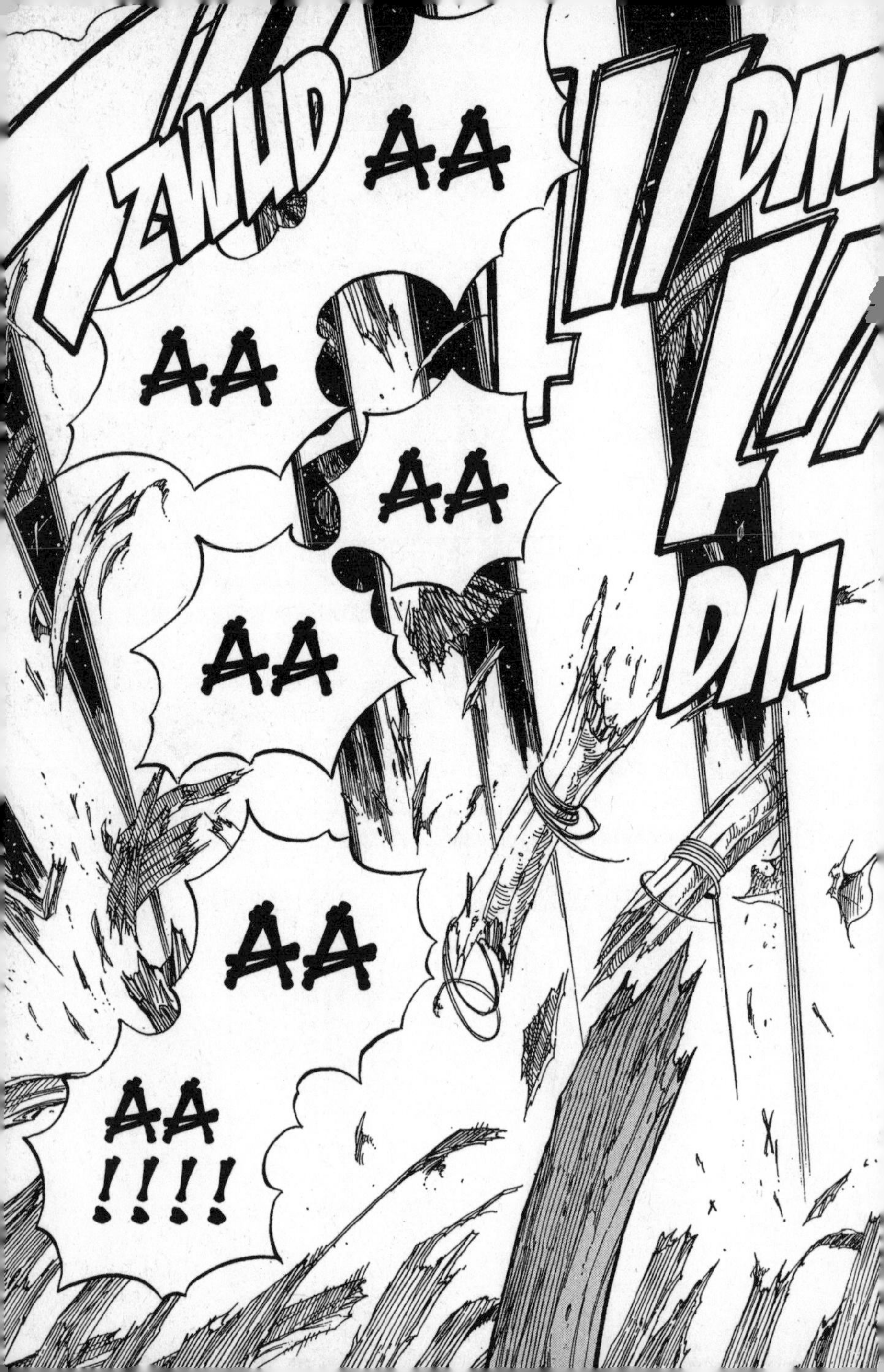
DM
AA
AA
AA
AA
AA
AA
!!!!

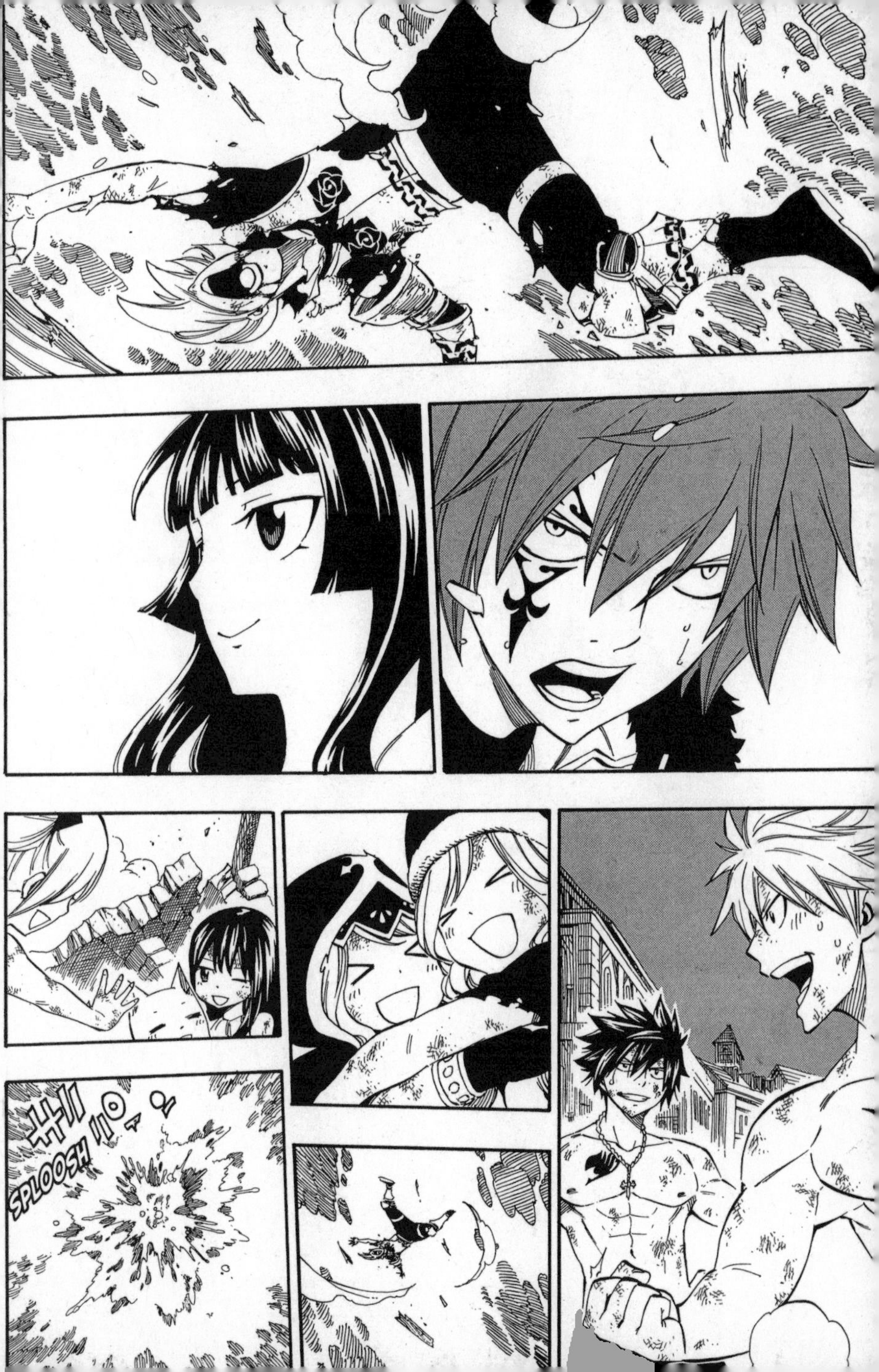
SPLOOSH

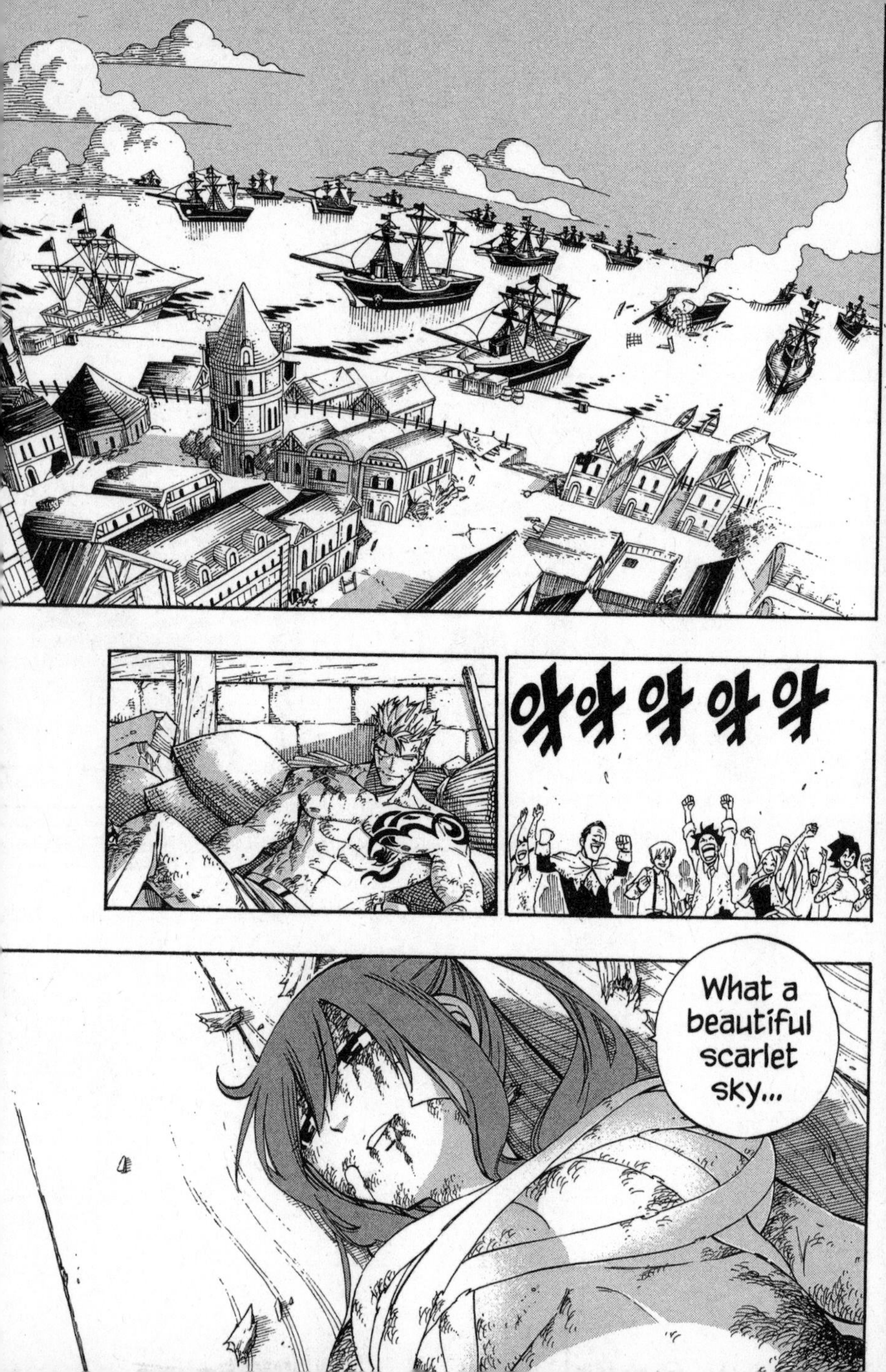
와와와와와
What a beautiful scarlet sky...

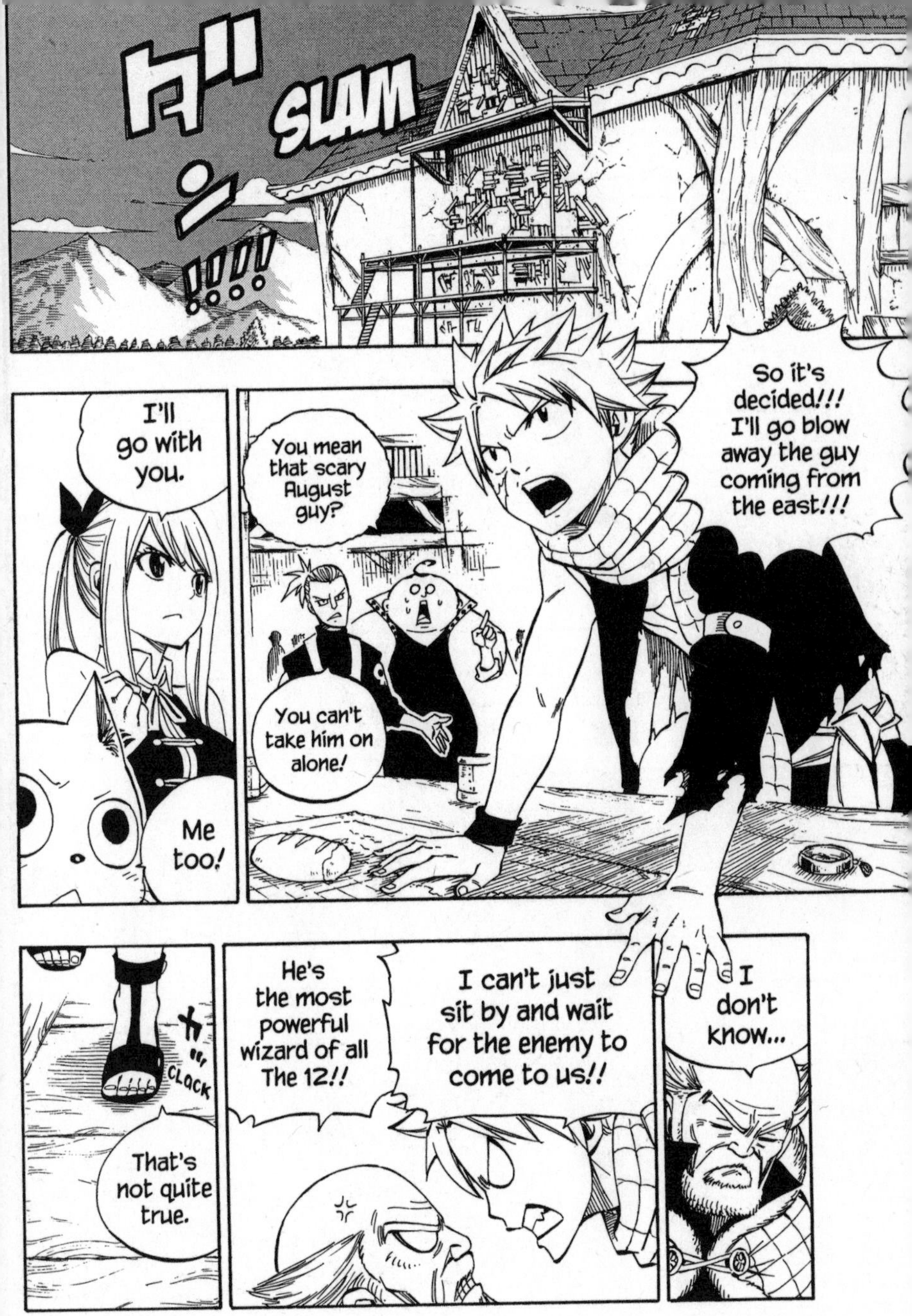
SLAM
!!!!
So it's decided!!! I'll go blow away the guy coming from the east!!!
You mean that scary August guy?
You can't take him on alone!
I'll go with you.
Me too!
I don't know...
I can't just sit by and wait for the enemy to come to us!!
He's the most powerful wizard of all The 12!!
CLACK
That's not quite true.

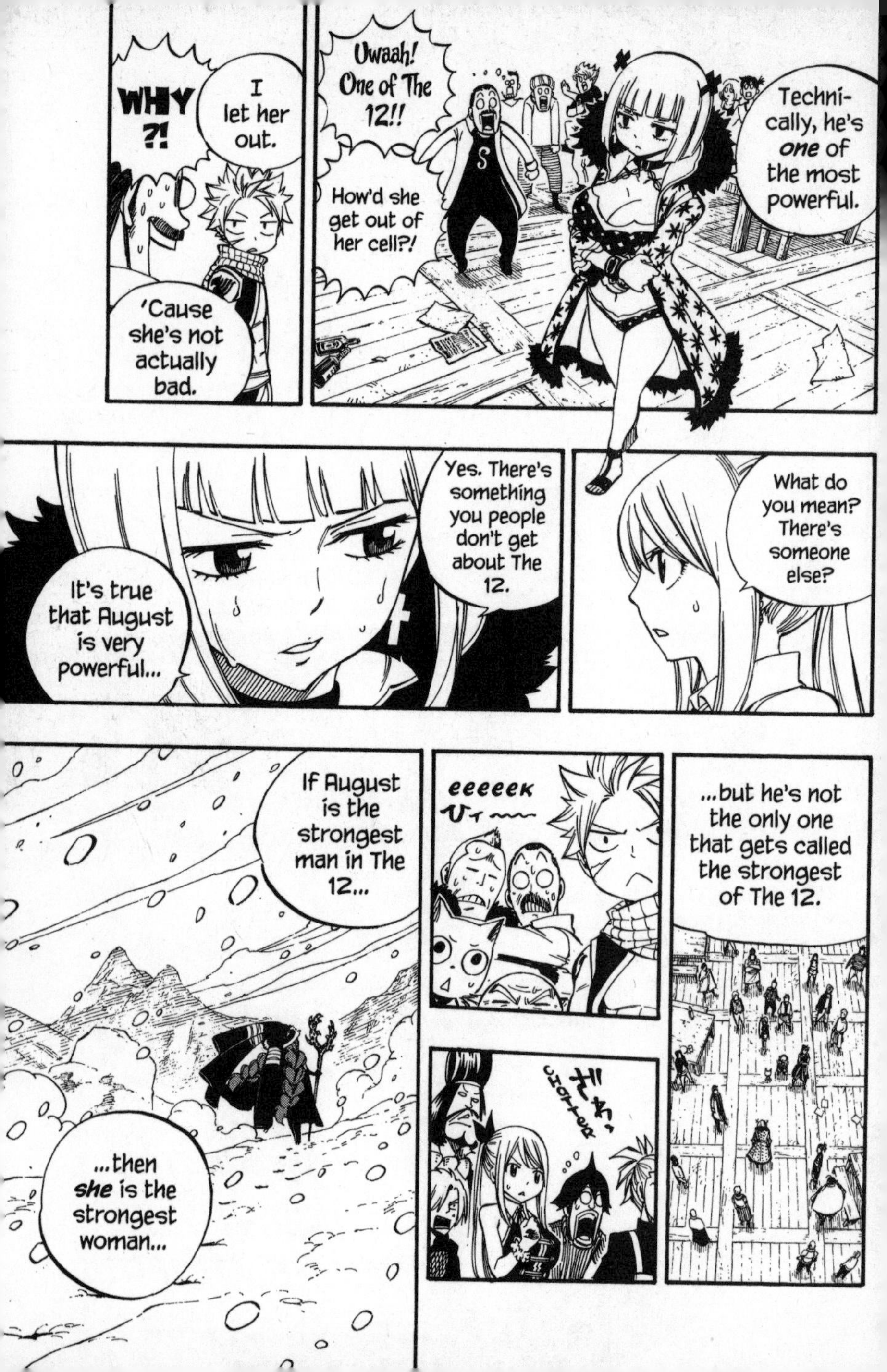
Techni-cally, he's *one* of the most powerful.
Uwaah! One of The 12!!
How'd she get out of her cell?!
I let her out.
WHY ?!
'Cause she's not actually bad.
What do you mean? There's someone else?
Yes. There's something you people don't get about The 12.
It's true that August is very powerful...
...but he's not the only one that gets called the strongest of The 12.
eeeeek
CHATTER
If August is the strongest man in The 12...
...then *she* is the strongest woman...

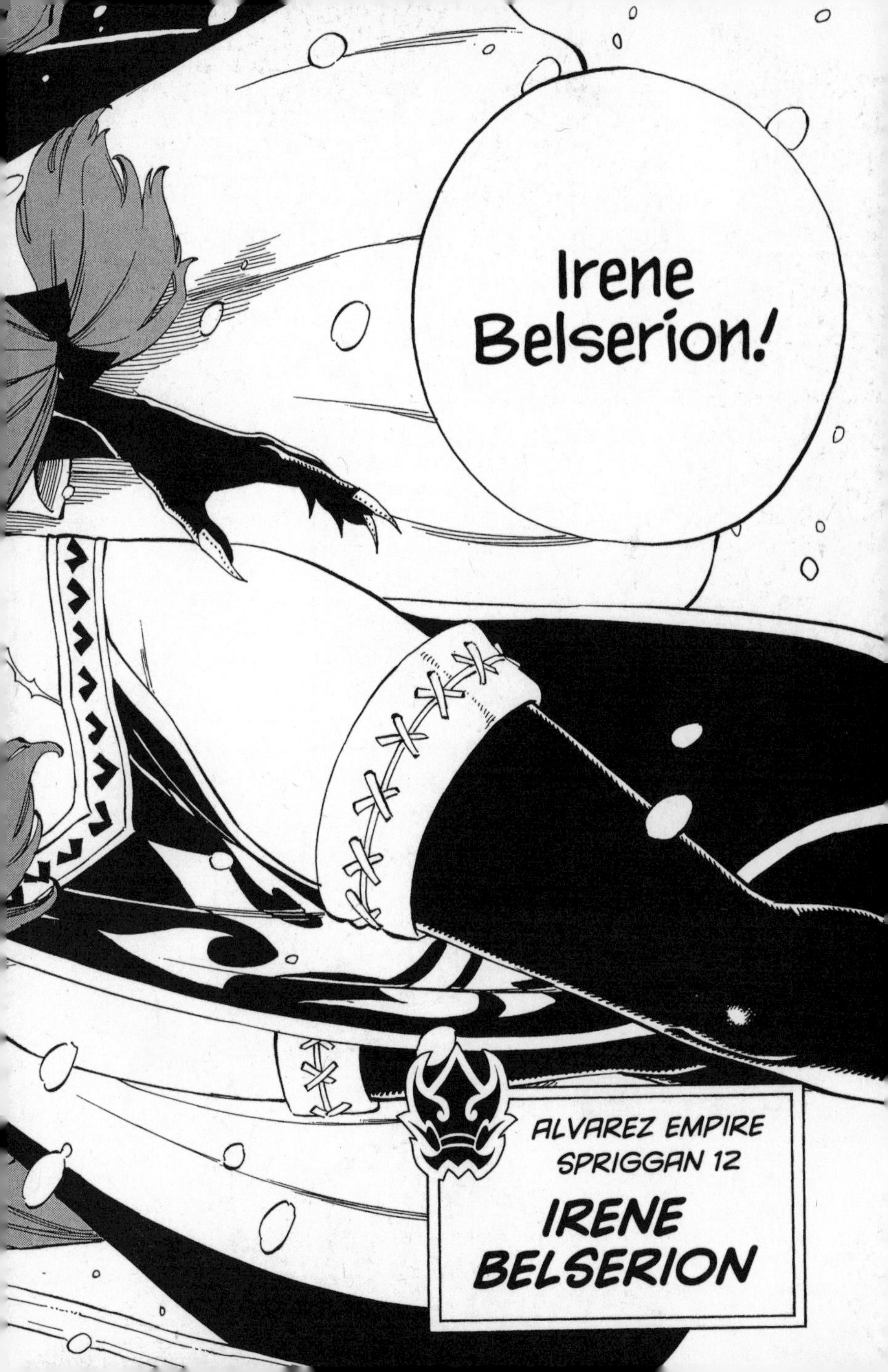
Irene Belserion!
ALVAREZ EMPIRE SPRIGGAN 12
IRENE BELSERION

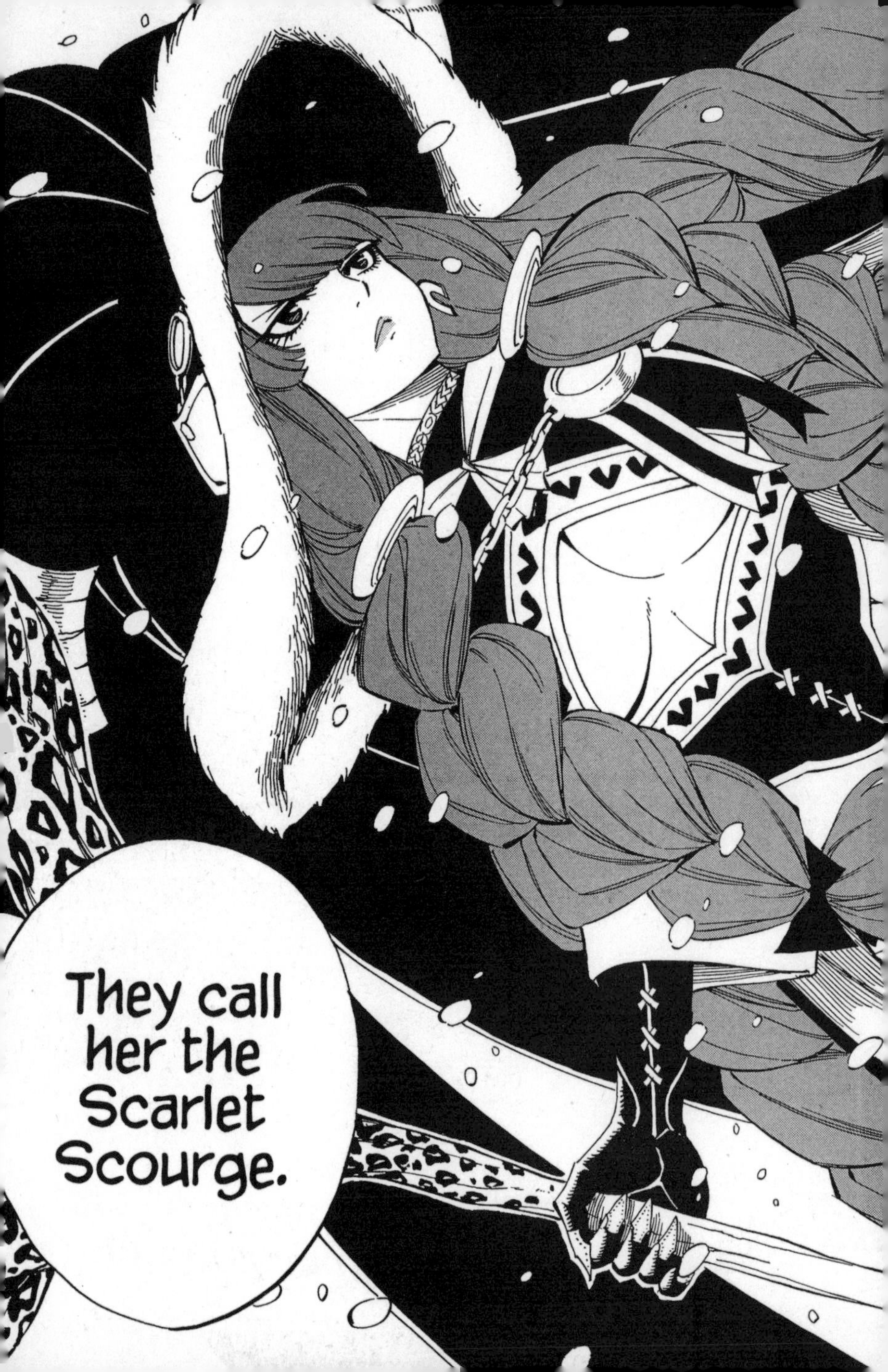
They call her the Scarlet Scourge.

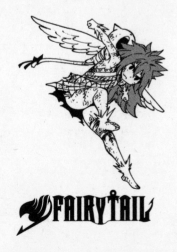

FAIRYTAIL

FAIRY TAIL

フェアリーテイル

Chapter 484: Savage Six

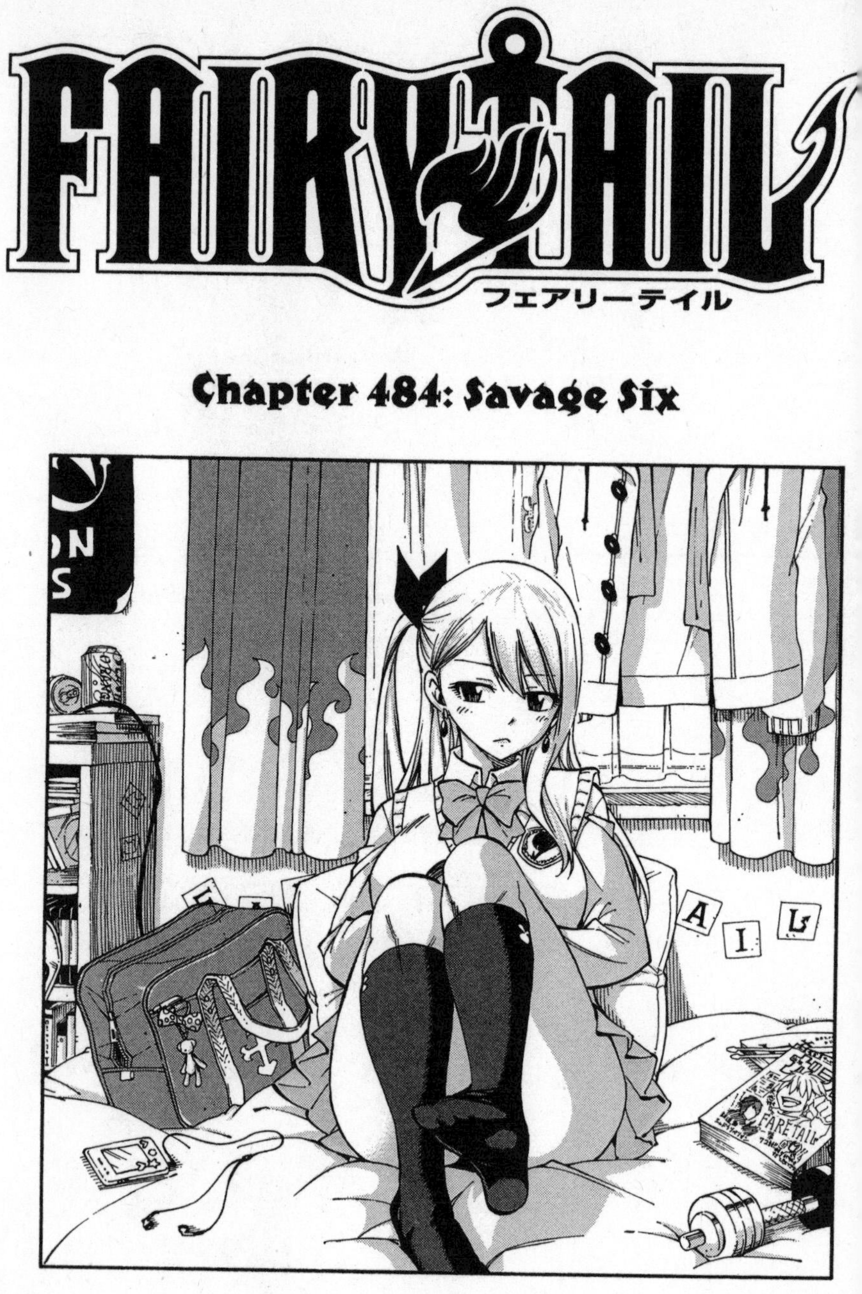
A
I
FARETAIL

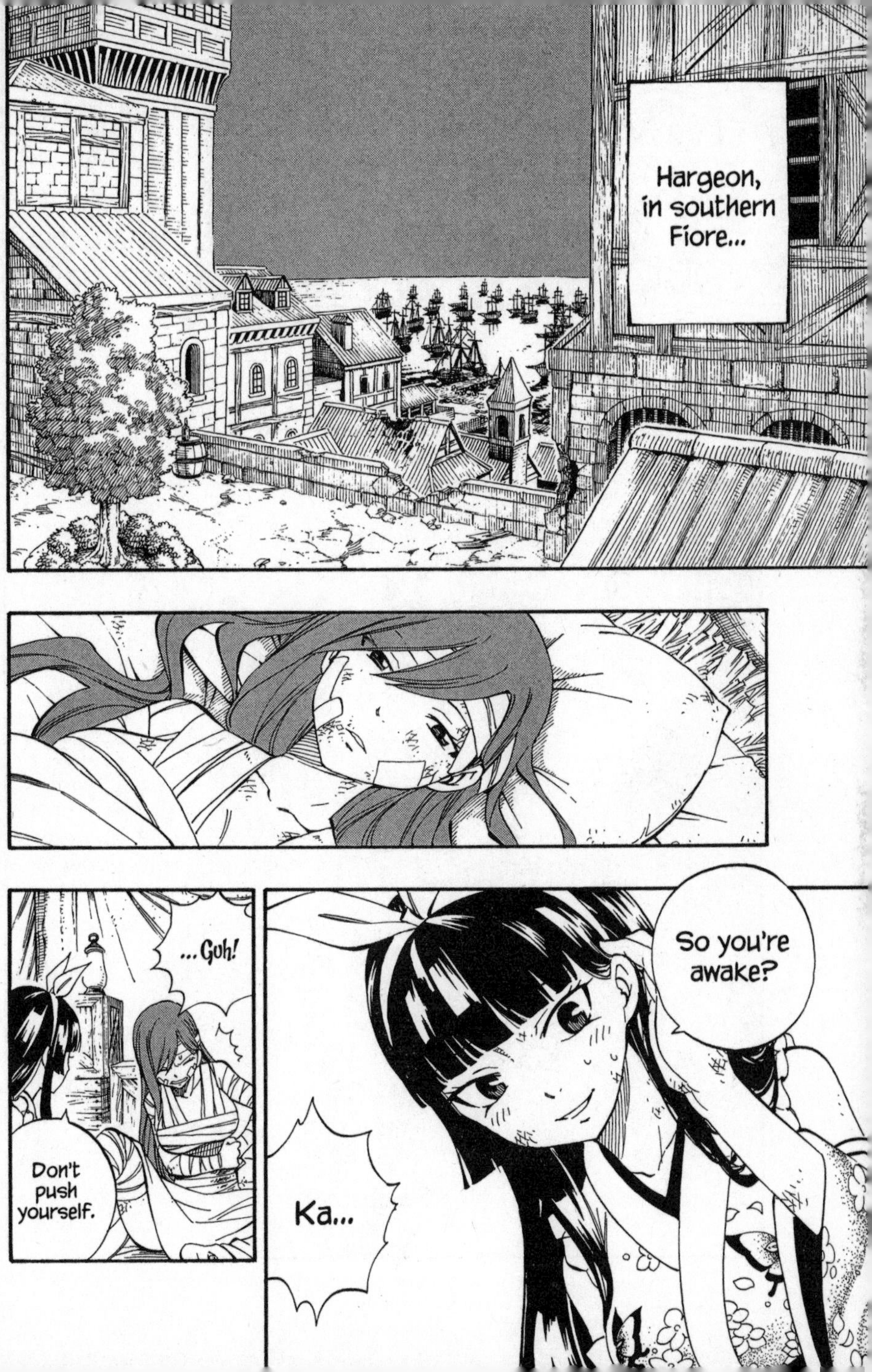
Hargeon, in southern Fiore...
So you're awake?
Ka...
...Guh!
Don't push yourself.

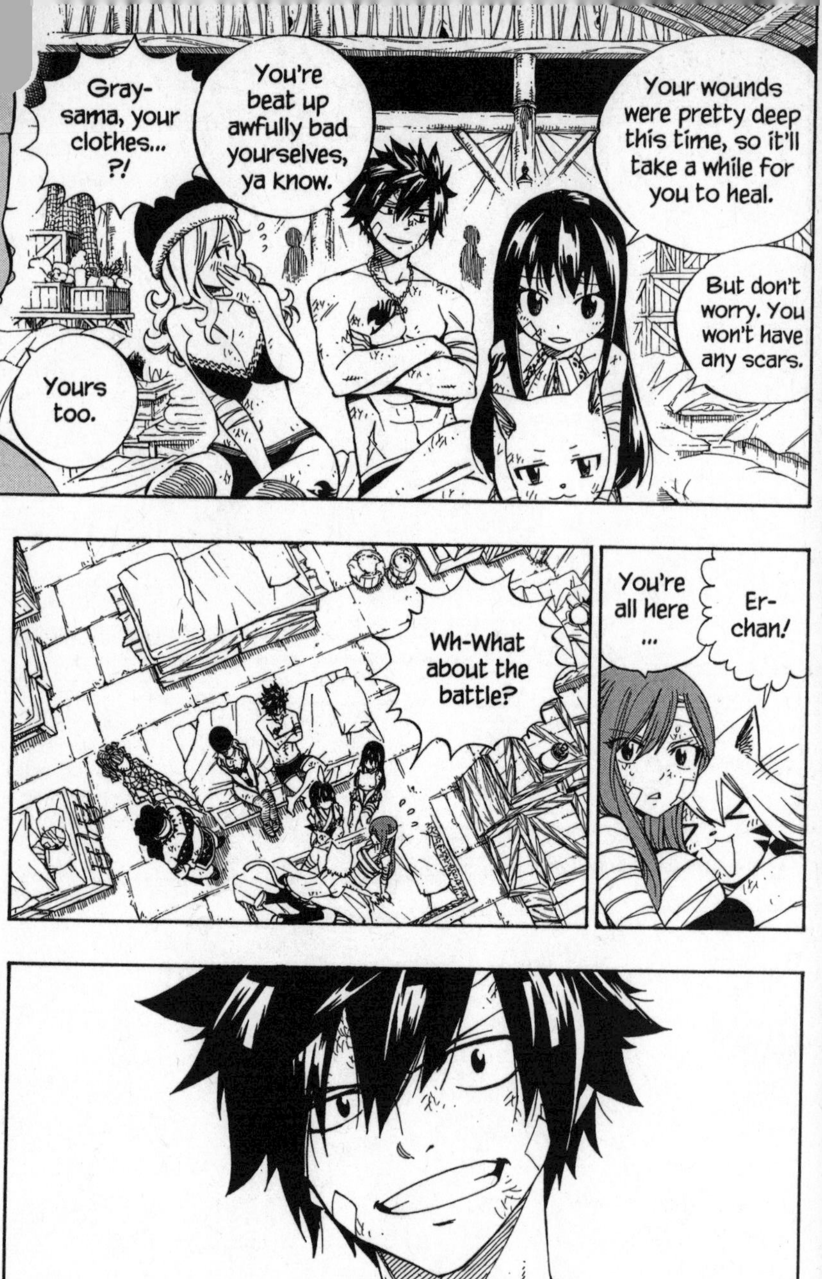
Your wounds were pretty deep this time, so it'll take a while for you to heal.
But don't worry. You won't have any scars.
You're beat up awfully bad yourselves, ya know.
Gray-sama, your clothes...?!
Yours too.
Er-chan!
You're all here...
Wh-What about the battle?

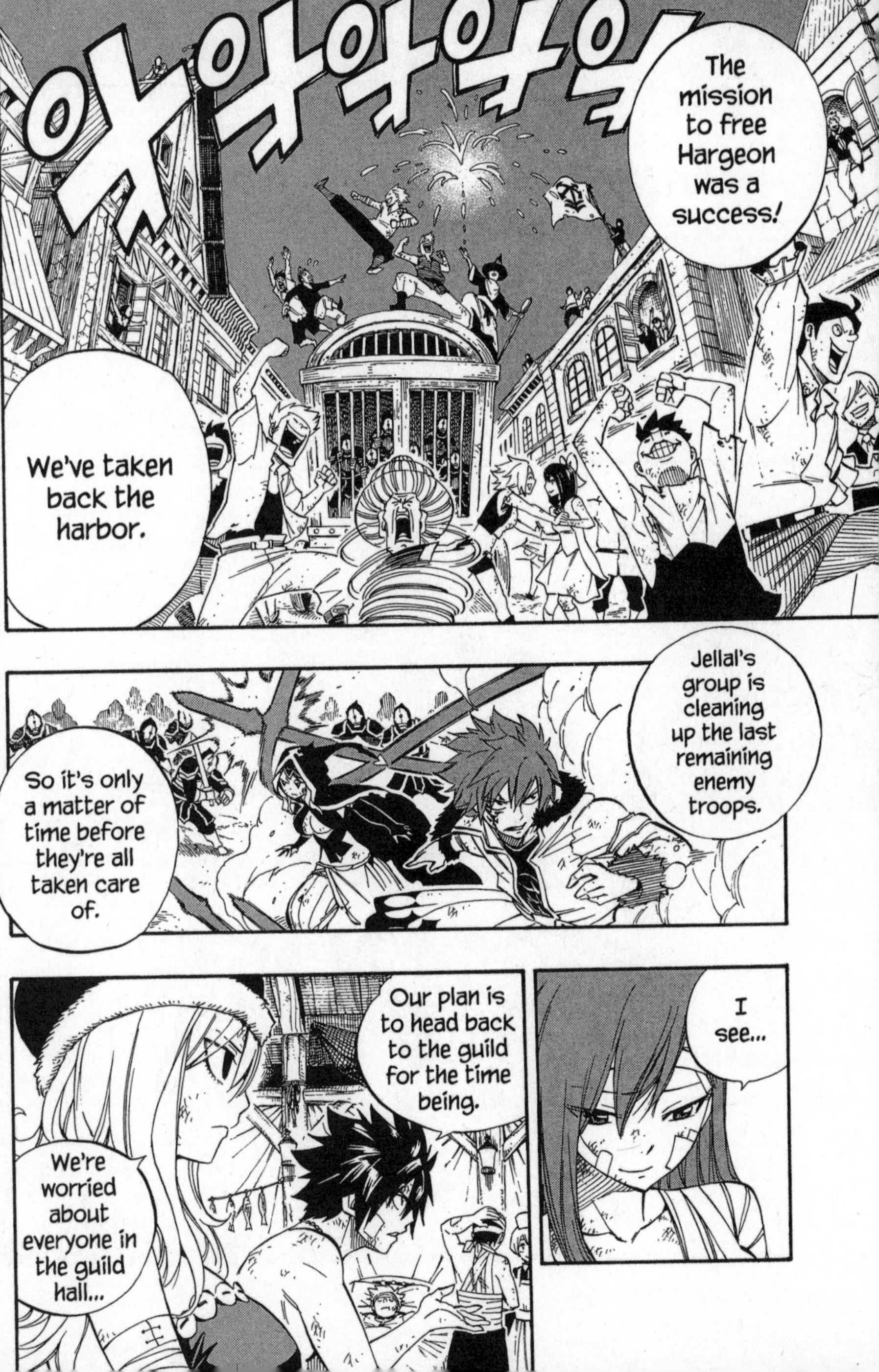
The mission to free Hargeon was a success!
We've taken back the harbor.
Jellal's group is cleaning up the last remaining enemy troops.
So it's only a matter of time before they're all taken care of.
I see...
Our plan is to head back to the guild for the time being.
We're worried about everyone in the guild hall...

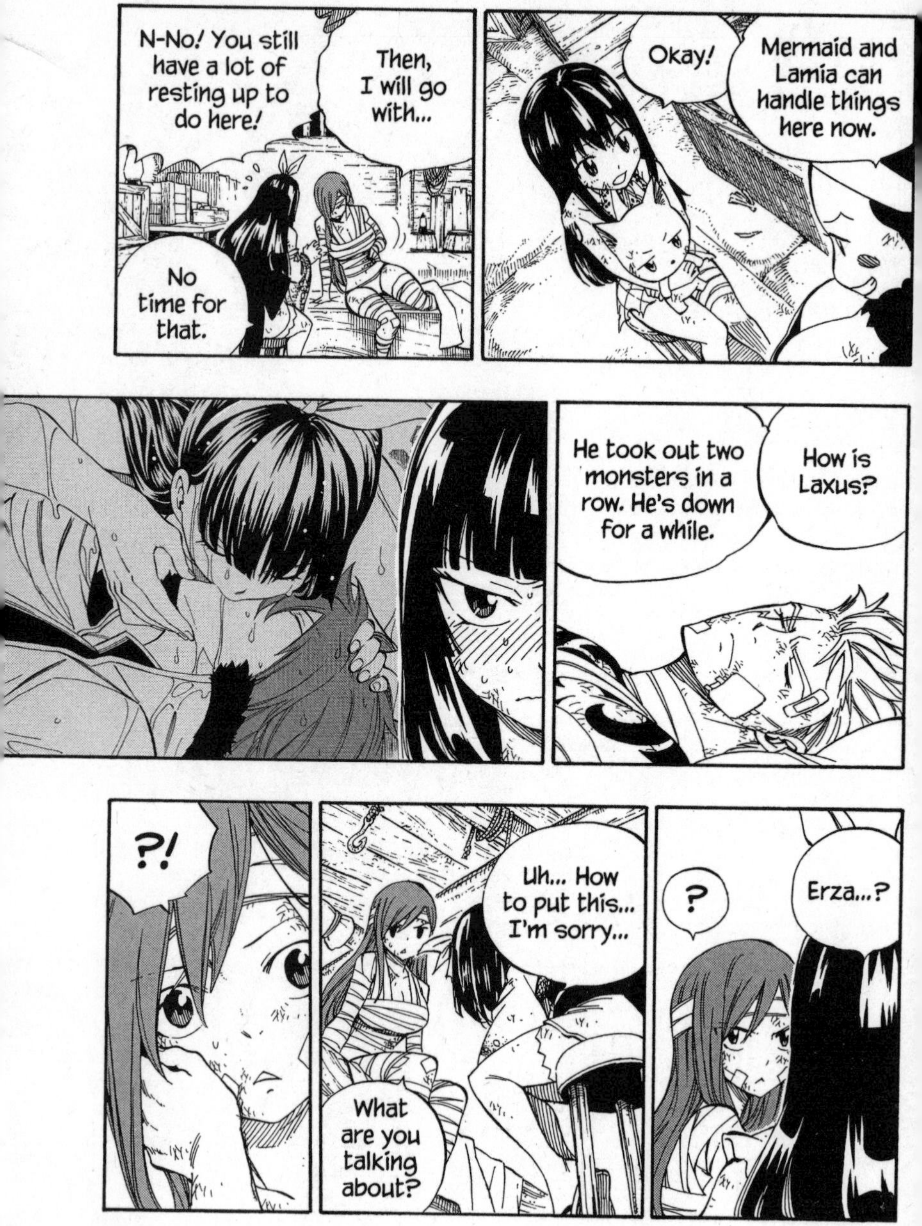
Mermaid and Lamia can handle things here now.
Okay!
Then, I will go with...
N-No! You still have a lot of resting up to do here!
No time for that.
How is Laxus?
He took out two monsters in a row. He's down for a while.
Erza...?
?
Uh... How to put this... I'm sorry...
What are you talking about?
?!

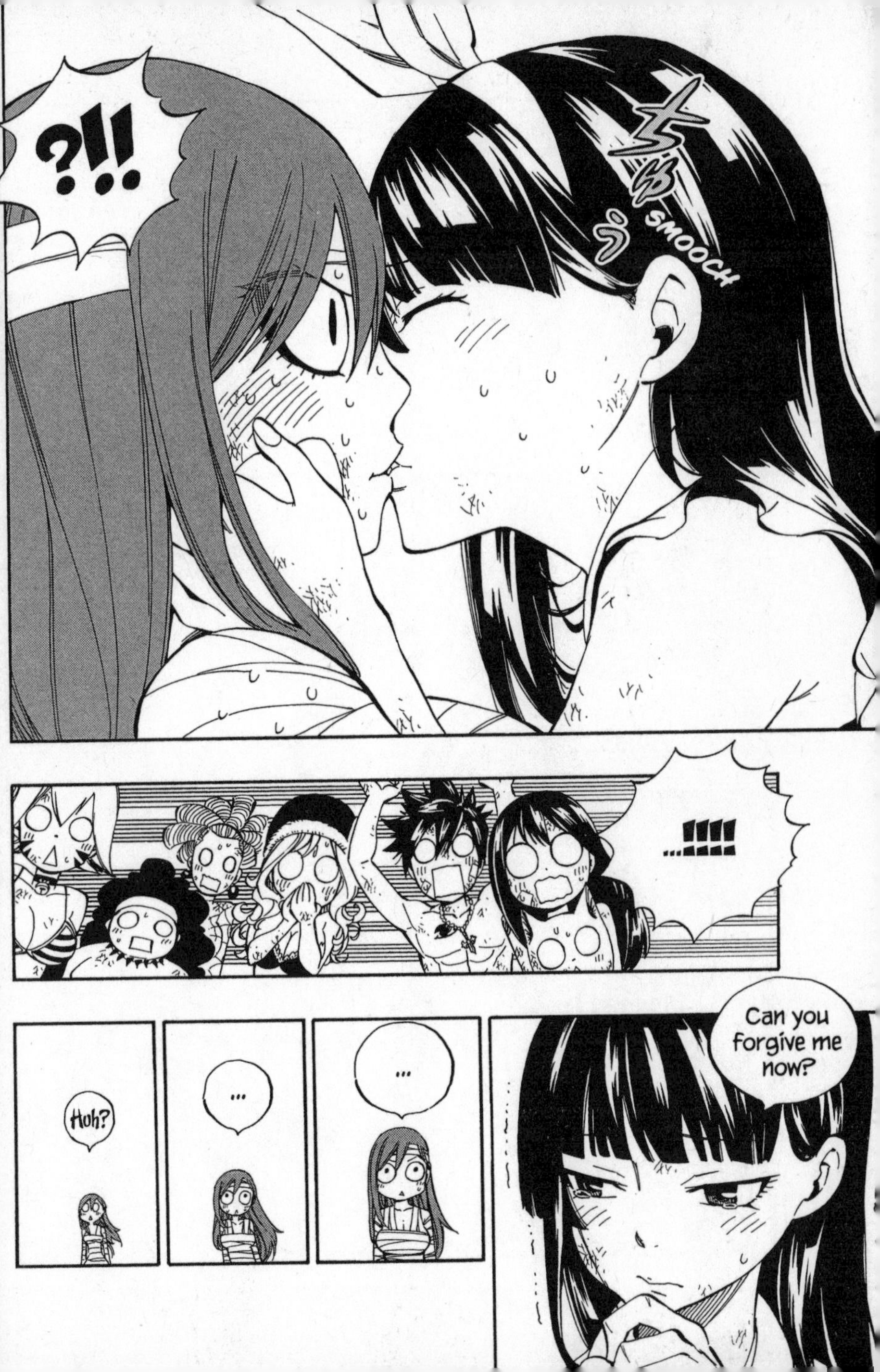

ちゅっ SMOOCH
?!!
...!!!!
Can you forgive me now?
...
...
Huh?

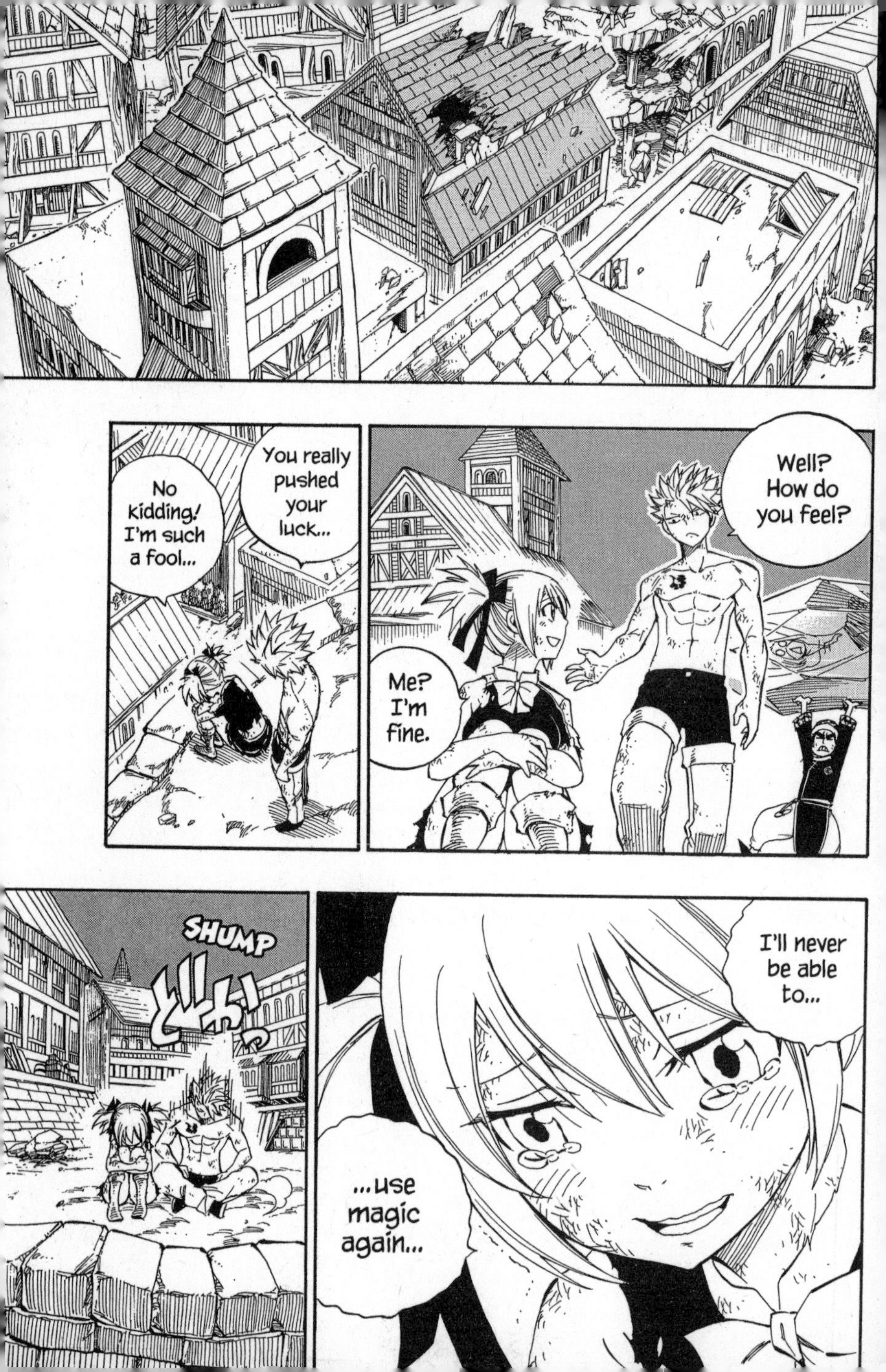
Well? How do you feel?
Me? I'm fine.
You really pushed your luck...
No kidding! I'm such a fool...
I'll never be able to...
...use magic again...
SHUMP

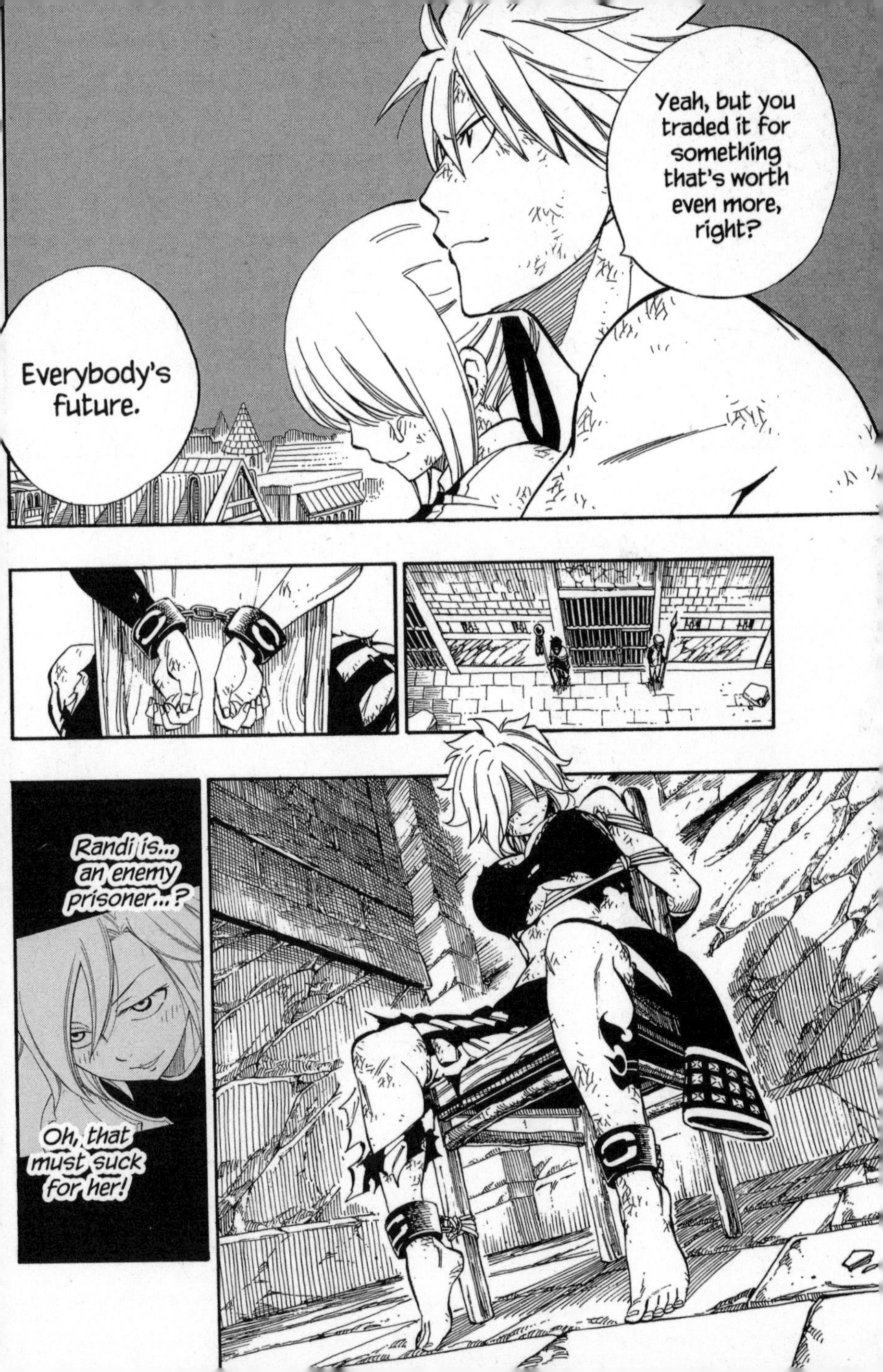
Yeah, but you traded it for something that's worth even more, right?
Everybody's future.
Randi is... an enemy prisoner...?
Oh, that must suck for her!

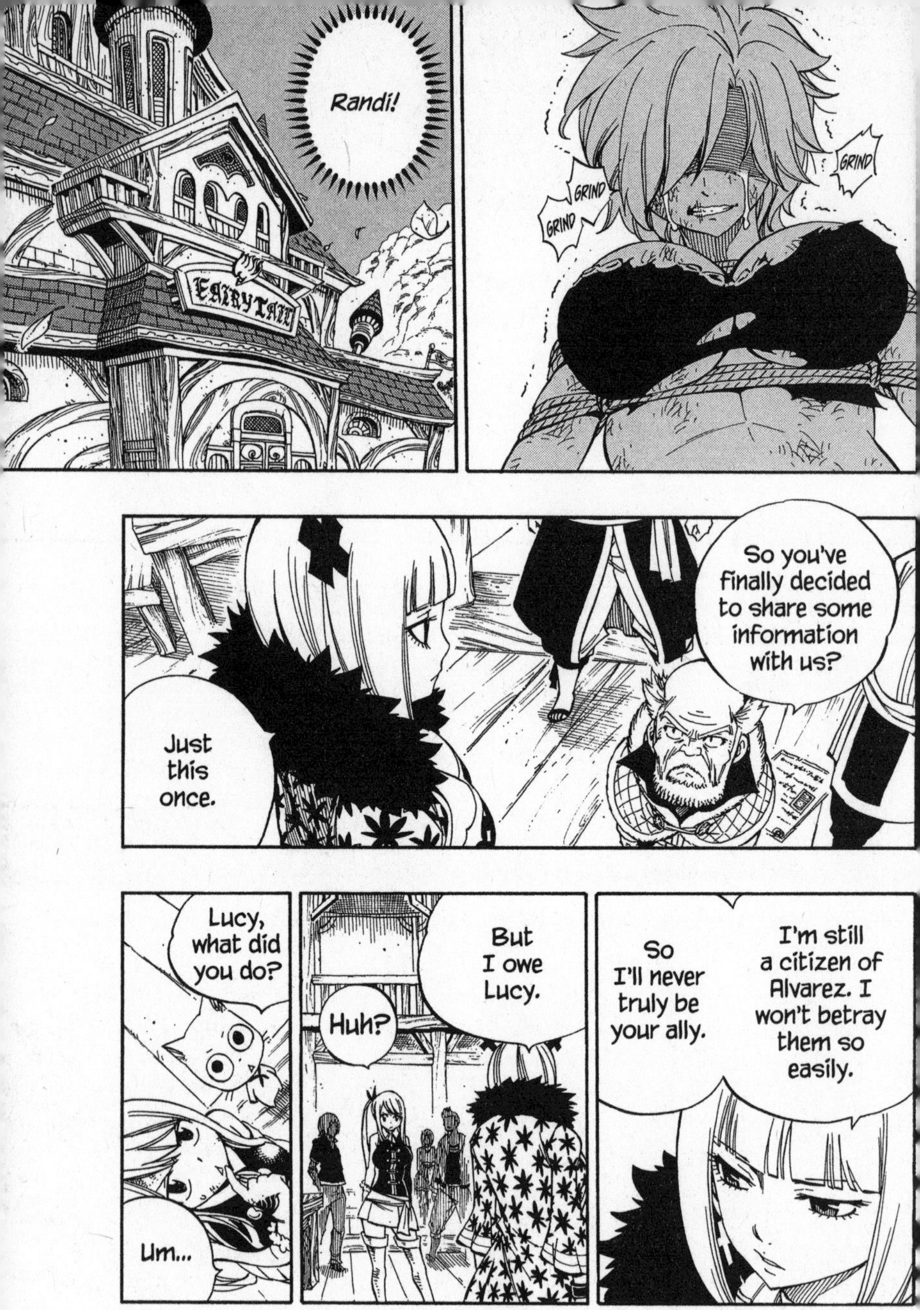
GRIND
GRIND
GRIND
Randi!
So you've finally decided to share some information with us?
Just this once.
I'm still a citizen of Alvarez. I won't betray them so easily.
So I'll never truly be your ally.
But I owe Lucy.
Huh?
Lucy, what did you do?
Um...

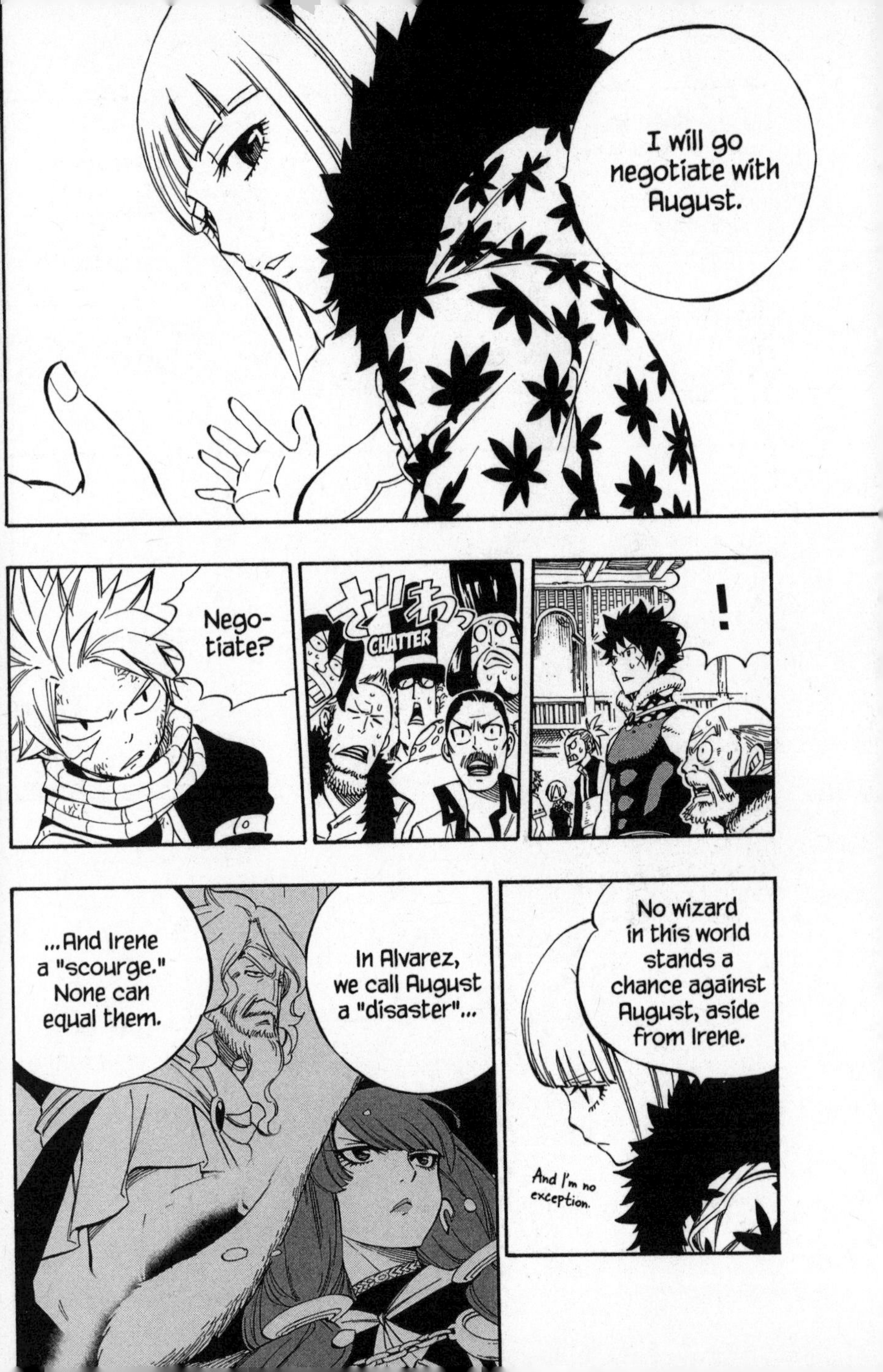
I will go negotiate with August.
!
CHATTER
Nego-tiate?
No wizard in this world stands a chance against August, aside from Irene.
And I'm no exception.
In Alvarez, we call August a "disaster"...
...And Irene a "scourge." None can equal them.

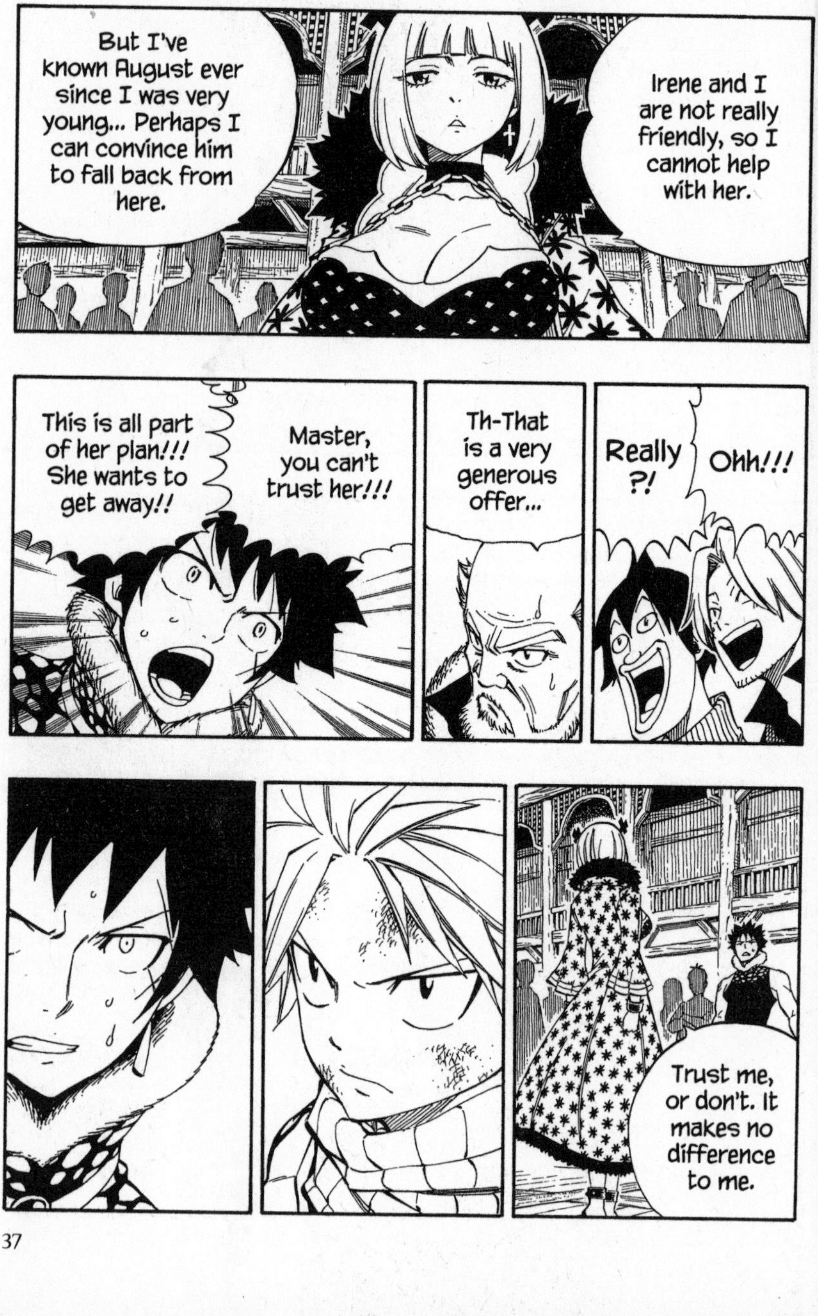
Irene and I are not really friendly, so I cannot help with her.
But I've known August ever since I was very young... Perhaps I can convince him to fall back from here.
Ohh!!!
Really?!
Th-That is a very generous offer...
Master, you can't trust her!!!
This is all part of her plan!!! She wants to get away!!
Trust me, or don't. It makes no difference to me.

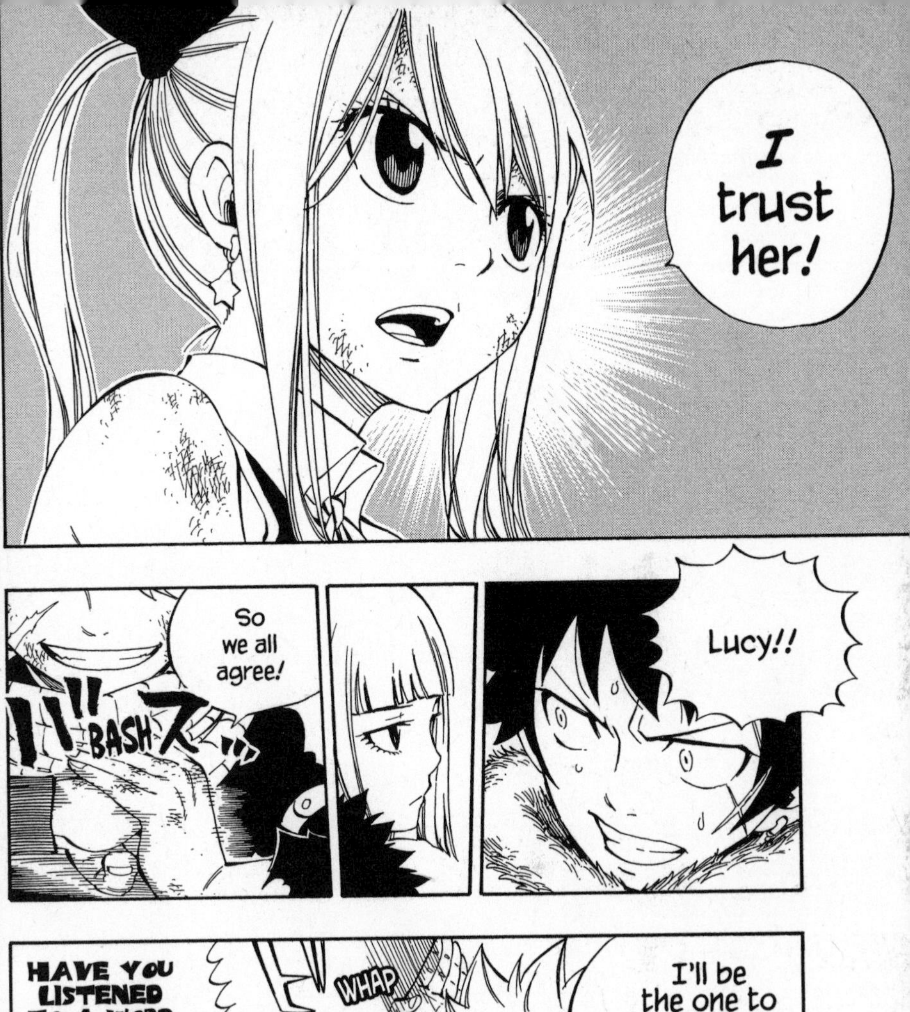
I trust her!
Lucy!!
So we all agree!
BASH
I'll be the one to take down August!!!!
WHAP
HAVE YOU LISTENED TO A WORD ANYONE HAS SAID ?!

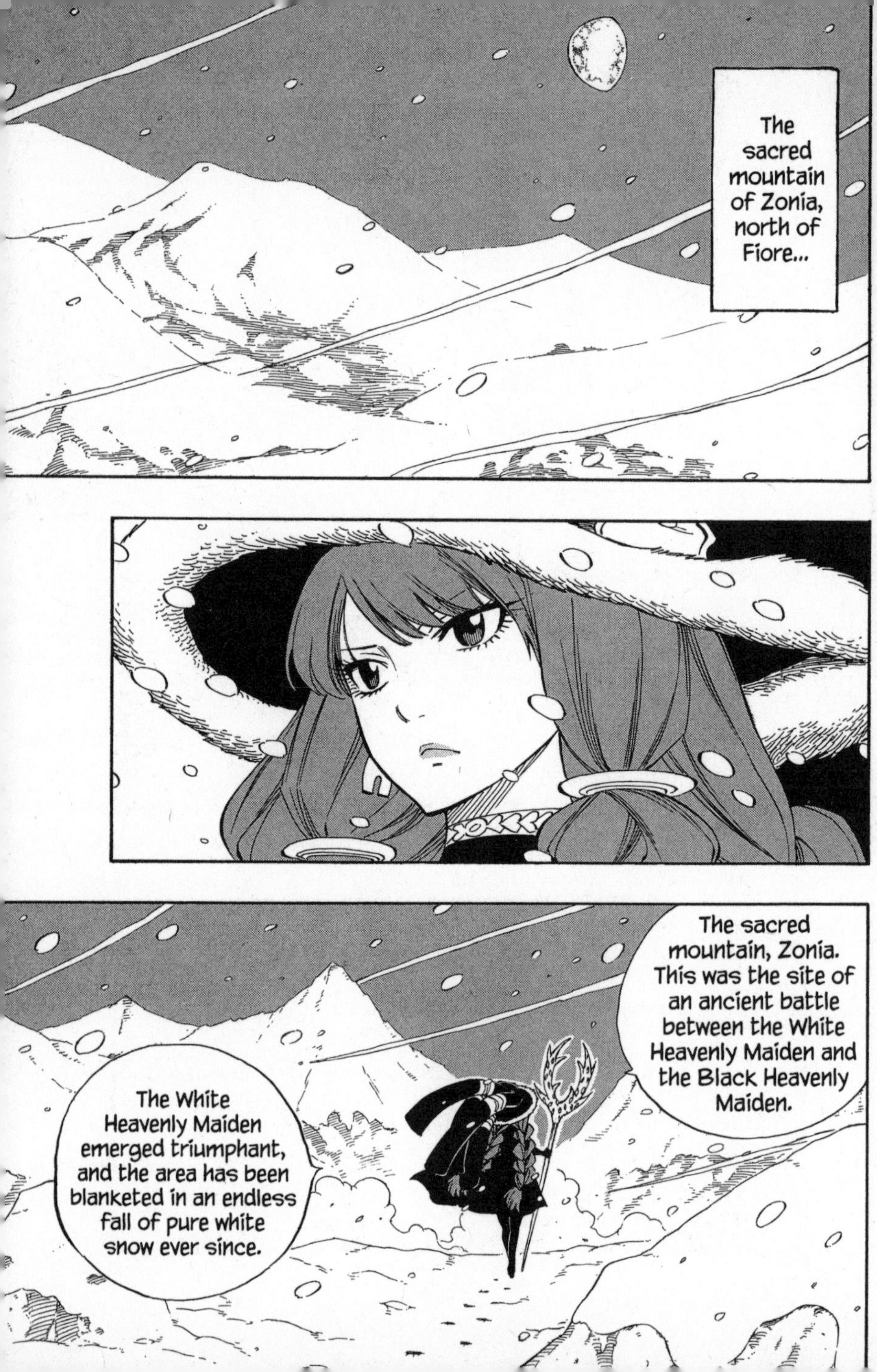
The sacred mountain of Zonia, north of Fiore...
The sacred mountain, Zonia. This was the site of an ancient battle between the White Heavenly Maiden and the Black Heavenly Maiden.
The White Heavenly Maiden emerged triumphant, and the area has been blanketed in an endless fall of pure white snow ever since.

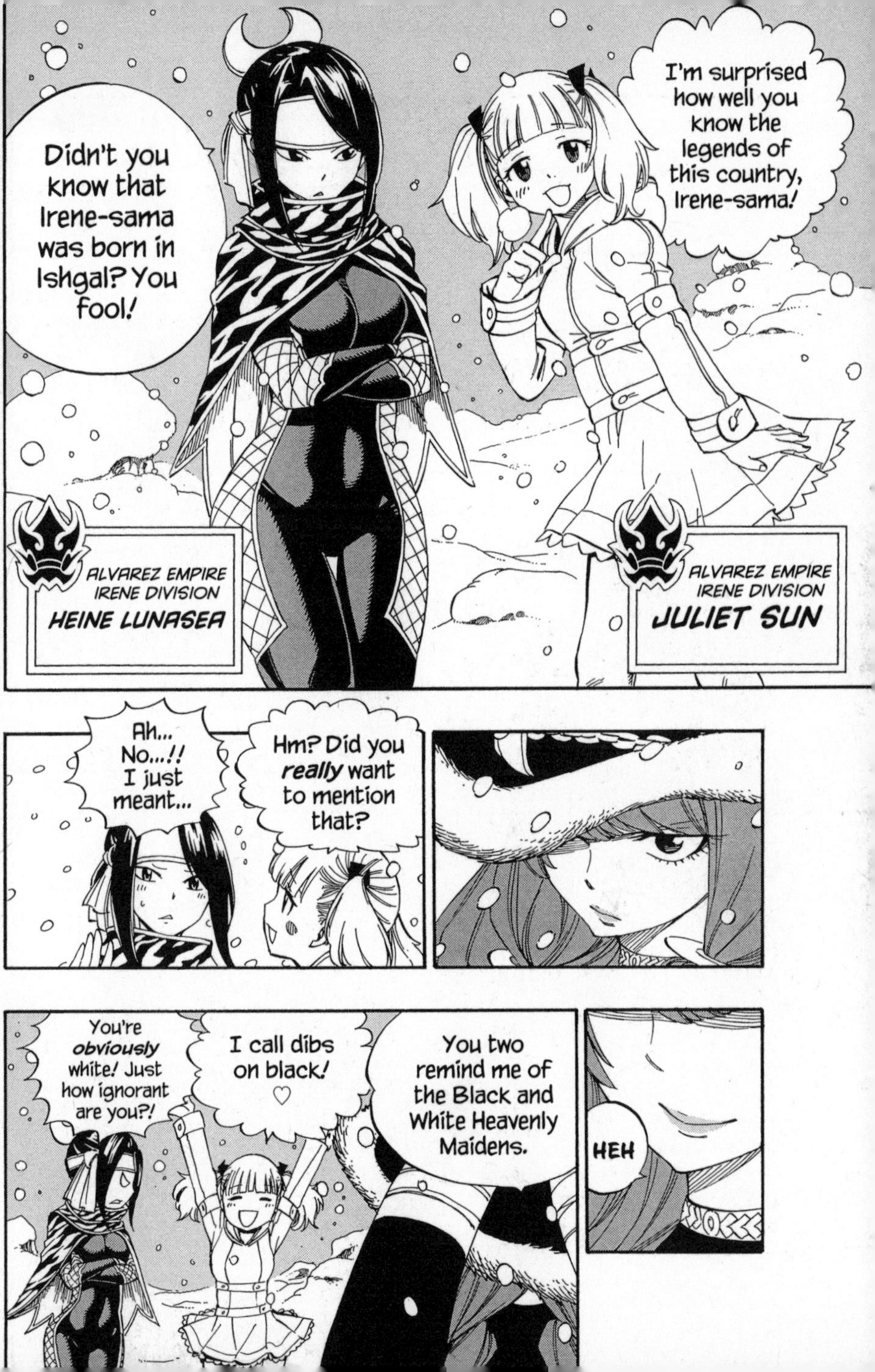
I'm surprised how well you know the legends of this country, Irene-sama!
Didn't you know that Irene-sama was born in Ishgal? You fool!
ALVAREZ EMPIRE IRENE DIVISION JULIET SUN
ALVAREZ EMPIRE IRENE DIVISION HEINE LUNASEA
Hm? Did you *really* want to mention that?
Ah... No...!! I just meant...
HEH
You two remind me of the Black and White Heavenly Maidens.
I call dibs on black! ♡
You're *obviously* white! Just how ignorant are you?!

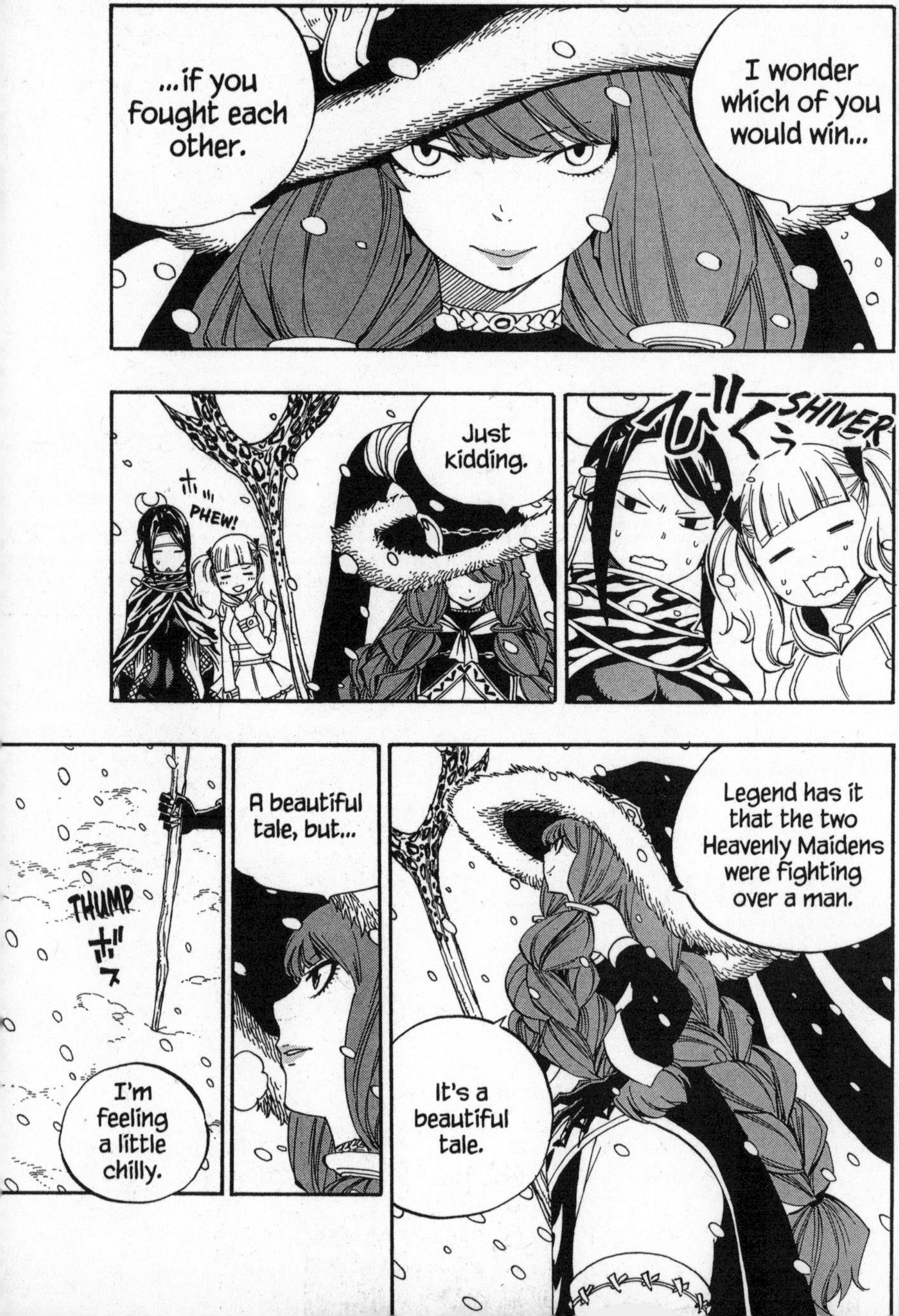
I wonder which of you would win...
...if you fought each other.
SHIVER
Just kidding.
PHEW!
Legend has it that the two Heavenly Maidens were fighting over a man.
It's a beautiful tale.
A beautiful tale, but...
THUMP
I'm feeling a little chilly.

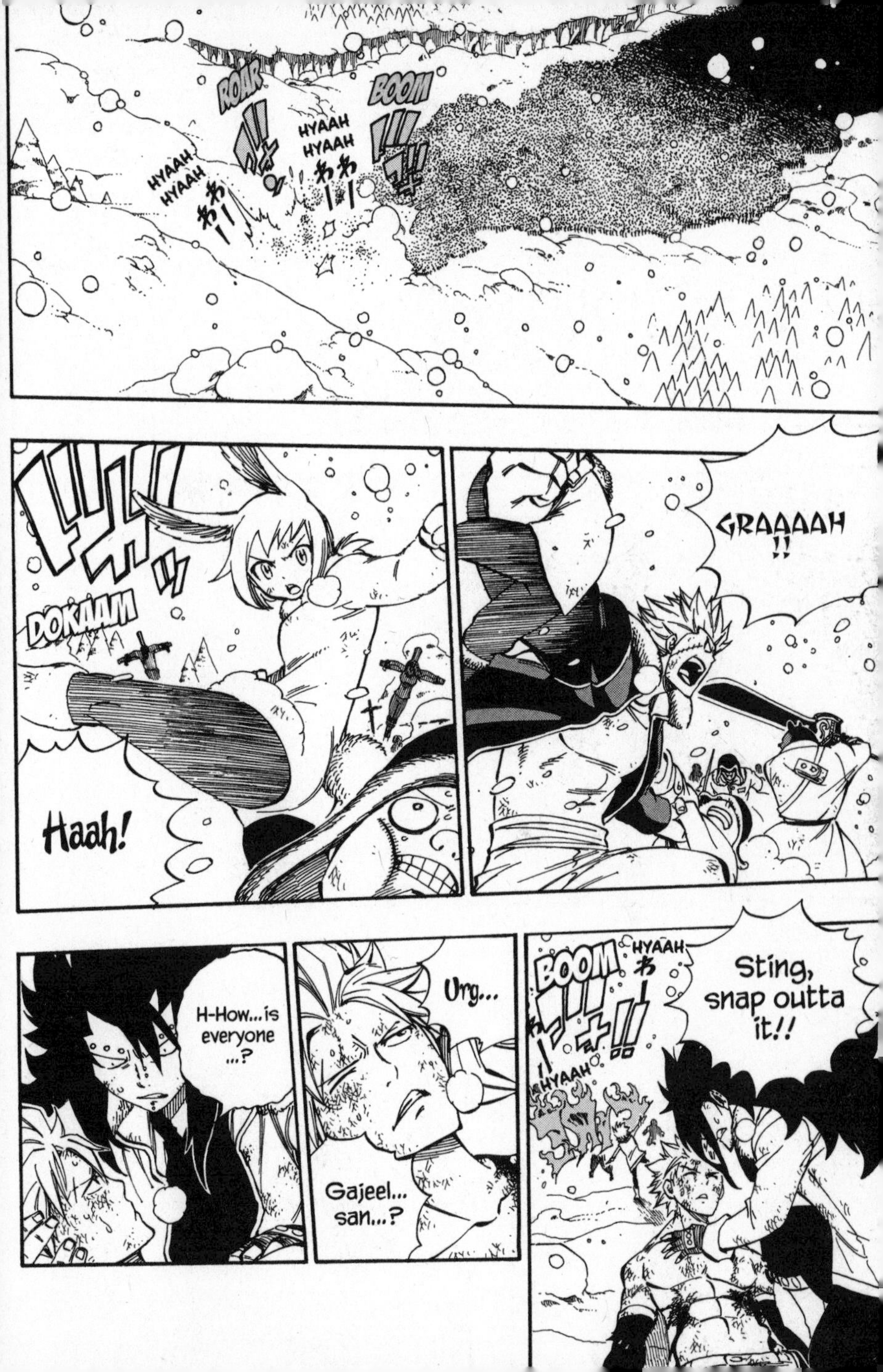
BOOM
HYAAH HYAAH
ROAR
HYAAH HYAAH
GRAAAAH!!
DOKAAM
Haah!
Sting, snap outta it!!
BOOM
HYAAH
HYAAH
Urg...
Gajeel... san...?
H-How...is everyone ...?

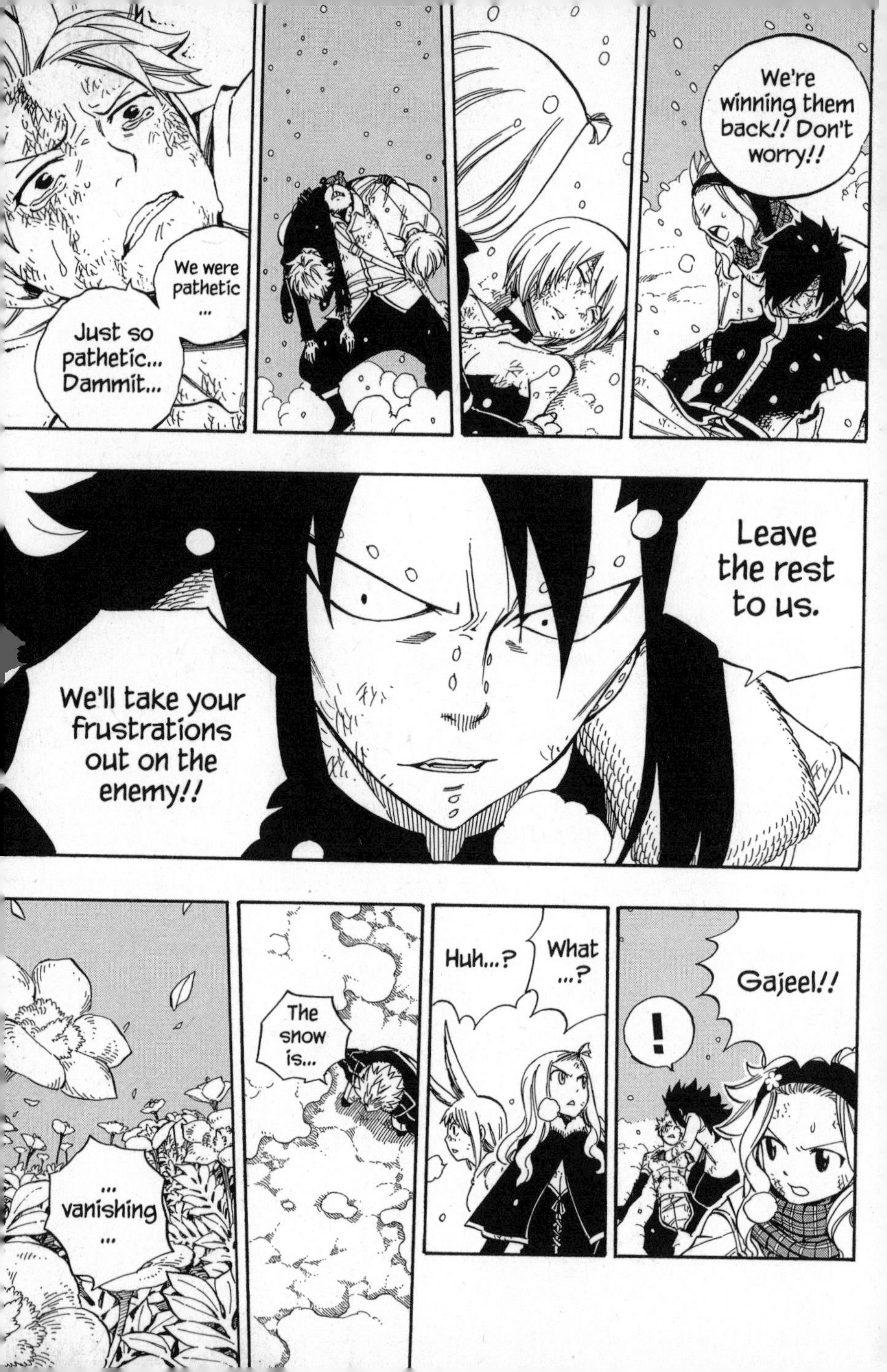
We're winning them back!! Don't worry!!
We were pathetic ...
Just so pathetic... Dammit...
Leave the rest to us.
We'll take your frustrations out on the enemy!!
Gajeel!!
!
What ...?
Huh...?
The snow is...
... vanishing ...

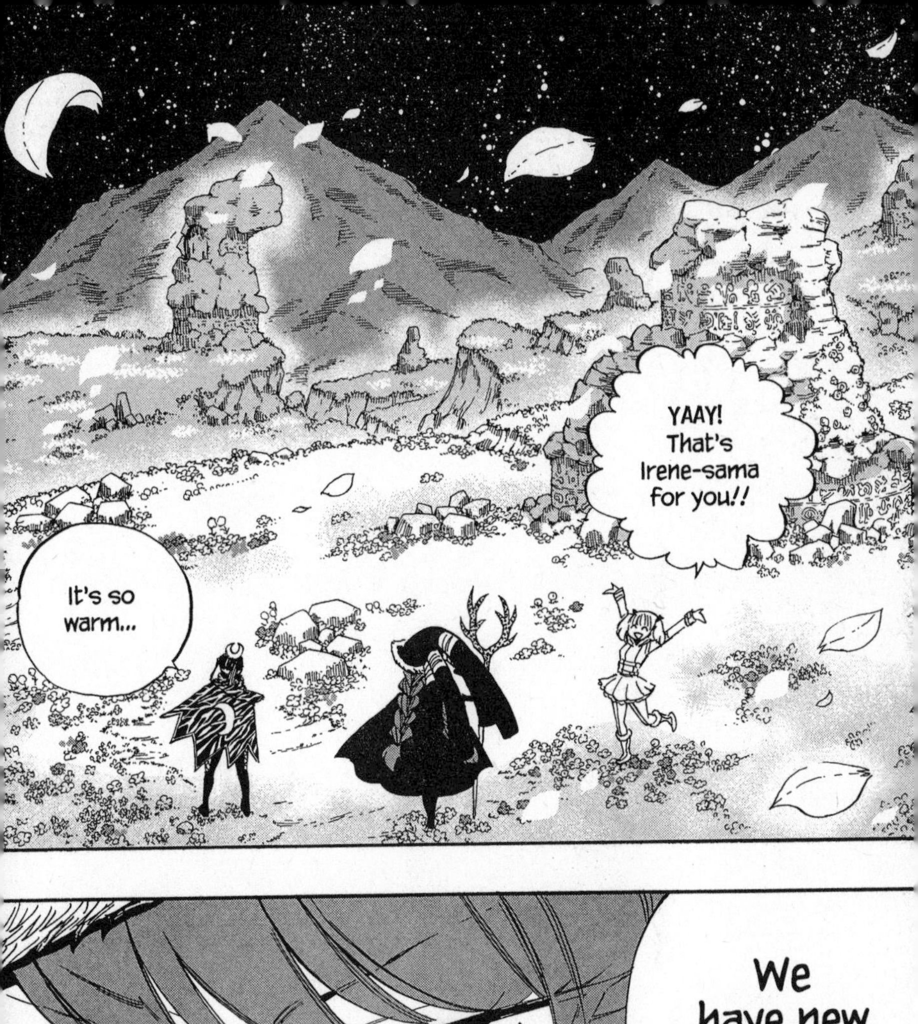
YAAY! That's Irene-sama for you!!
It's so warm...

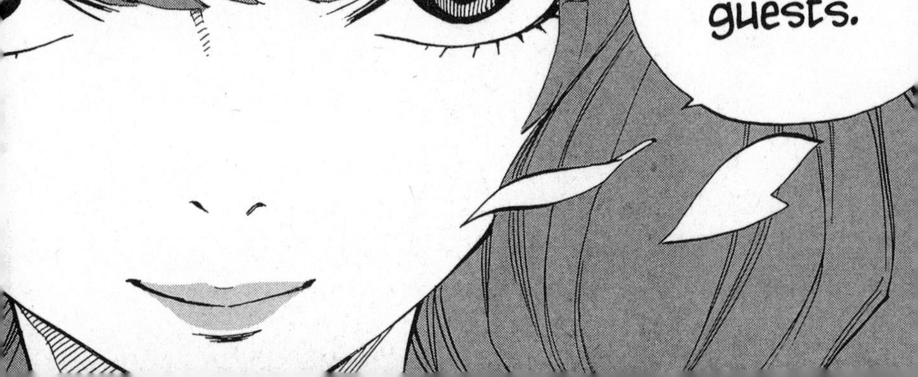
We have new guests.

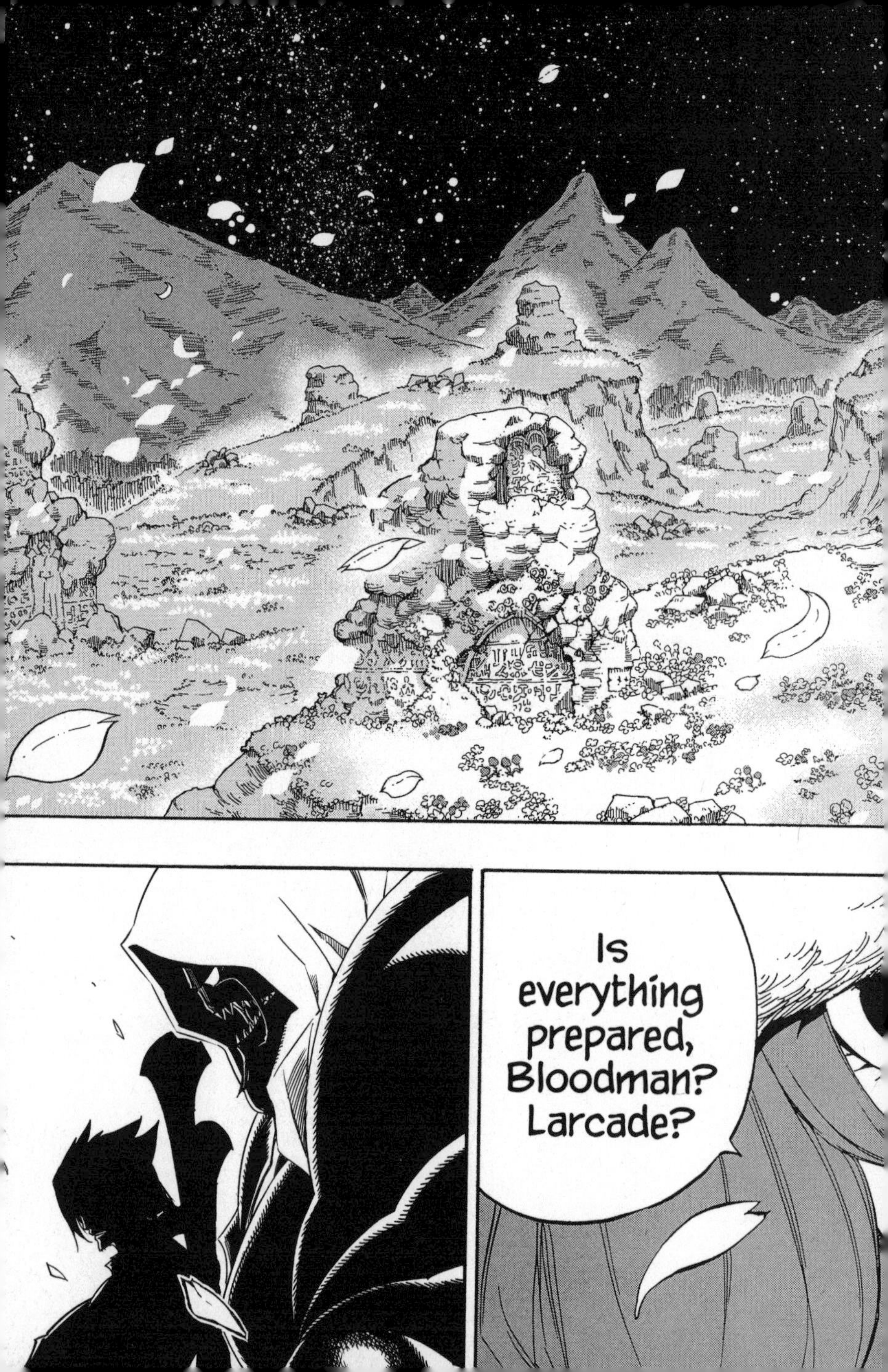
Is everything prepared, Bloodman? Larcade?

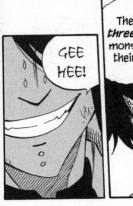

GEE
HEE!

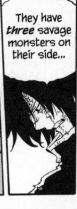

They have *three* savage monsters on their side...

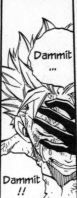

Dammit
...

Dammit
!!

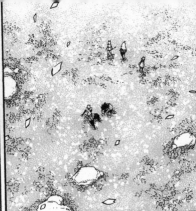

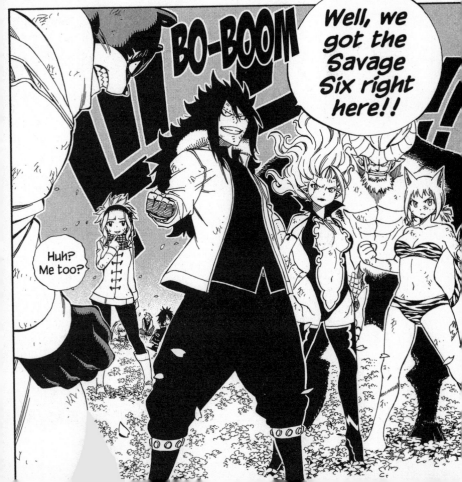

BO-BOOM

Well, we got the Savage Six right here!!

Huh? Me too?

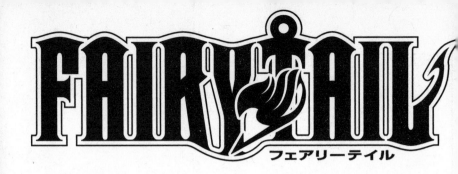

Chapter 485: The First Dinner in Five Days

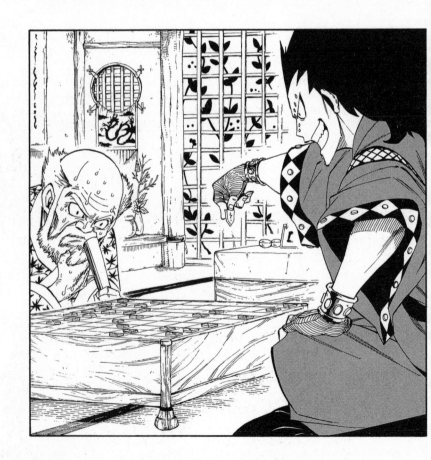

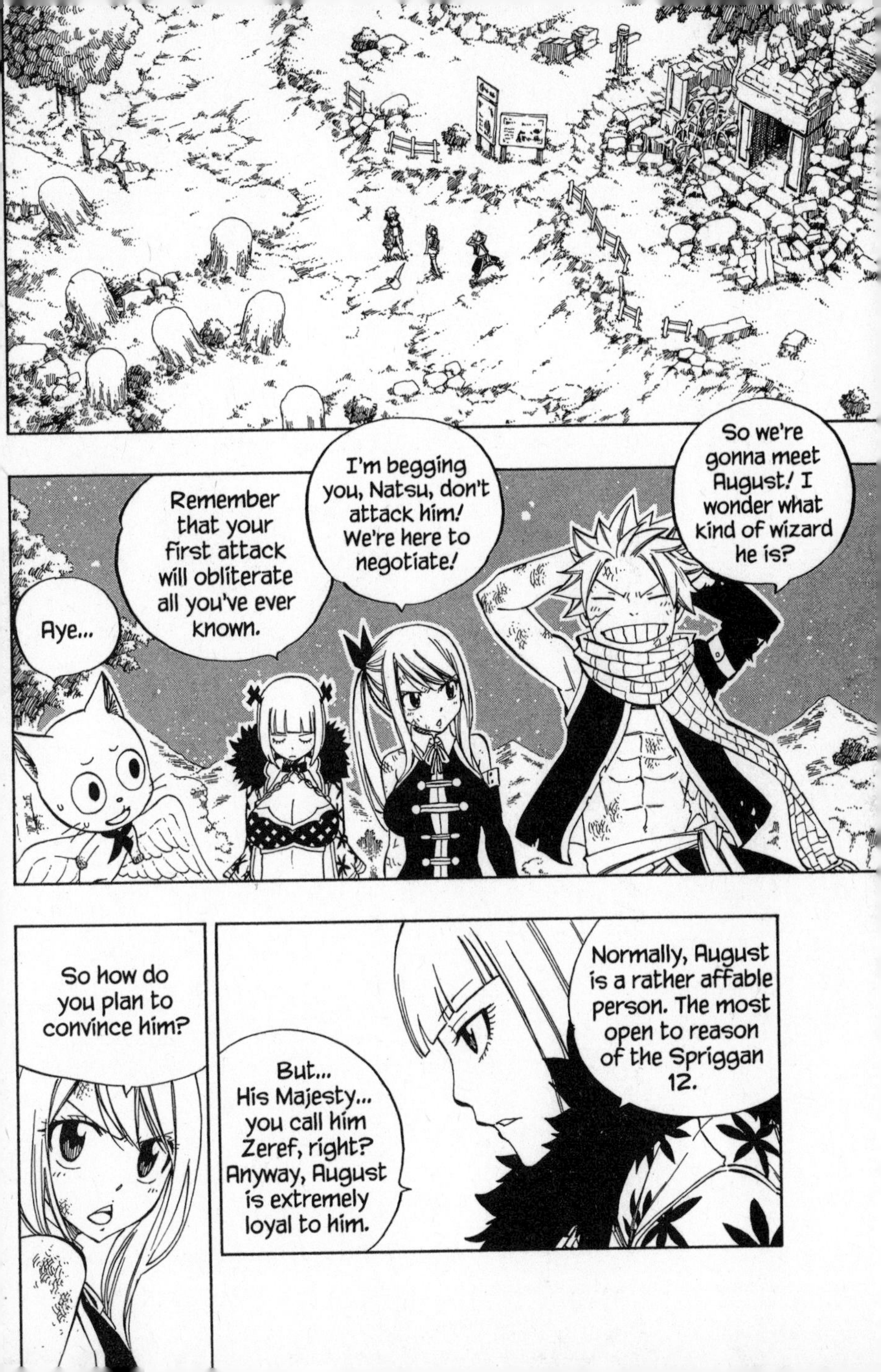
So we're gonna meet August! I wonder what kind of wizard he is?
I'm begging you, Natsu, don't attack him! We're here to negotiate!
Remember that your first attack will obliterate all you've ever known.
Aye...
Normally, August is a rather affable person. The most open to reason of the Spriggan 12.
But... His Majesty... you call him Zeref, right? Anyway, August is extremely loyal to him.
So how do you plan to convince him?

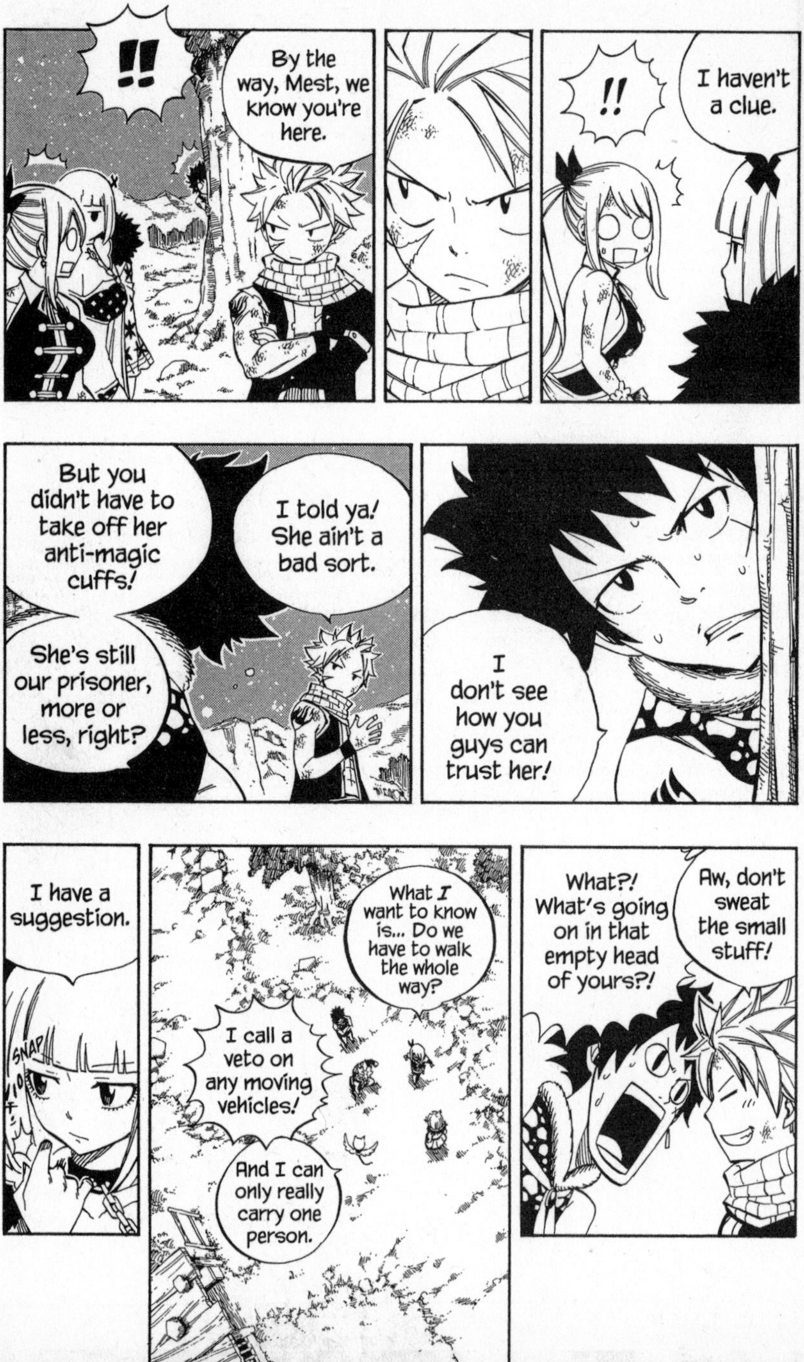
I haven't a clue.
!!
By the way, Mest, we know you're here.
!!
I don't see how you guys can trust her!
I told ya! She ain't a bad sort.
But you didn't have to take off her anti-magic cuffs!
She's still our prisoner, more or less, right?
Aw, don't sweat the small stuff!
What?! What's going on in that empty head of yours?!
What *I* want to know is... Do we have to walk the whole way?
I call a veto on any moving vehicles!
And I can only really carry one person.
I have a suggestion.
SNAP

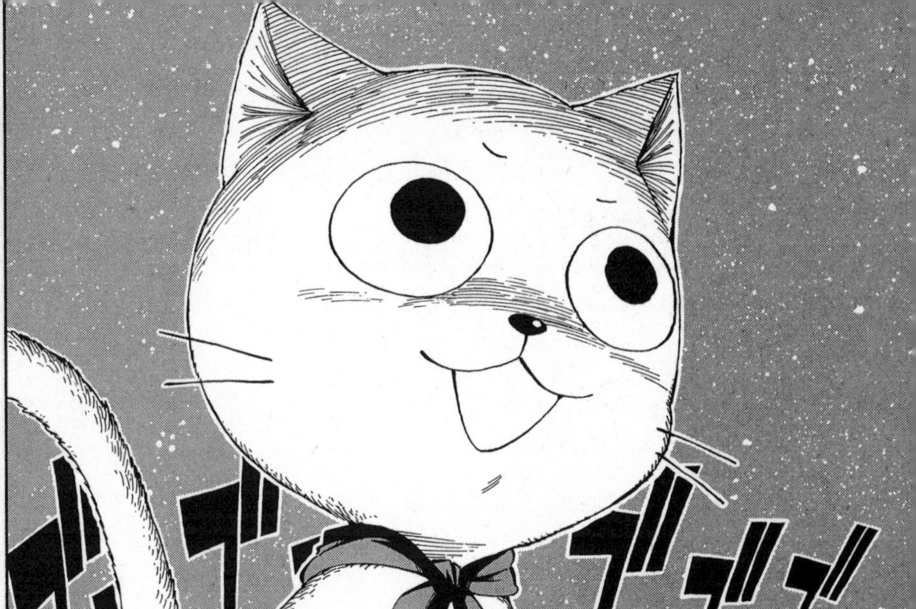
RUM
MMBBLE

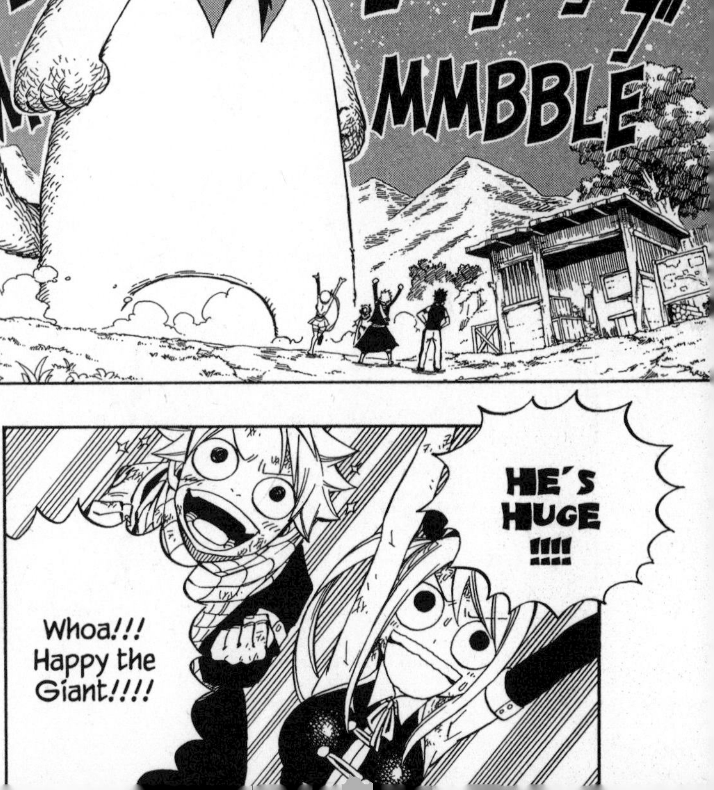
HE´S HUGE !!!!
Whoa!!! Happy the Giant!!!!

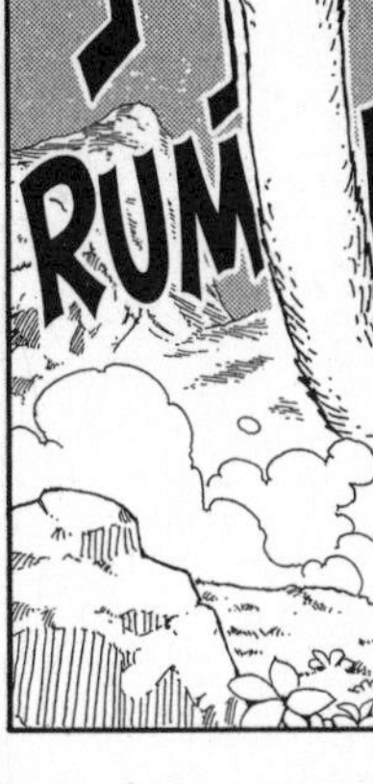
Now we can all get on board. ♡

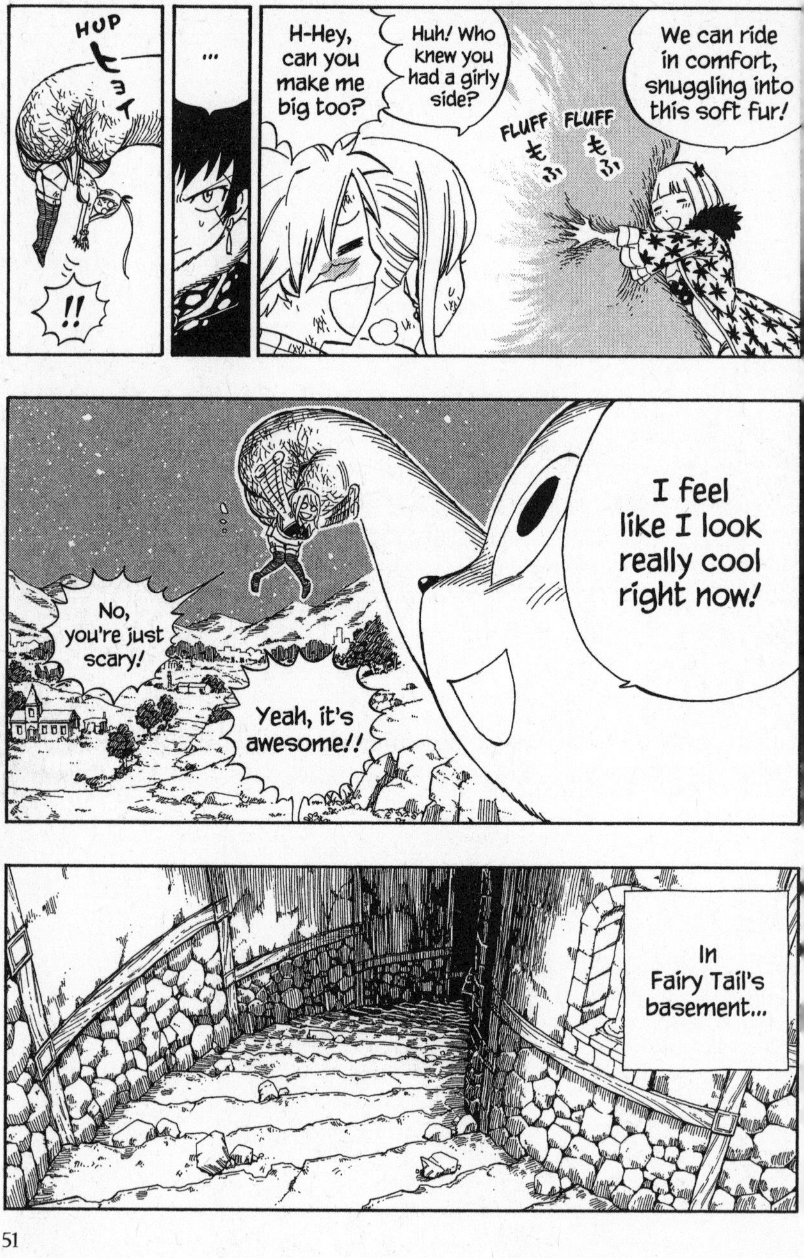
We can ride in comfort, snuggling into this soft fur!
FLUFF もふ
FLUFF もふ
Huh! Who knew you had a girly side?
H-Hey, can you make me big too?
...
HUP ヒョイ
!!
I feel like I look really cool right now!
Yeah, it's awesome!!
No, you're just scary!
In Fairy Tail's basement...

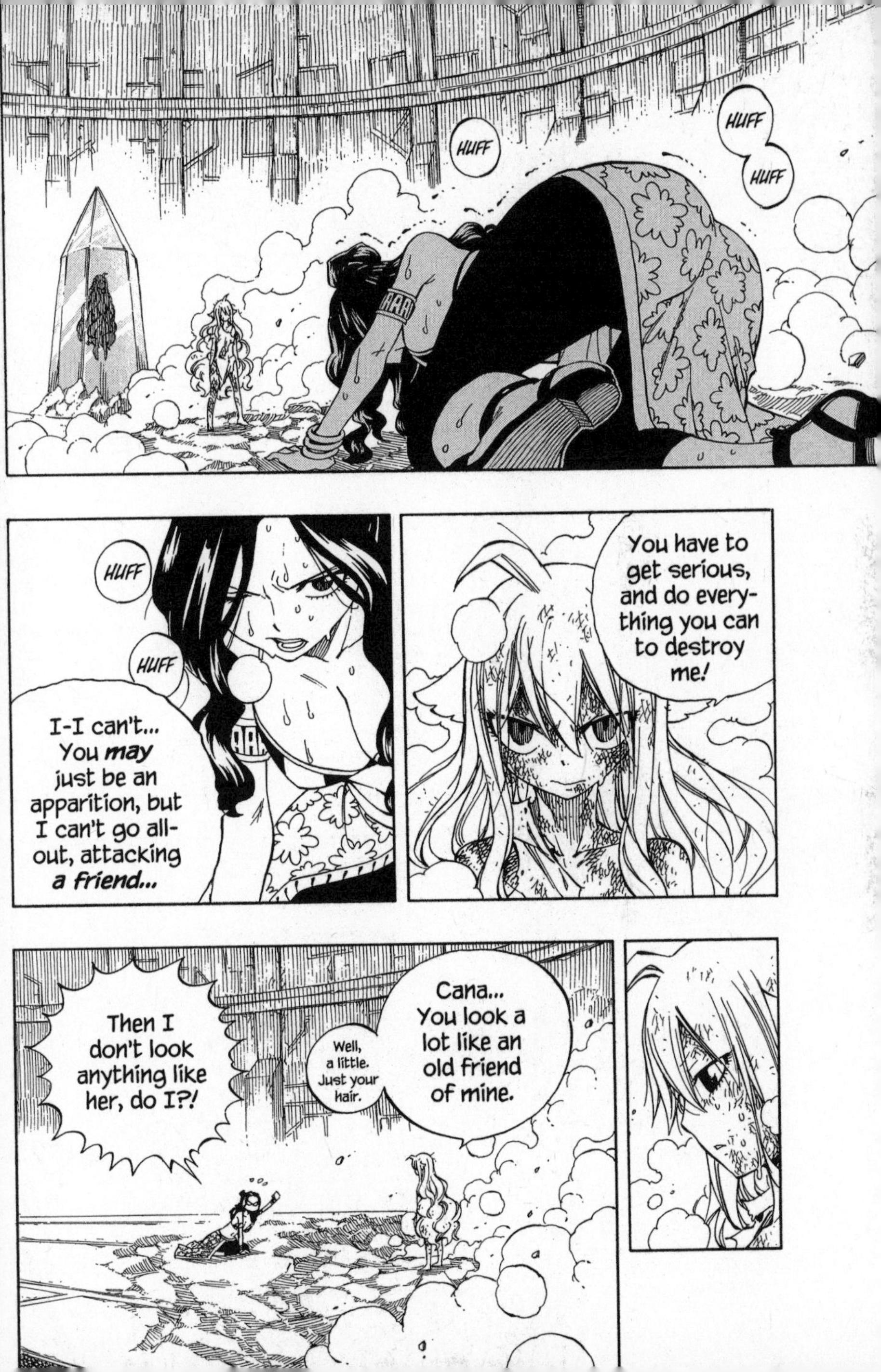
HUFF
HUFF
HUFF
You have to get serious, and do everything you can to destroy me!
HUFF
HUFF
I-I can't... You may just be an apparition, but I can't go all-out, attacking a friend...
Cana... You look a lot like an old friend of mine.
Well, a little. Just your hair.
Then I don't look anything like her, do I?!

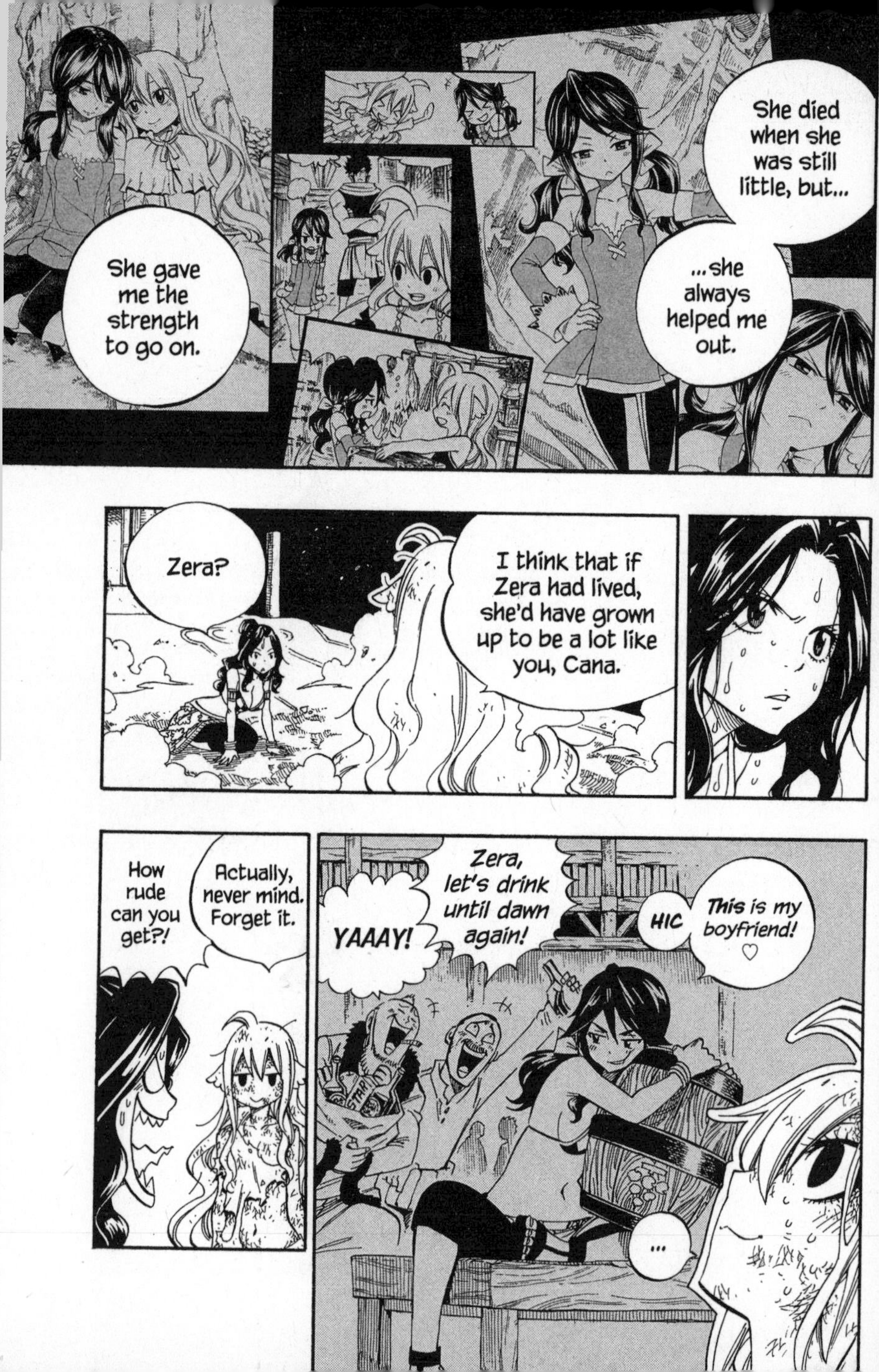
She died when she was still little, but...
...she always helped me out.
She gave me the strength to go on.
I think that if Zera had lived, she'd have grown up to be a lot like you, Cana.
Zera?
This is my boyfriend! ♡
HIC
Zera, let's drink until dawn again!
YAAAY!
...
Actually, never mind. Forget it.
How rude can you get?!

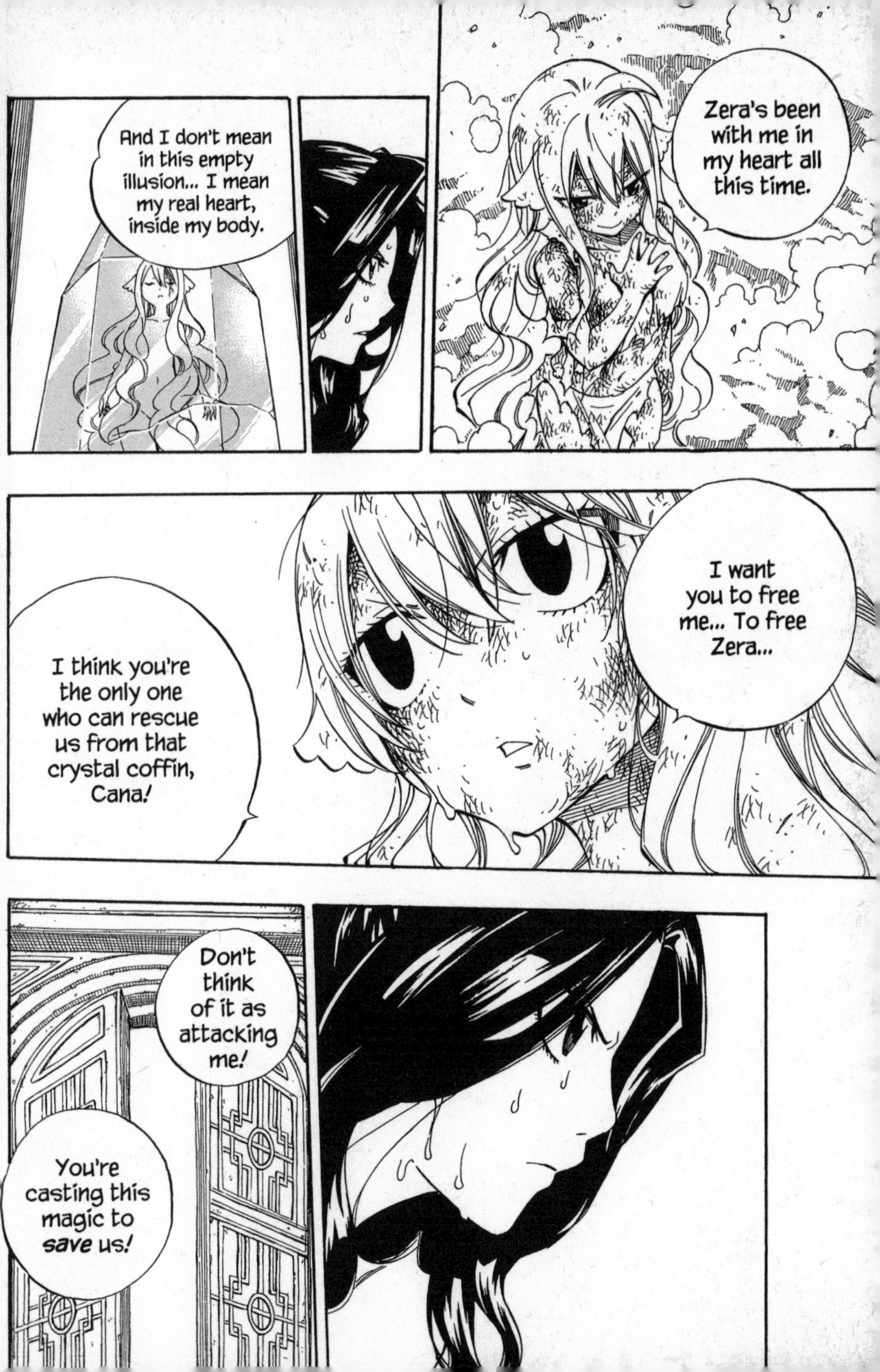
Zera's been with me in my heart all this time.
And I don't mean in this empty illusion... I mean my real heart, inside my body.
I want you to free me... To free Zera...
I think you're the only one who can rescue us from that crystal coffin, Cana!
Don't think of it as attacking me!
You're casting this magic to *save* us!

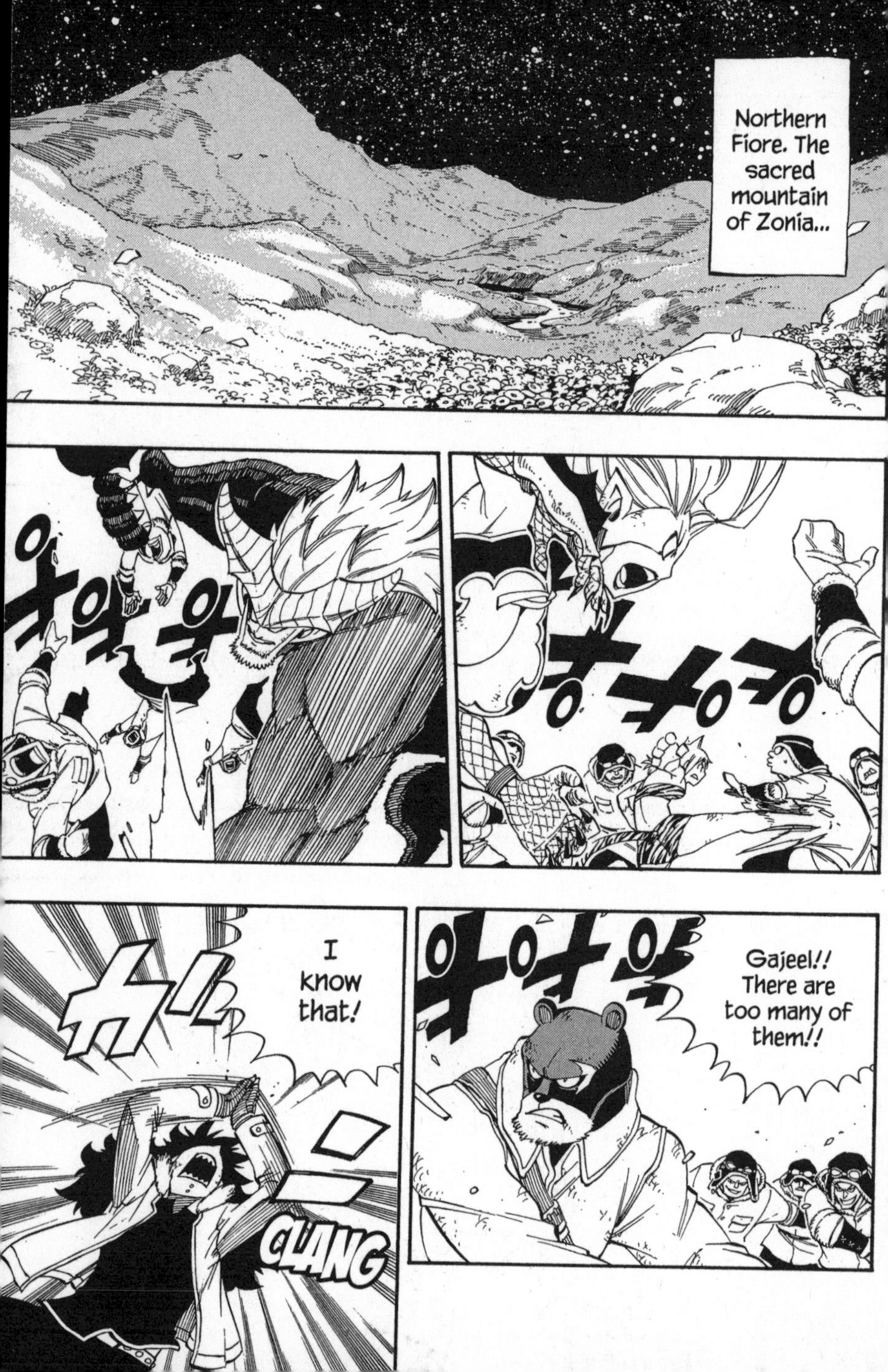
Northern Fiore. The sacred mountain of Zonia...
Gajeel!! There are too many of them!!
I know that!
CLANG

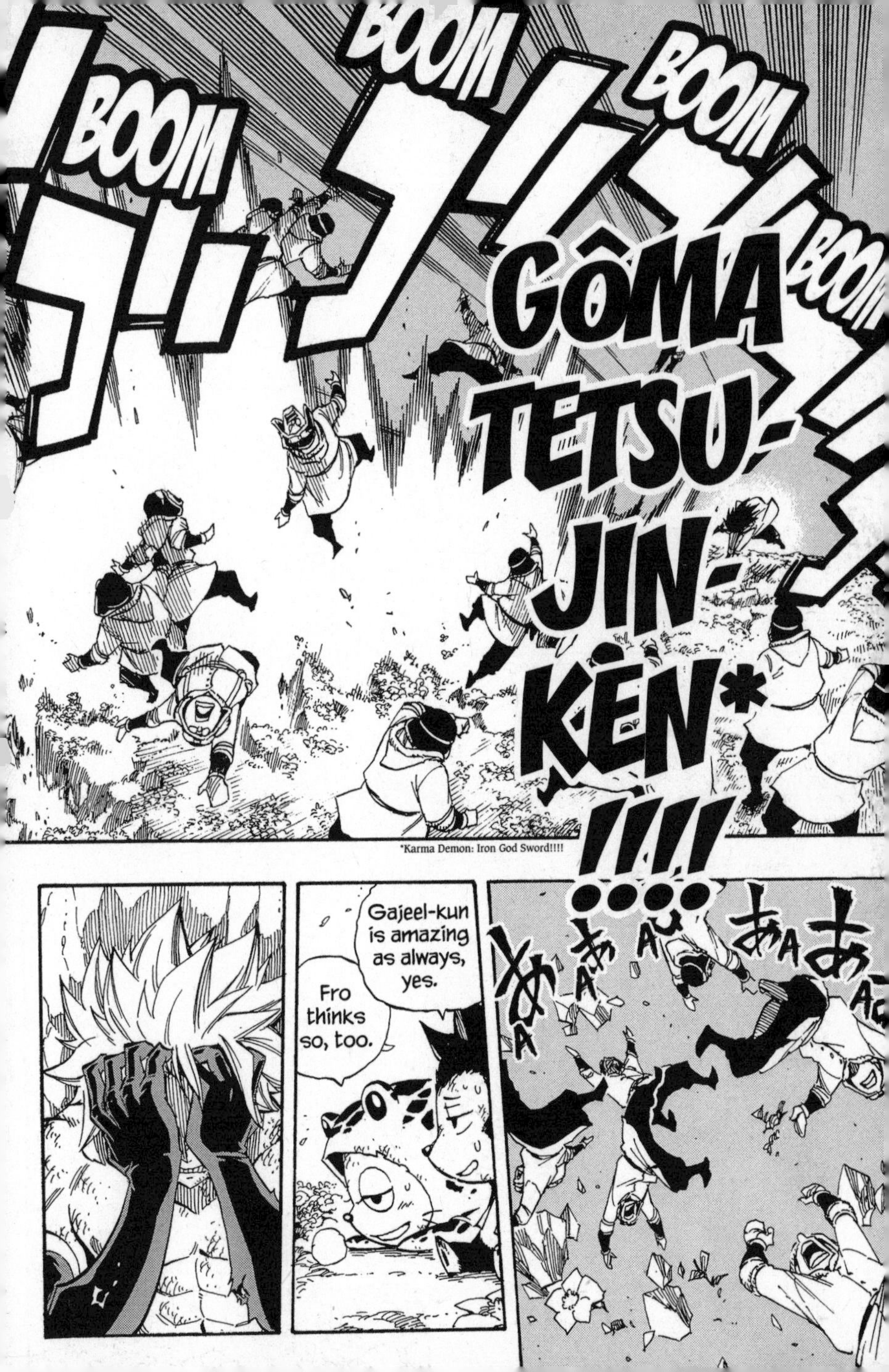
BOOM
BOOM
BOOM
BOOM
GÔMA TETSU-JIN-KÊN*!!!!
*Karma Demon: Iron God Sword!!!!
Gajeel-kun is amazing as always, yes.
Fro thinks so, too.

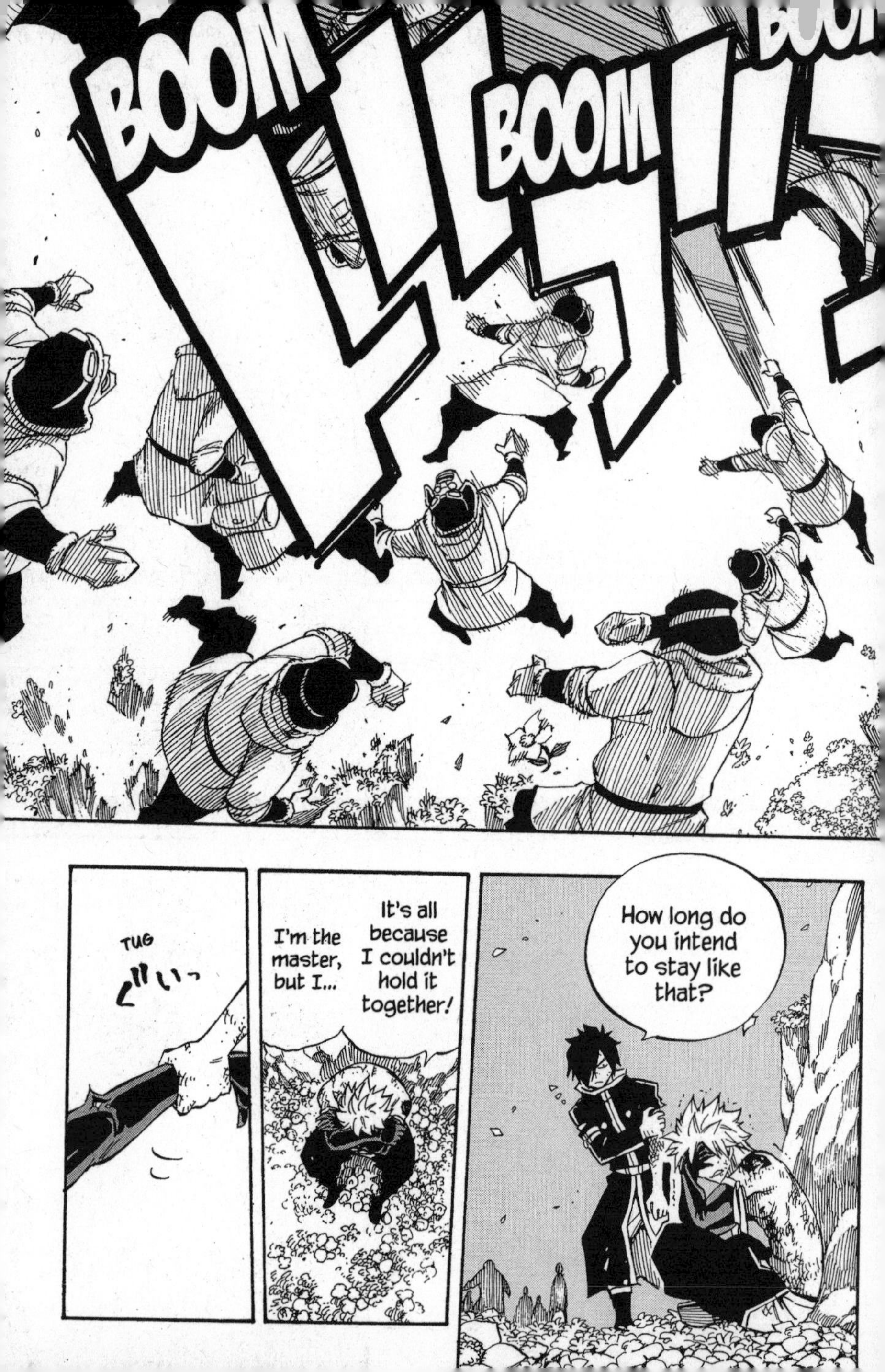
BOOM
BOOM
How long do you intend to stay like that?
It's all because I couldn't hold it together!
I'm the master, but I...
TUG

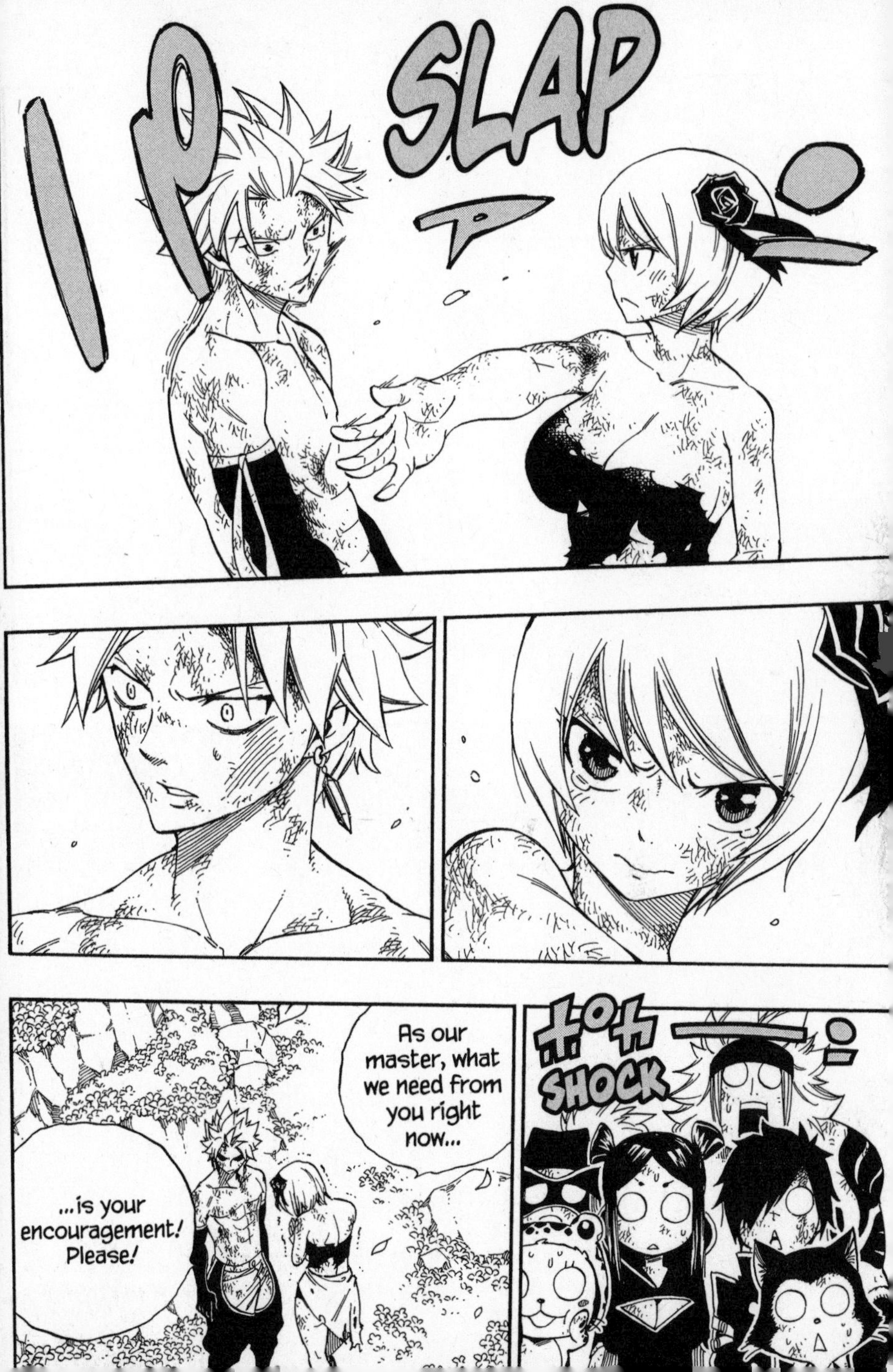
SLAP
SHOCK
As our master, what we need from you right now...
...is your encouragement! Please!

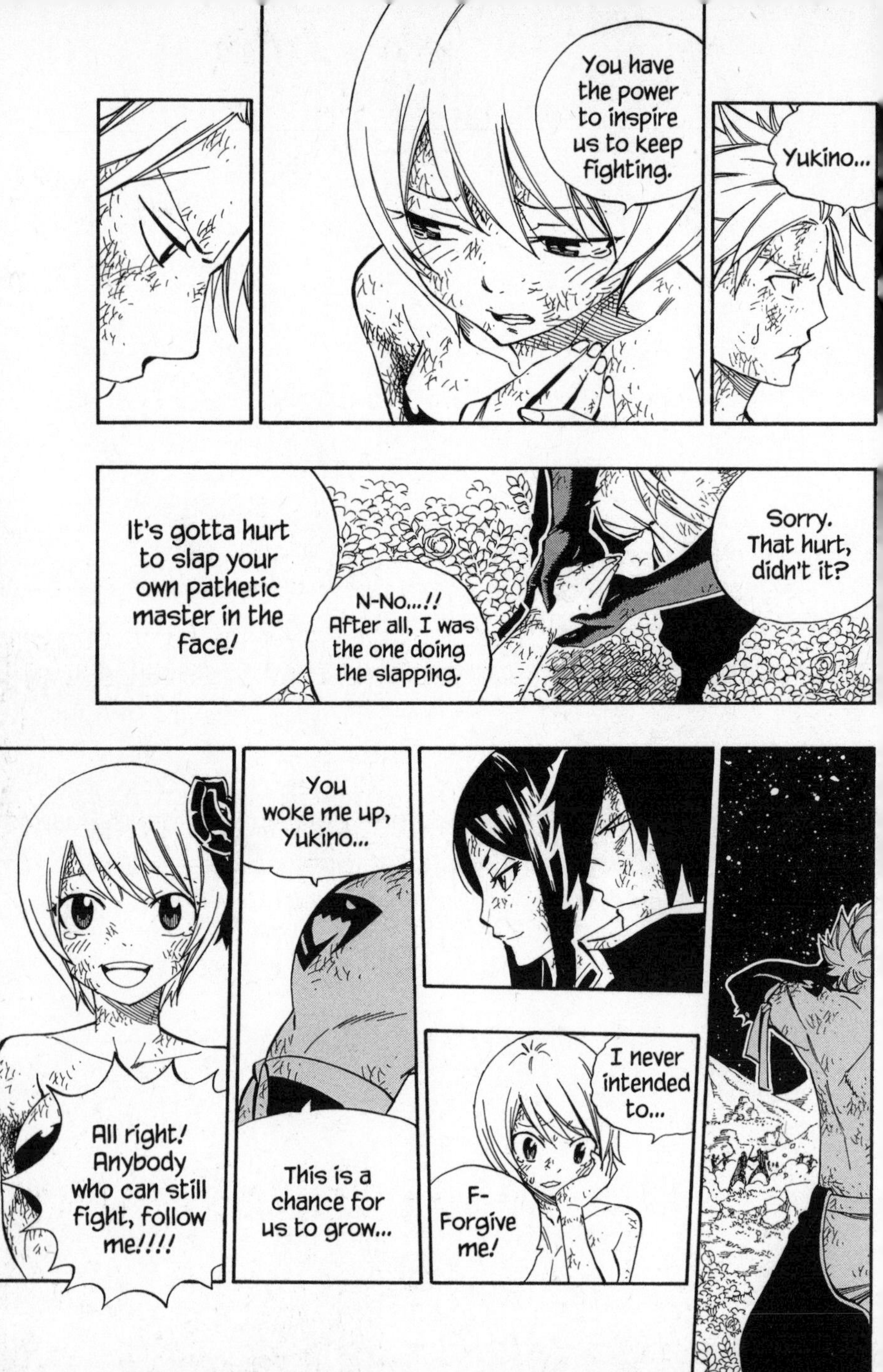
Yukino...
You have the power to inspire us to keep fighting.
Sorry. That hurt, didn't it?
N-No...!! After all, I was the one doing the slapping.
It's gotta hurt to slap your own pathetic master in the face!
I never intended to...
F- Forgive me!
You woke me up, Yukino...
This is a chance for us to grow...
All right! Anybody who can still fight, follow me!!!!

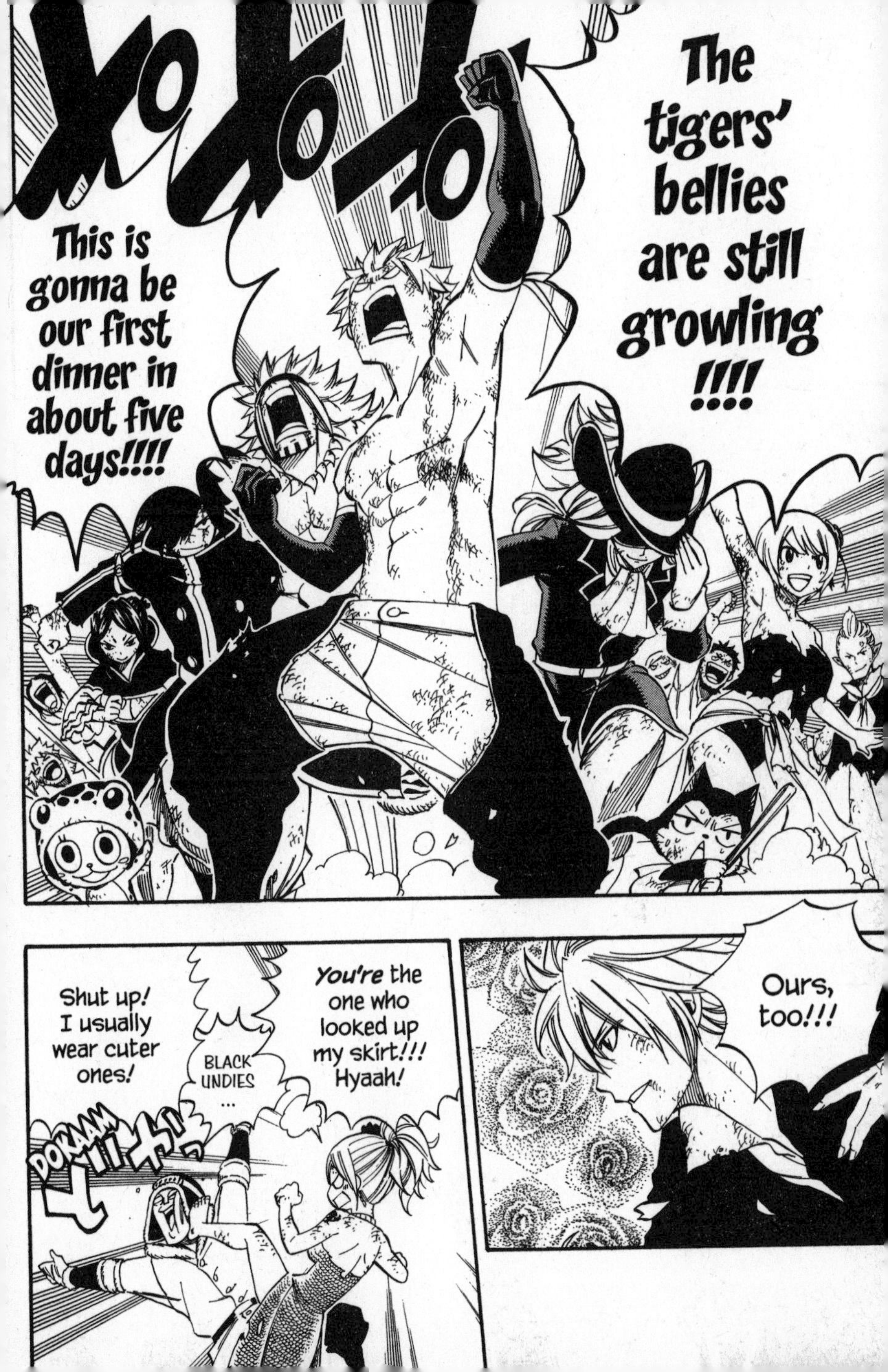
The tigers' bellies are still growling!!!!
This is gonna be our first dinner in about five days!!!!
Ours, too!!!
You're the one who looked up my skirt!!! Hyaah!
BLACK UNDIES ...
Shut up! I usually wear cuter ones!
DOKAAM

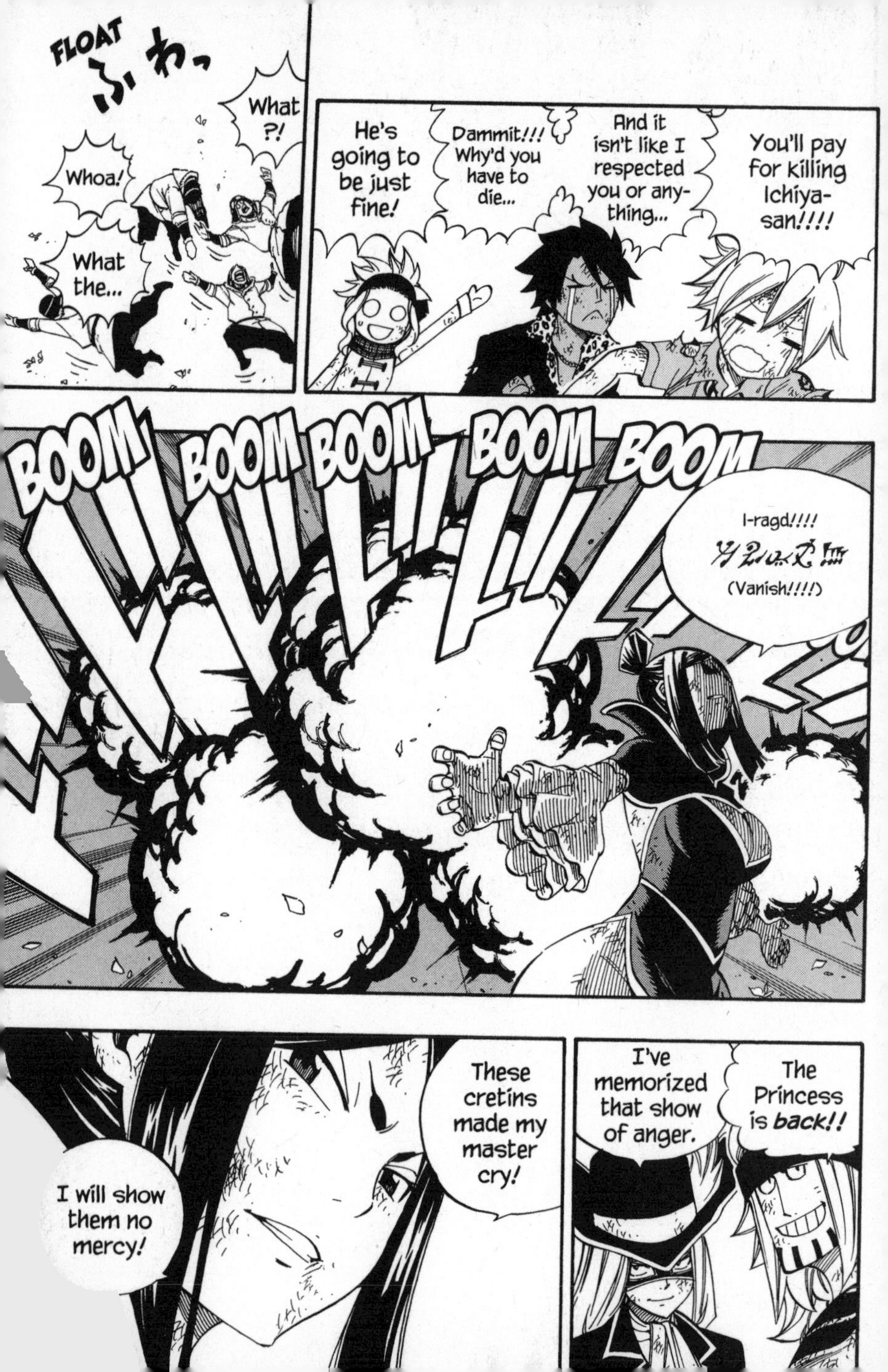
You'll pay for killing Ichiya-san!!!!
And it isn't like I respected you or anything...
Dammit!!! Why'd you have to die...
He's going to be just fine!
What ?!
FLOAT
ふわっ
Whoa!
What the...
BOOM BOOM BOOM BOOM BOOM
I-ragd!!!!
(Vanish!!!!)
The Princess is back!!
I've memorized that show of anger.
These cretins made my master cry!
I will show them no mercy!

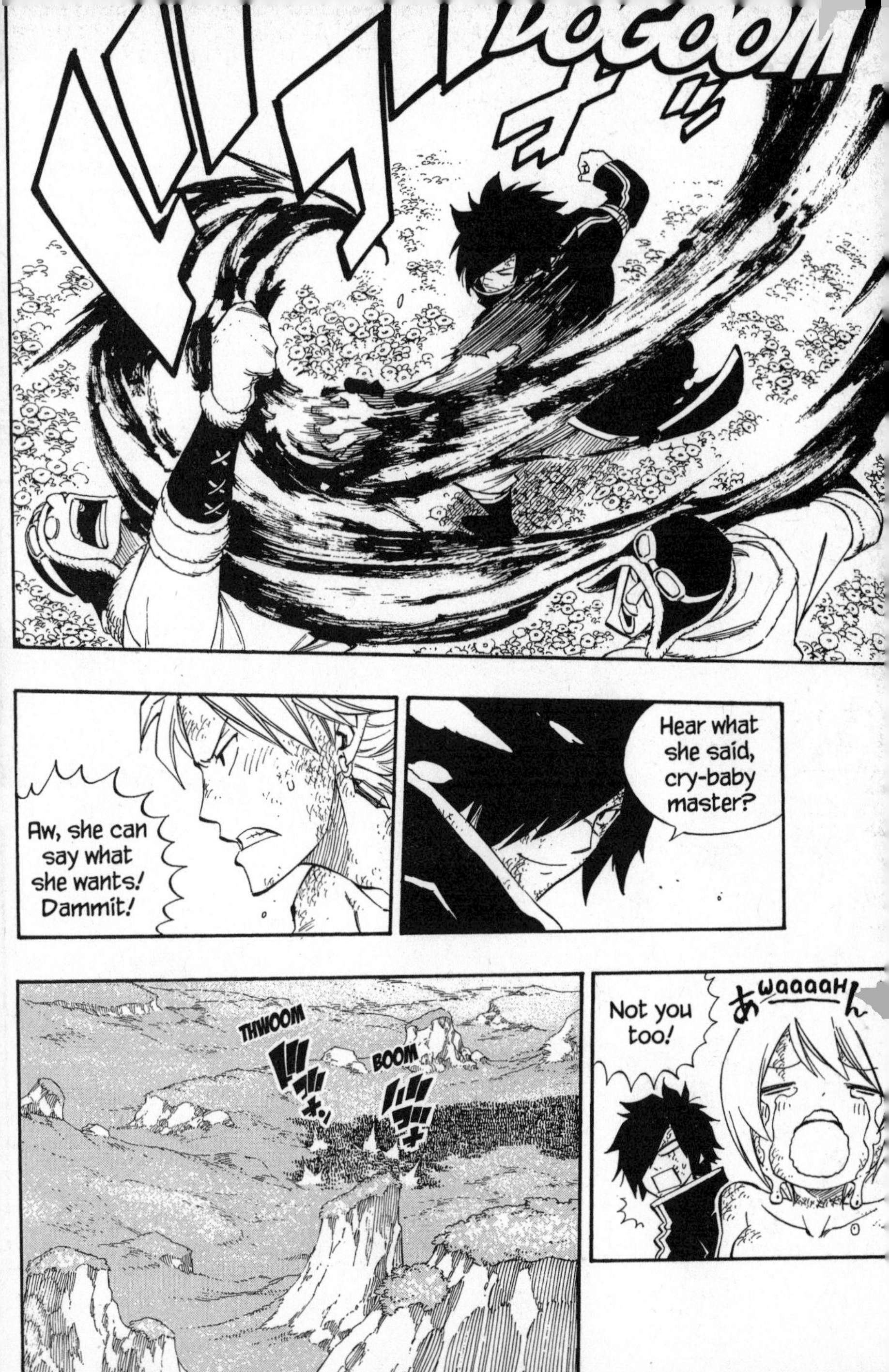
DOGOOM
Hear what she said, cry-baby master?
Aw, she can say what she wants! Dammit!
WAAAAH
Not you too!
THWOOM
BOOM

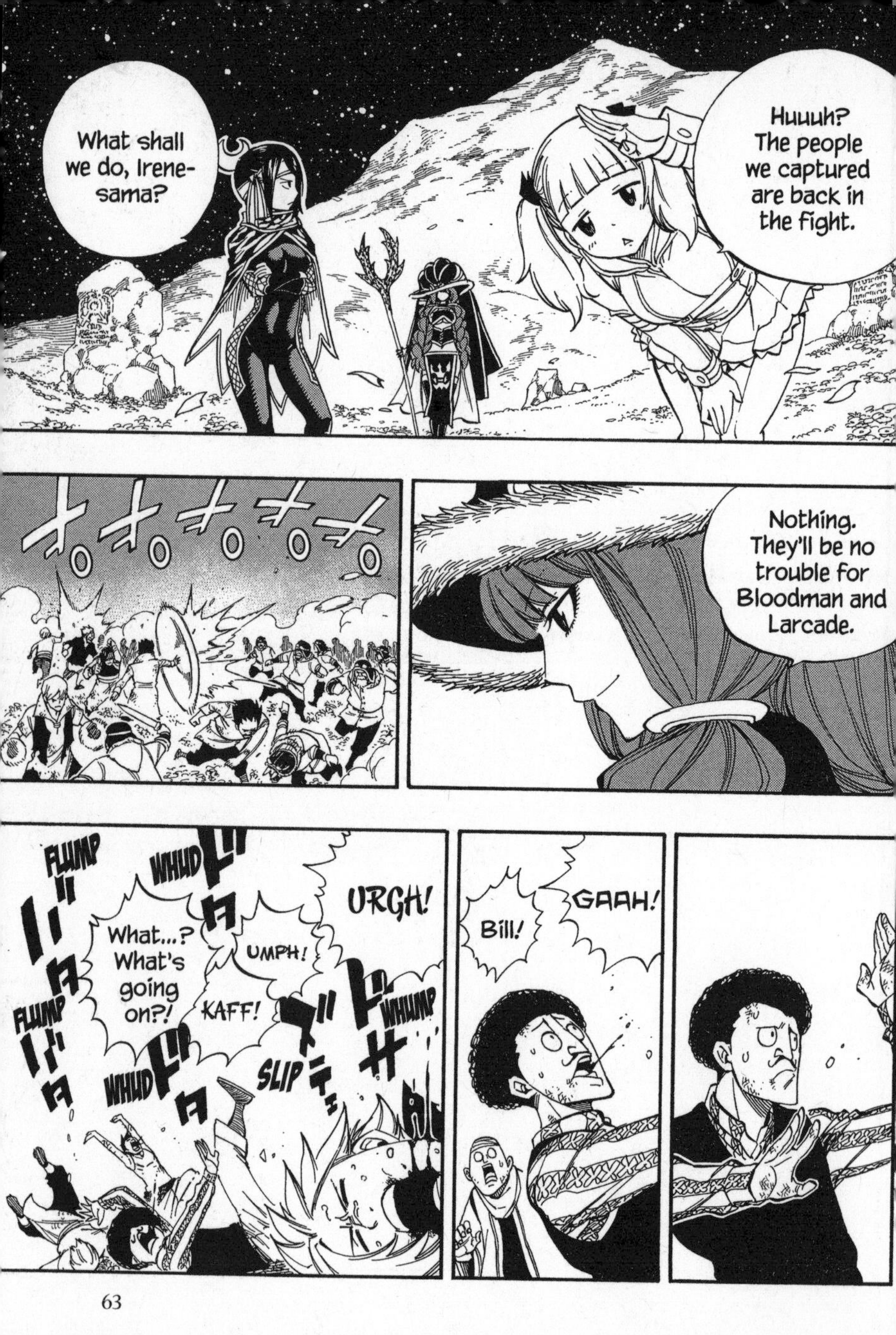
Huuuh? The people we captured are back in the fight.
What shall we do, Irene-sama?
Nothing. They'll be no trouble for Bloodman and Larcade.
GAAH!
Bill!
URGH!
WHUMP
UMPH!
WHUD
What...? What's going on?!
KAFF!
SLIP
FLUMP
FLUMP
WHUD

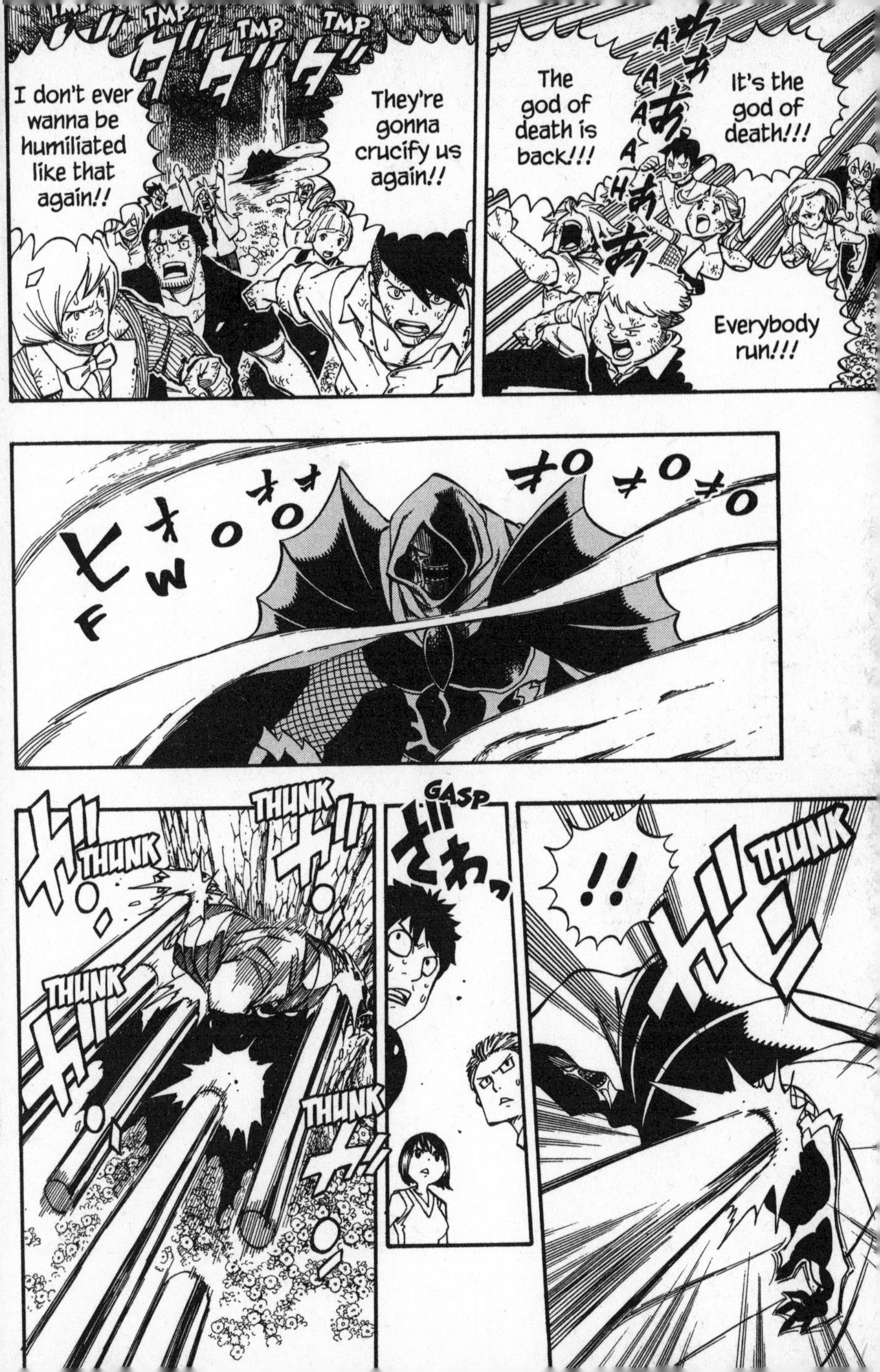
A A A A A H
It's the god of death!!!
The god of death is back!!!
Everybody run!!!
TMP TMP TMP
They're gonna crucify us again!!
I don't ever wanna be humiliated like that again!!
FW
THUNK
!!
GASP
THUNK
THUNK
THUNK
THUNK

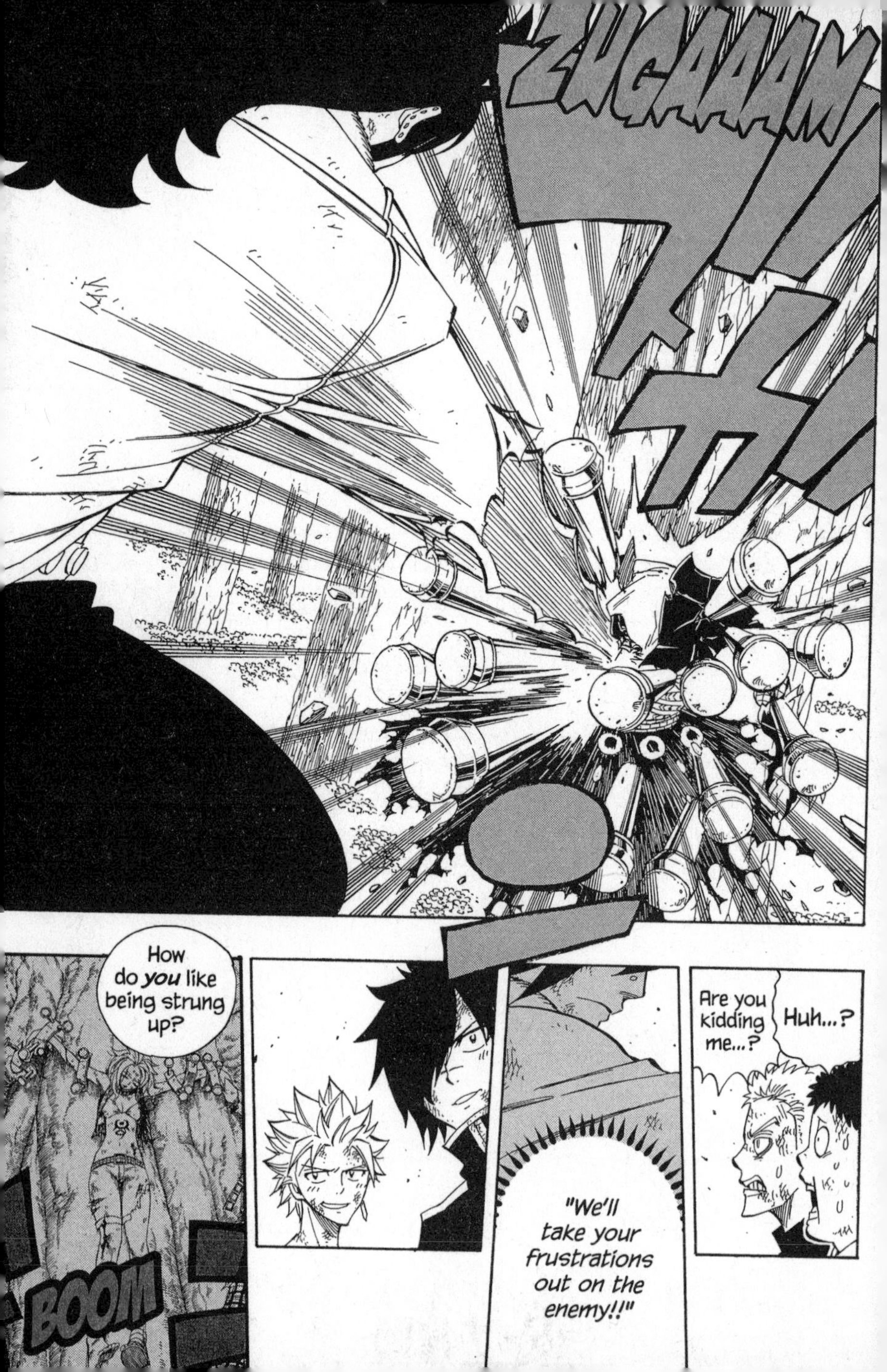
ZUGAAAM
Huh...?
Are you kidding me...?
"We'll take your frustrations out on the enemy!!"
How do *you* like being strung up?
BOOM

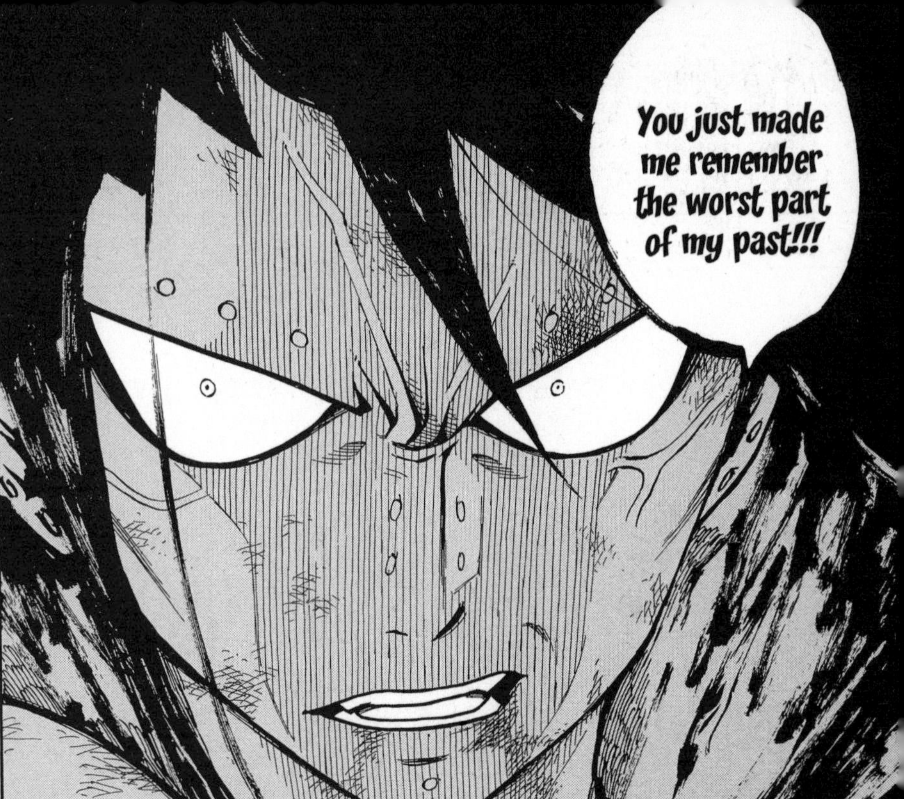
You just made me remember the worst part of my past!!!

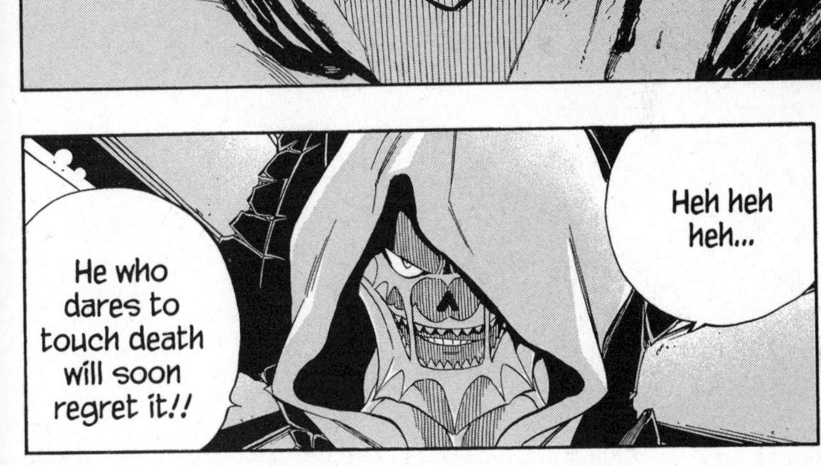
Heh heh heh...
He who dares to touch death will soon regret it!!

FAIRY TAIL
フェアリーテイル

Chapter 486: The Fourth Guest

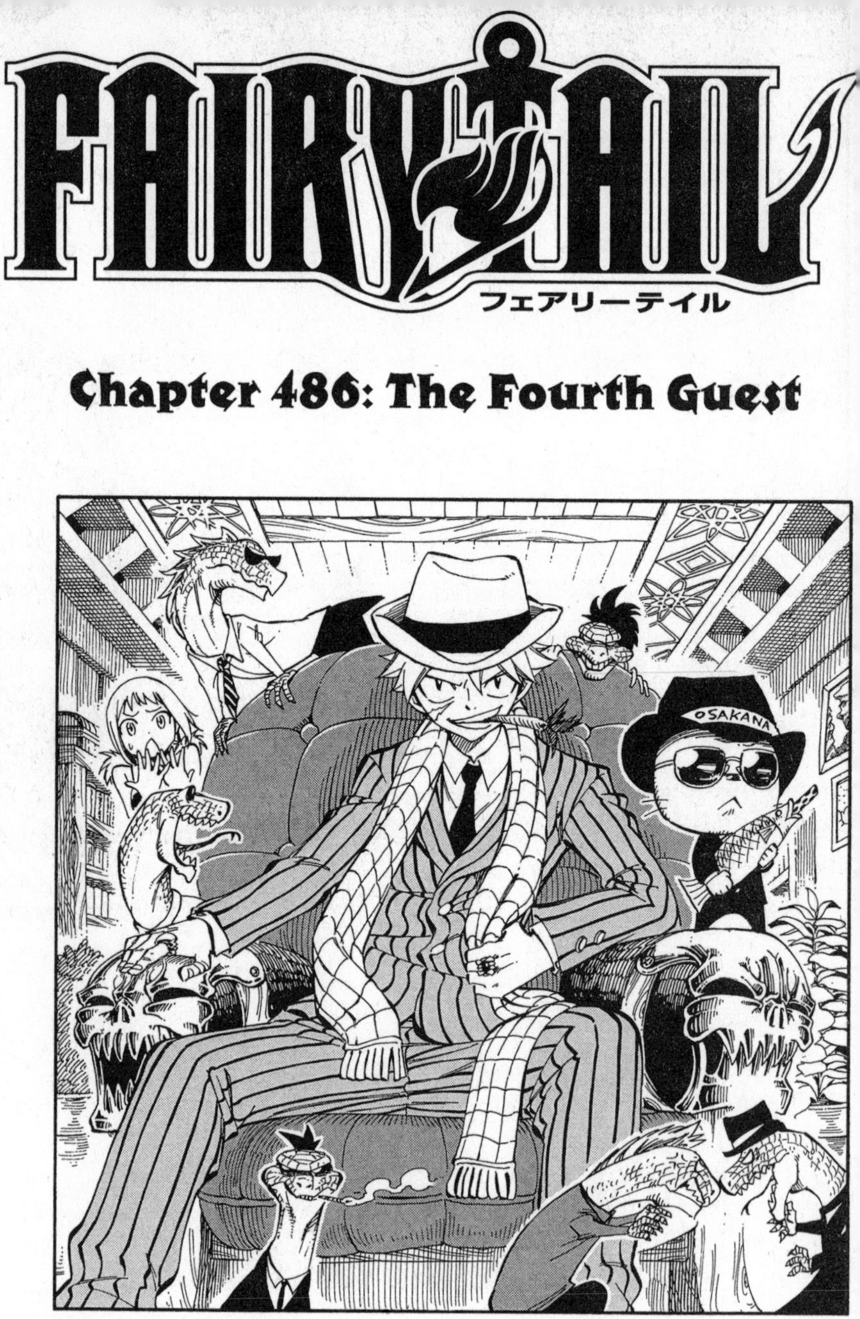
OSAKANA

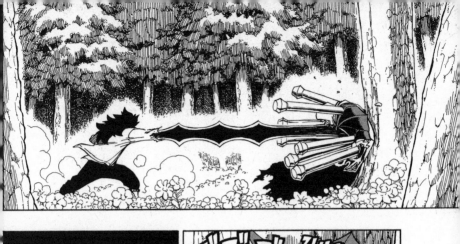

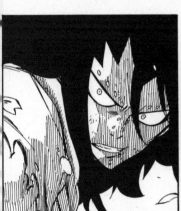

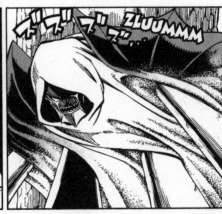

ズ"ズ" ブ"ズ" ZLUUMMM

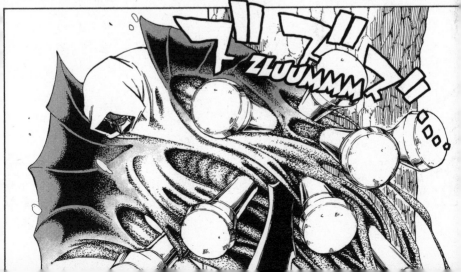

ブ"ブ"ZLUUMMM ブ"ズ"

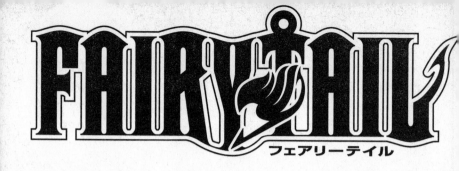

Chapter 486: The Fourth Guest

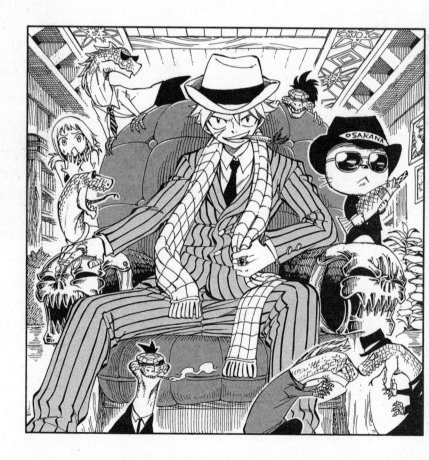

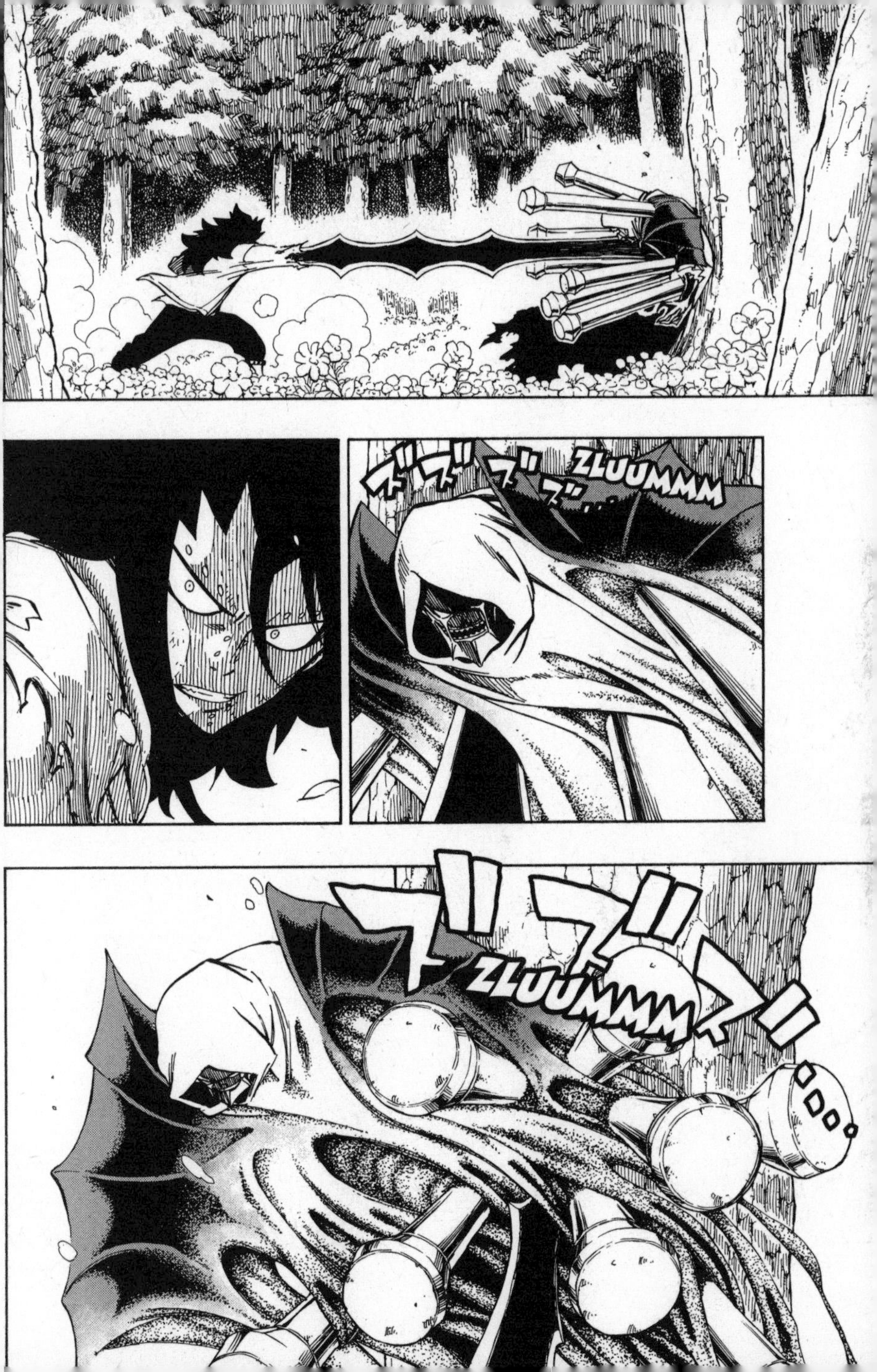
ZLUUMMM
ZLUUMMM

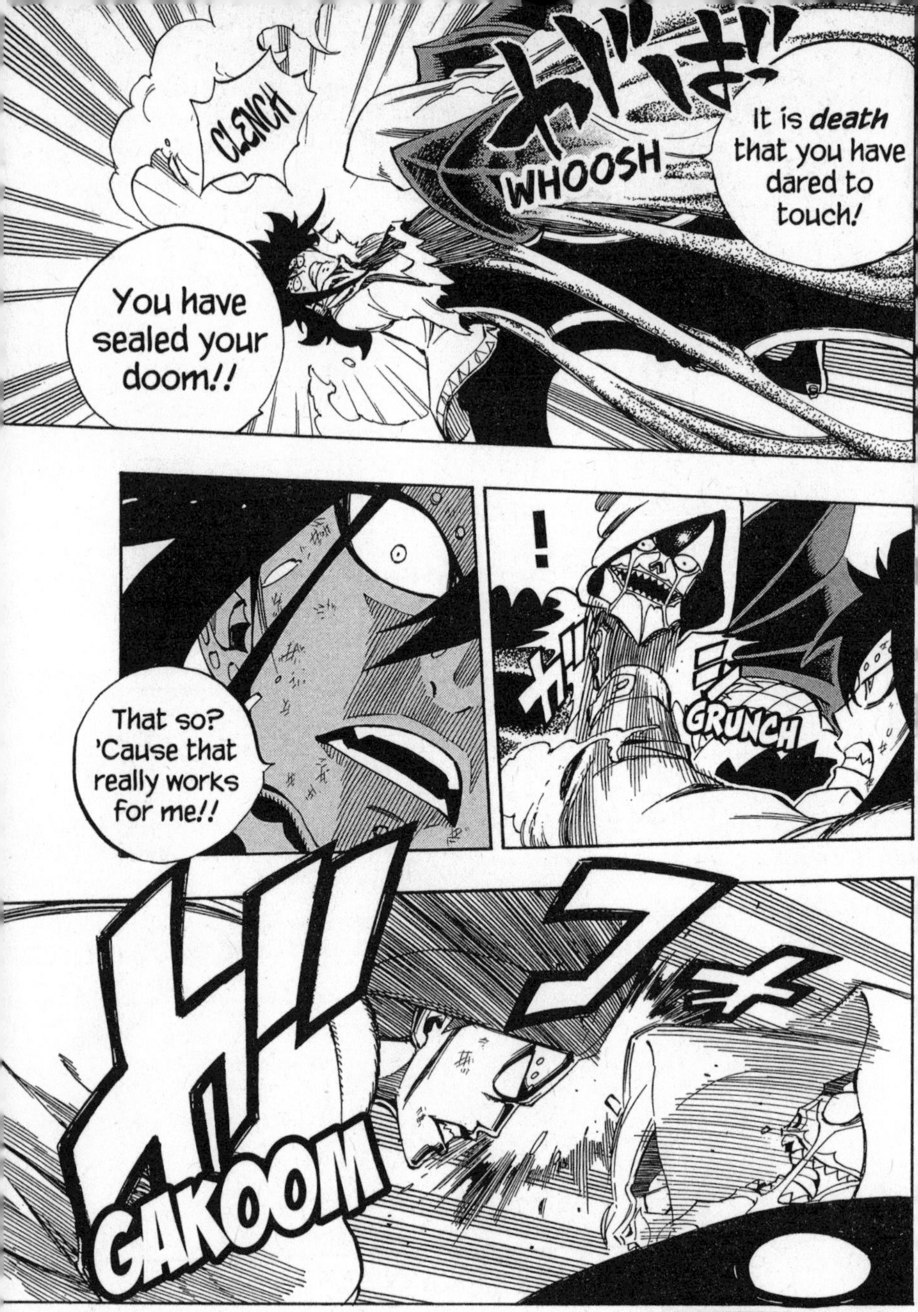
It is *death* that you have dared to touch!
WHOOSH
CLENCH
You have sealed your doom!!
!
GRUNCH
That so? 'Cause that really works for me!!
GAKOOM

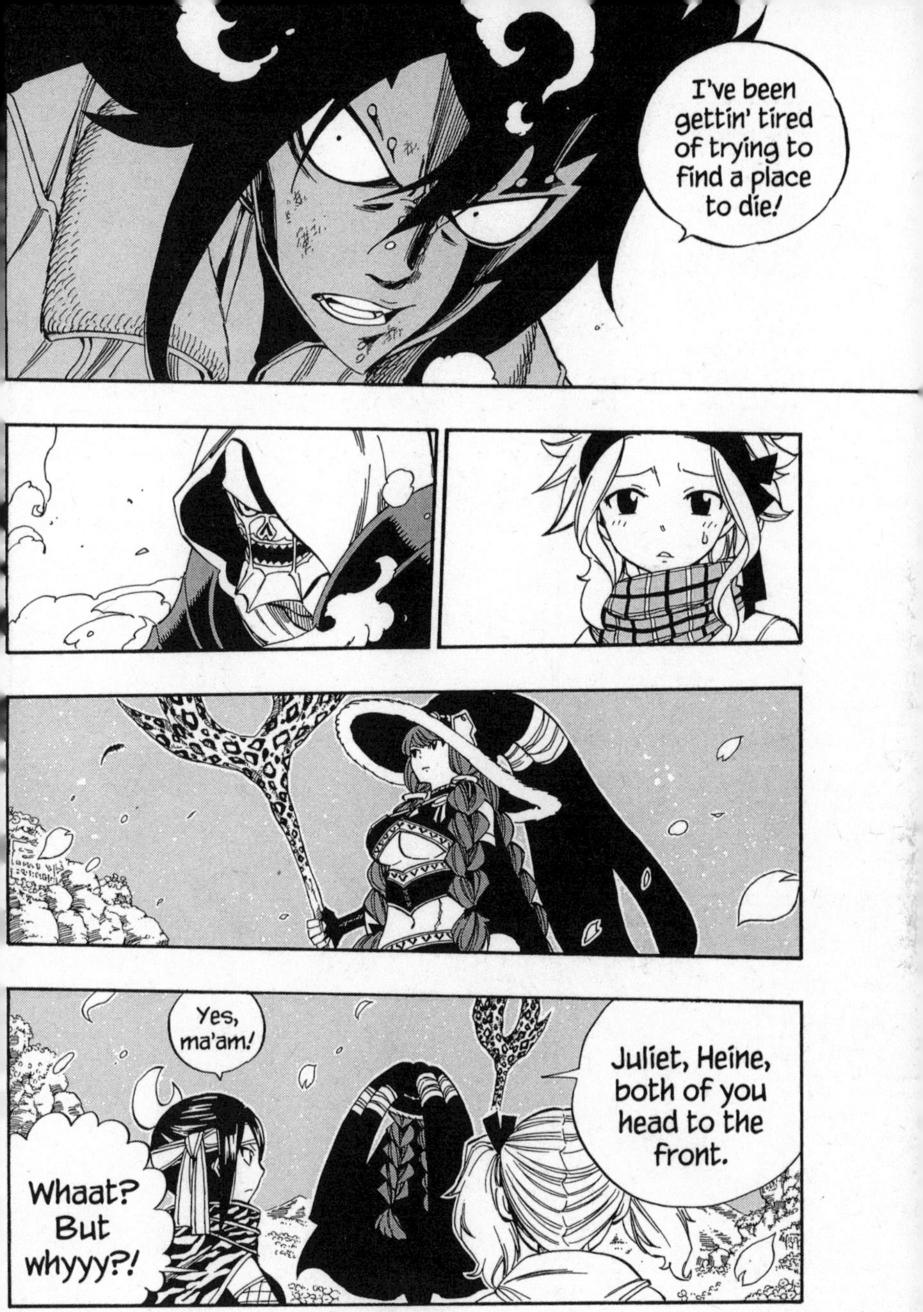
I've been gettin' tired of trying to find a place to die!
Juliet, Heine, both of you head to the front.
Yes, ma'am!
Whaat? But whyyy?!

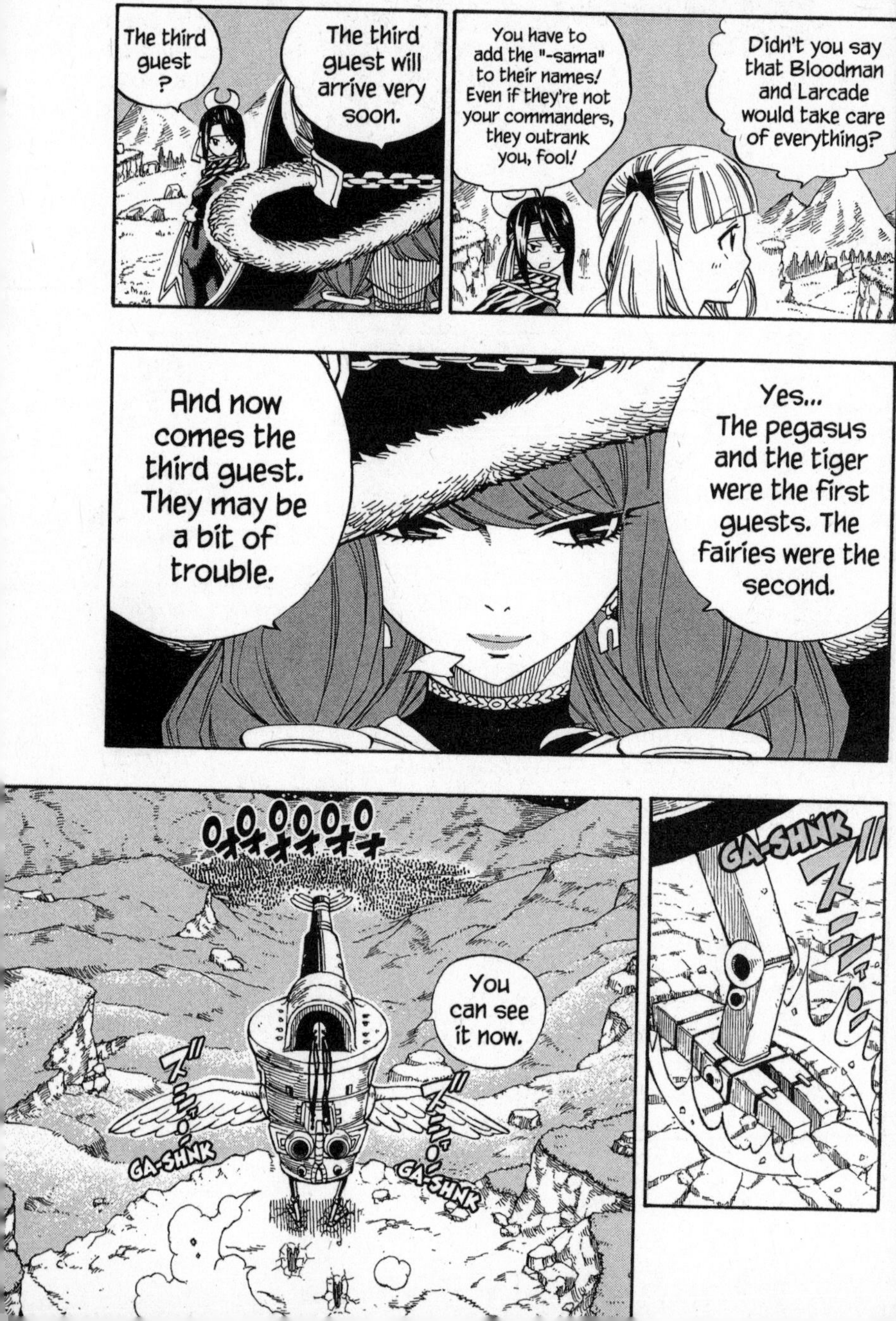
Didn't you say that Bloodman and Larcade would take care of everything?
You have to add the "-sama" to their names! Even if they're not your commanders, they outrank you, fool!
The third guest will arrive very soon.
The third guest ?
Yes... The pegasus and the tiger were the first guests. The fairies were the second.
And now comes the third guest. They may be a bit of trouble.
GA-SHNK
OOOOOO
You can see it now.
GA-SHNK
GA-SHNK

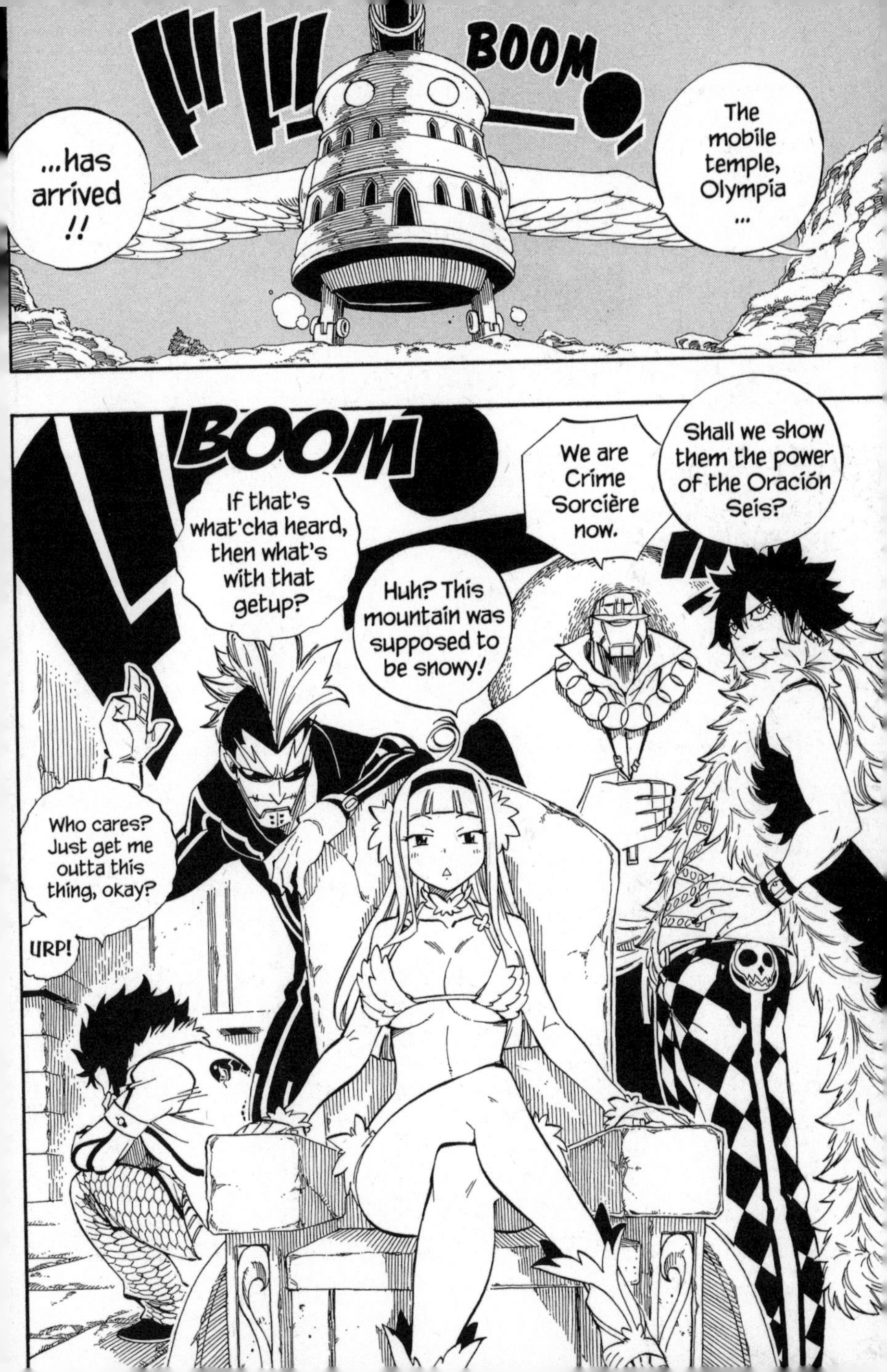
The mobile temple, Olympia ...
BOOM
...has arrived !!
Shall we show them the power of the Oración Seis?
We are Crime Sorcière now.
BOOM
If that's what'cha heard, then what's with that getup?
Huh? This mountain was supposed to be snowy!
Who cares? Just get me outta this thing, okay?
URP!

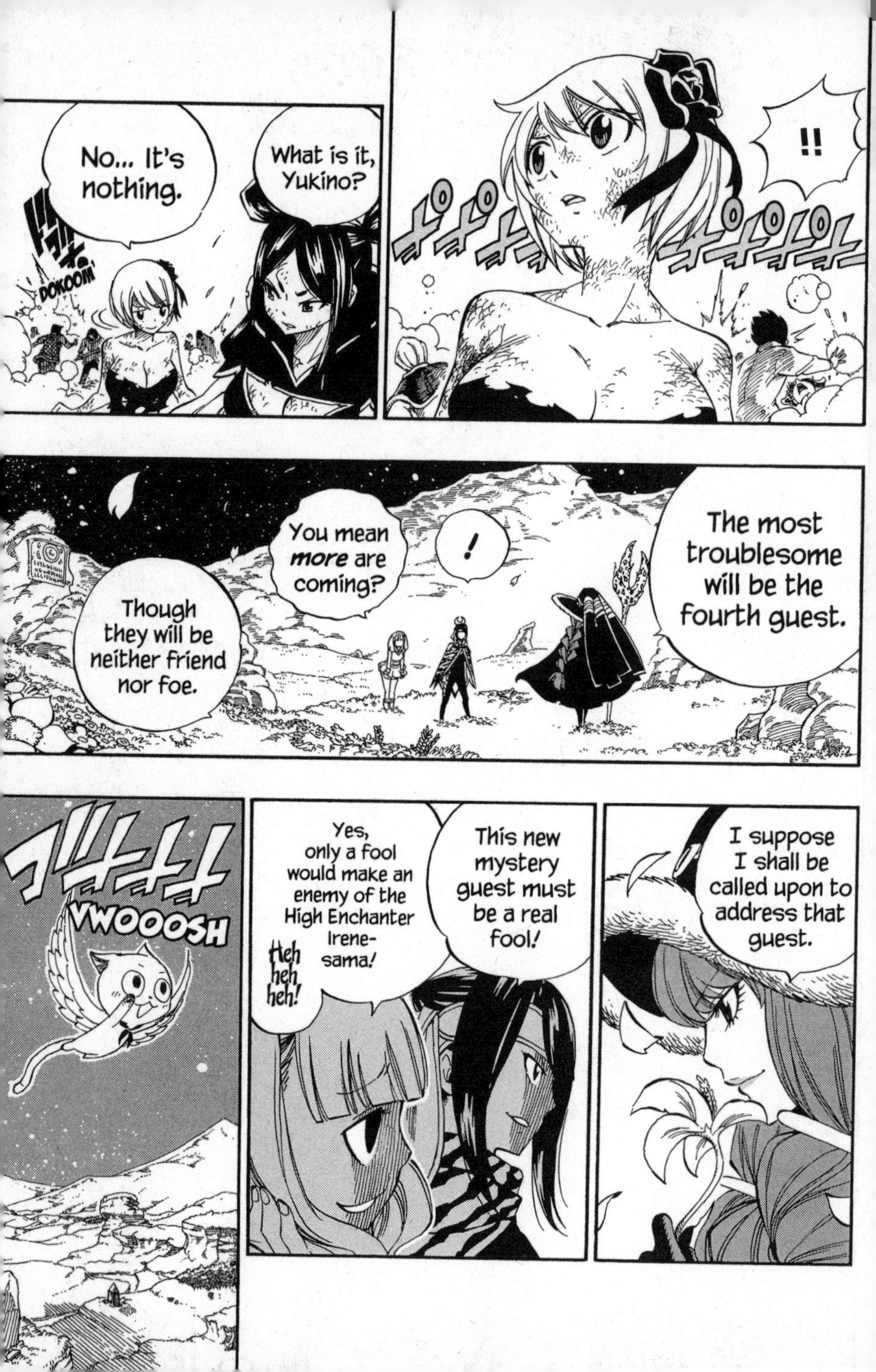
!!
What is it, Yukino?
No... It's nothing.
DOKOOM
The most troublesome will be the fourth guest.
!
You mean *more* are coming?
Though they will be neither friend nor foe.
I suppose I shall be called upon to address that guest.
This new mystery guest must be a real fool!
Yes, only a fool would make an enemy of the High Enchanter Irene-sama!
Heh heh heh!
VWOOOSH

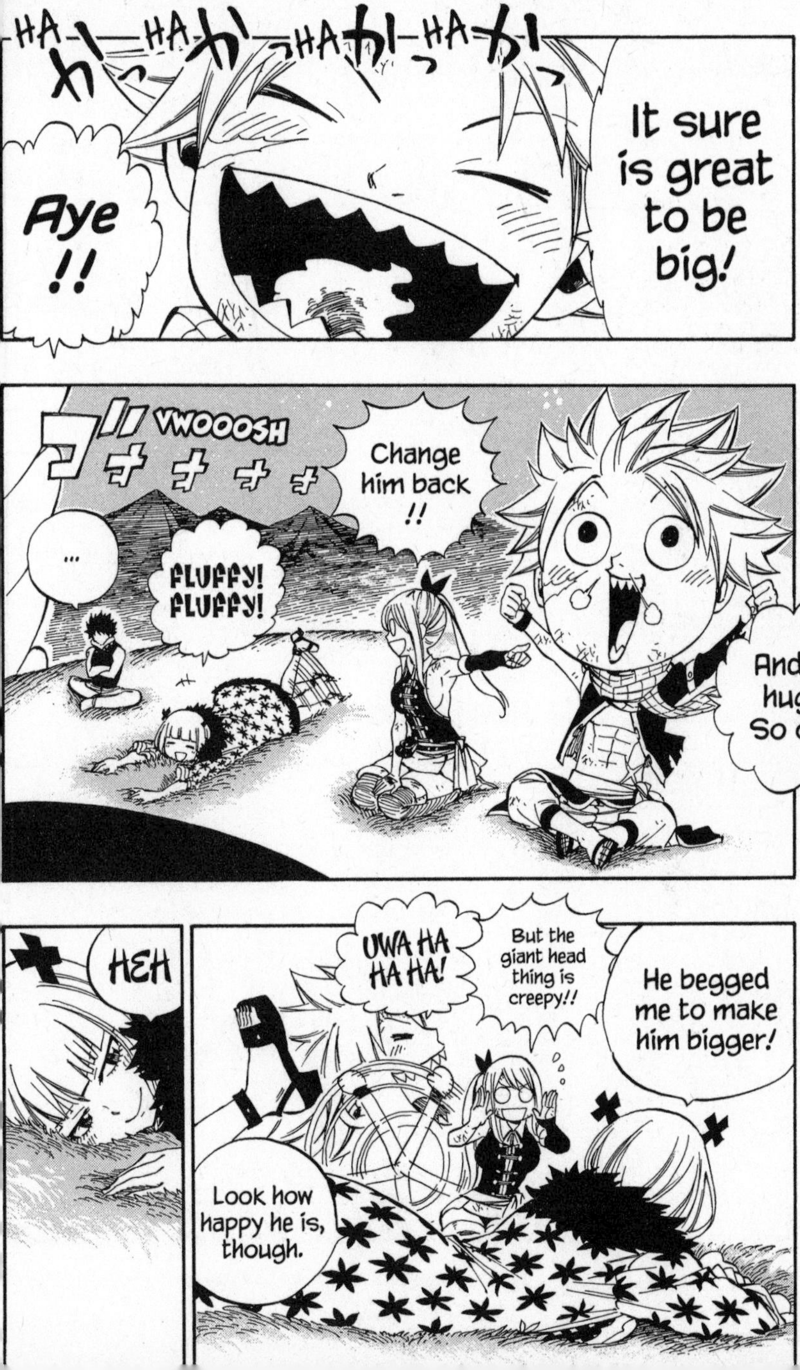
HA HA HA HA
It sure is great to be big!
Aye!!
And I'm huge!! So cool!
Change him back!!
VWOOOSH
FLUFFY! FLUFFY!
...
He begged me to make him bigger!
But the giant head thing is creepy!!
UWA HA HA HA!
Look how happy he is, though.
HEH

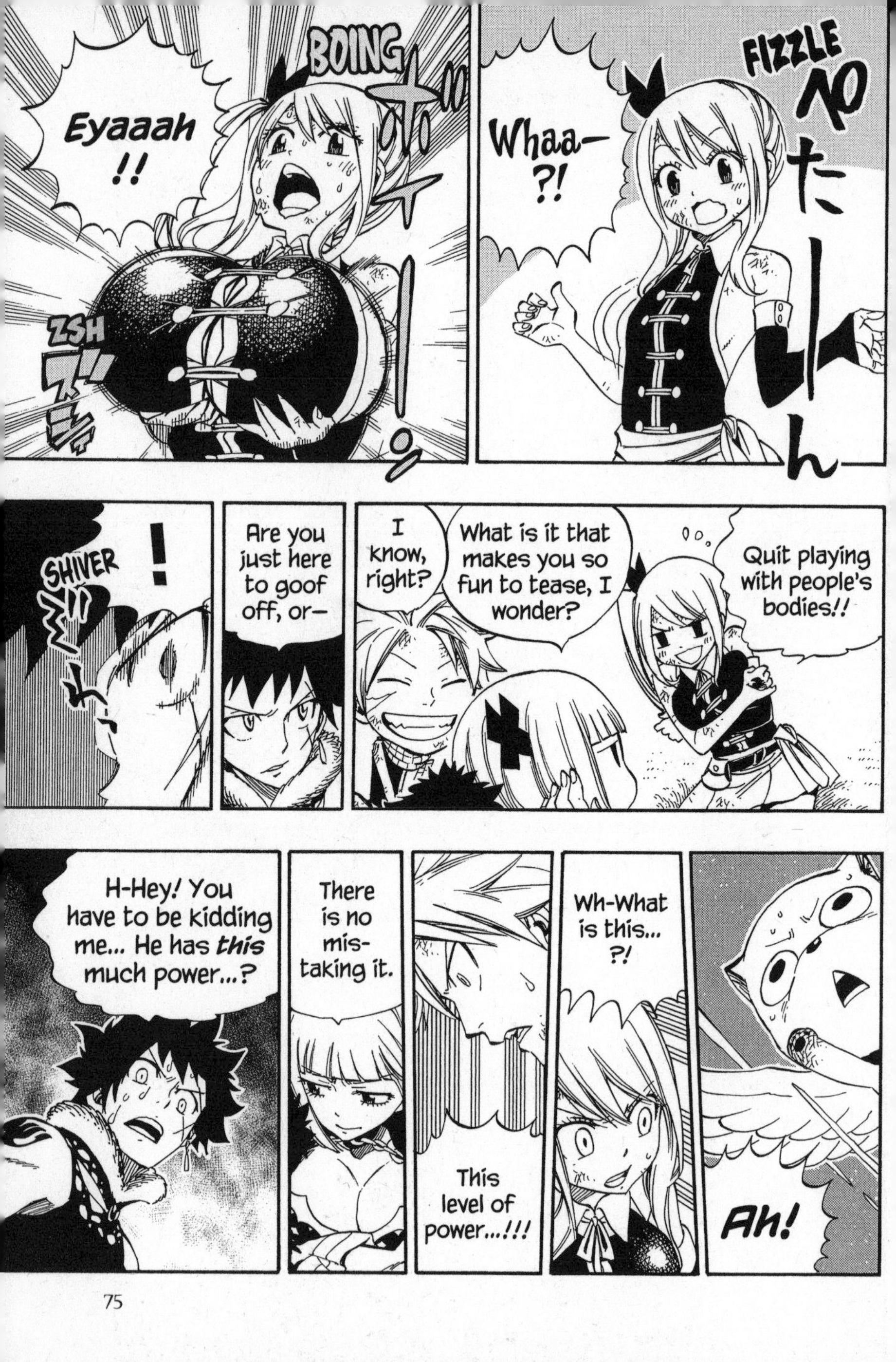
FIZZLE
Whaa-?!
BOING
Eyaaah!!
ZSH
Quit playing with people's bodies!!
What is it that makes you so fun to tease, I wonder?
I know, right?
Are you just here to goof off, or—
!
SHIVER
Ah!
Wh-What is this...?!
This level of power...!!!
There is no mis-taking it.
H-Hey! You have to be kidding me... He has *this* much power...?

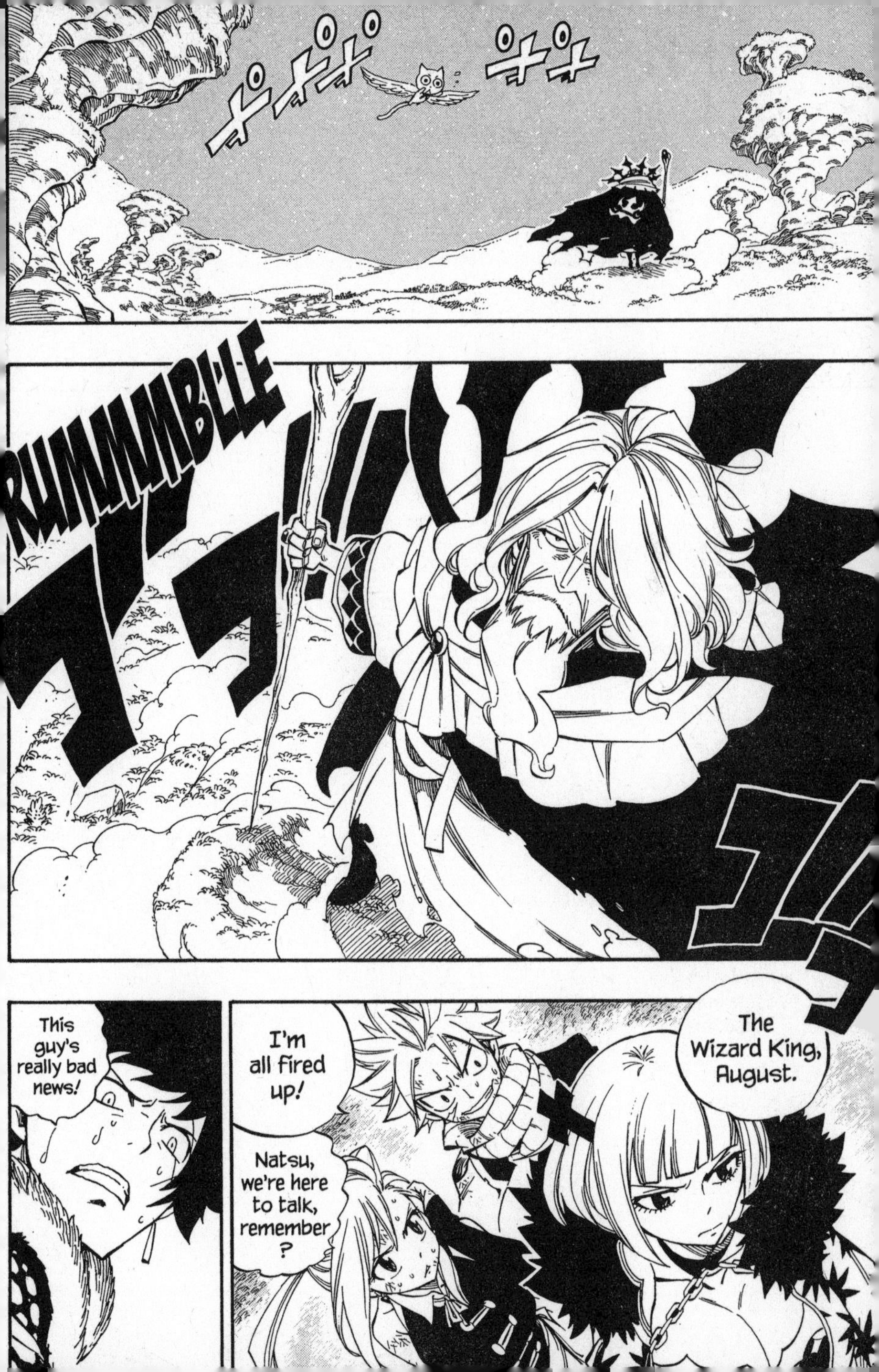
RUMMMBLE
The Wizard King, August.
I'm all fired up!
Natsu, we're here to talk, remember?
This guy's really bad news!

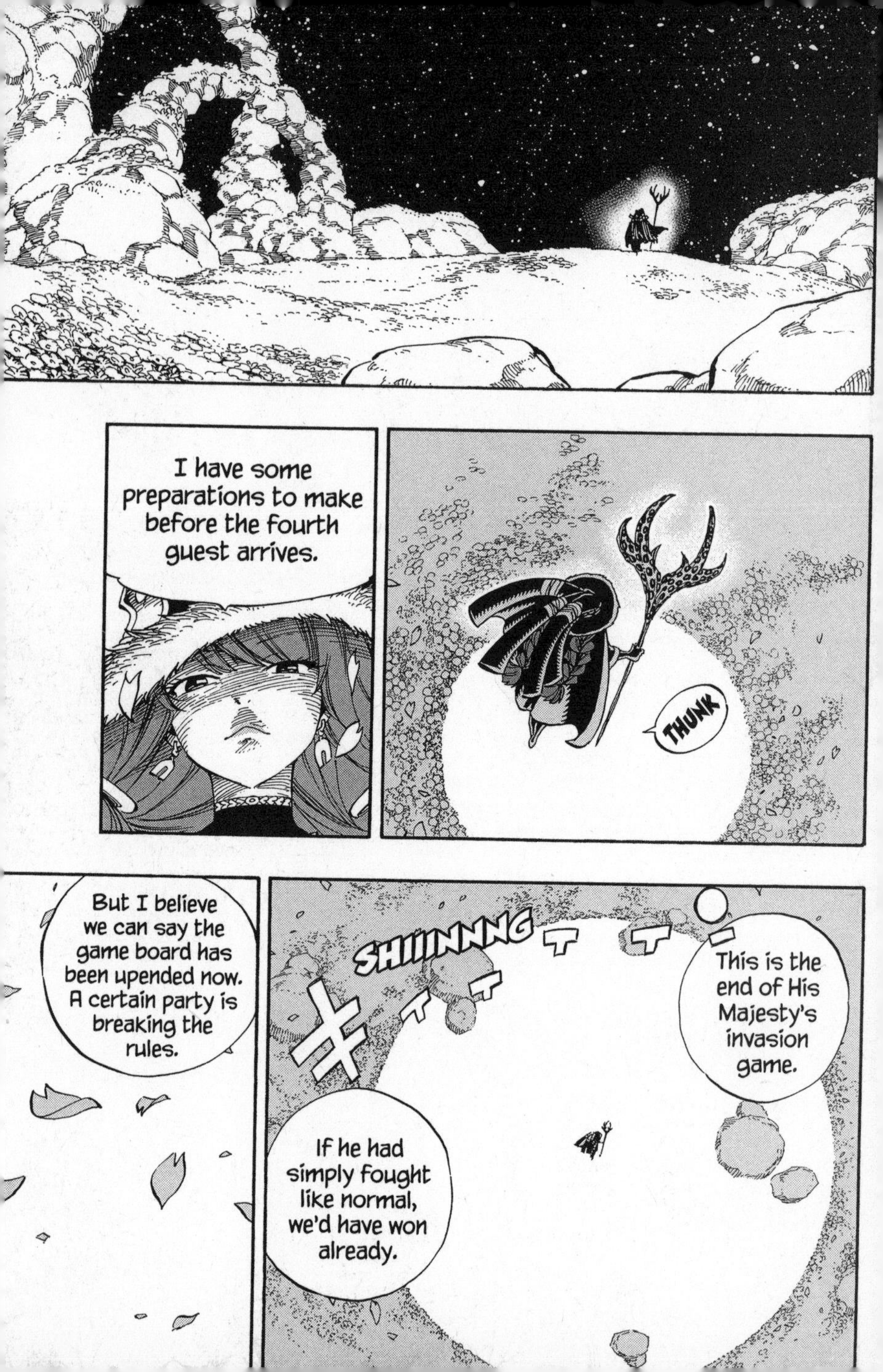
THUNK
I have some preparations to make before the fourth guest arrives.
This is the end of His Majesty's invasion game.
SHIIINNNG
If he had simply fought like normal, we'd have won already.
But I believe we can say the game board has been upended now. A certain party is breaking the rules.

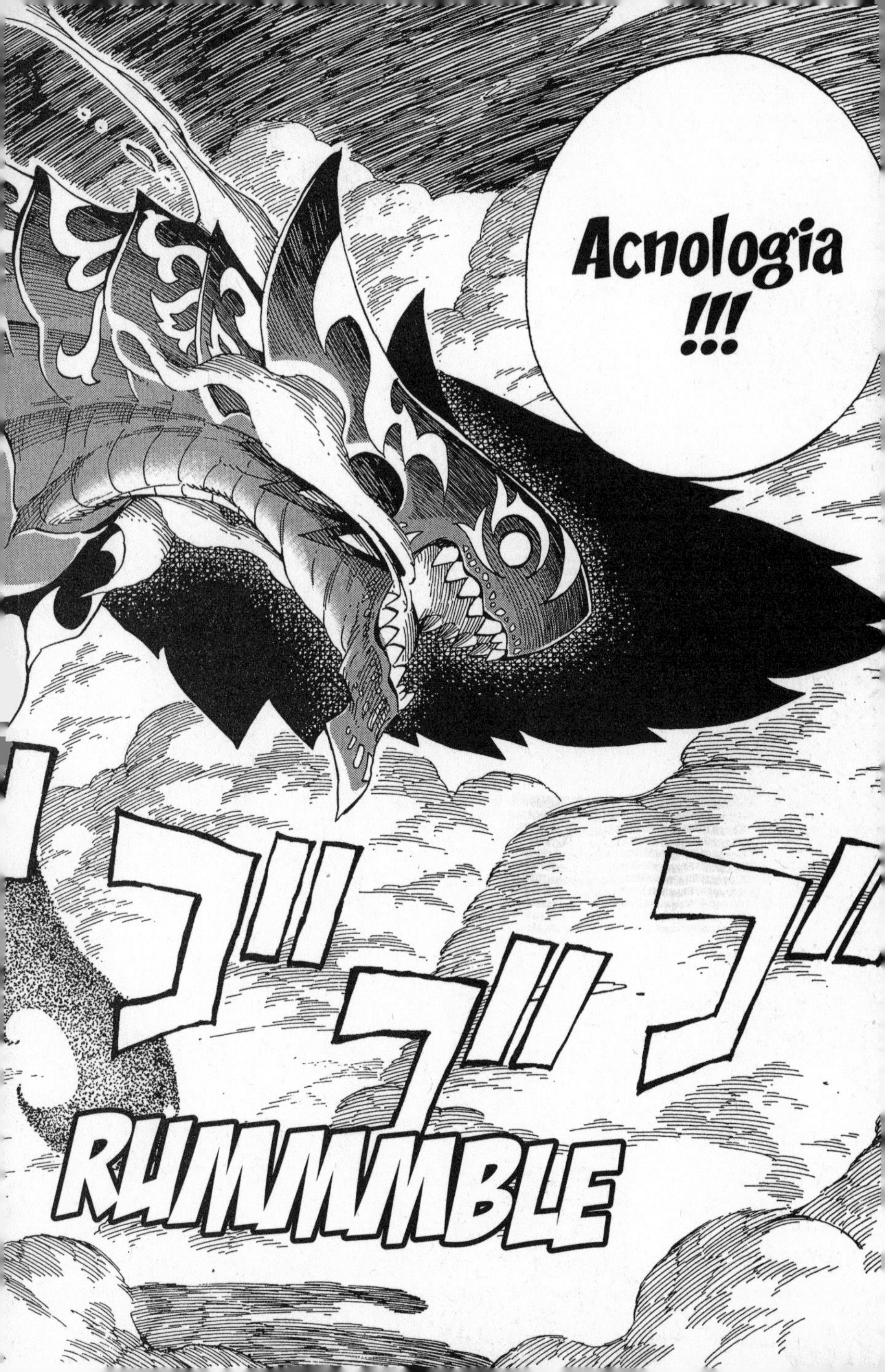
Acnologia !!!
ゴゴゴ
RUMMMMBLE

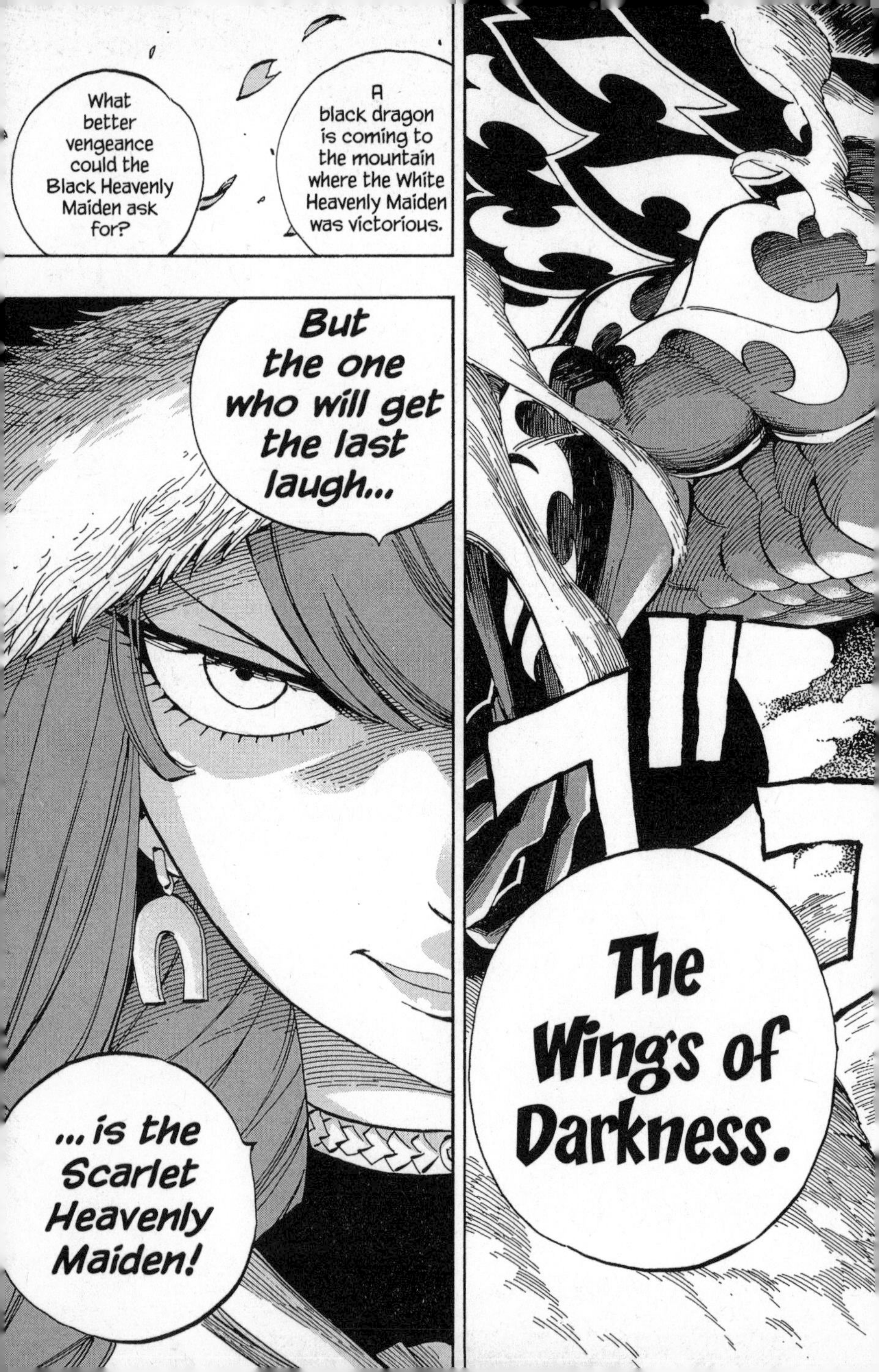
The Wings of Darkness.
A black dragon is coming to the mountain where the White Heavenly Maiden was victorious.
What better vengeance could the Black Heavenly Maiden ask for?
But the one who will get the last laugh...
...is the Scarlet Heavenly Maiden!

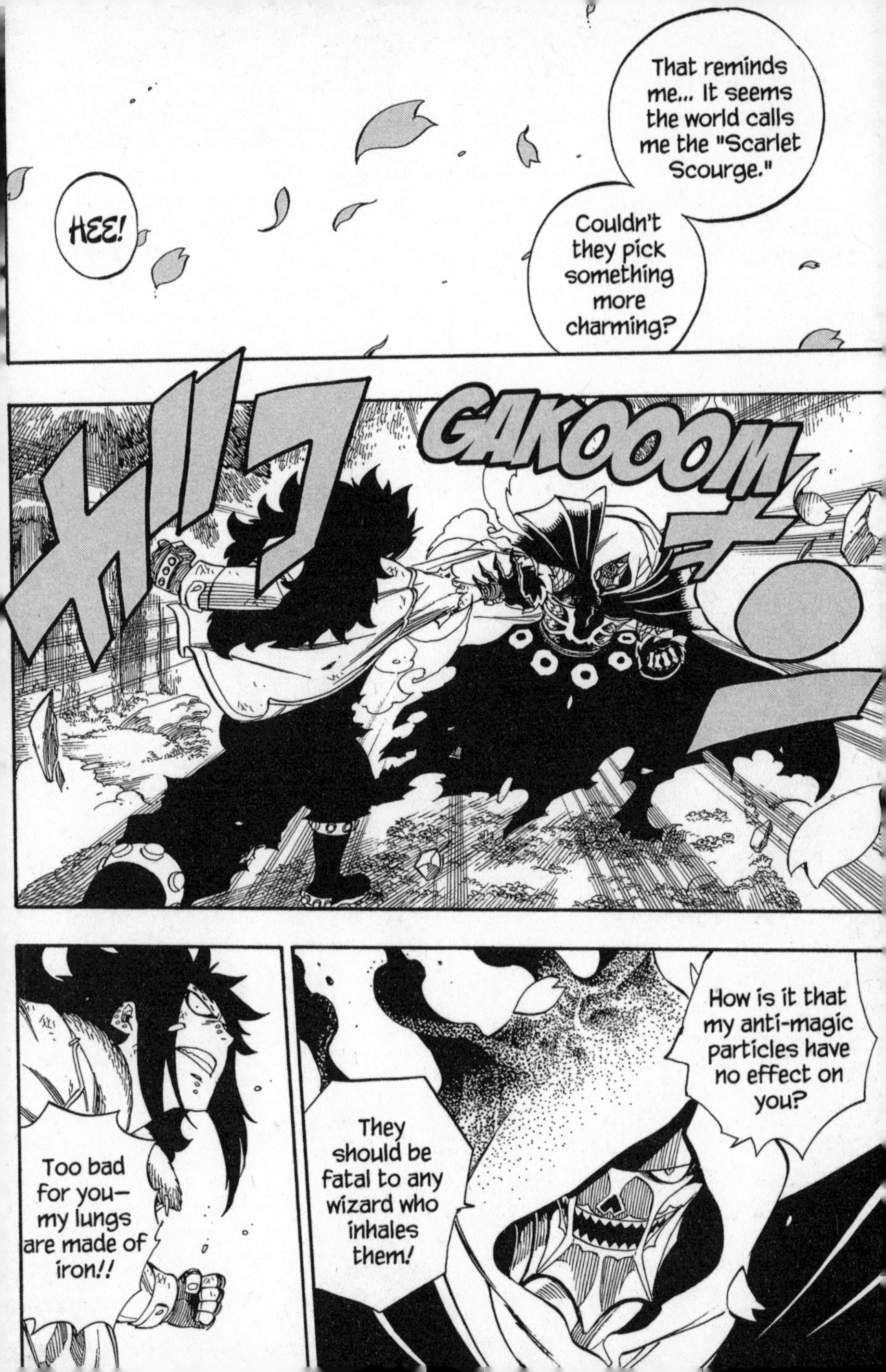
That reminds me... It seems the world calls me the "Scarlet Scourge."
Couldn't they pick something more charming?
HEE!
GAKOOOM
How is it that my anti-magic particles have no effect on you?
They should be fatal to any wizard who inhales them!
Too bad for you—my lungs are made of iron!!

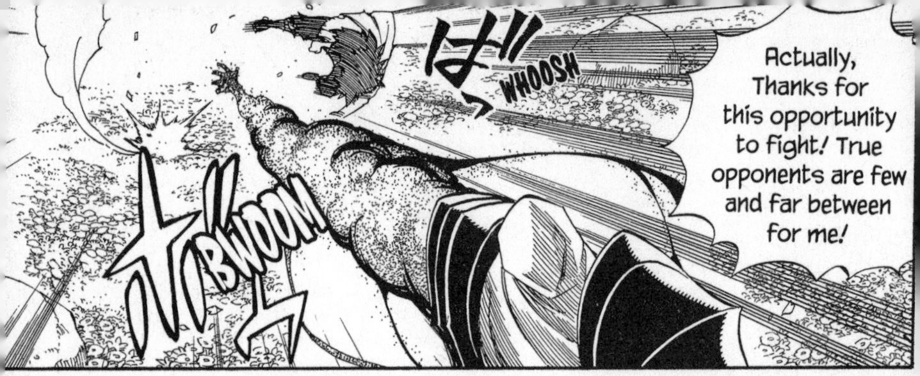
Actually, Thanks for this opportunity to fight! True opponents are few and far between for me!
は WHOOSH
BWOOM
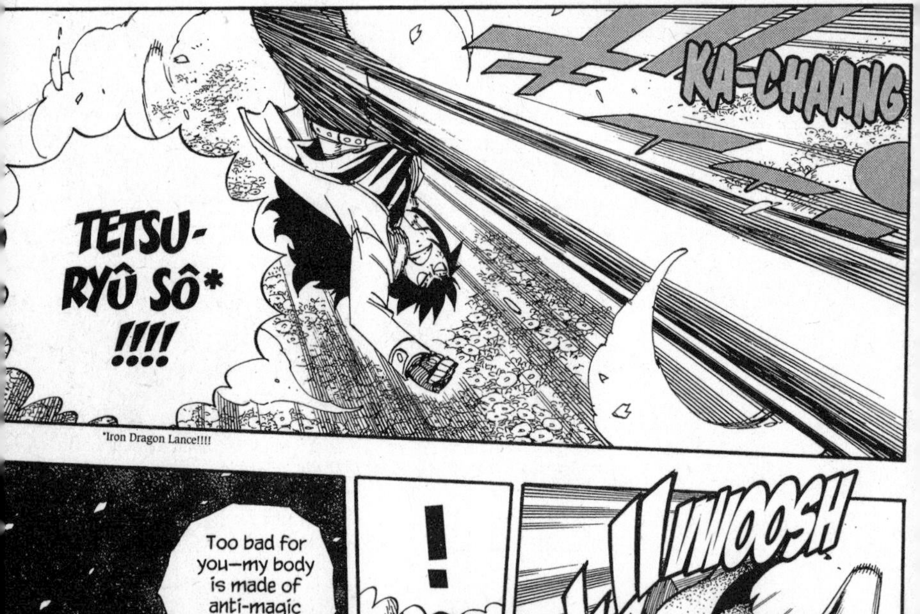
KA-CHAANG
TETSU-RYÛ SÔ* !!!!
*Iron Dragon Lance!!!!
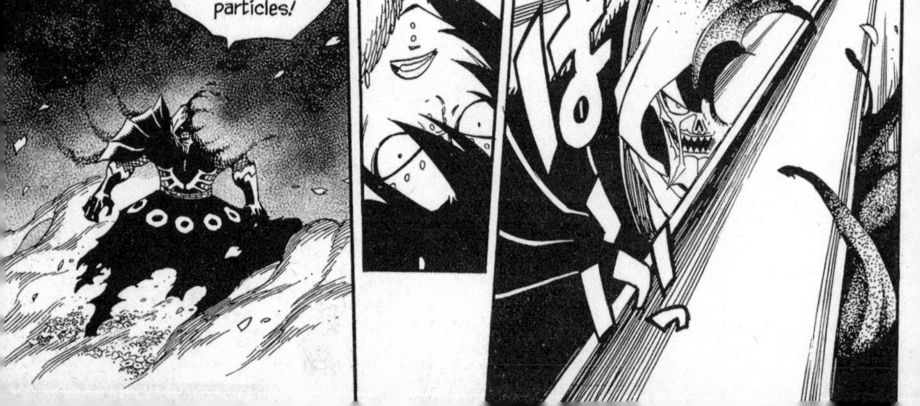
WOOSH
!
Too bad for you—my body is made of anti-magic particles!

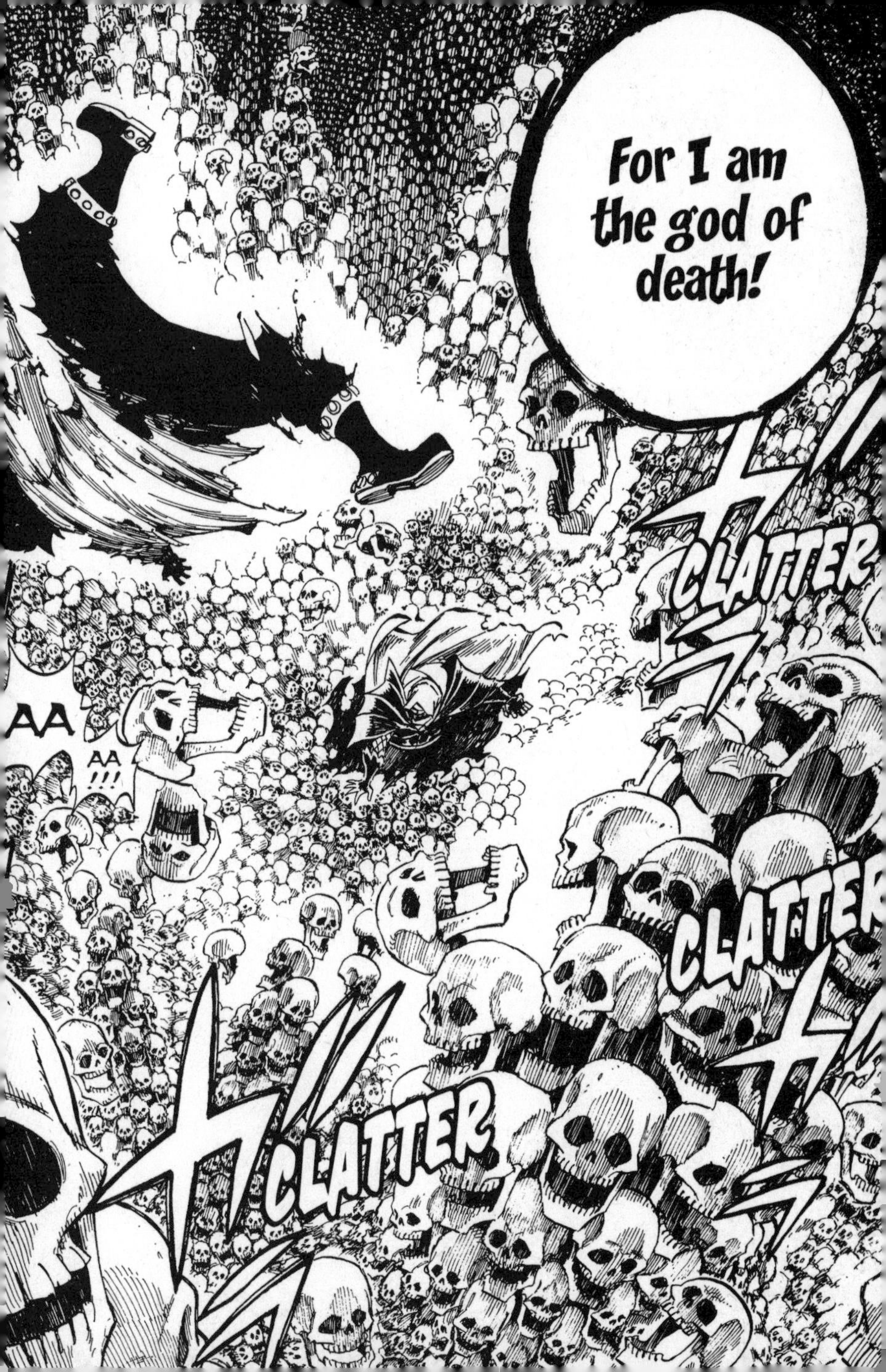
For I am the god of death!
CLATTER
CLATTER
CLATTER
AA
AA !!!

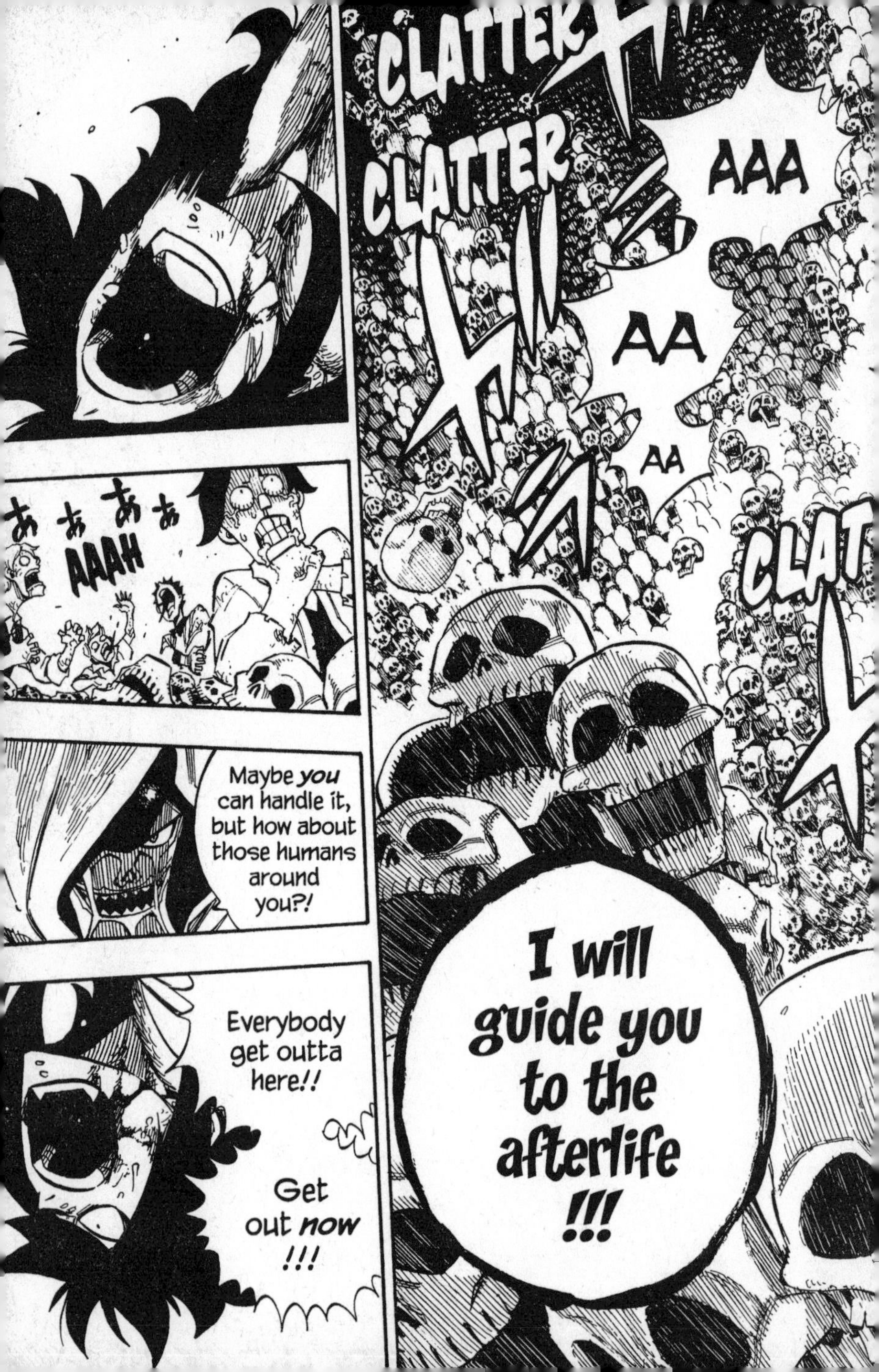
CLATTER
AAA
CLATTER
AA
AA
CLAT
I will guide you to the afterlife !!!
あぁあぁ
AAAH
Maybe *you* can handle it, but how about those humans around you?!
Everybody get outta here!!
Get out *now* !!!

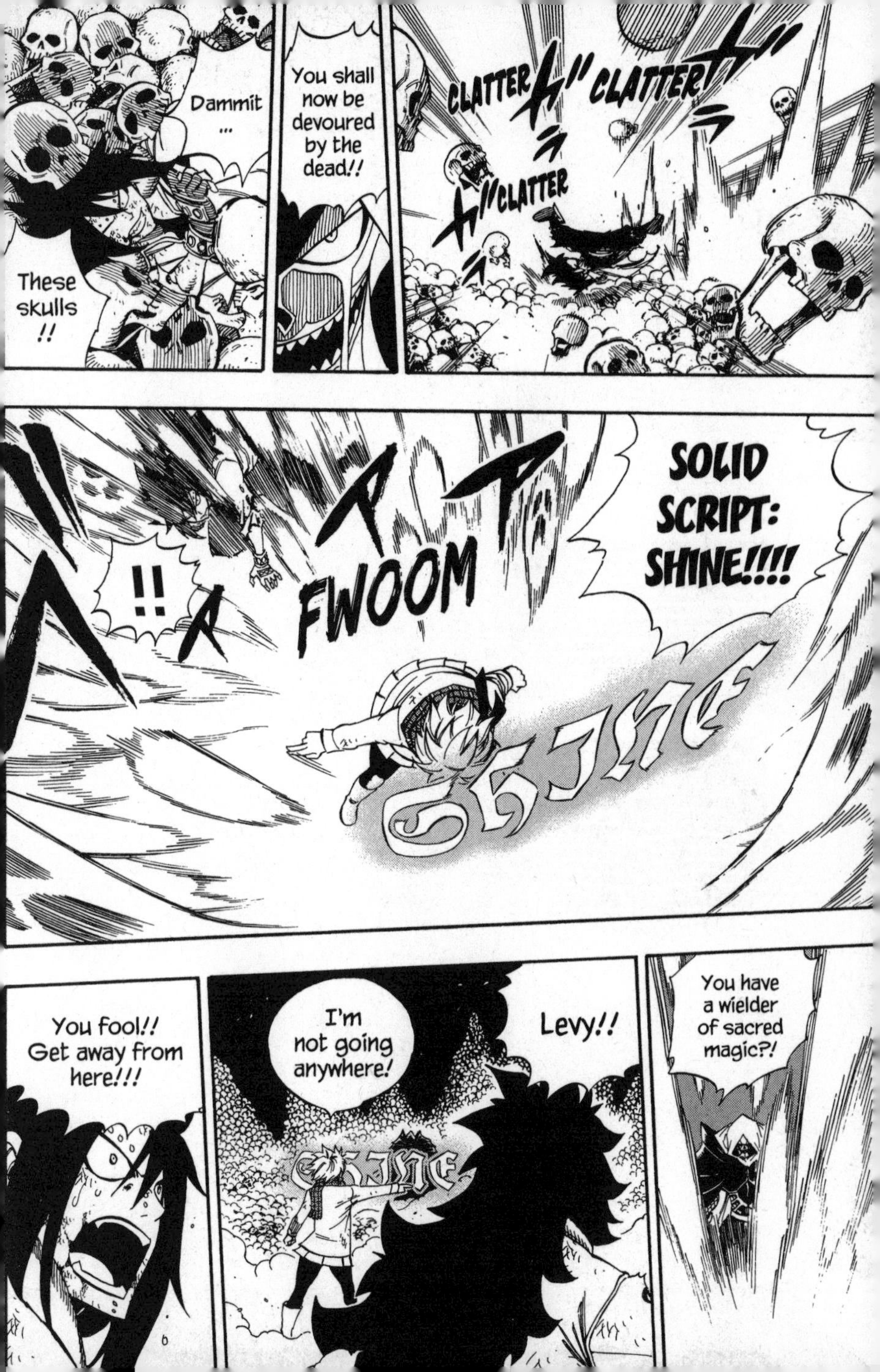
CLATTER
CLATTER
CLATTER
You shall now be devoured by the dead!!
Dammit ...
These skulls !!
SOLID SCRIPT: SHINE!!!!
FWOOM
!!
You have a wielder of sacred magic?!
Levy!!
I'm not going anywhere!
You fool!! Get away from here!!!

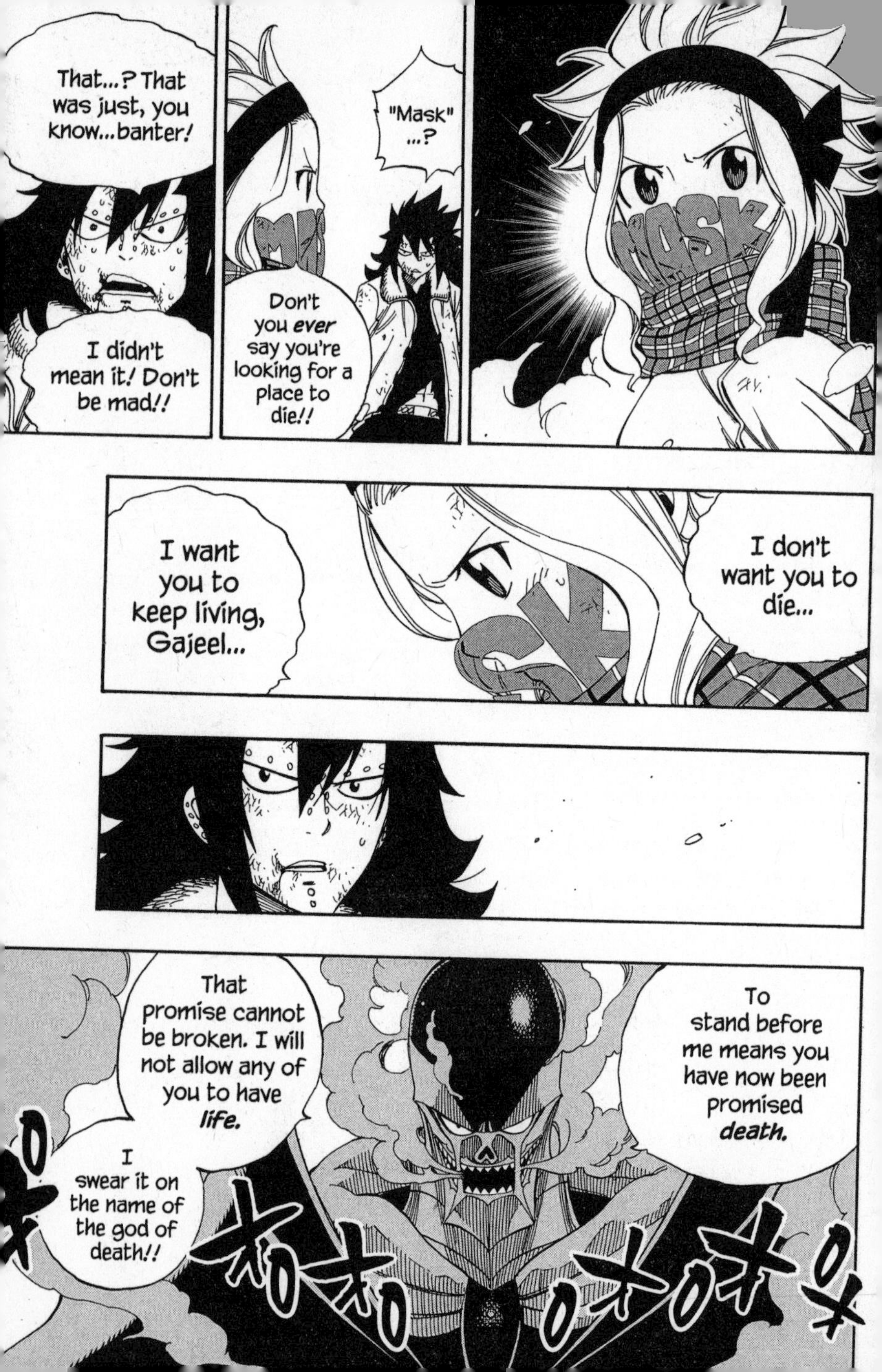
"Mask" ...?
Don't you *ever* say you're looking for a place to die!!
That...? That was just, you know...banter!
I didn't mean it! Don't be mad!!
I don't want you to die...
I want you to keep living, Gajeel...
To stand before me means you have now been promised *death.*
That promise cannot be broken. I will not allow any of you to have *life.*
I swear it on the name of the god of death!!

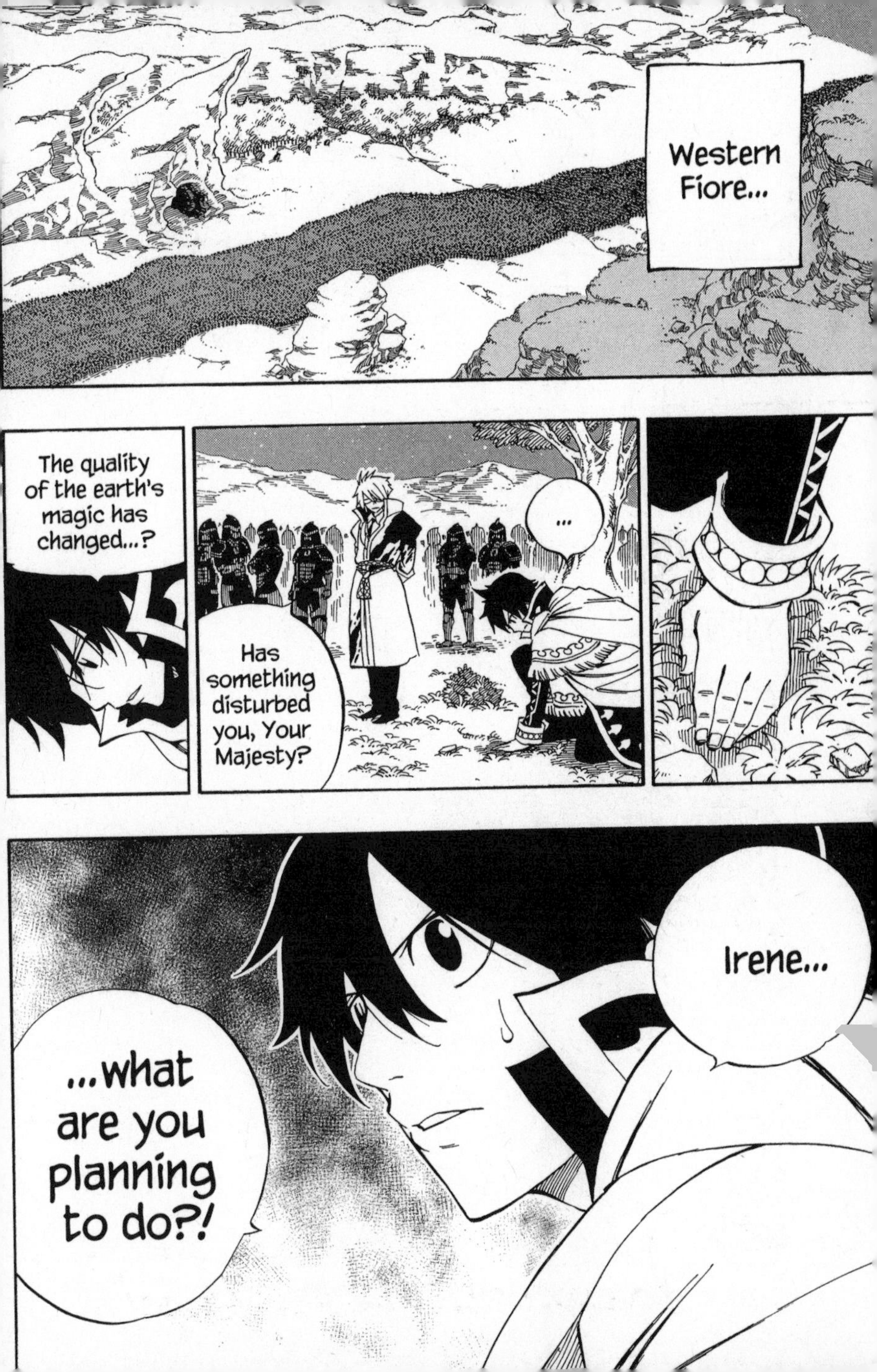
Western Fiore...
...
Has something disturbed you, Your Majesty?
The quality of the earth's magic has changed...?
Irene...
...what are you planning to do?!

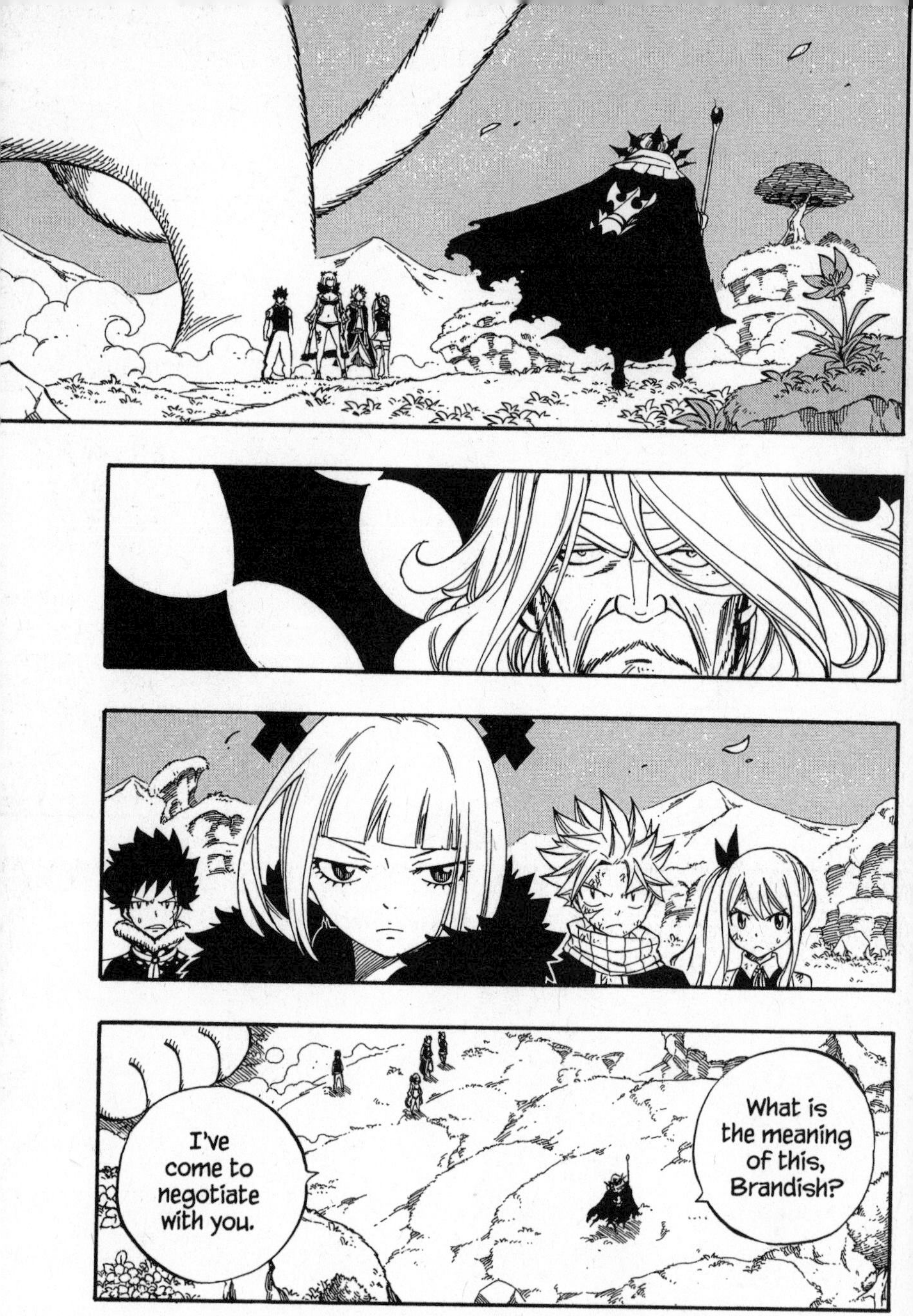
What is the meaning of this, Brandish?
I've come to negotiate with you.

Chapter 487: The Third Seal

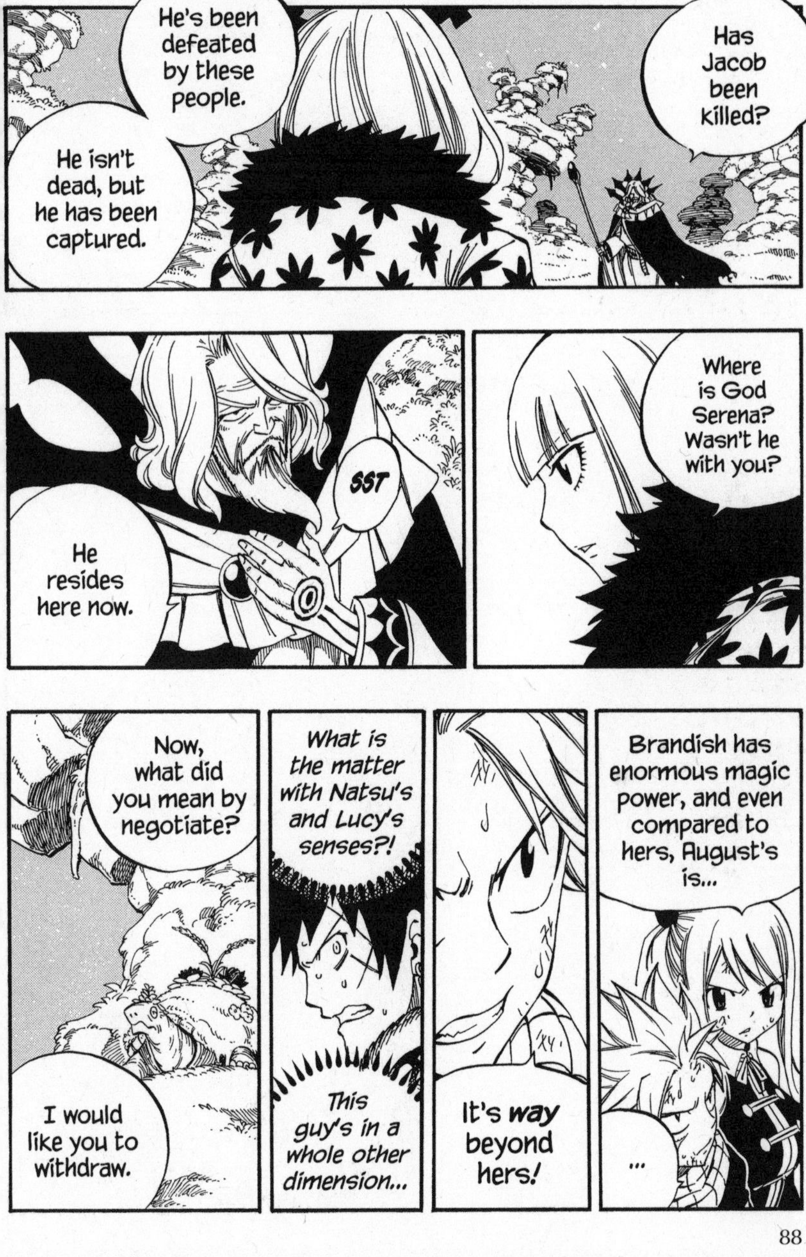
Has Jacob been killed?
He's been defeated by these people.
He isn't dead, but he has been captured.
Where is God Serena? Wasn't he with you?
SST
He resides here now.
Brandish has enormous magic power, and even compared to hers, August's is...
...
It's *way* beyond hers!
What is the matter with Natsu's and Lucy's senses?!
This guy's in a whole other dimension...
Now, what did you mean by negotiate?
I would like you to withdraw.

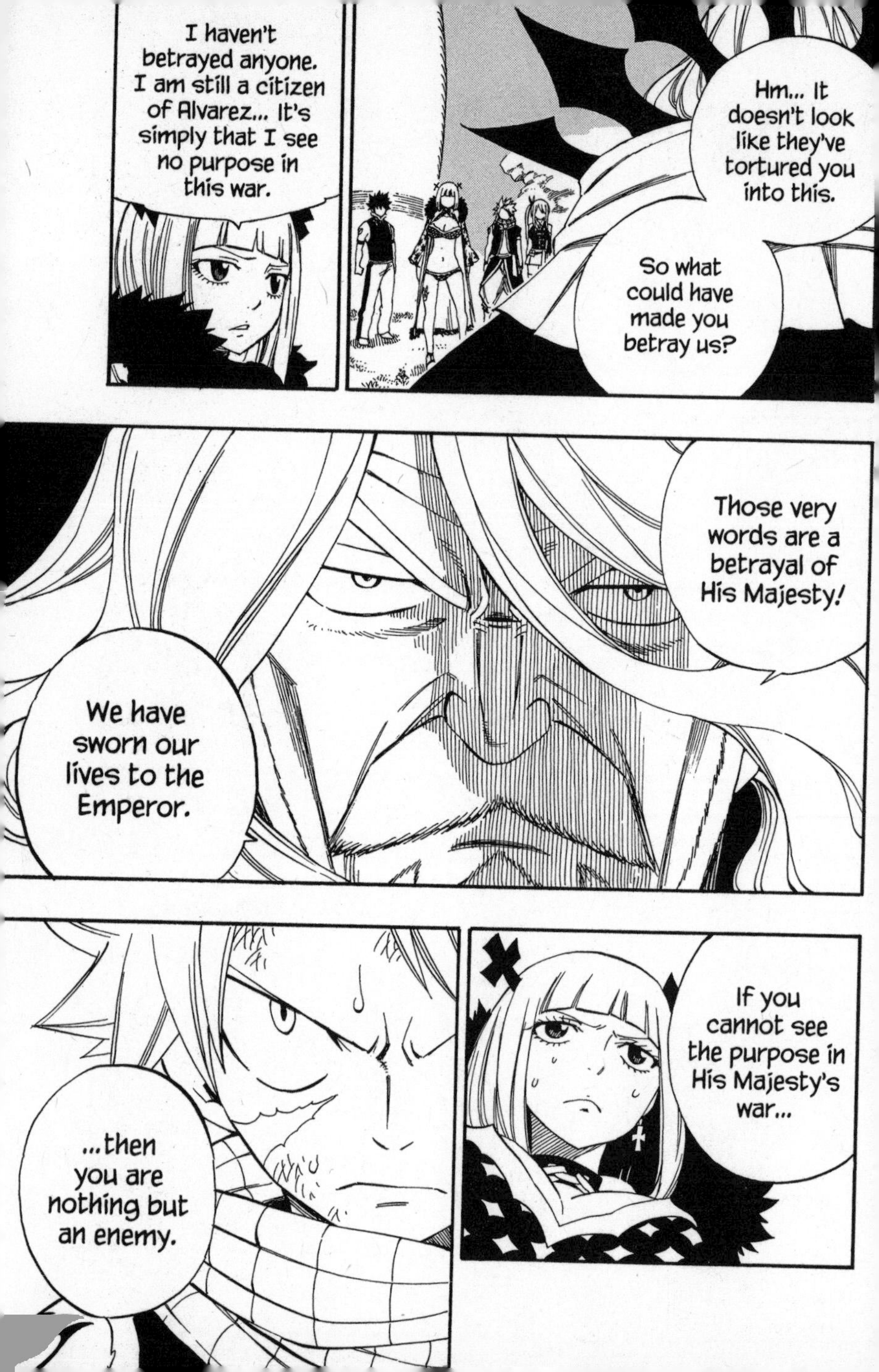
Hm... It doesn't look like they've tortured you into this.
So what could have made you betray us?
I haven't betrayed anyone. I am still a citizen of Alvarez... It's simply that I see no purpose in this war.
Those very words are a betrayal of His Majesty!
We have sworn our lives to the Emperor.
If you cannot see the purpose in His Majesty's war...
...then you are nothing but an enemy.

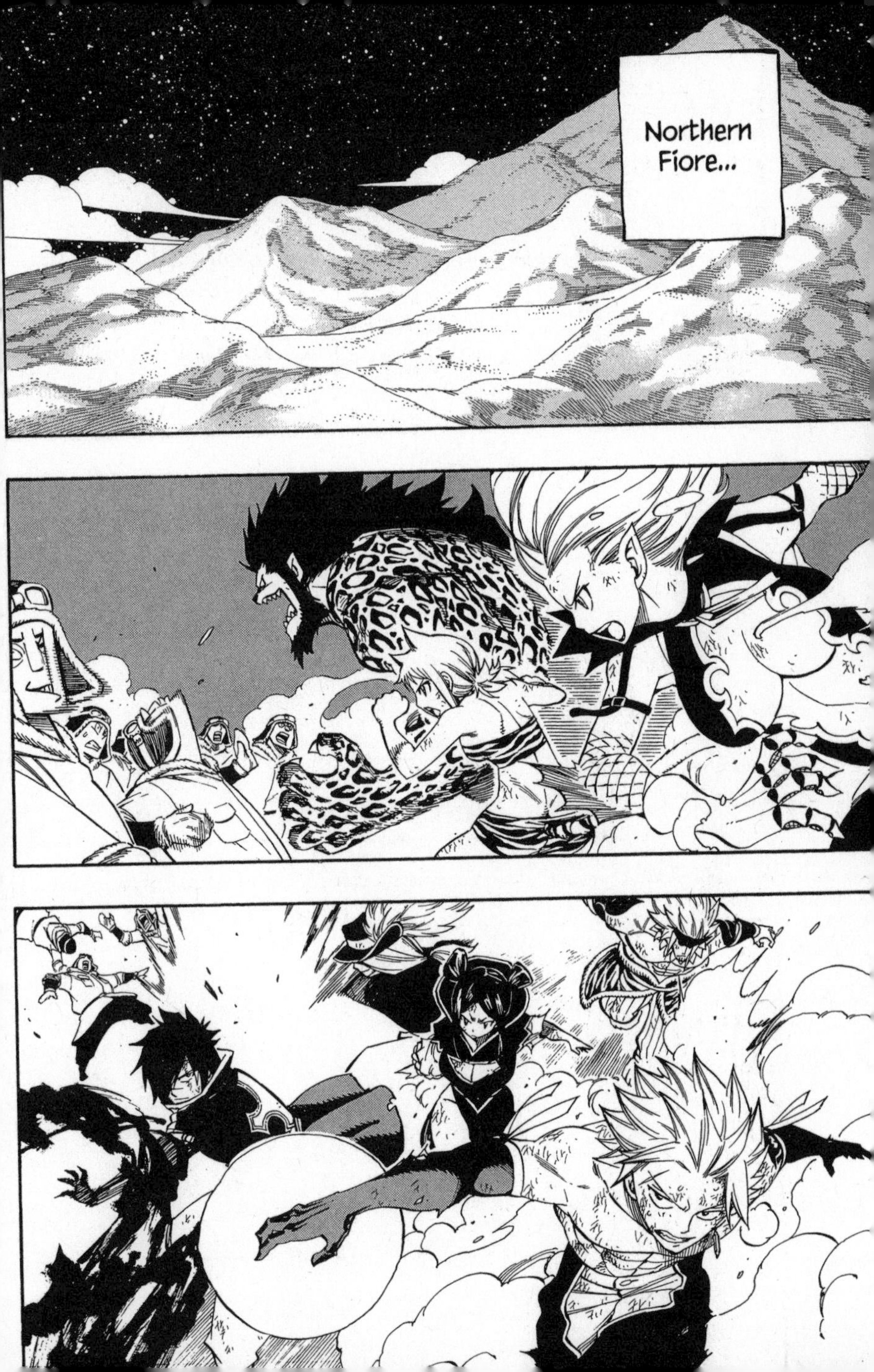
Northern Fiore...

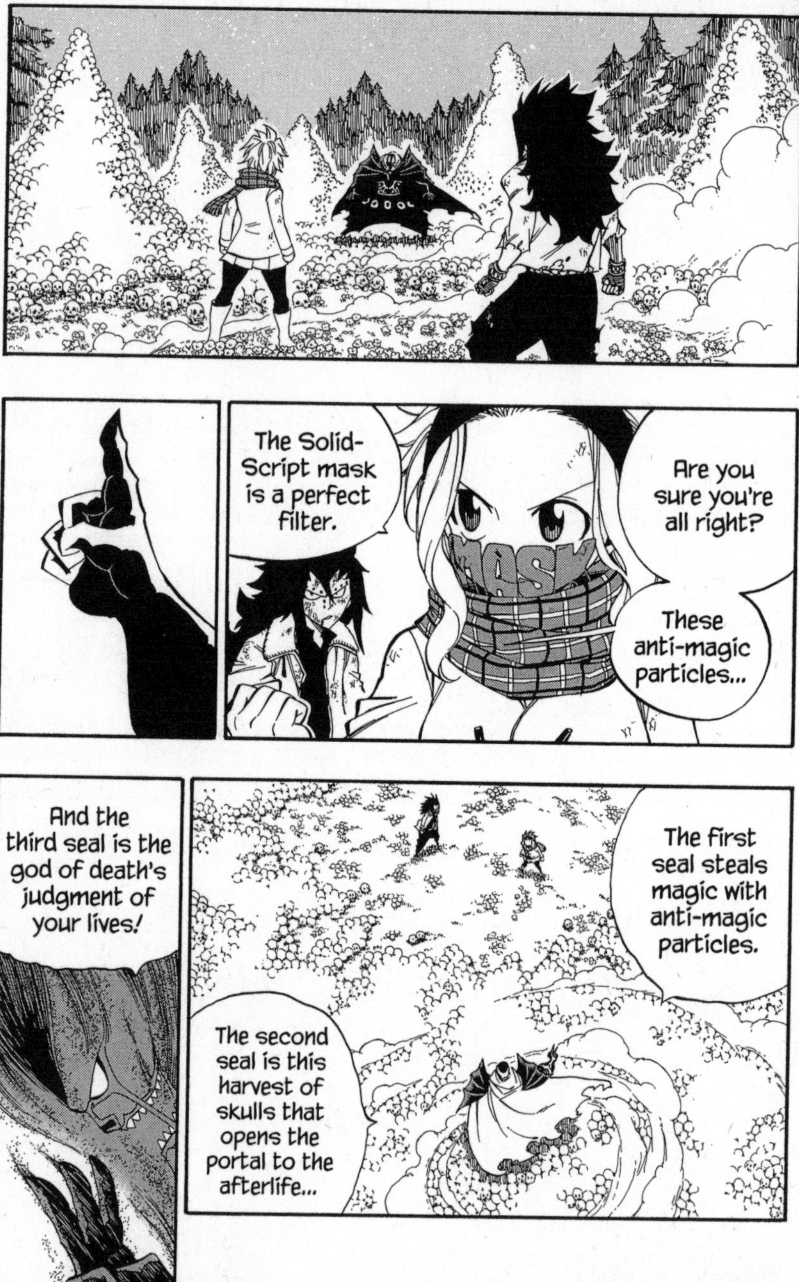

Are you sure you're all right?
These anti-magic particles...
The Solid-Script mask is a perfect filter.
The first seal steals magic with anti-magic particles.
The second seal is this harvest of skulls that opens the portal to the afterlife...
And the third seal is the god of death's judgment of your lives!

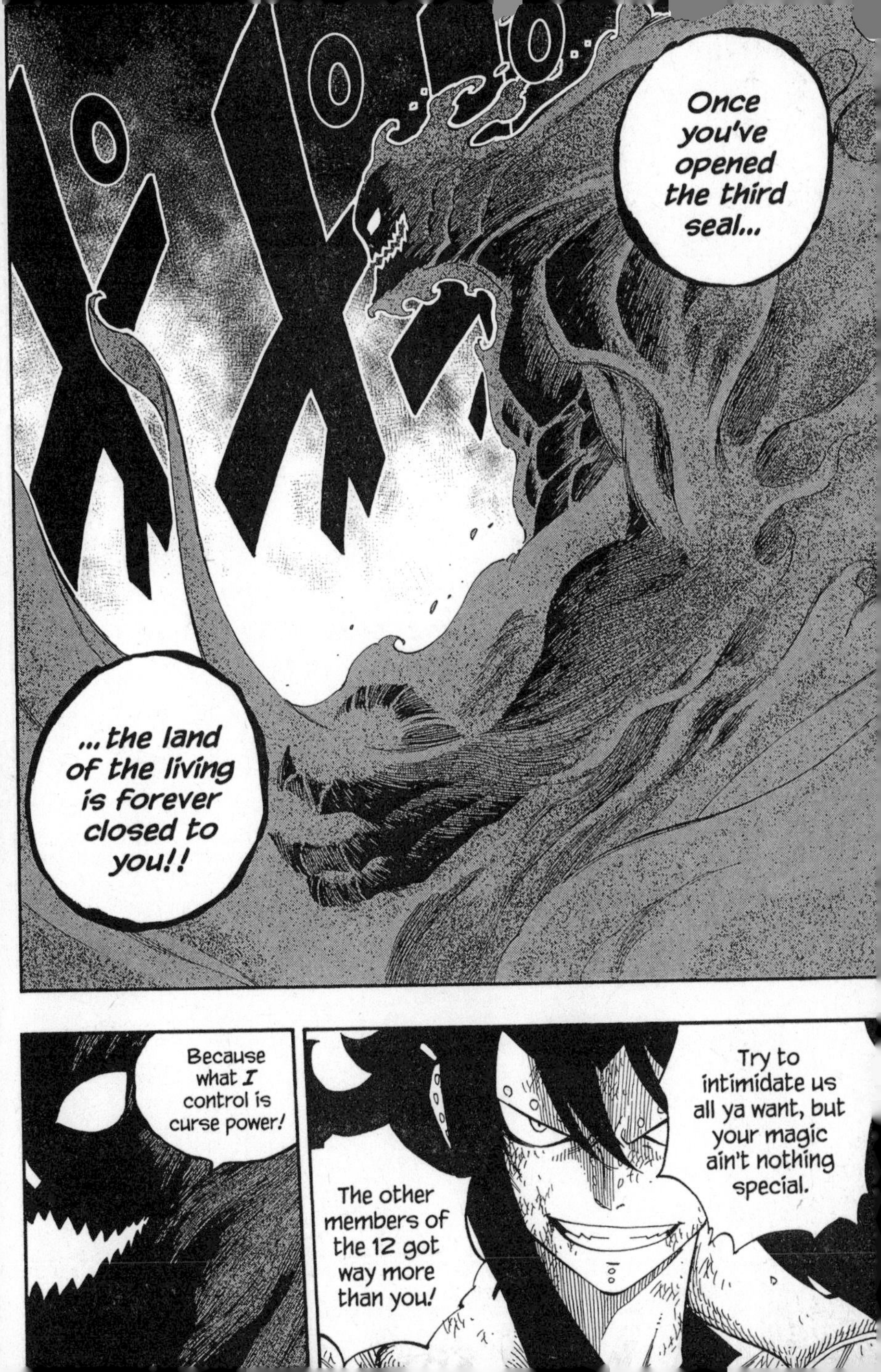
Once you've opened the third seal...
...the land of the living is forever closed to you!!
Try to intimidate us all ya want, but your magic ain't nothing special.
The other members of the 12 got way more than you!
Because what I control is curse power!

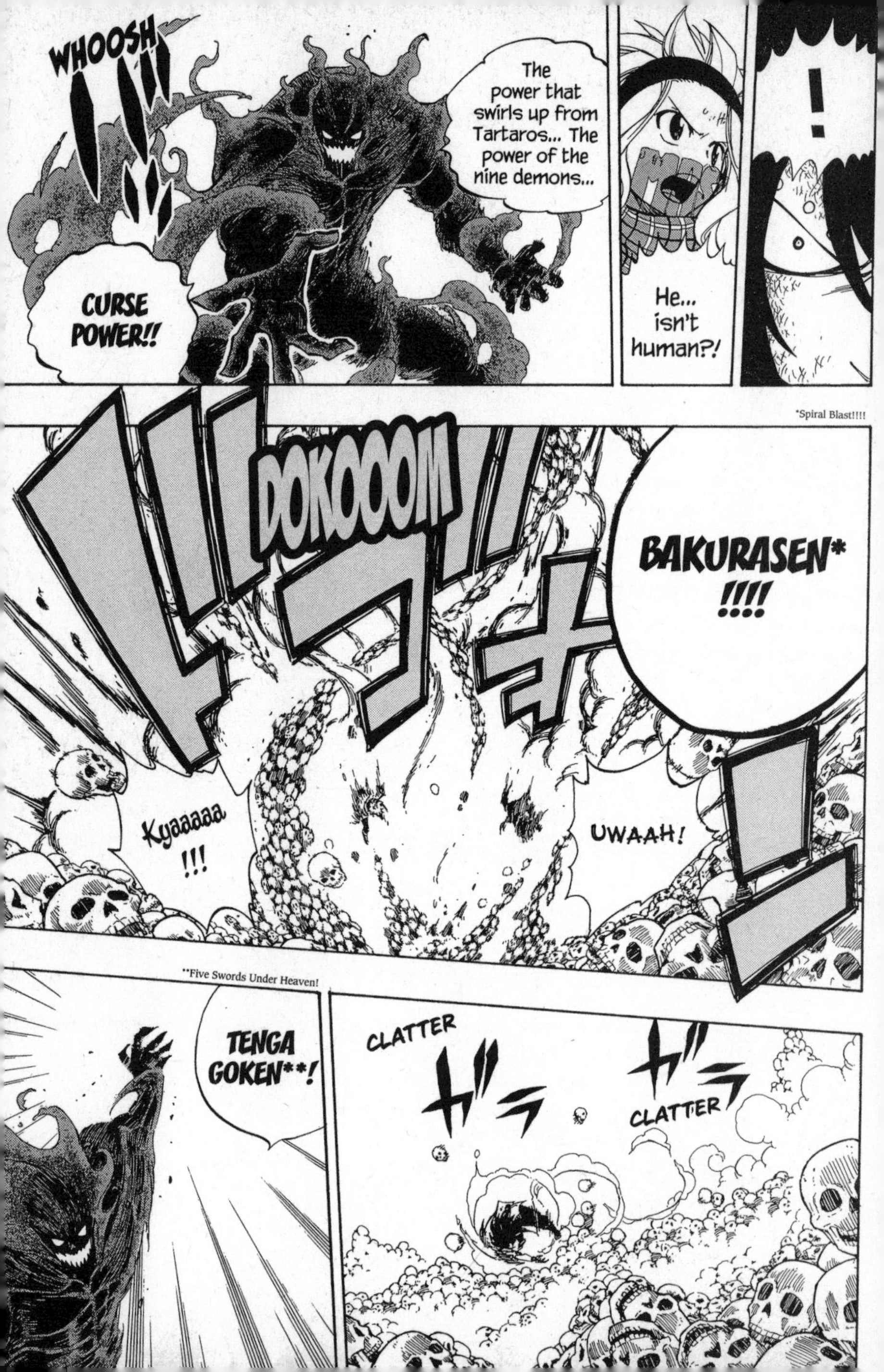
!
He... isn't human?!
The power that swirls up from Tartaros... The power of the nine demons...
WHOOSH
CURSE POWER!!
BAKURASEN* !!!!
DOKOOOM
UWAAH!
Kyaaaaa !!!
CLATTER
CLATTER
TENGA GOKEN**!

*Spiral Blast!!!!

**Five Swords Under Heaven!

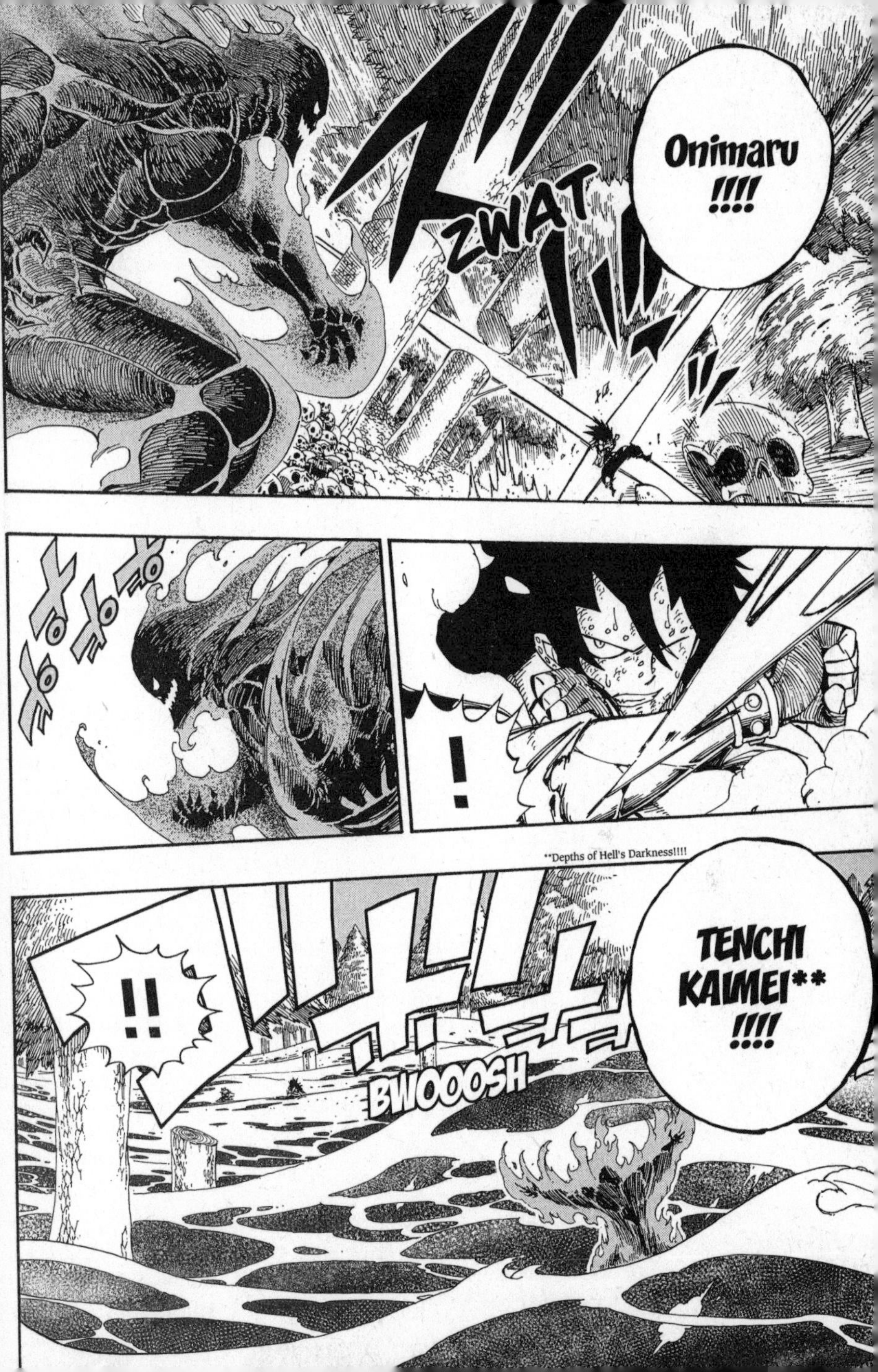
Onimaru !!!!
ZWAT
!
TENCHI KAIMEI** !!!!
!!
BWOOOSH
**Depths of Hell's Darkness!!!!

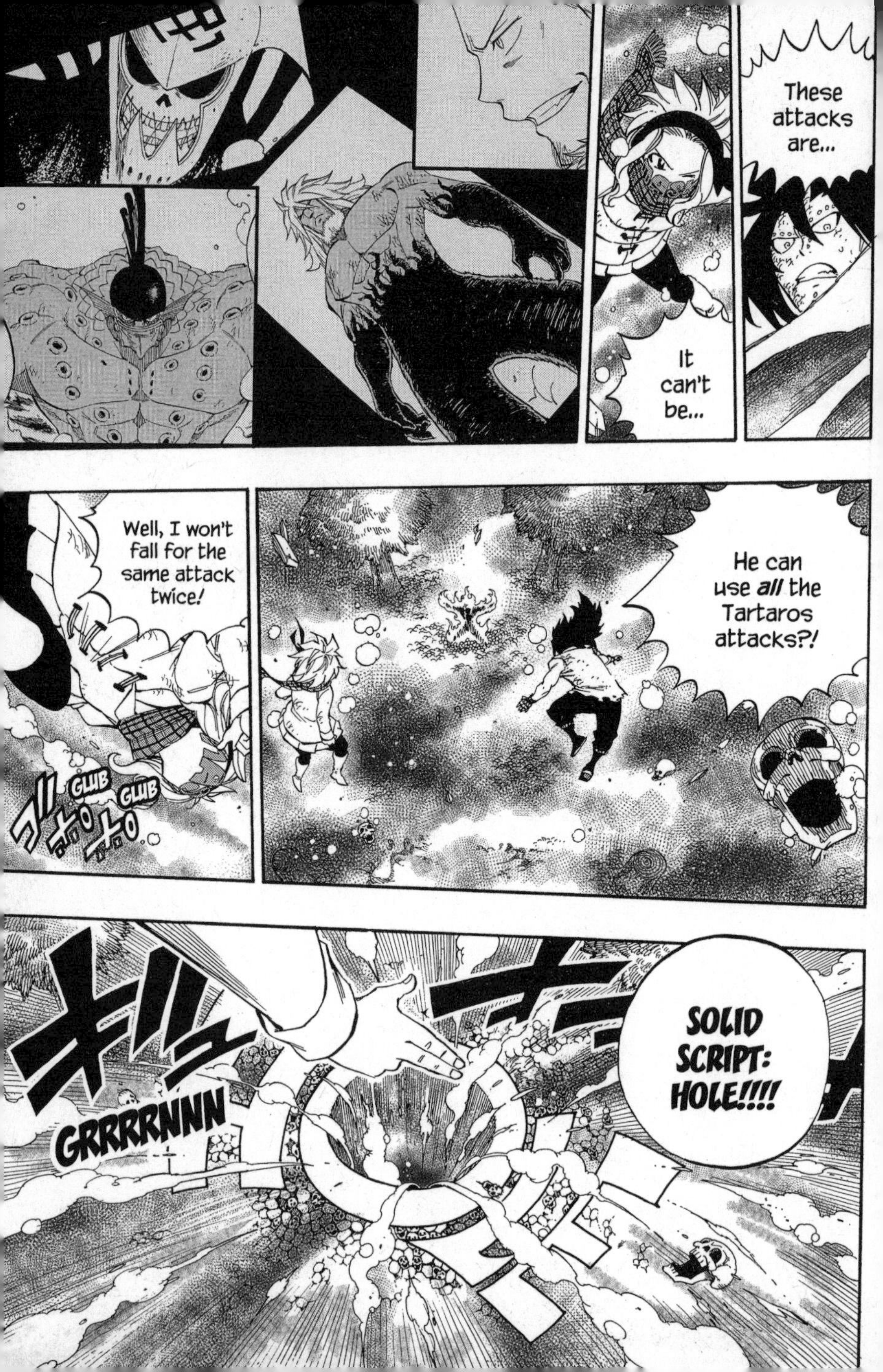
These attacks are...
It can't be...
He can use *all* the Tartaros attacks?!
Well, I won't fall for the same attack twice!
GLUB
GLUB
SOLID SCRIPT: HOLE!!!!
GRRRNNN

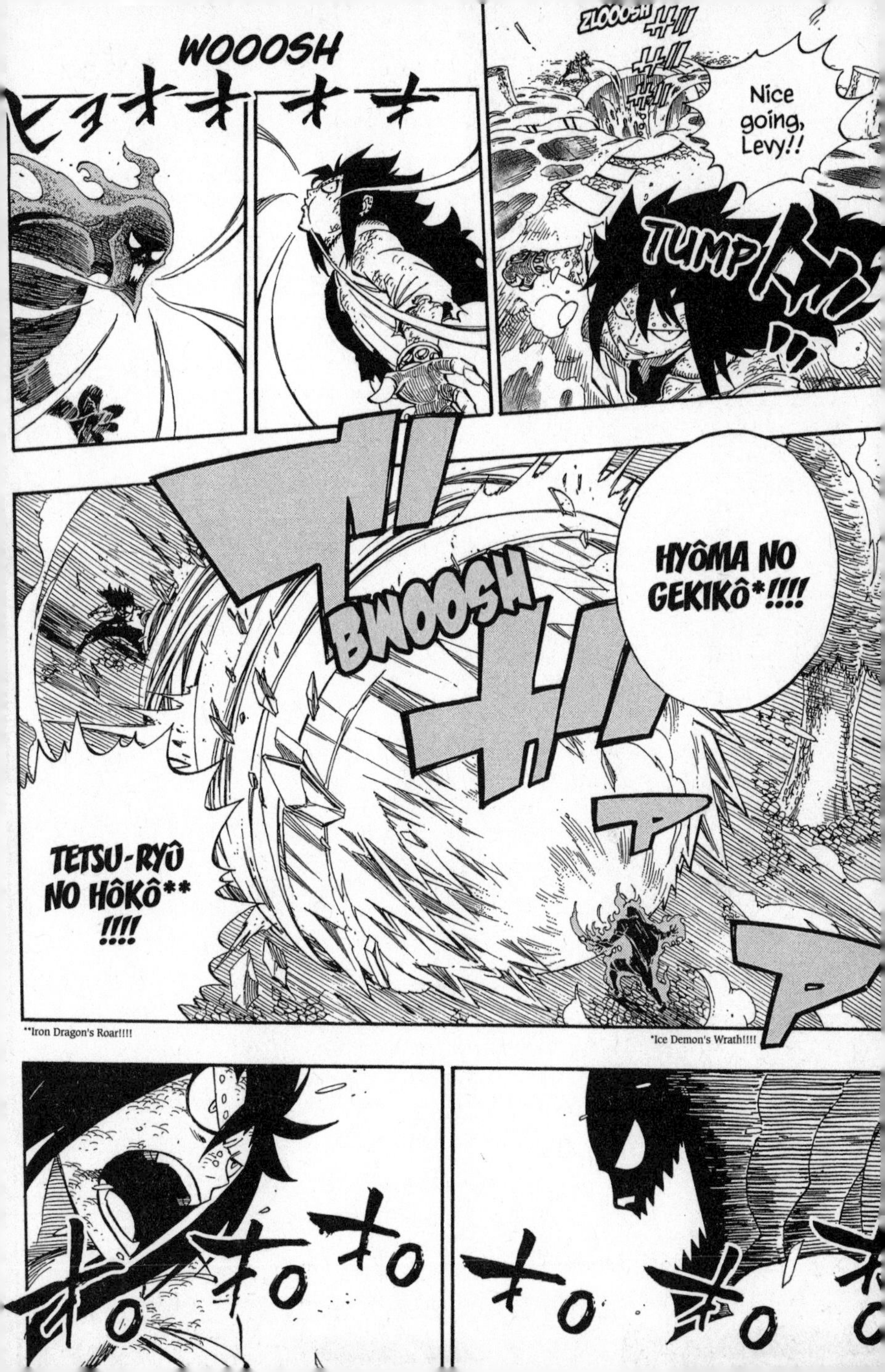
ZLOOOSH
Nice going, Levy!!
TUMP
WOOOSH
HYÔMA NO GEKIKÔ*!!!!
BWOOSH
TETSU-RYÛ NO HÔKÔ** !!!!

*Ice Demon's Wrath!!!!

**Iron Dragon's Roar!!!!

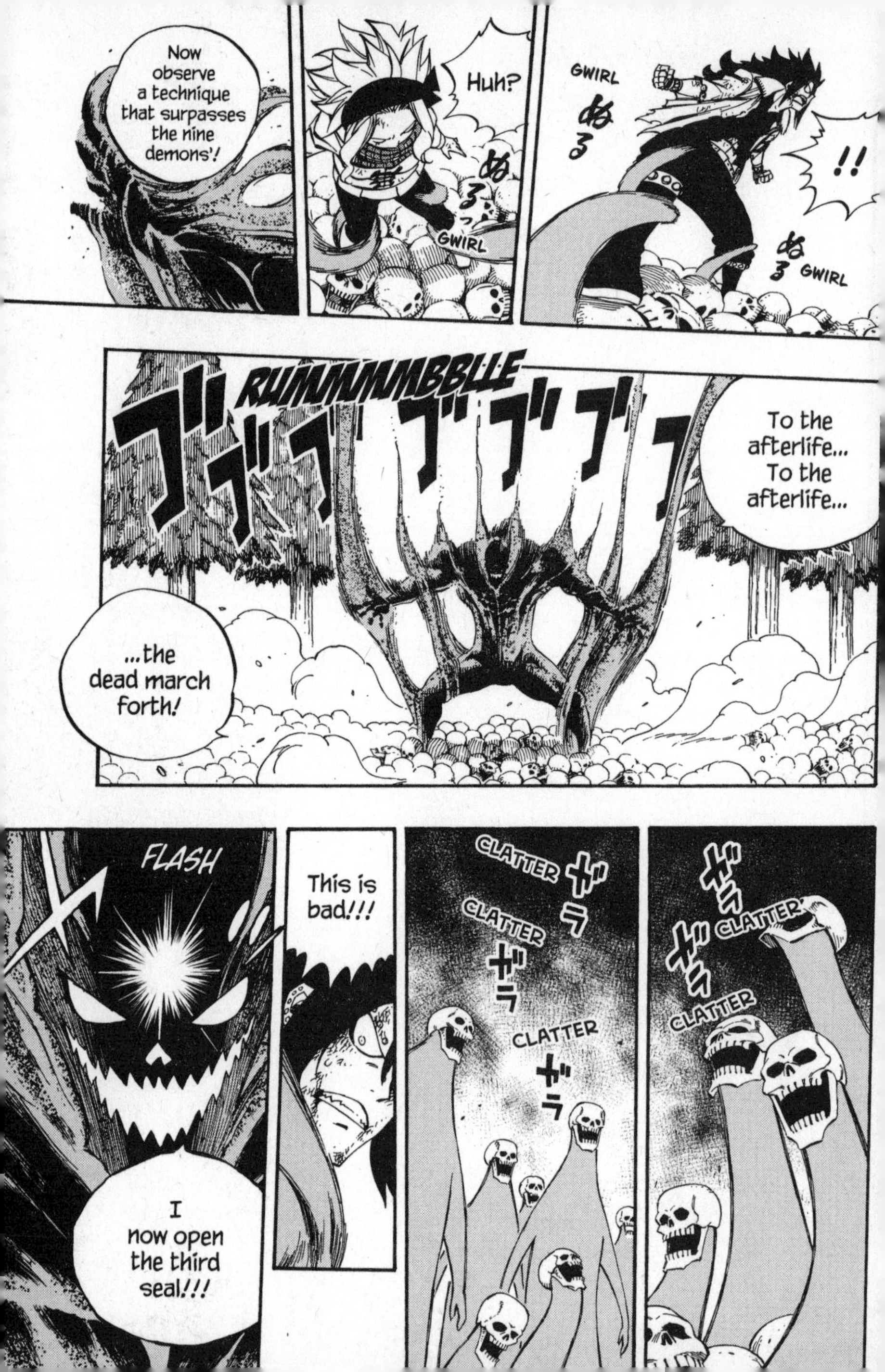
!!
GWIRL
ぬる
ぬる
GWIRL
Huh?
ぬるっ
GWIRL
Now observe a technique that surpasses the nine demons'!
RUMMMMBBLLE
ゴゴゴゴゴゴゴ
To the afterlife... To the afterlife...
...the dead march forth!
ザラ
CLATTER
ザラ
CLATTER
CLATTER
ザラ
CLATTER
ザラ
CLATTER
ザラ
This is bad!!!
FLASH
I now open the third seal!!!

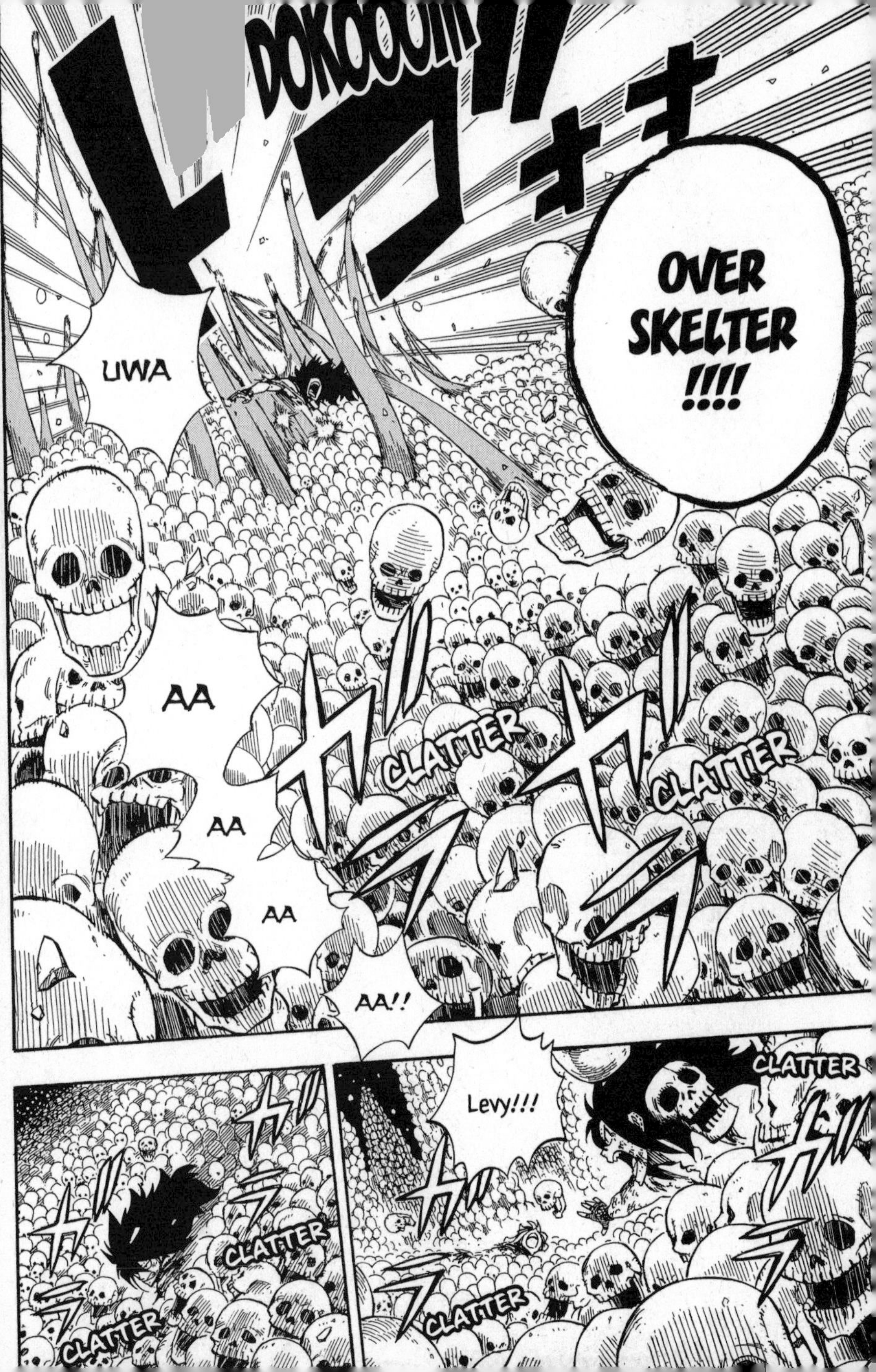
DOKOOOM!!
OVER SKELTER!!!!
UWA
AA
AA
AA
AA!!
CLATTER
CLATTER
CLATTER
Levy!!!
CLATTER
CLATTER
CLATTER

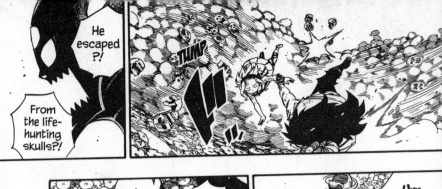

He escaped?!

From the life-hunting skulls?!

TLUMP

KAFF

KAFF

KAFF

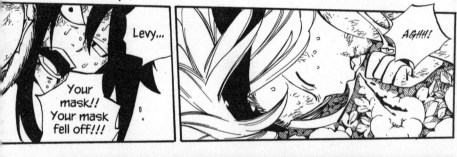

Urr...

Urh...

Urrgh...

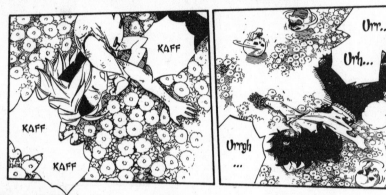

Levy...

Your mask!! Your mask fell off!!!

AGHH!

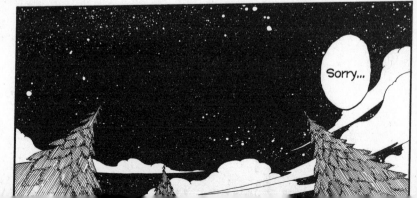

Sorry...

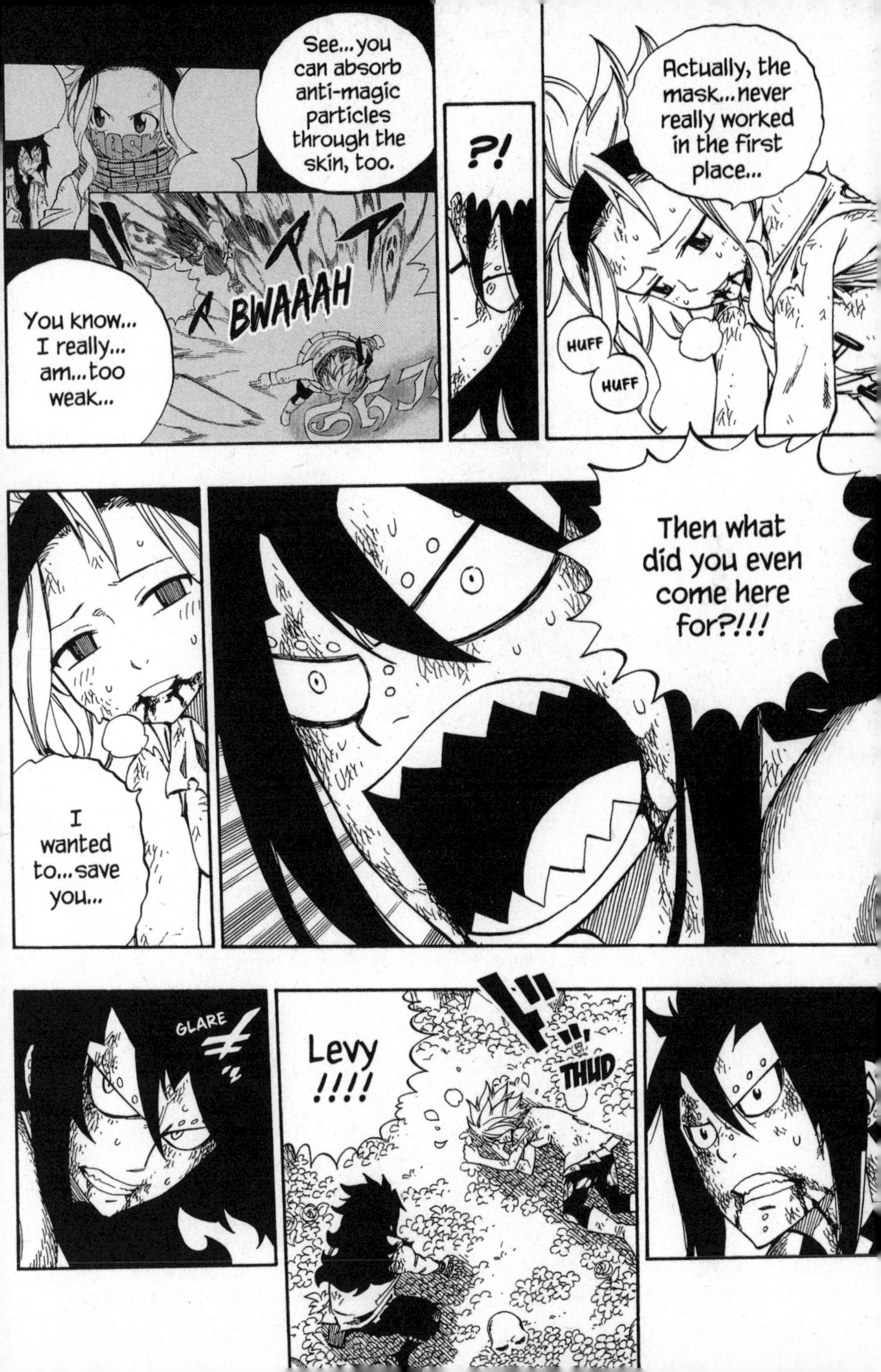
Actually, the mask...never really worked in the first place...
HUFF
HUFF
?!
See...you can absorb anti-magic particles through the skin, too.
BWAAAH
You know... I really... am...too weak...
Then what did you even come here for?!!!
I wanted to...save you...
THUD
Levy !!!!
GLARE

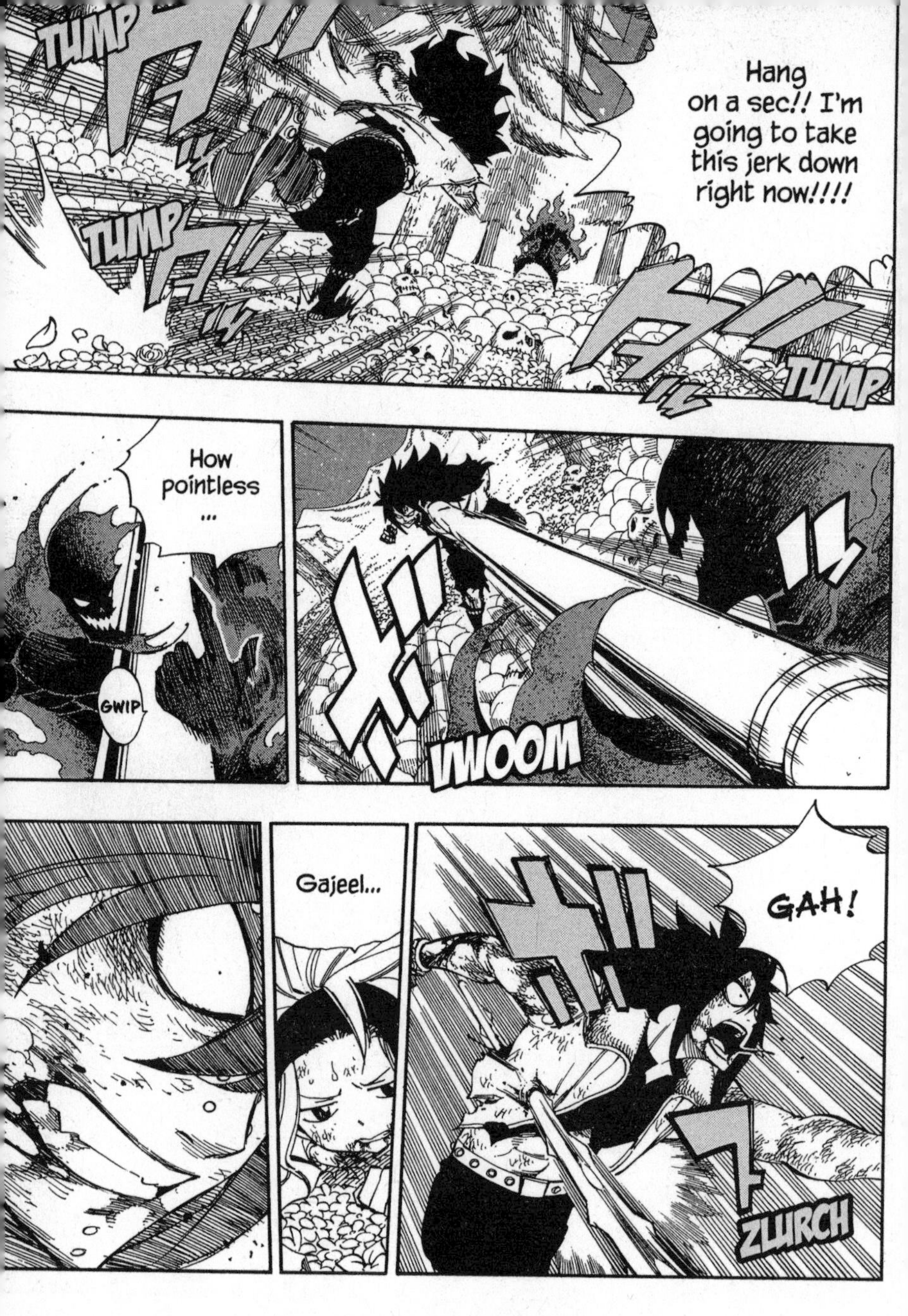
Hang on a sec!! I'm going to take this jerk down right now!!!!
TUMP
TUMP
TUMP
VWOOM
How pointless ...
GWIP
GAH!
ZLURCH
Gajeel...

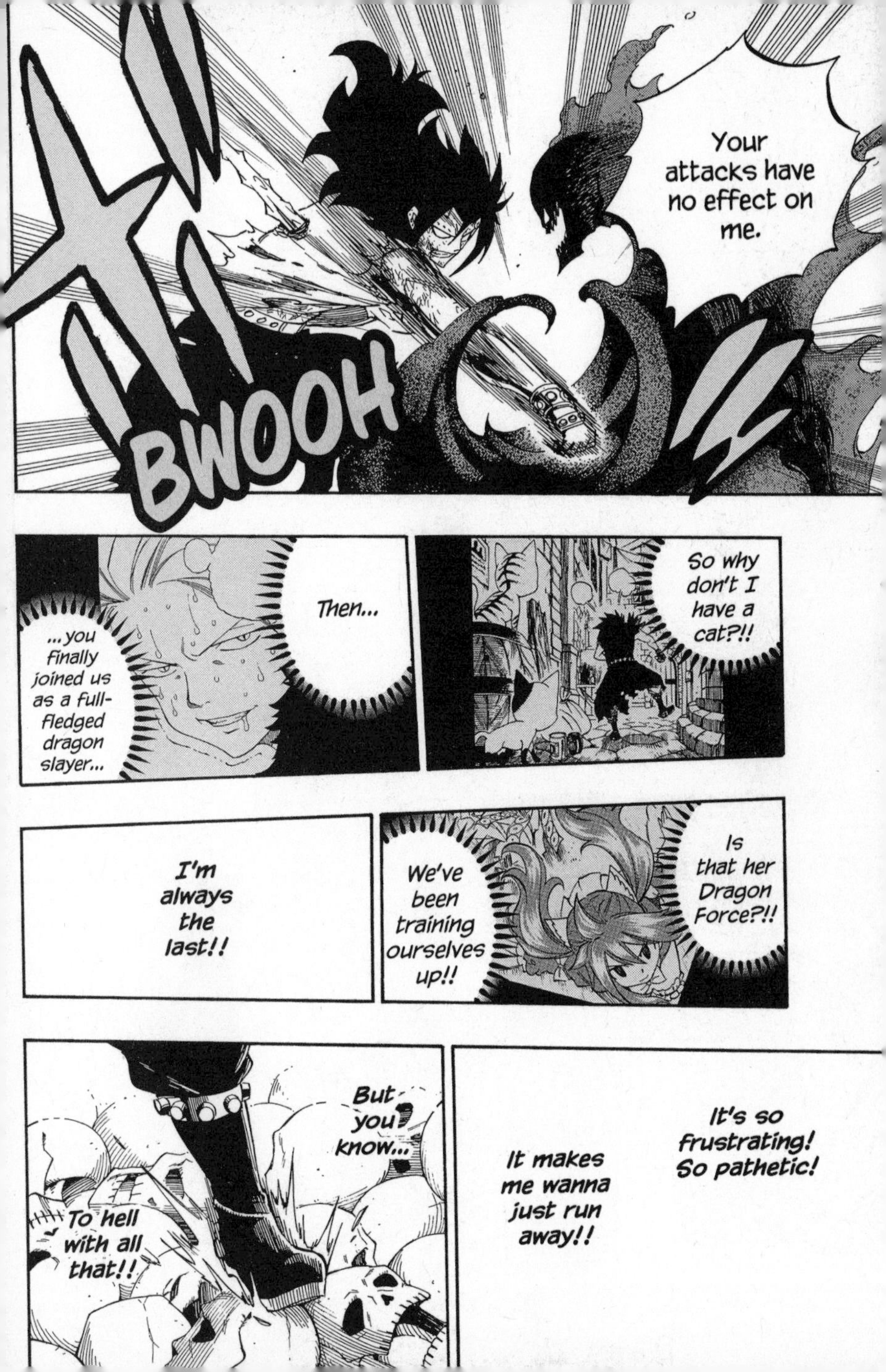
Your attacks have no effect on me.
BWOOH
So why don't I have a cat?!!
Then...
...you finally joined us as a full-fledged dragon slayer...
Is that her Dragon Force?!!
We've been training ourselves up!!
I'm always the last!!
It's so frustrating! So pathetic!
It makes me wanna just run away!!
But you know...
To hell with all that!!

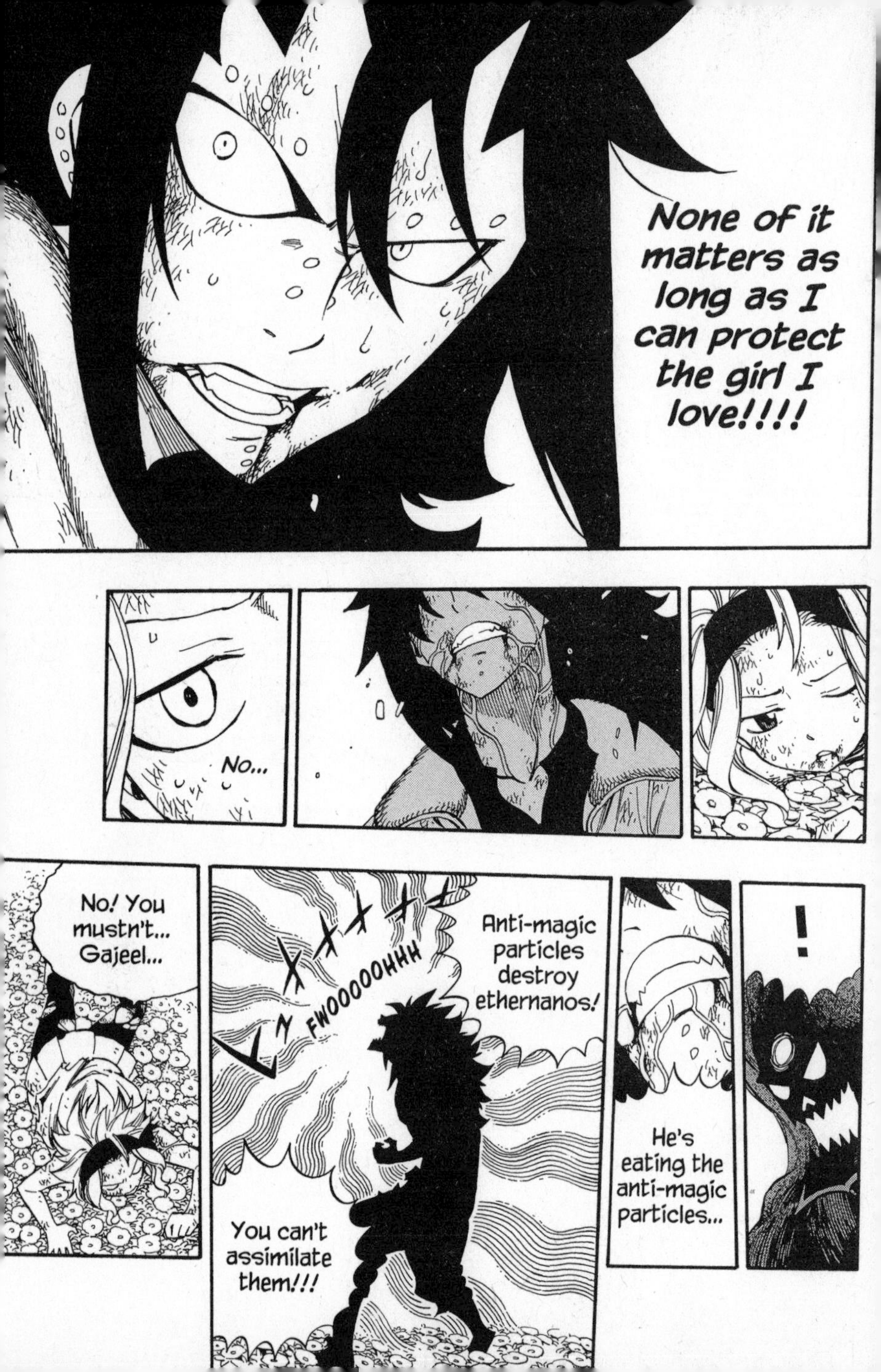
None of it matters as long as I can protect the girl I love!!!!
No...
!
He's eating the anti-magic particles...
Anti-magic particles destroy ethernanos!
FWOOOOOHHH
You can't assimilate them!!!
No! You mustn't... Gajeel...

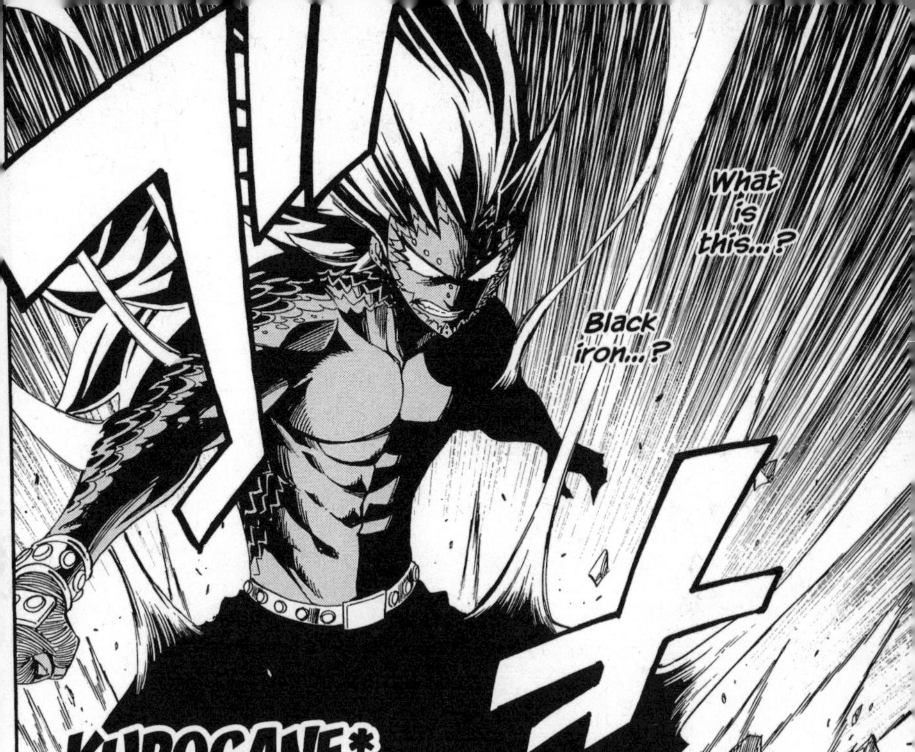
What is this...?
Black iron...?
KUROGANE*...
ROAR

*Black iron.

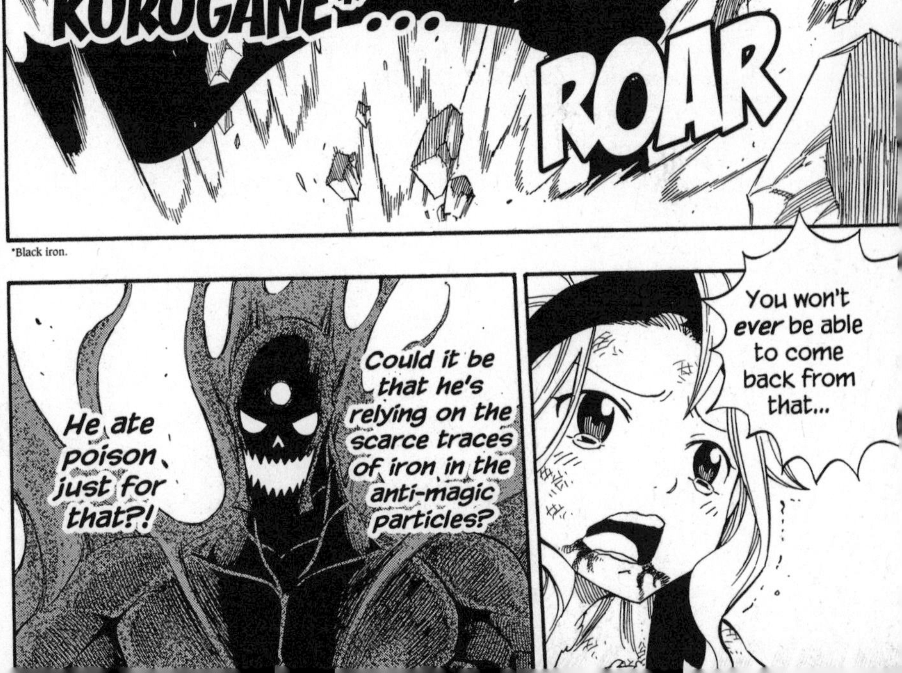
You won't *ever* be able to come back from that...
Could it be that he's relying on the scarce traces of iron in the anti-magic particles?
He ate poison just for that?!

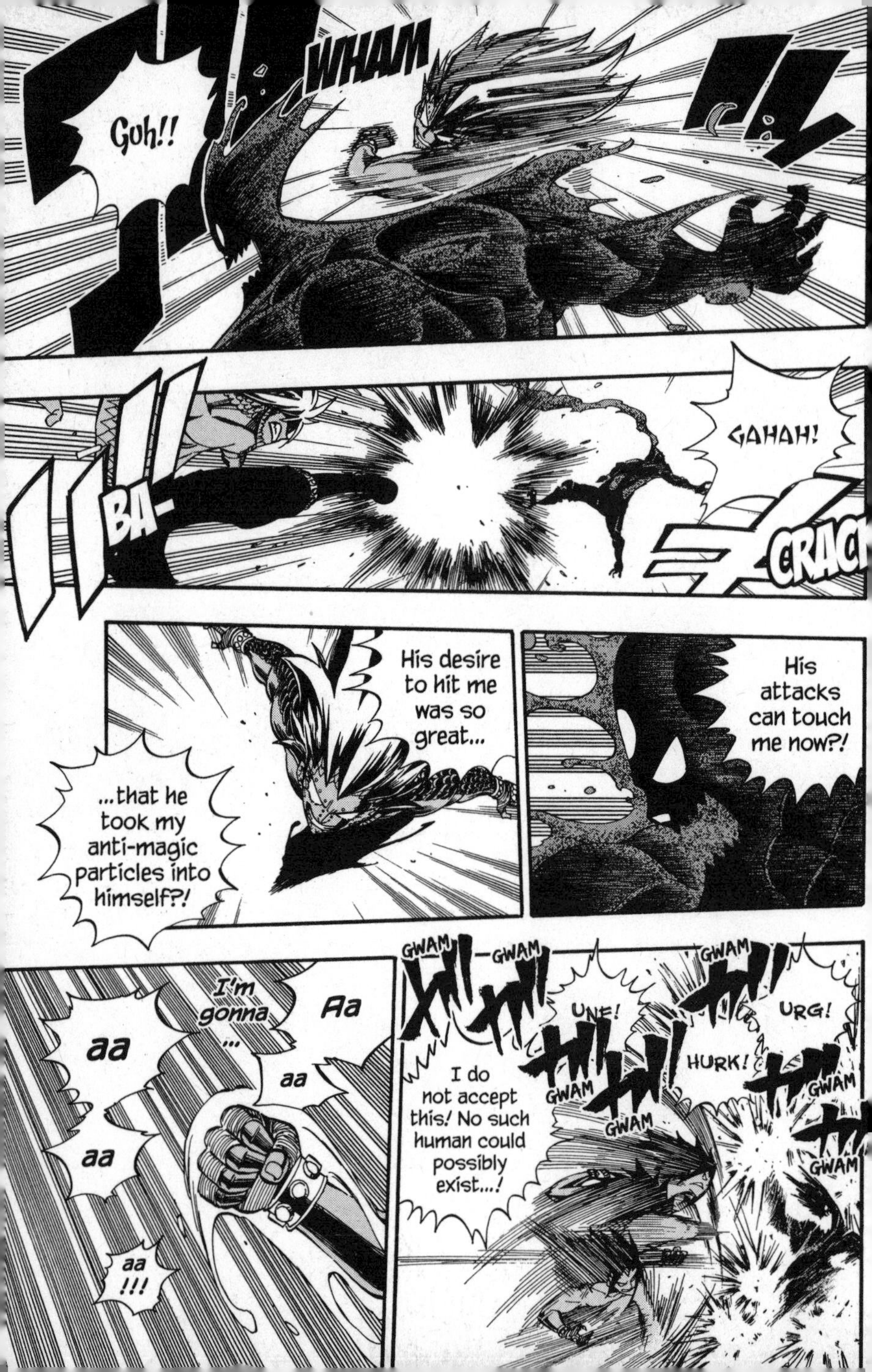
WHAM
Guh!!
GAHAH!
CRACK
BA-
His attacks can touch me now?!
His desire to hit me was so great...
...that he took my anti-magic particles into himself?!
GWAM
GWAM
GWAM
URG!
UNE!
HURK!
GWAM
GWAM
GWAM
GWAM
I do not accept this! No such human could possibly exist...!
I'm gonna...
Aa aa aa aa aa !!!

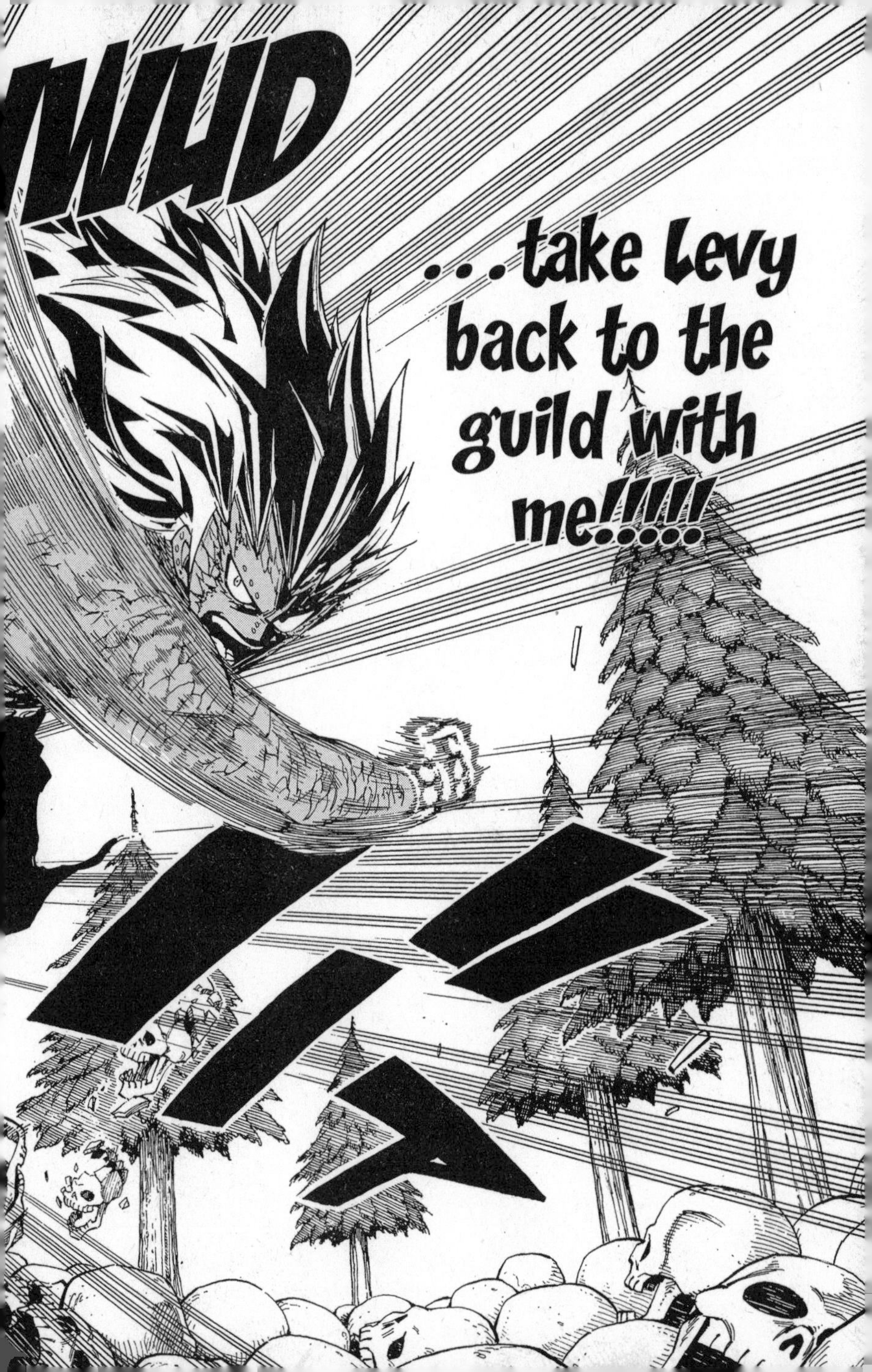
WHD
...take Levy back to the guild with me!!!!!

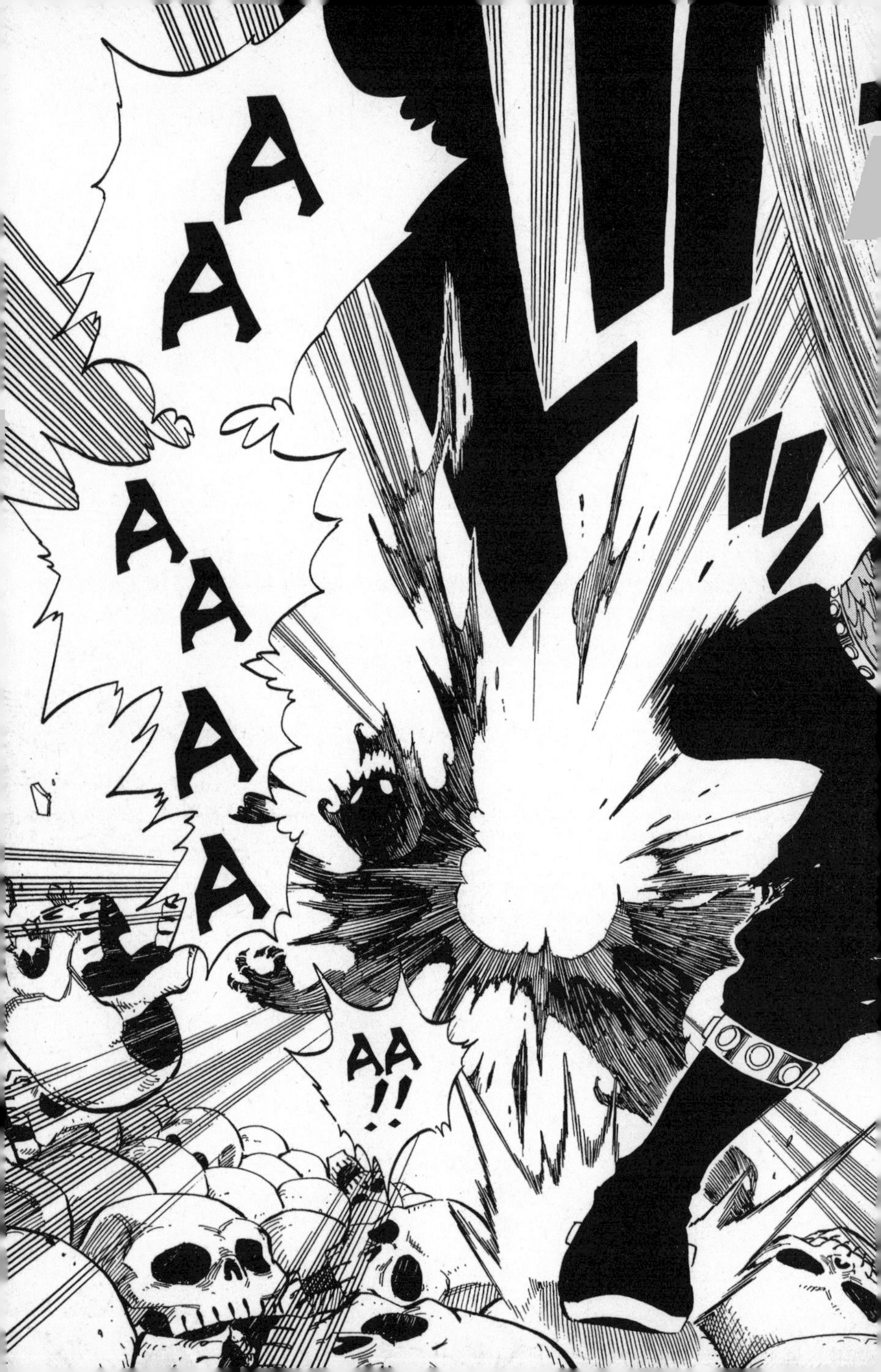
AAAAAA
AA!!

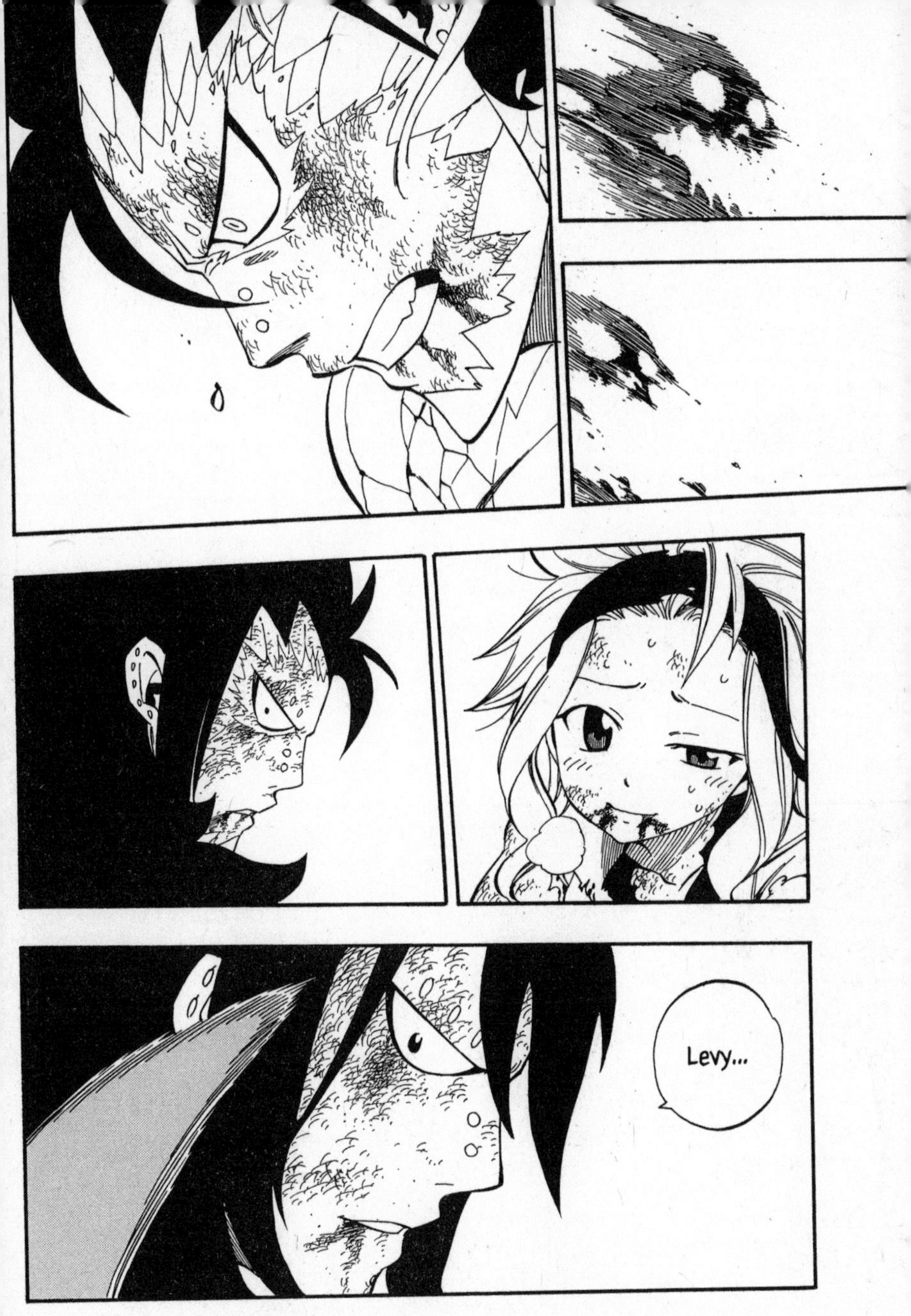
Levy...

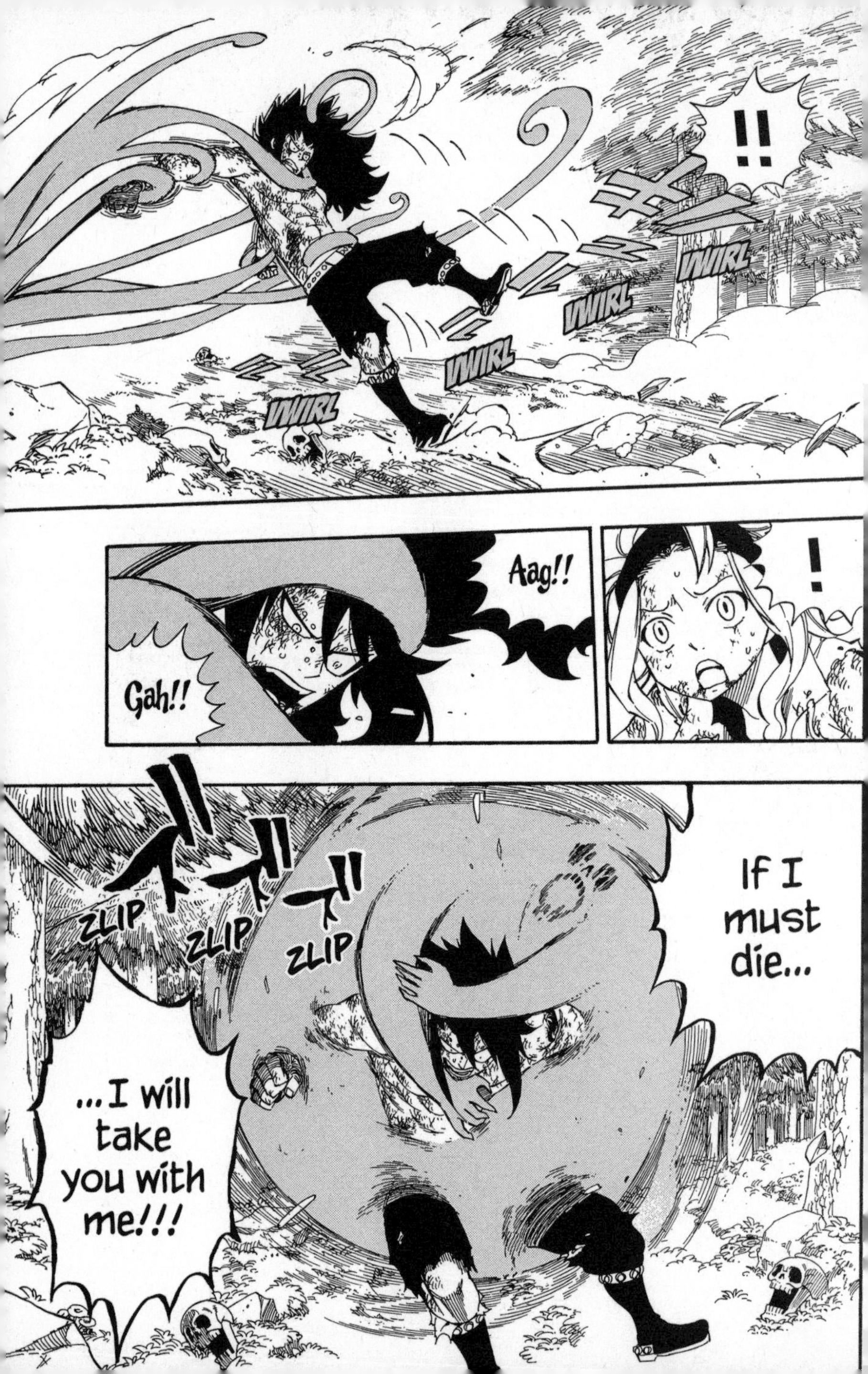
!!
VWIRL
VWIRL
VWIRL
VWIRL
!
Aag!!
Gah!!
If I must die...
ZLIP
ZLIP
ZLIP
...I will take you with me!!!

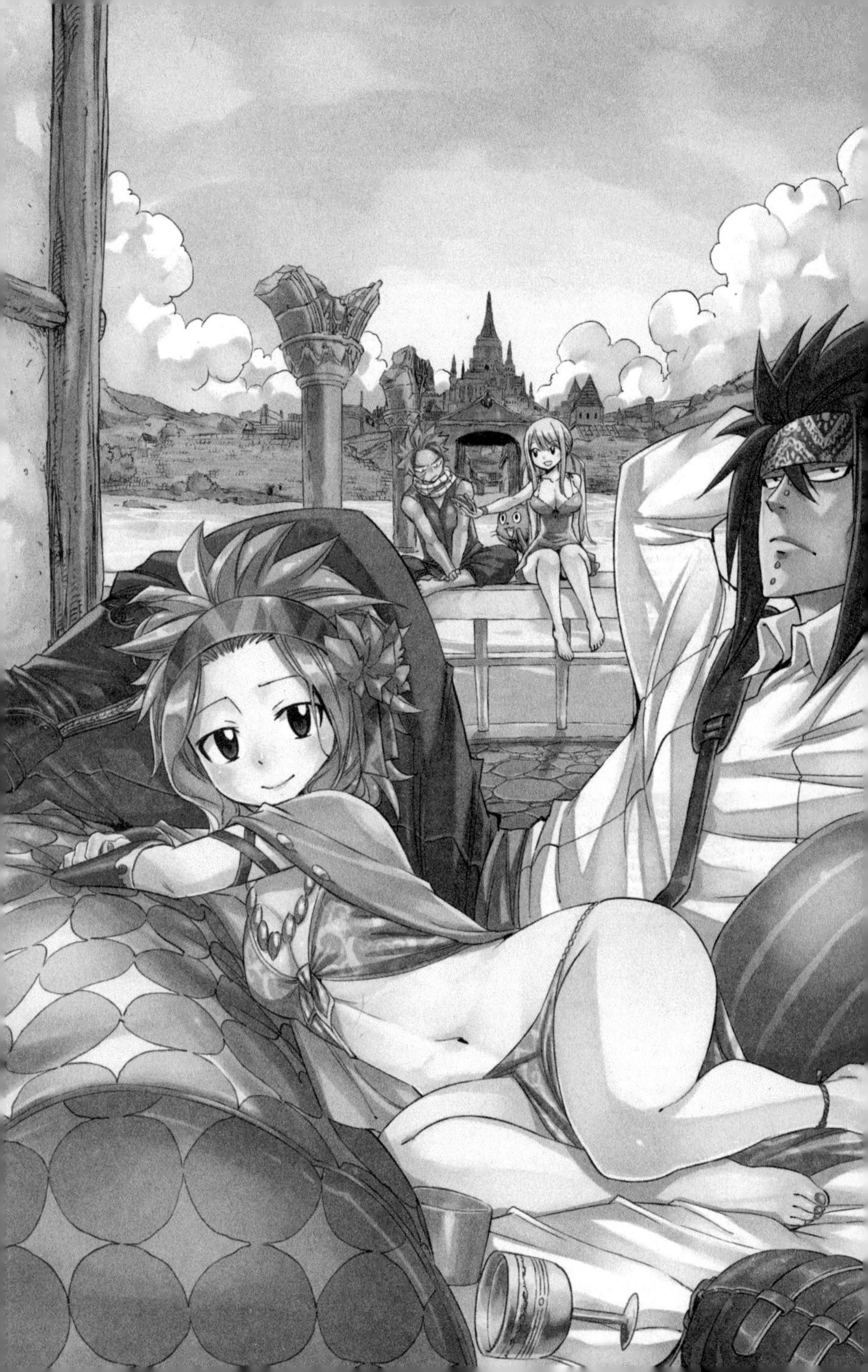

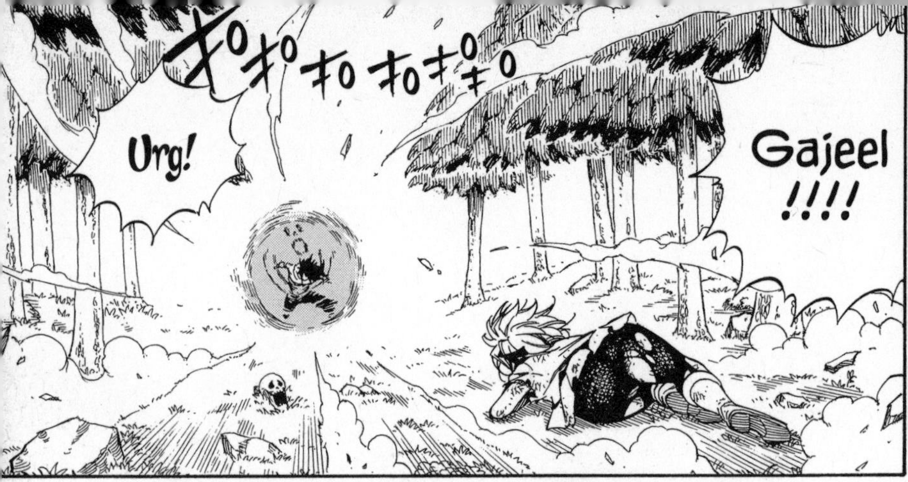
Gajeel !!!!
Urg!

FAIRY TAIL

フェアリーテイル

Chapter 488: The Two of U$, Forever

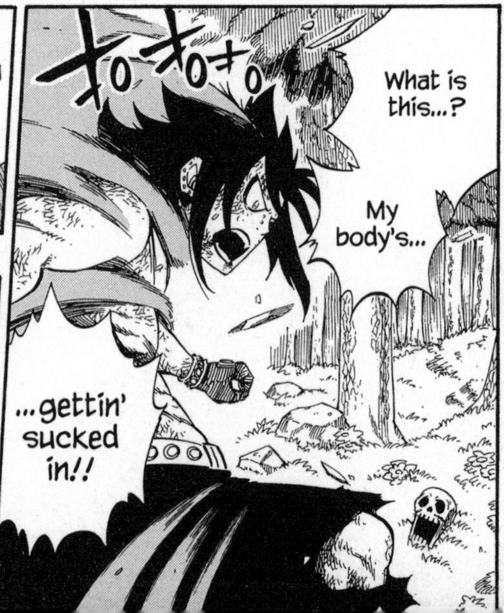
What is this...?
My body's...
...gettin' sucked in!!

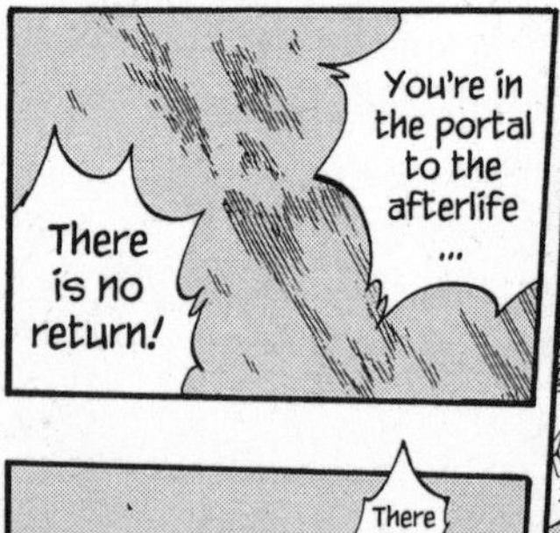
You're in the portal to the afterlife ...
There is no return!

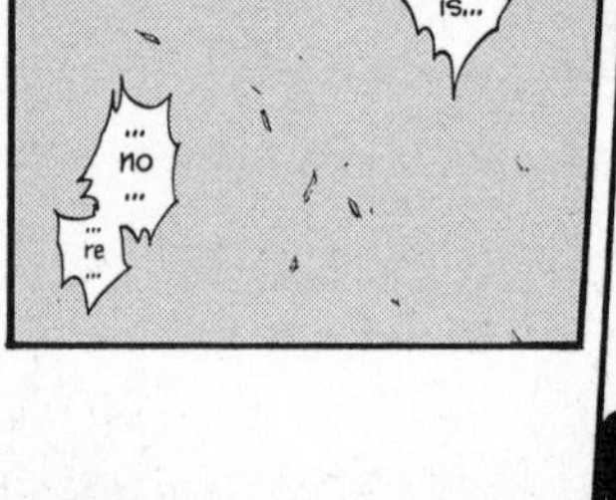
There is...
... no ...
... re ...

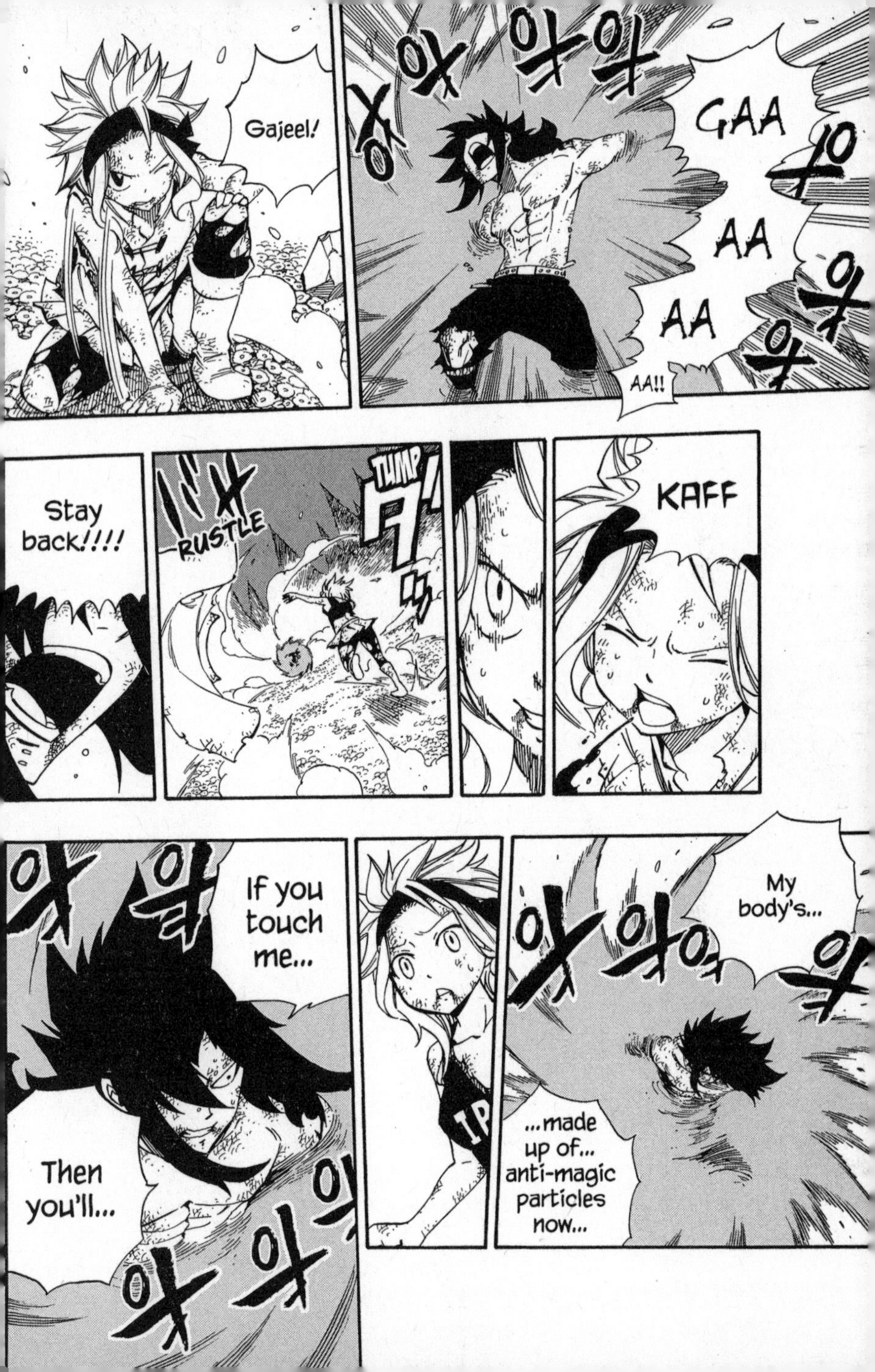
GAA
AA
AA
AA!!
Gajeel!
KAFF
TUMP
RUSTLE
Stay back!!!!
My body's...
...made up of... anti-magic particles now...
If you touch me...
Then you'll...

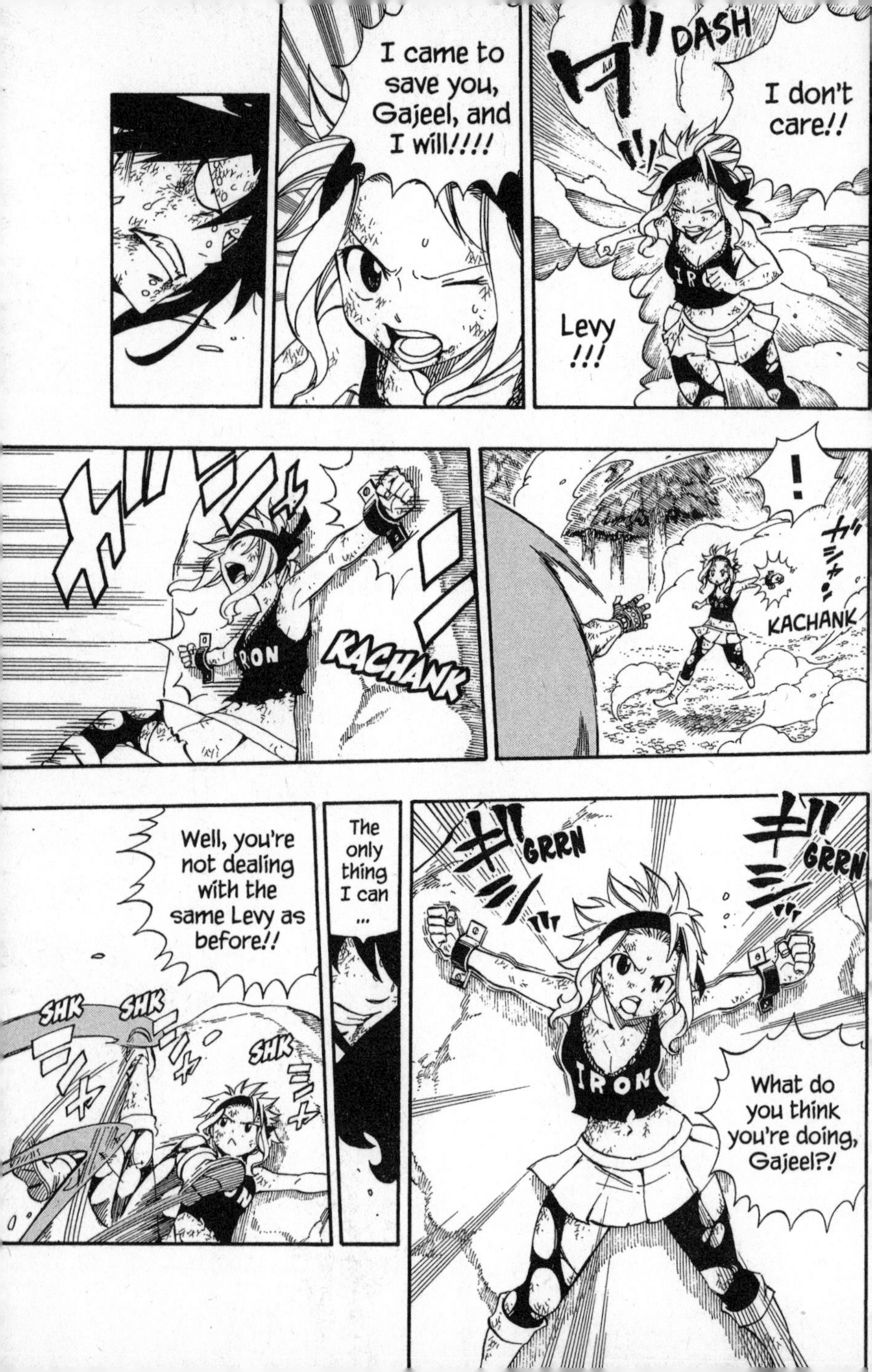
DASH
I don't care!!
Levy!!!
I came to save you, Gajeel, and I will!!!!
!
KACHANK
KACHANK
GRRN
GRRN
What do you think you're doing, Gajeel?!
The only thing I can ...
Well, you're not dealing with the same Levy as before!!
SHK
SHK
SHK

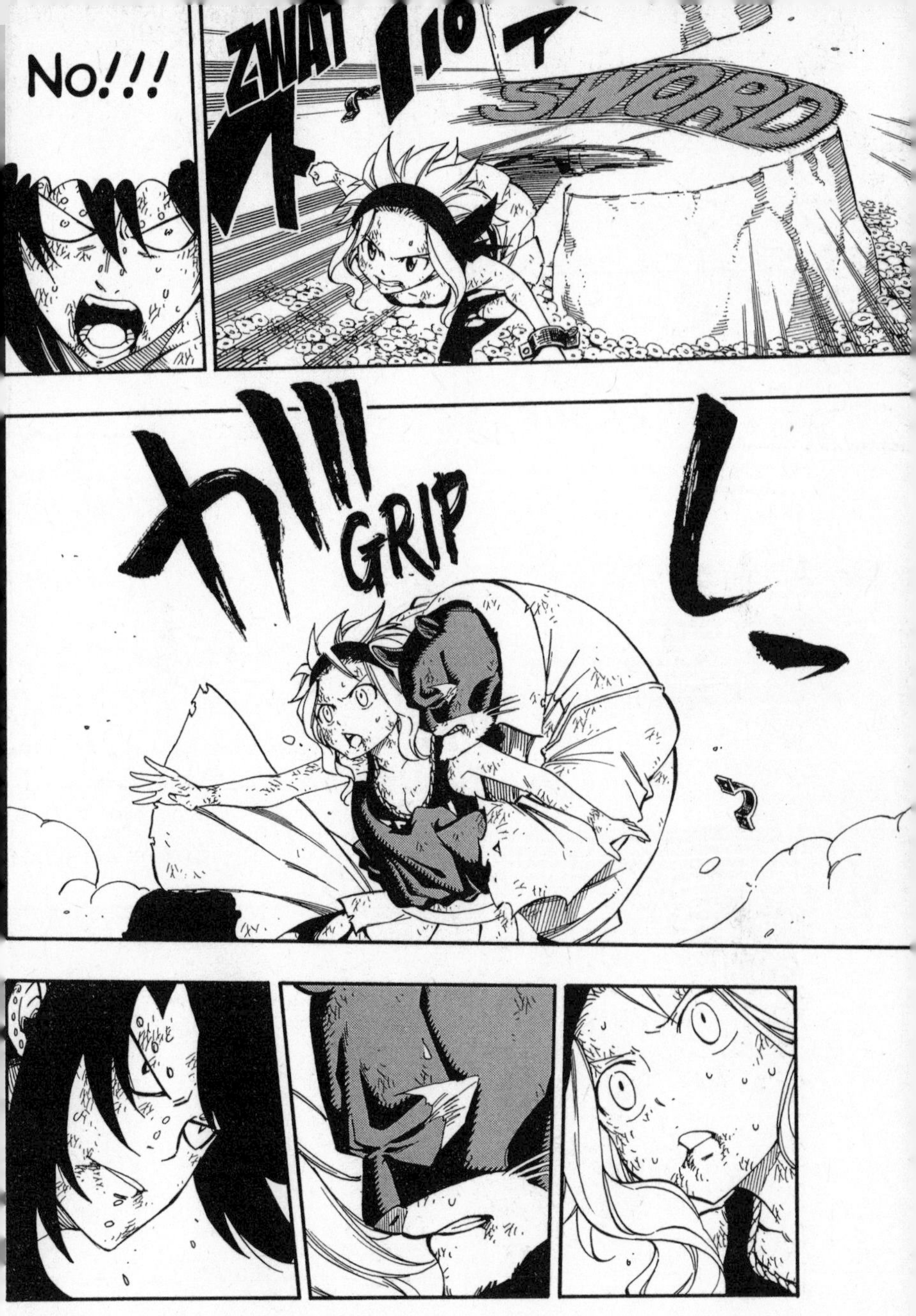
ZWAT
SWORD
No!!!
GRIP

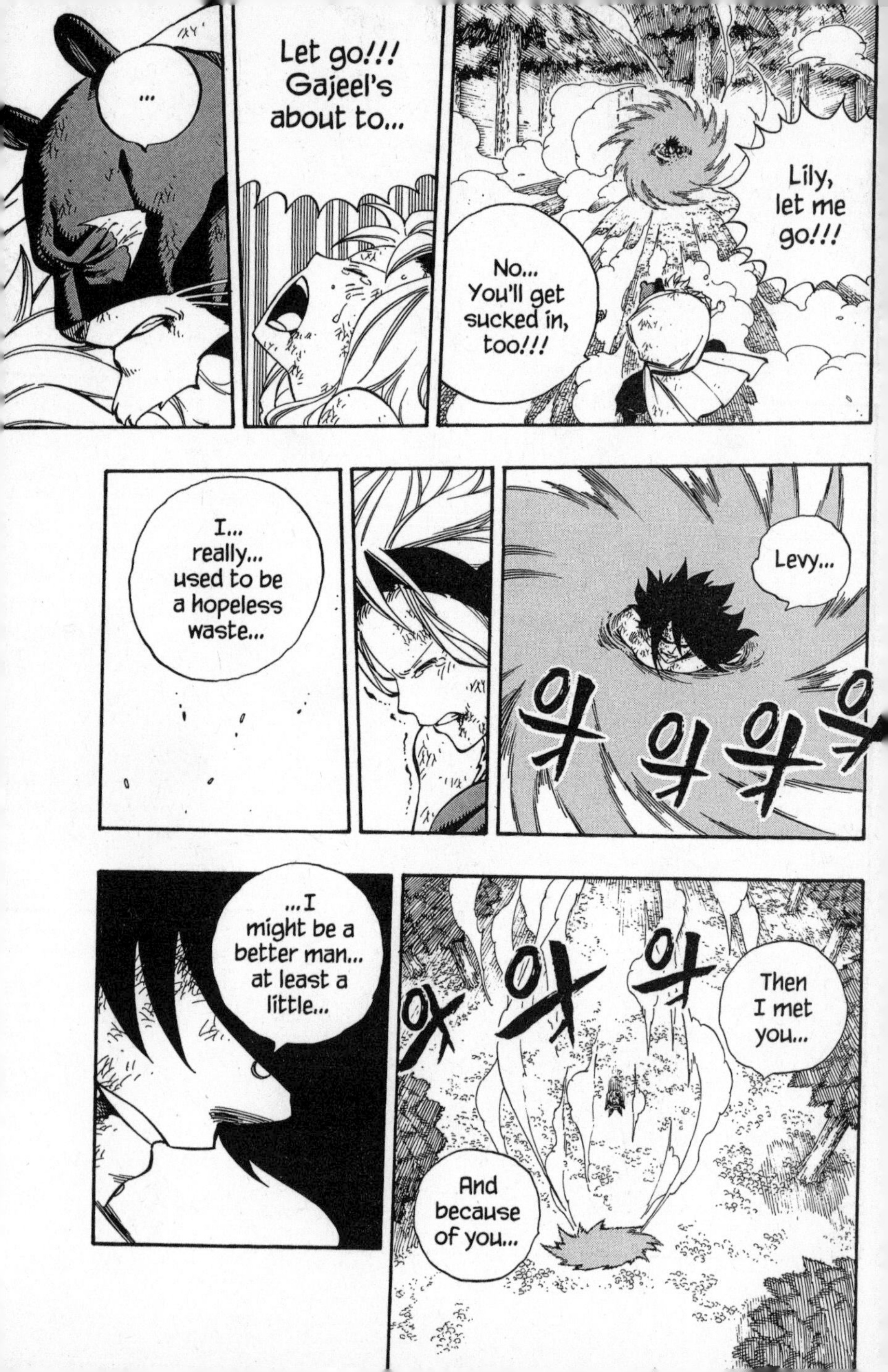
Lily, let me go!!!
No... You'll get sucked in, too!!!
Let go!!! Gajeel's about to...
...
Levy...
I... really... used to be a hopeless waste...
Then I met you...
And because of you...
...I might be a better man... at least a little...

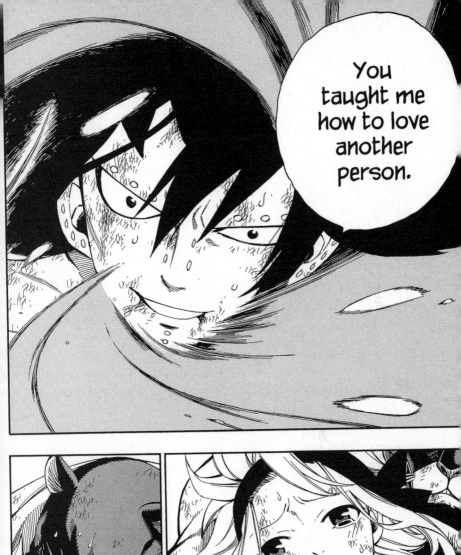

You
taught me
how to love
another
person.

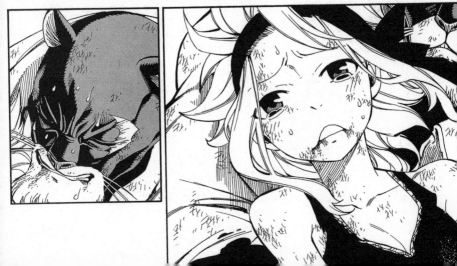

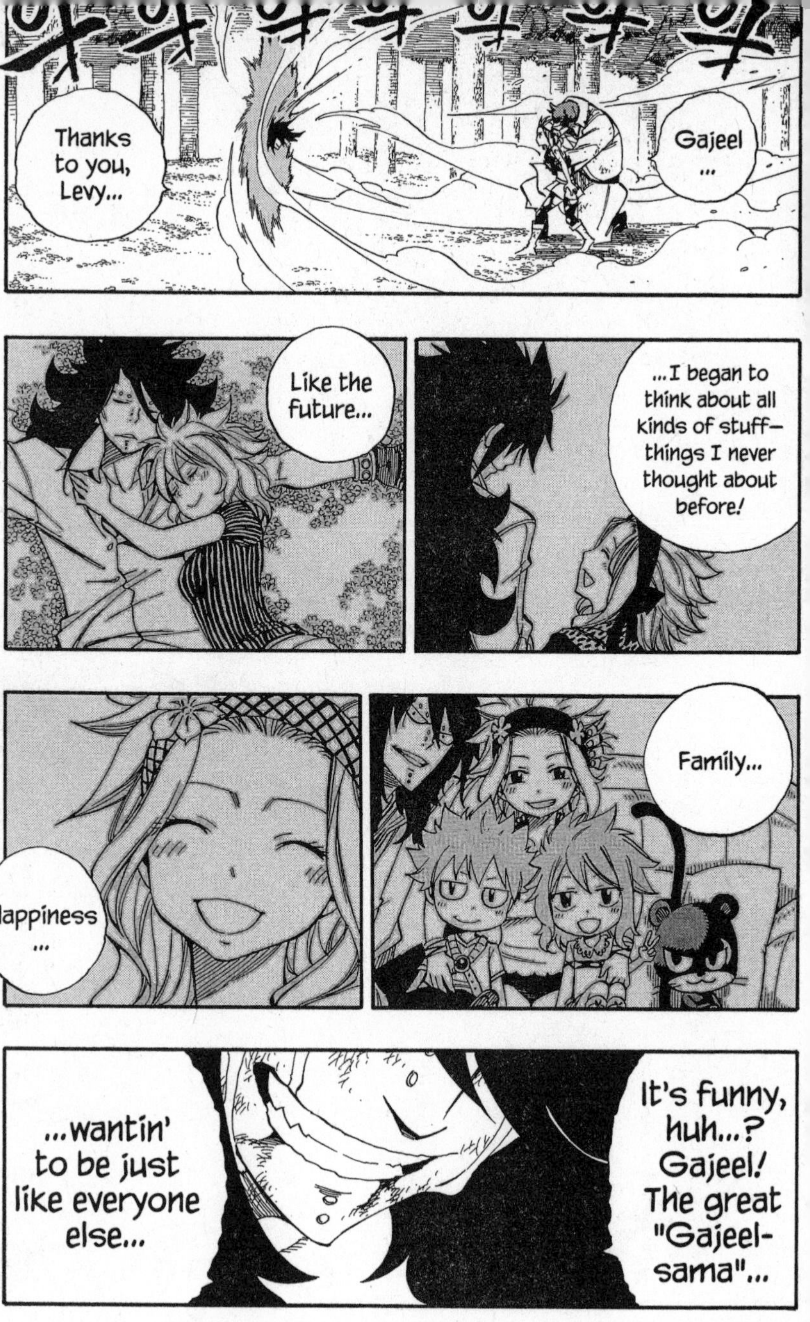
Gajeel ...
Thanks to you, Levy...
...I began to think about all kinds of stuff— things I never thought about before!
Like the future...
Family...
Happiness ...
It's funny, huh...? Gajeel! The great "Gajeel-sama"...
...wantin' to be just like everyone else...

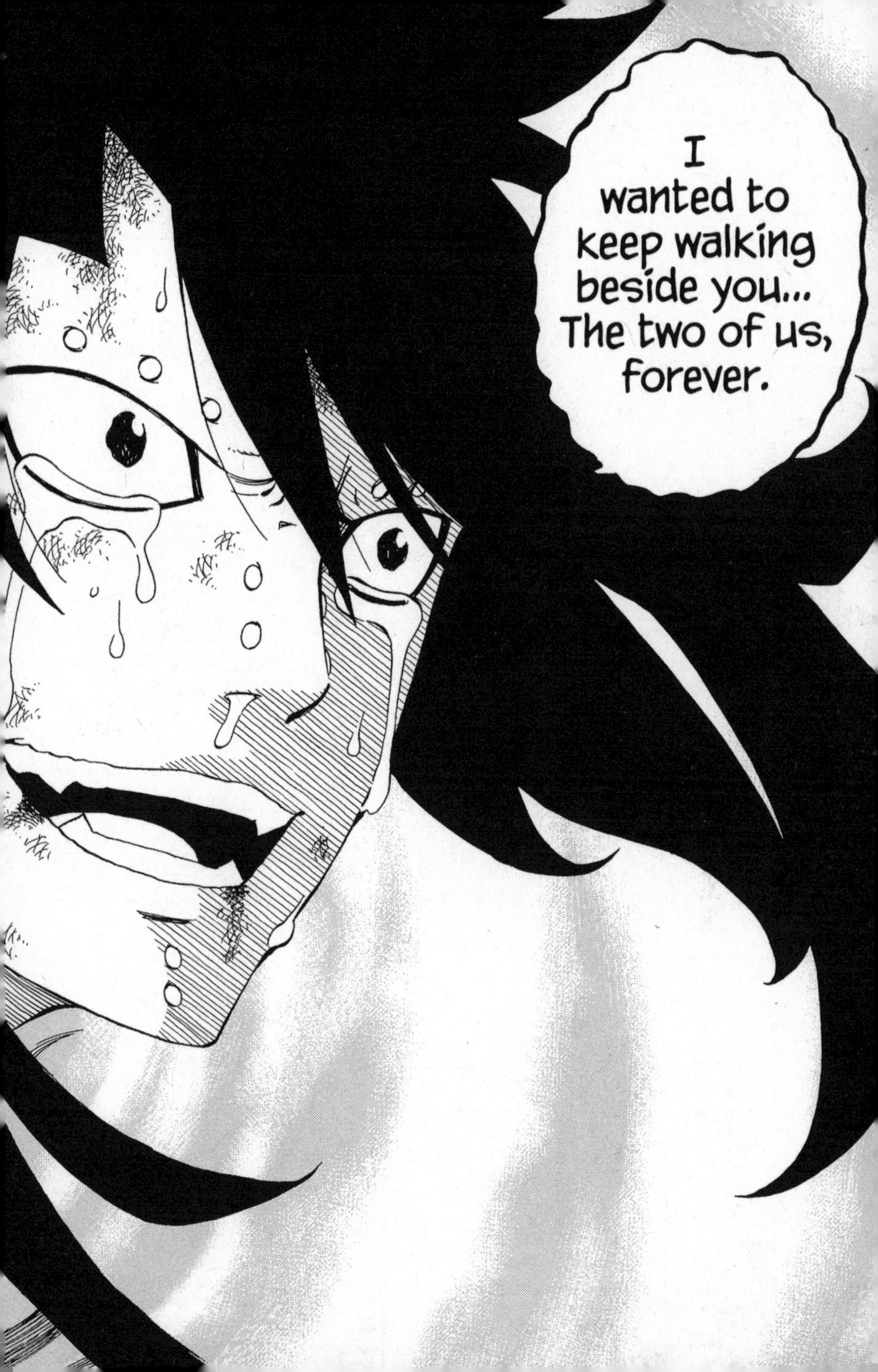
I wanted to keep walking beside you... The two of us, forever.

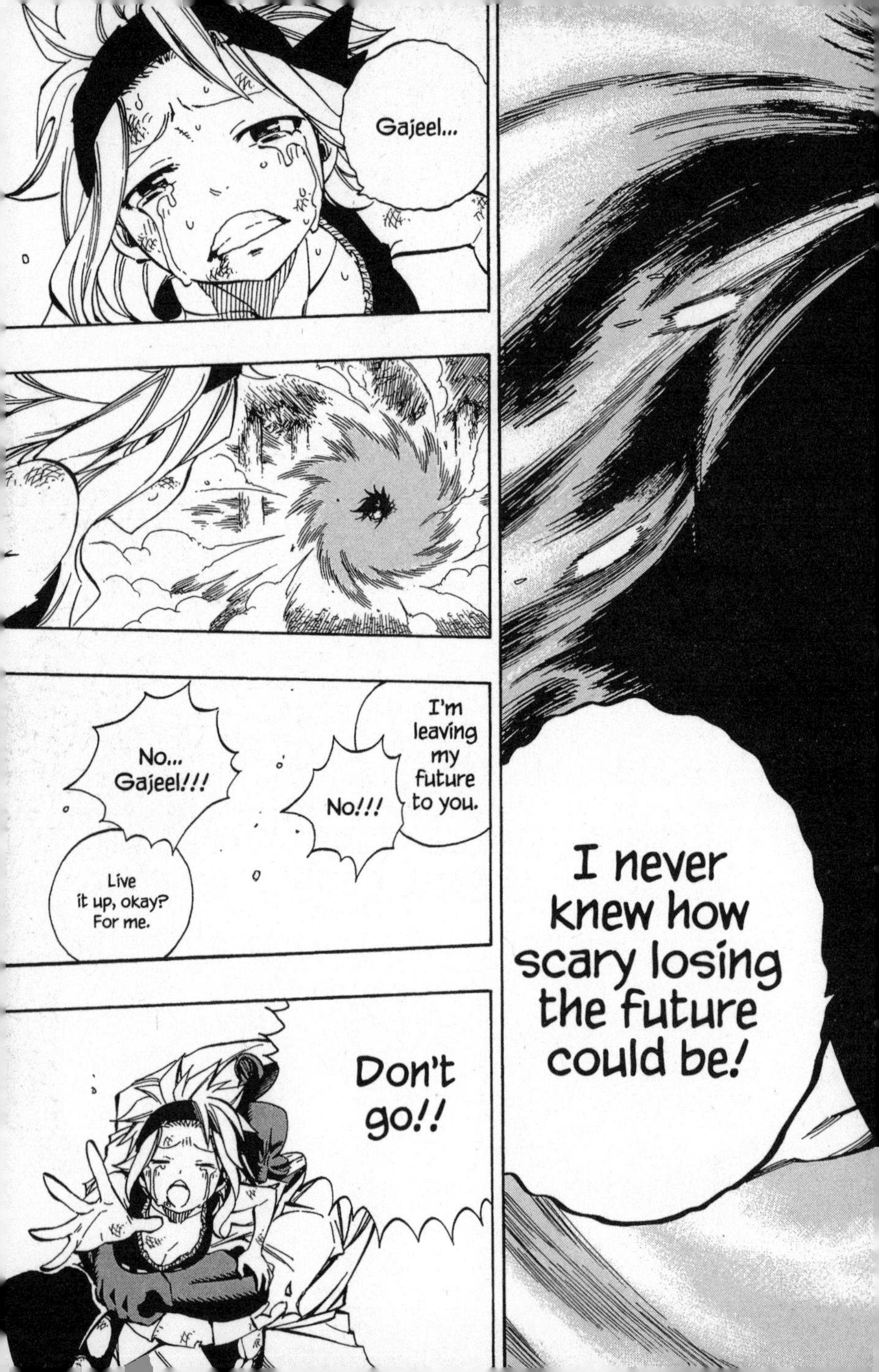
I never knew how scary losing the future could be!
Gajeel...
I'm leaving my future to you.
No!!!
No... Gajeel!!!
Live it up, okay? For me.
Don't go!!

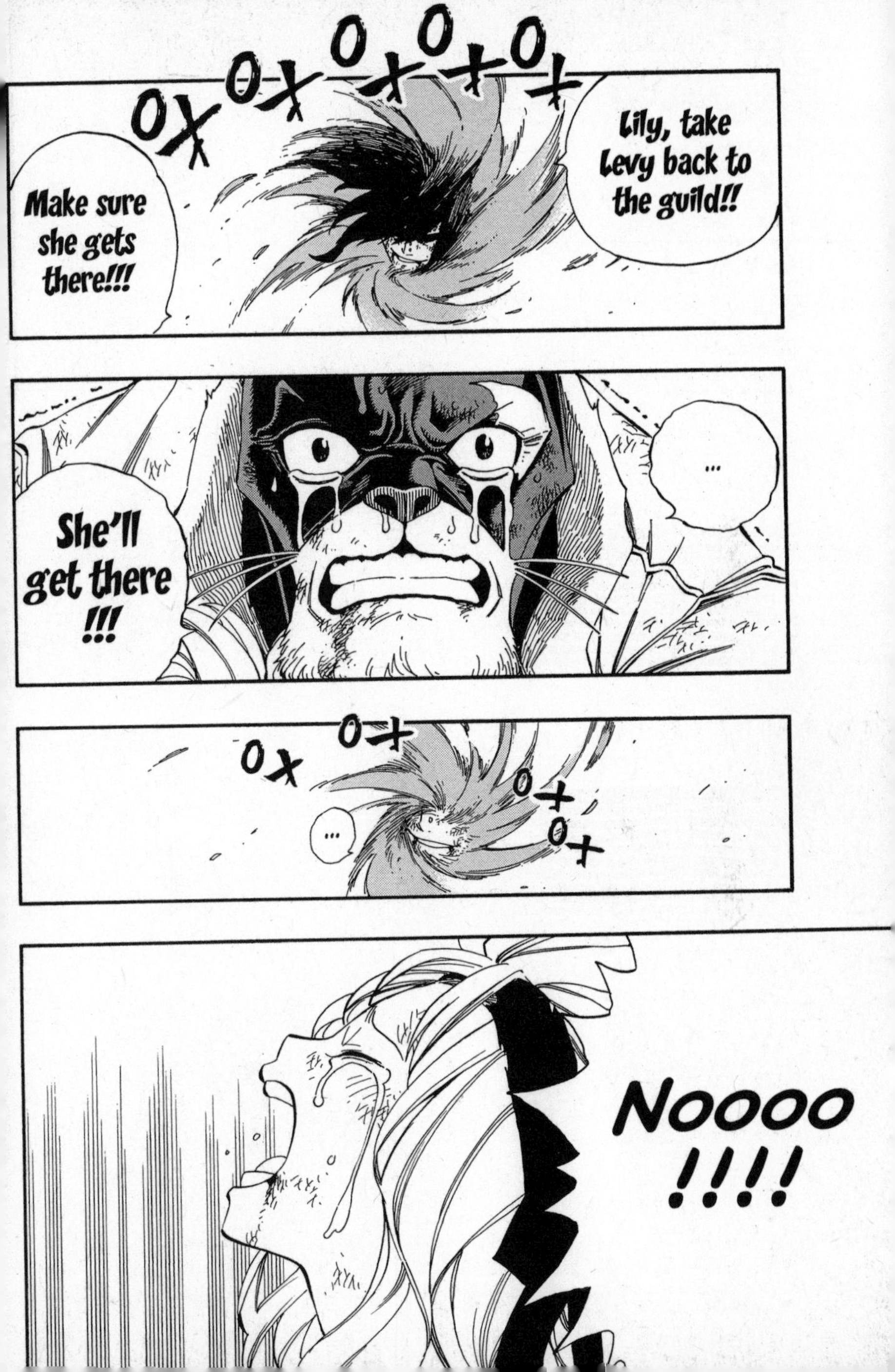
Lily, take Levy back to the guild!!
Make sure she gets there!!!
...
She'll get there!!!
...
NOOOO!!!!

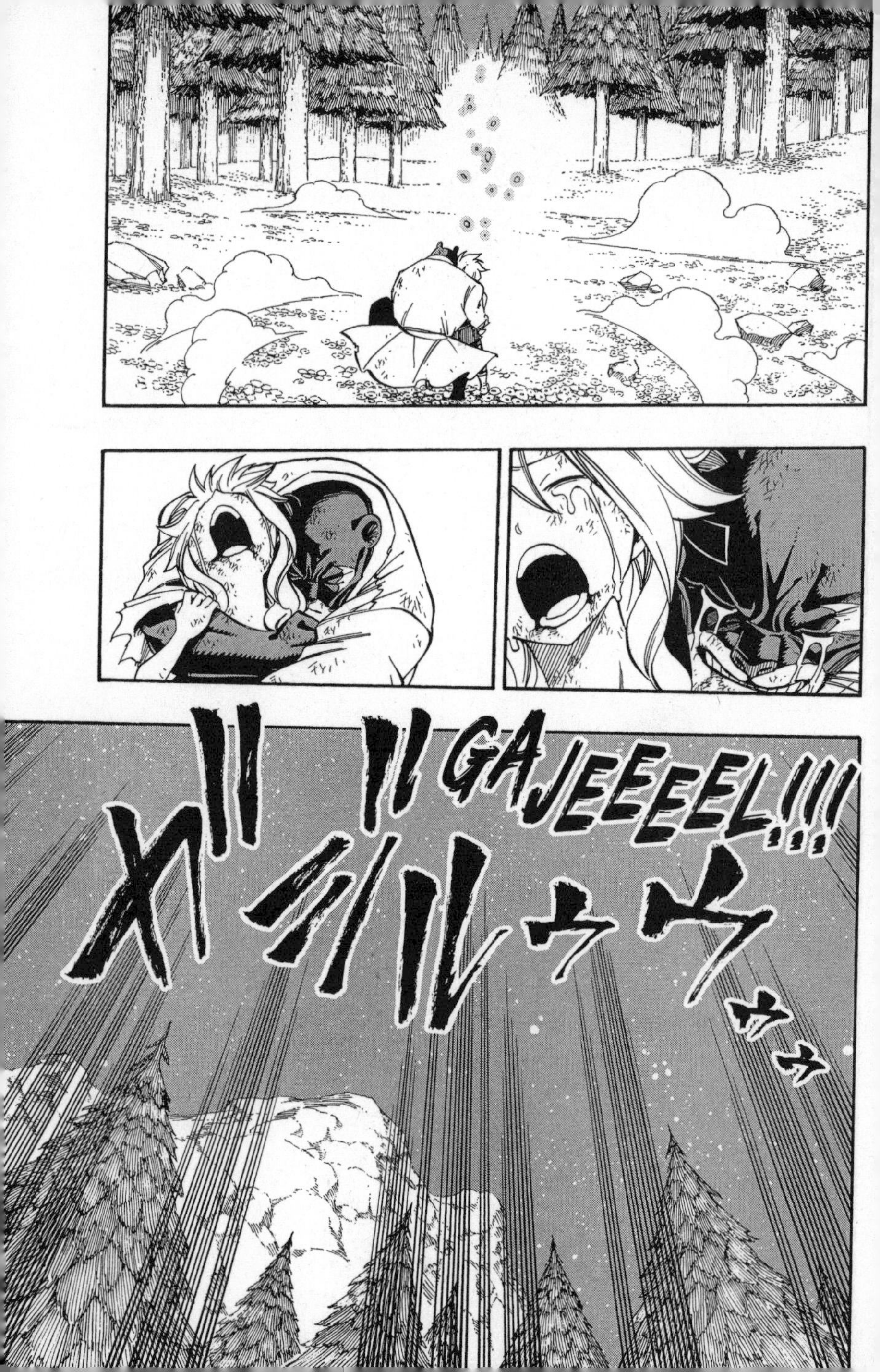
GAJEEEEL!!!

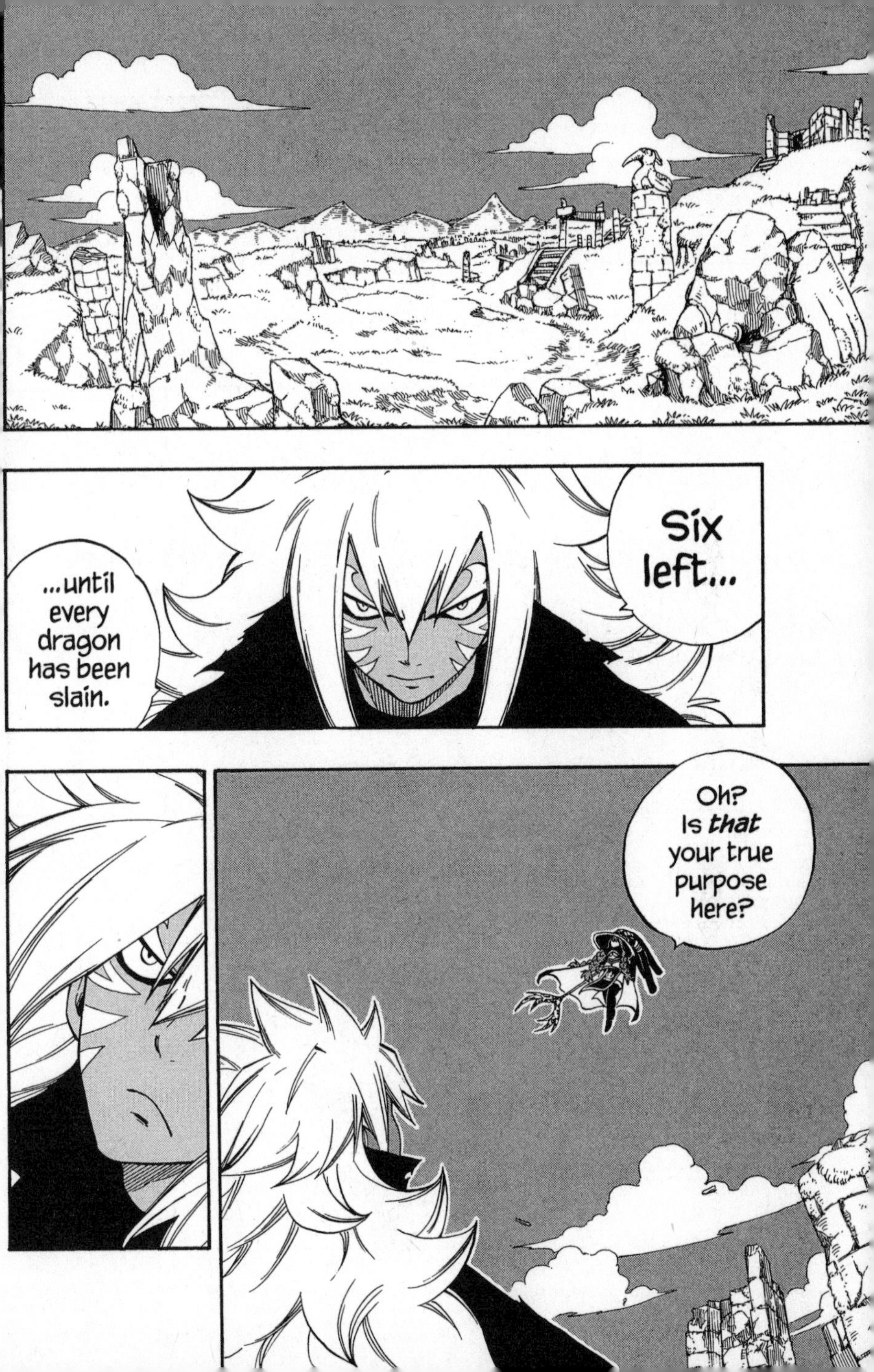
Six left...
...until every dragon has been slain.
Oh? Is *that* your true purpose here?

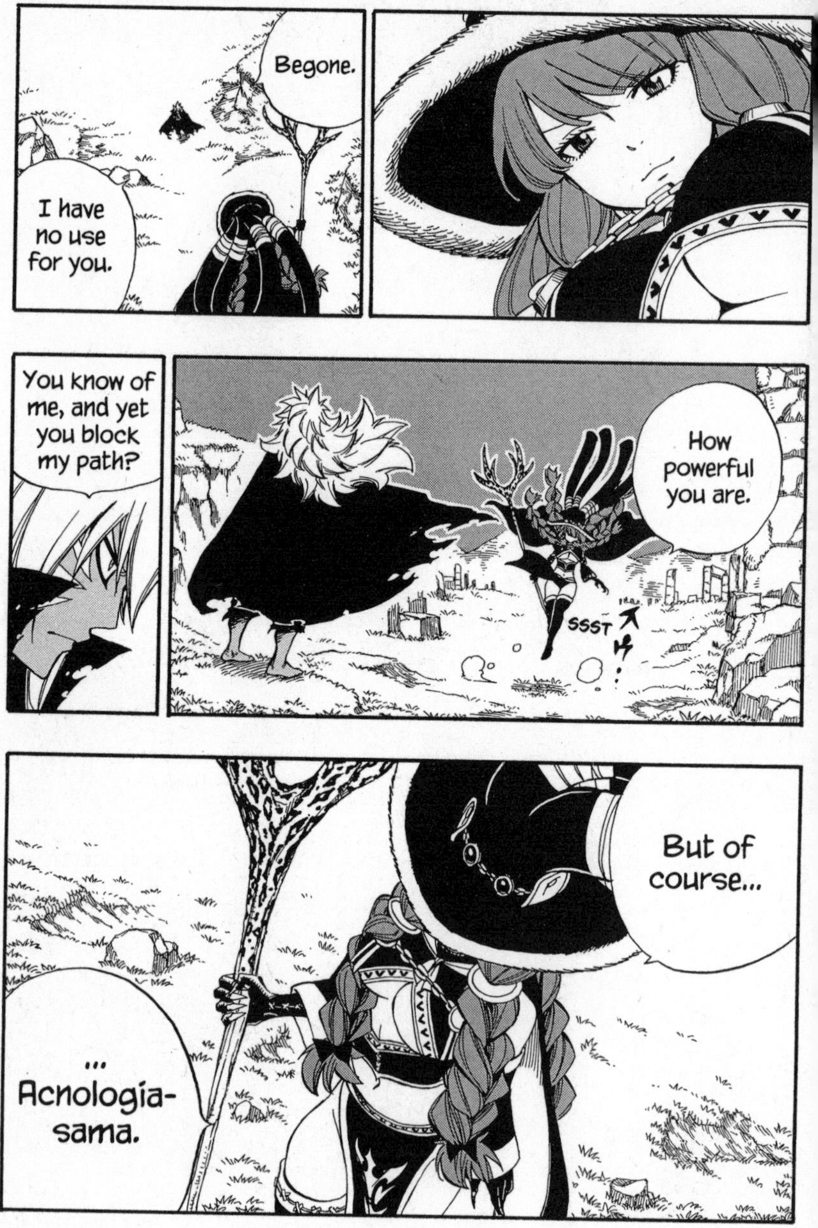
Begone.
I have no use for you.
How powerful you are.
SSST
You know of me, and yet you block my path?
But of course...
... Acnologia-sama.

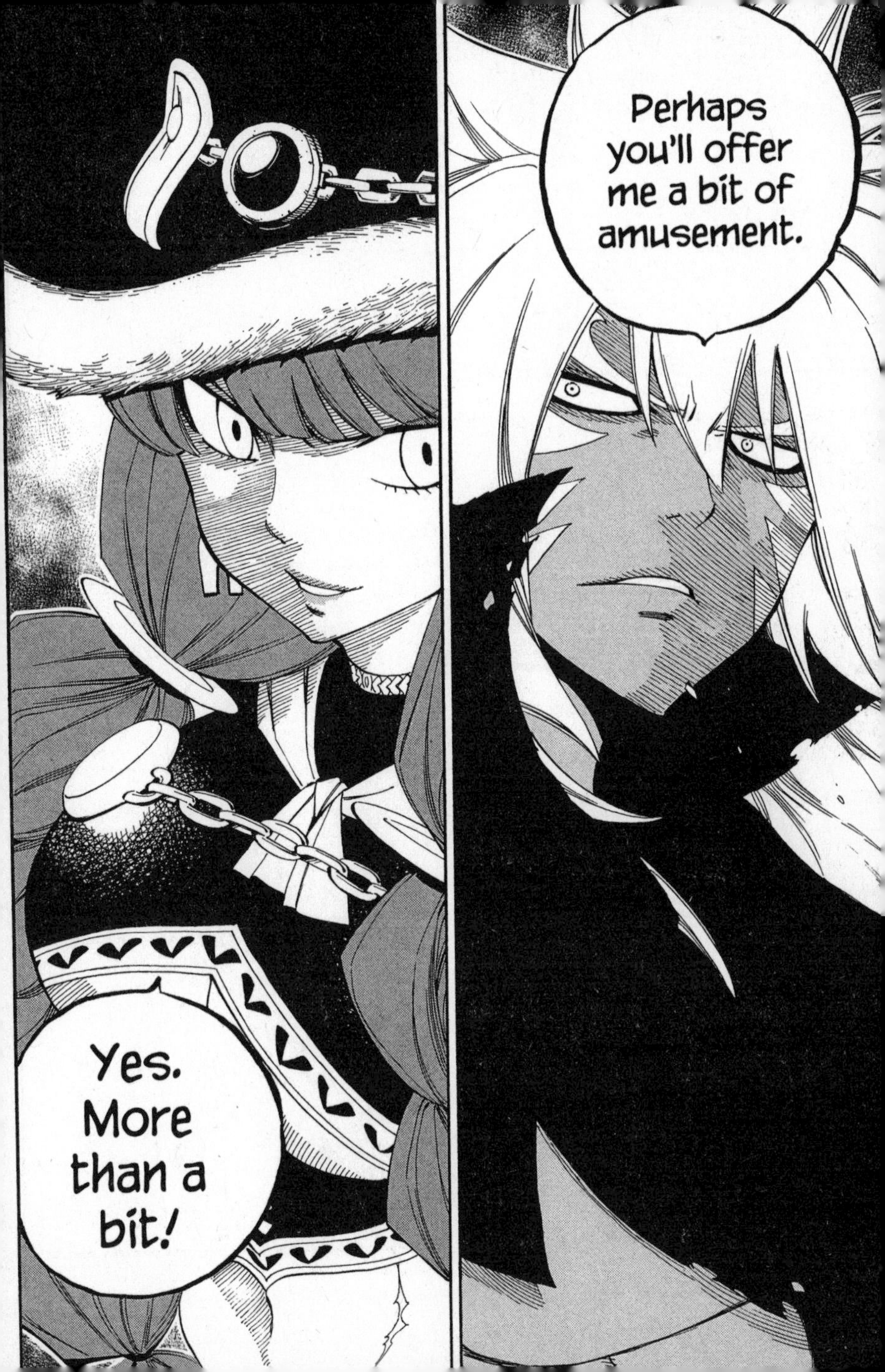
Perhaps you'll offer me a bit of amusement.
Yes. More than a bit!

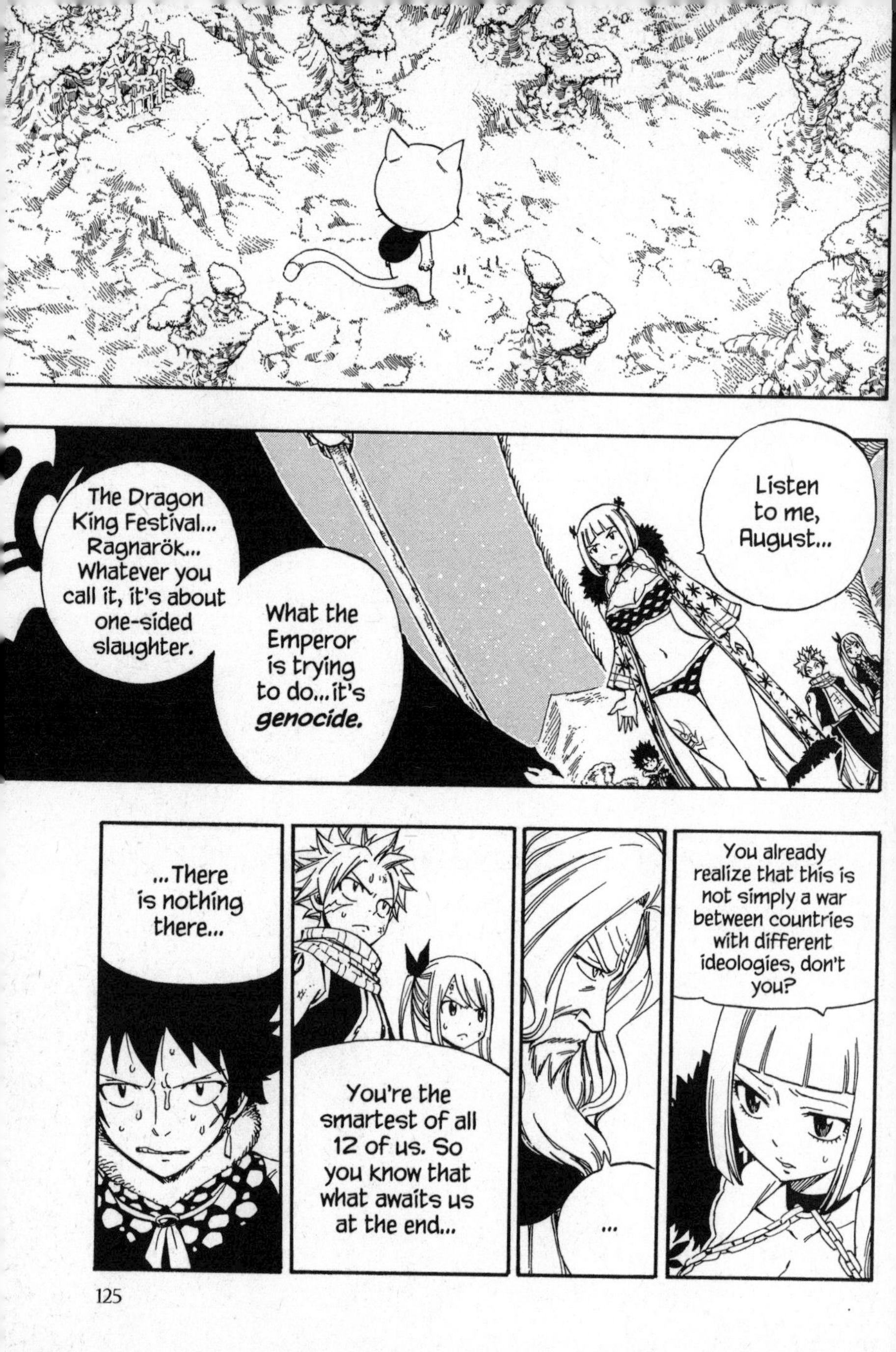
Listen to me, August...
What the Emperor is trying to do...it's *genocide.*
The Dragon King Festival... Ragnarök... Whatever you call it, it's about one-sided slaughter.
You already realize that this is not simply a war between countries with different ideologies, don't you?
...
You're the smartest of all 12 of us. So you know that what awaits us at the end...
...There is nothing there...

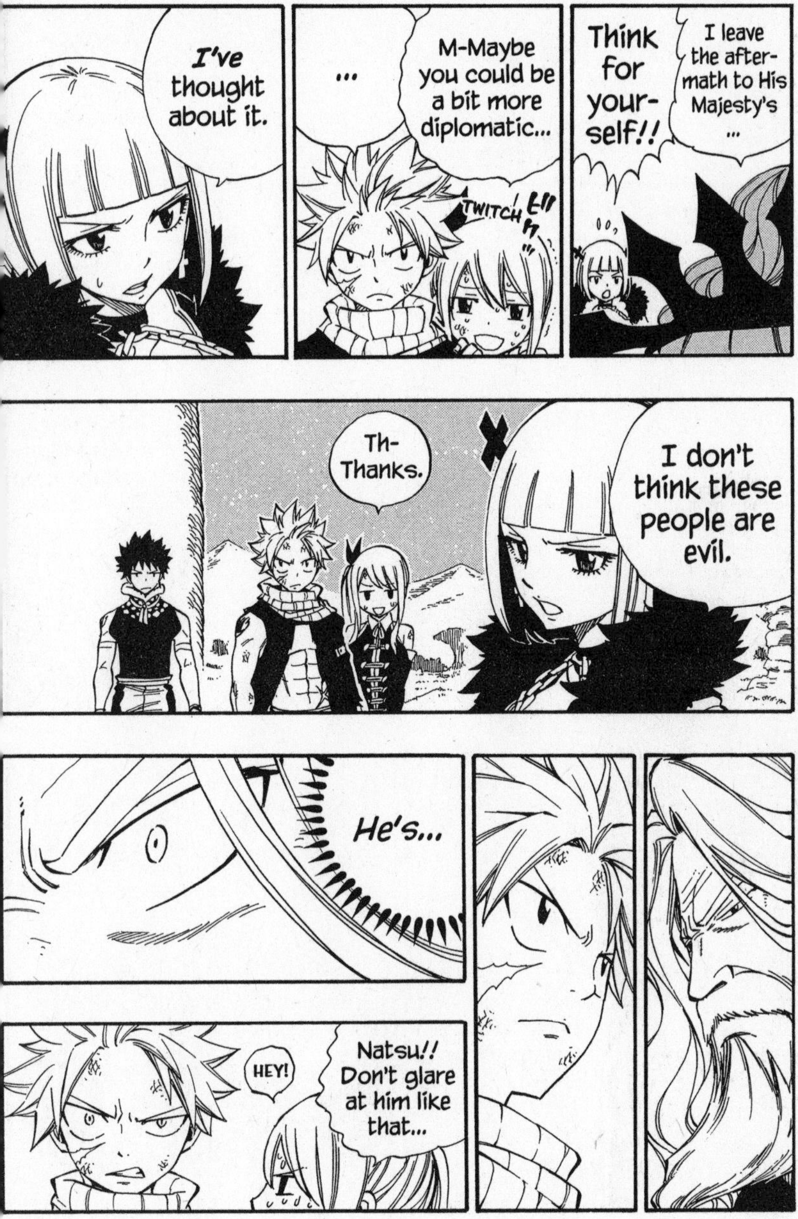
I leave the aftermath to His Majesty's ...
Think for yourself!!
M-Maybe you could be a bit more diplomatic...
...
TWITCH
I've thought about it.
I don't think these people are evil.
Th-Thanks.
He's...
Natsu!! Don't glare at him like that...
HEY!

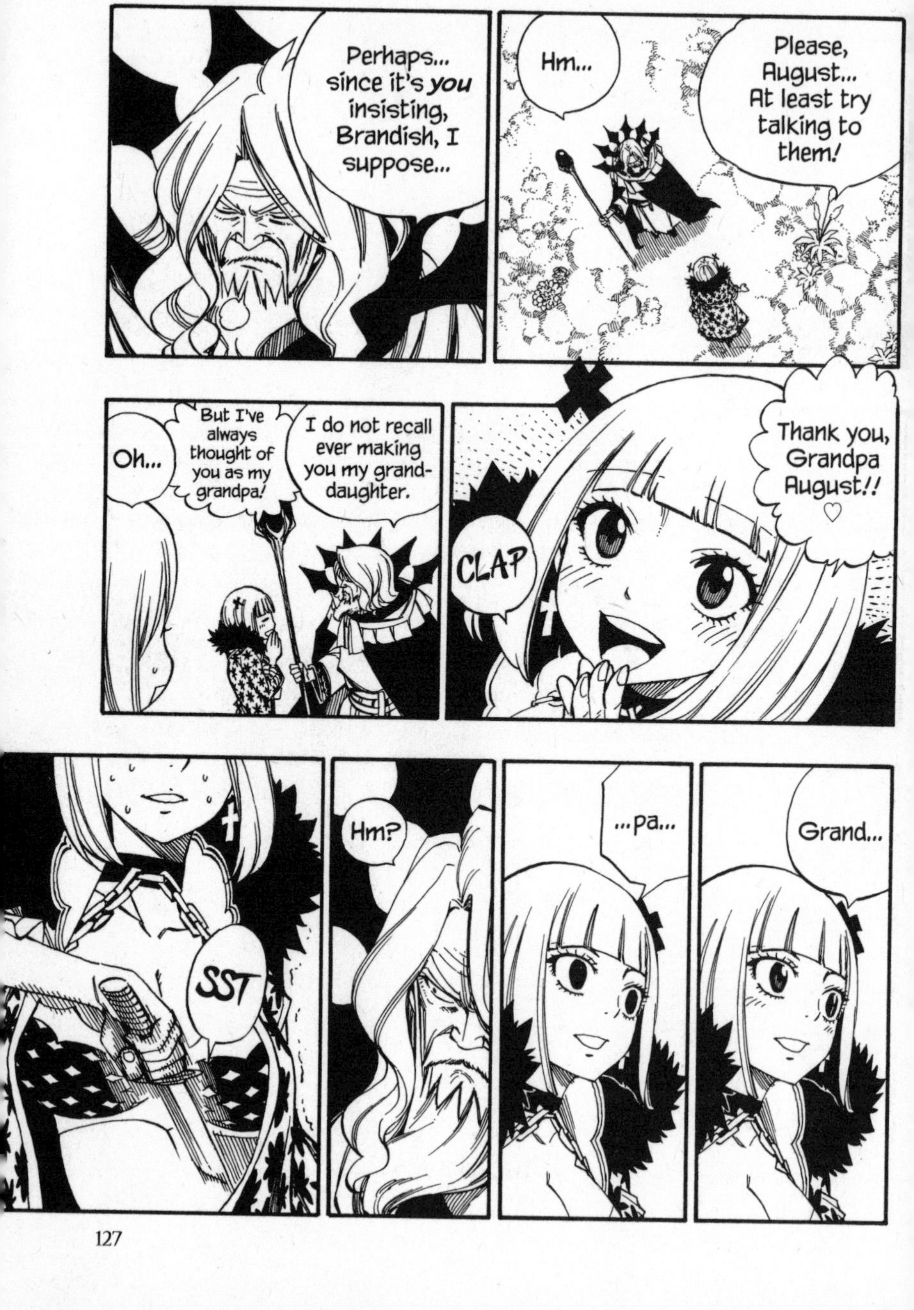
Please, August... At least try talking to them!
Hm...
Perhaps... since it's *you* insisting, Brandish, I suppose...
Thank you, Grandpa August!! ♡
CLAP
I do not recall ever making you my grand-daughter.
But I've always thought of you as my grandpa!
Oh...
Grand...
...pa...
Hm?
SST

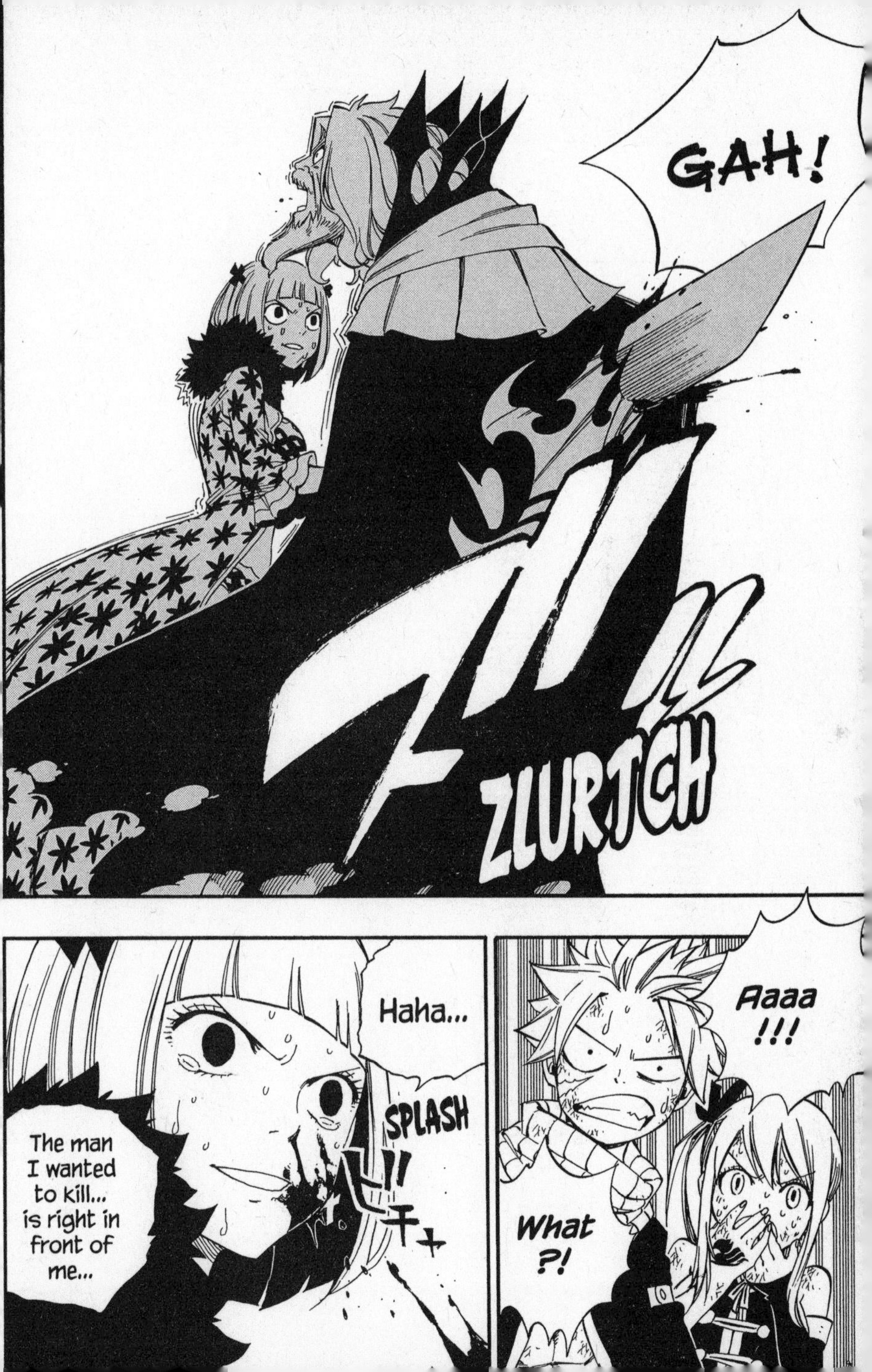
GAH!
ZLURTCH
Aaaa!!!
What?!
Haha...
SPLASH
The man I wanted to kill... is right in front of me...

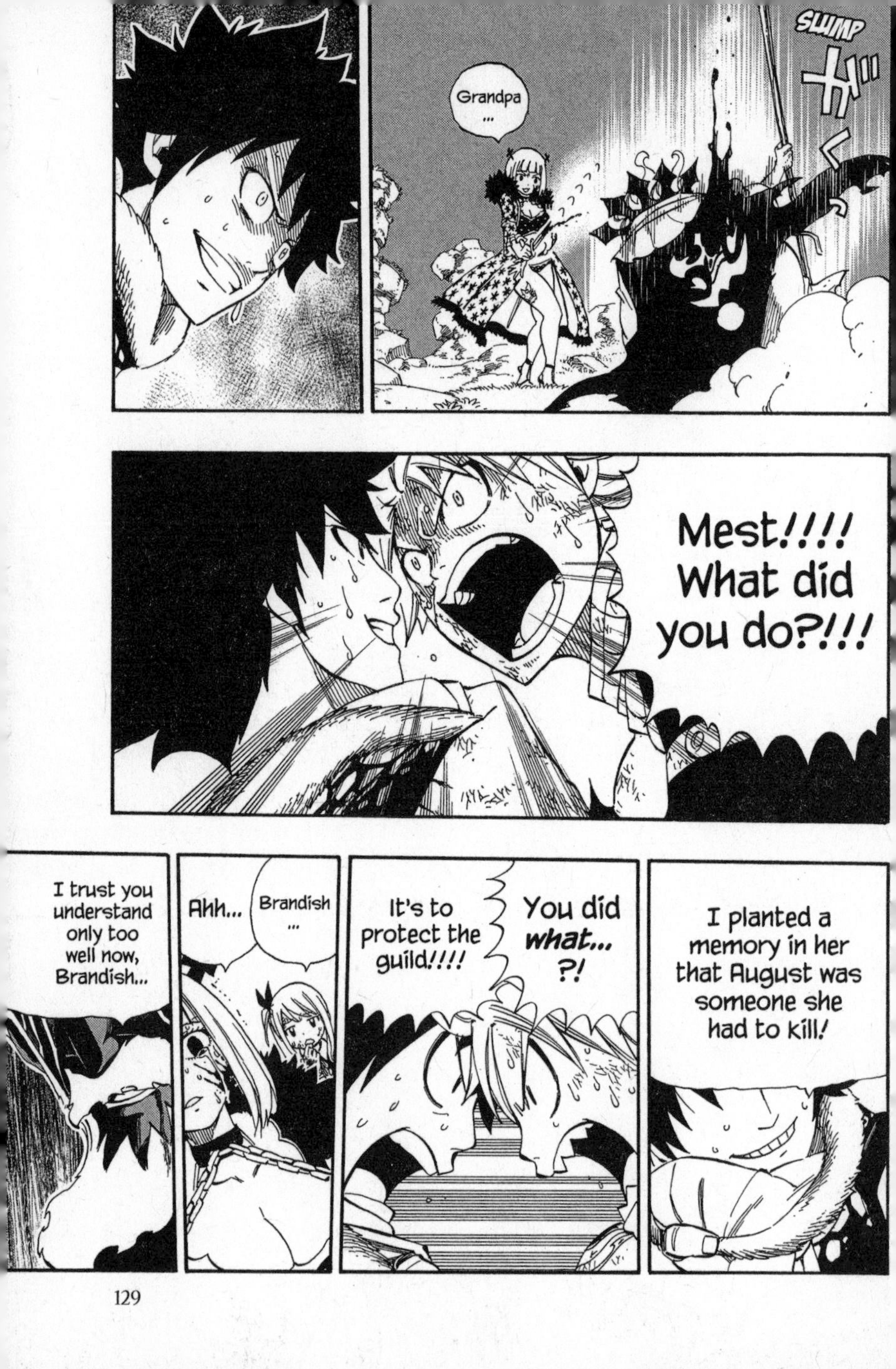
SLUMP
Grandpa ...
Mest!!!! What did you do?!!!
I planted a memory in her that August was someone she had to kill!
You did *what...* ?!
It's to protect the guild!!!!
Brandish ...
Ahh...
I trust you understand only too well now, Brandish...

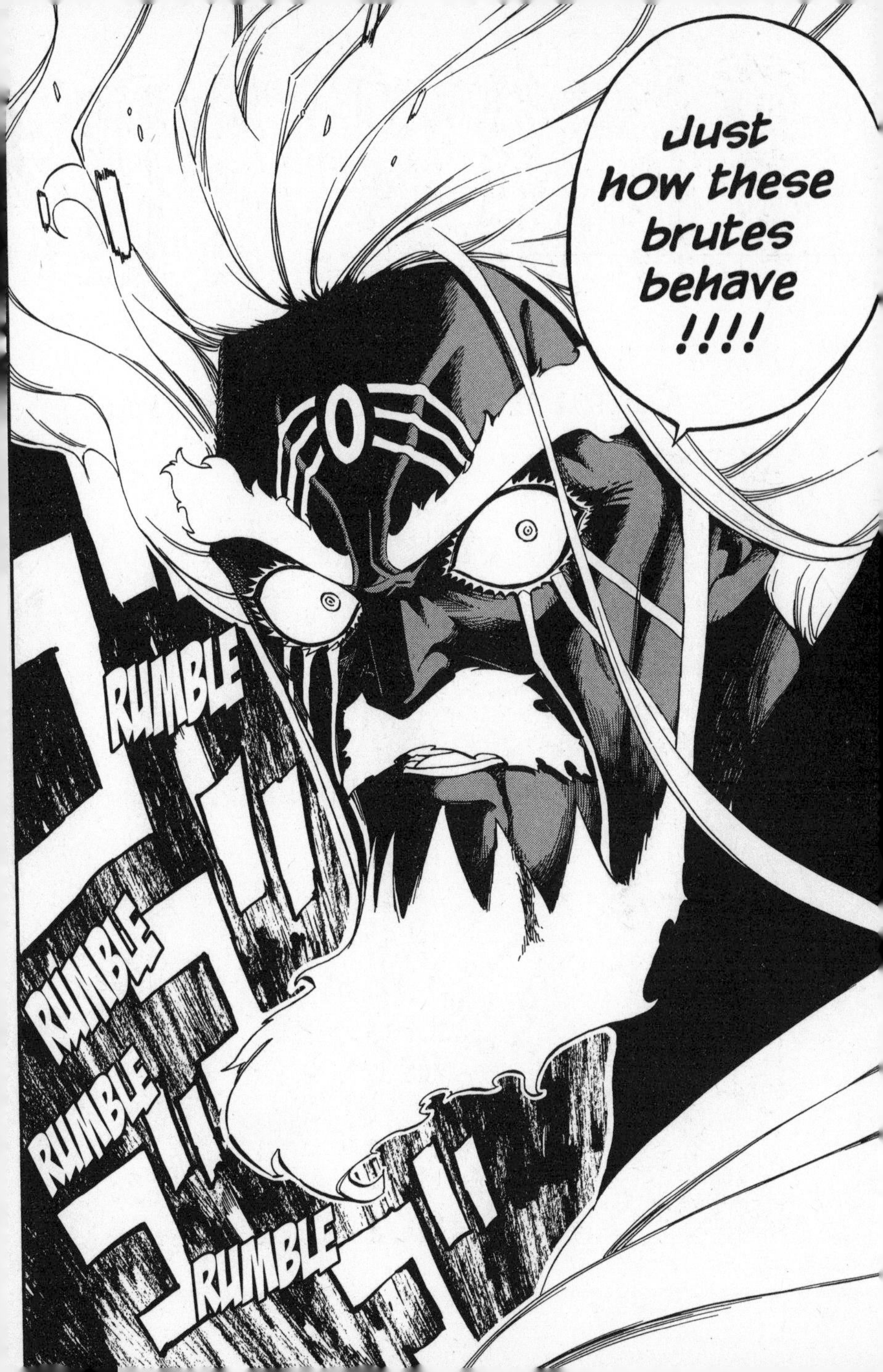
Just how these brutes behave !!!!
RUMBLE
RUMBLE
RUMBLE
RUMBLE

FAIRY TAIL

フェアリーテイル

Chapter 489: Universe One

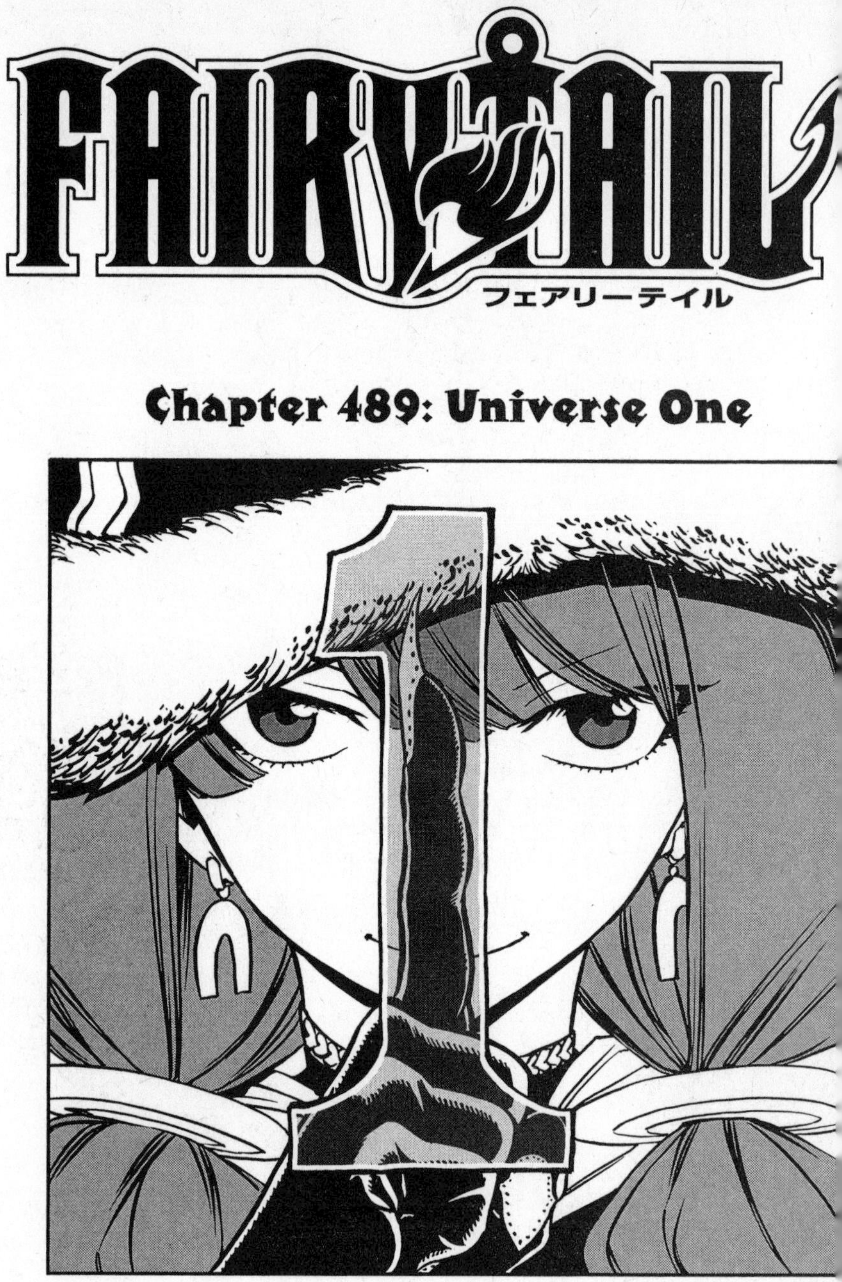

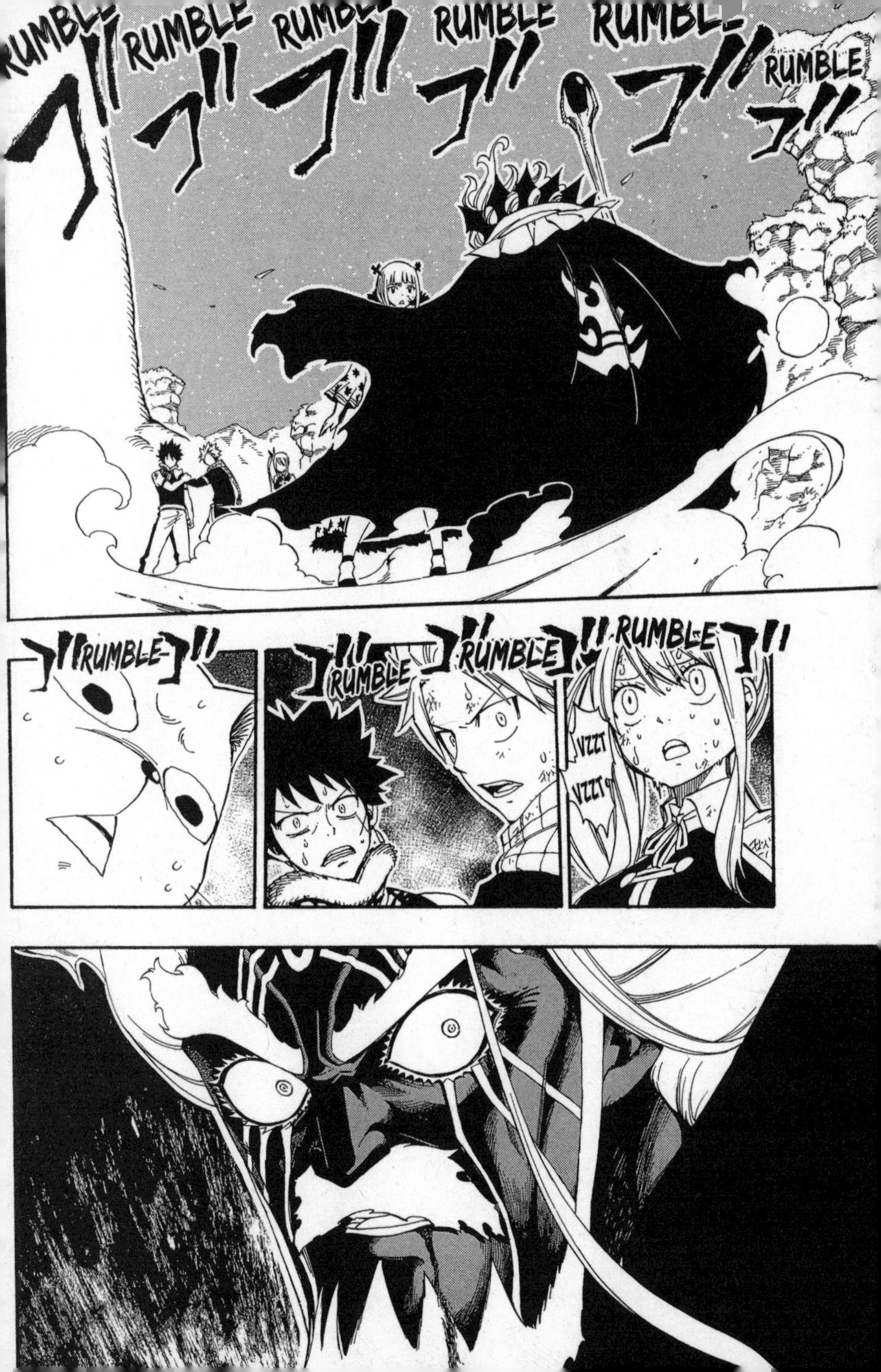
RUMBLE
RUMBLE
RUMBLE
RUMBLE
RUMBLE
RUMBLE
RUMBLE
VZZT
VZZT
RUMBLE
RUMBLE
RUMBLE

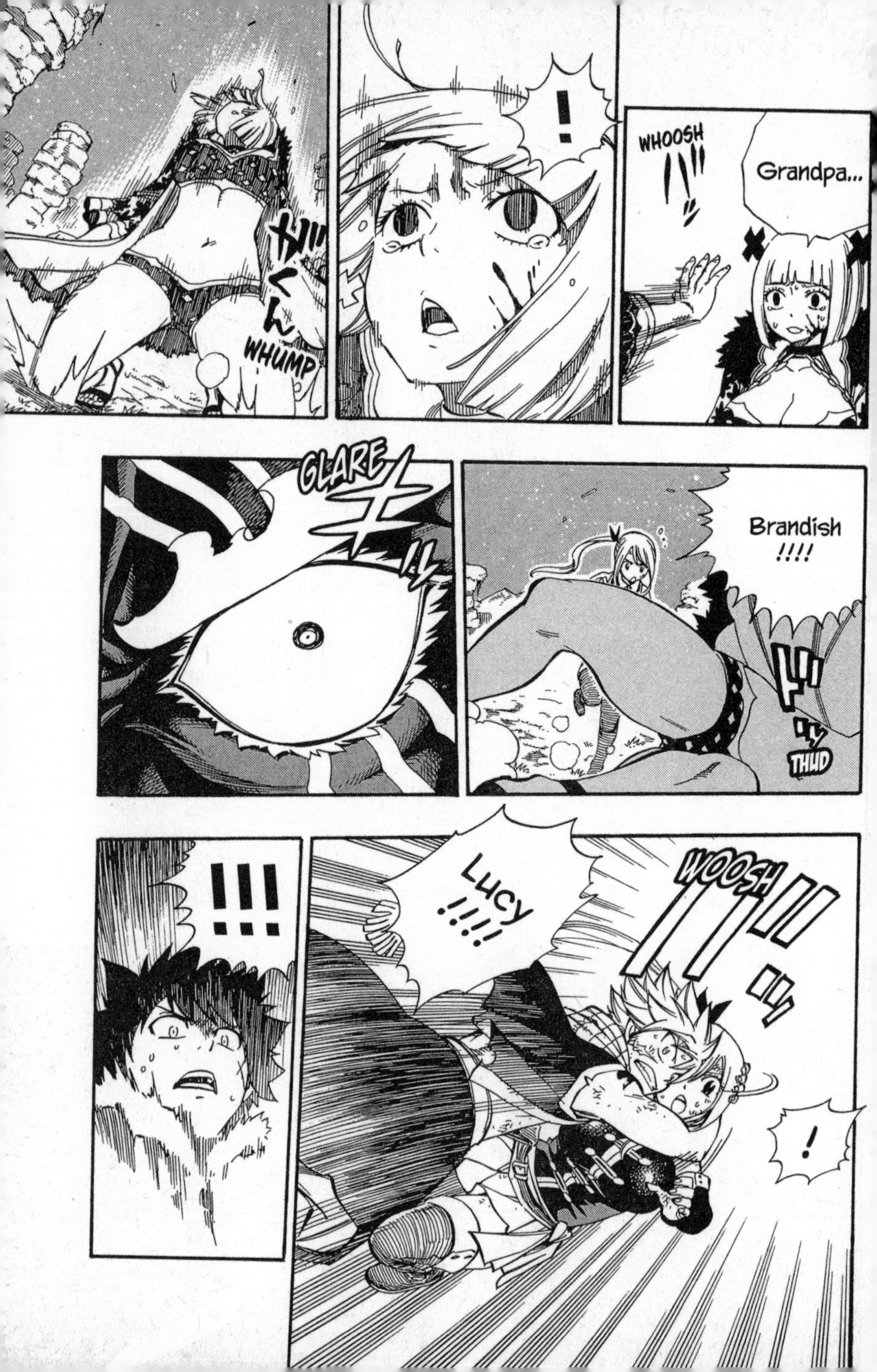
WHOOSH
Grandpa...
!
WHUMP
Brandish
!!!!
THUD
GLARE
WOOSH
Lucy
!!!!
!
!!!

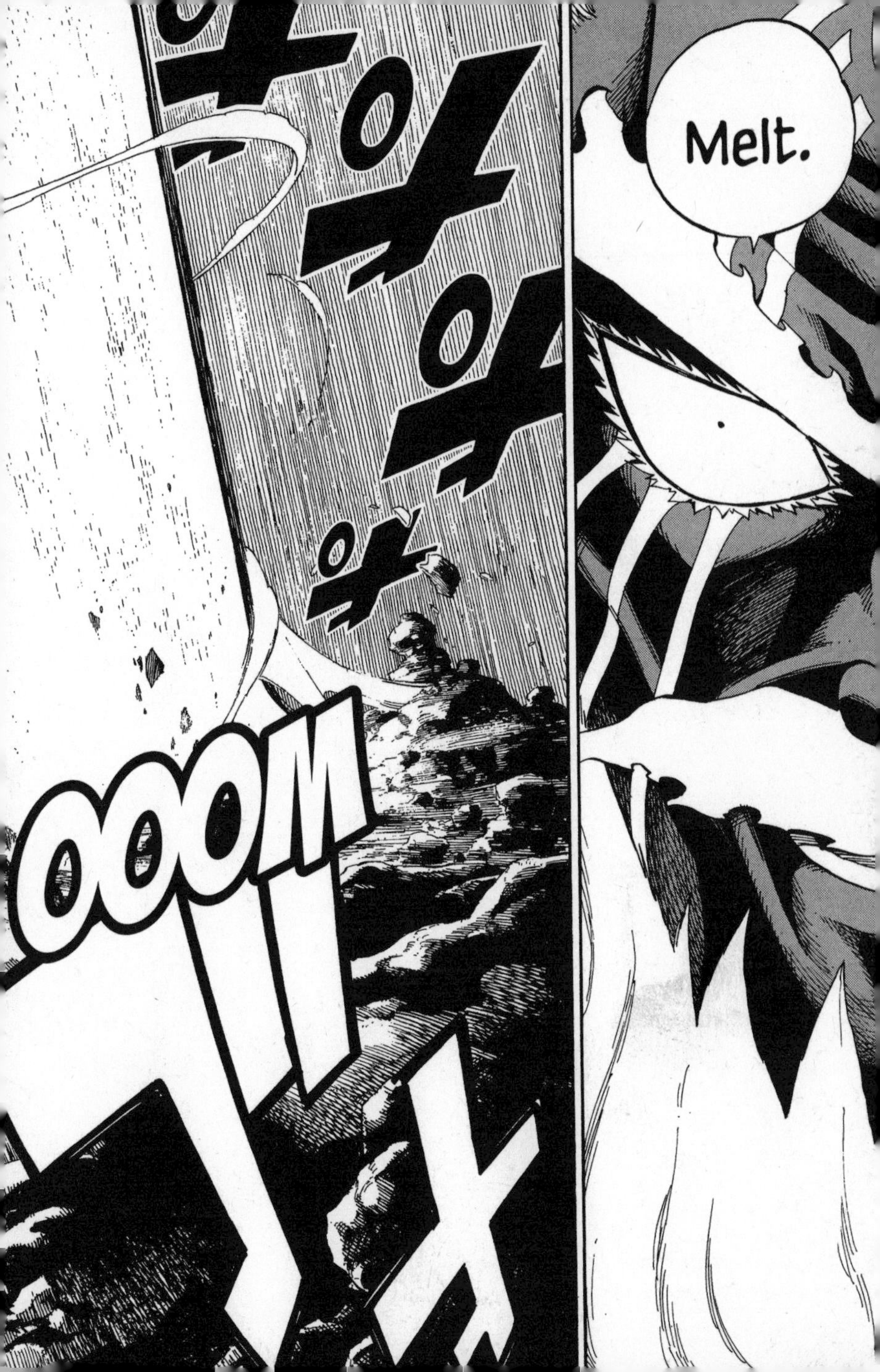
Melt.
OOOM

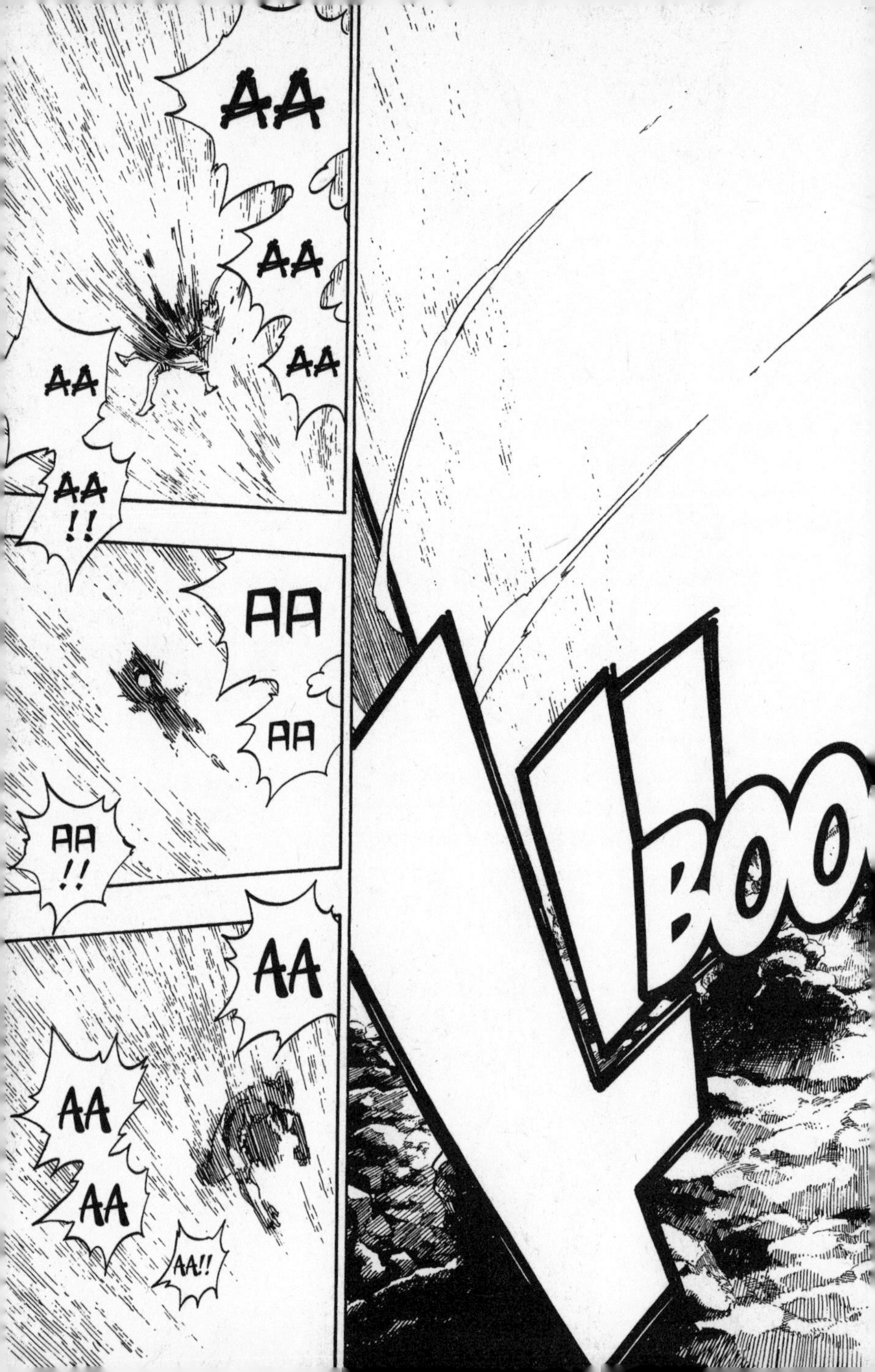
BOO
AA
AA
AA
AA
AA!!
AA
AA
AA!!
AA
AA
AA
AA!!

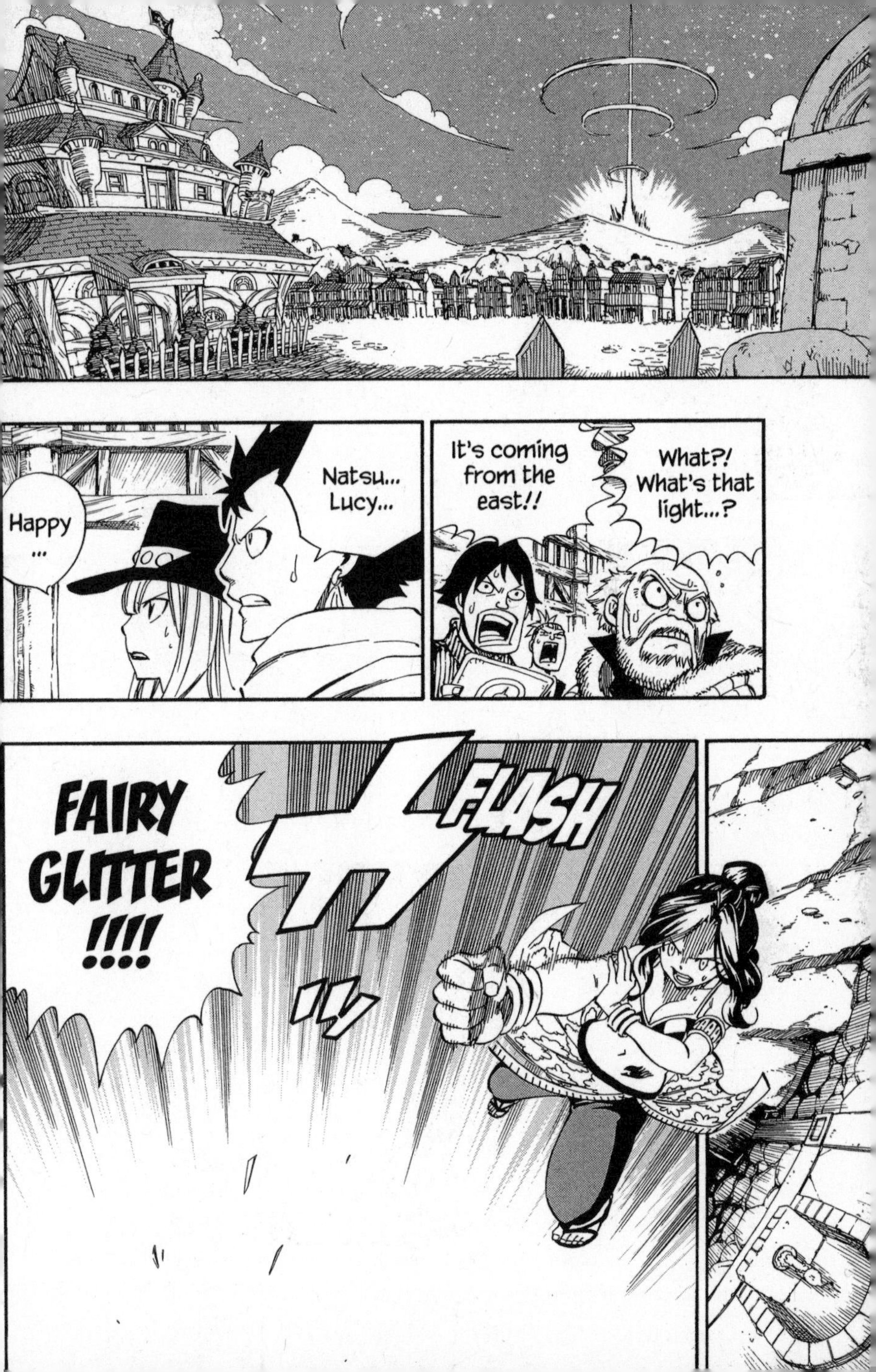
What?! What's that light...?
It's coming from the east!!
Natsu... Lucy...
Happy ...
FLASH
FAIRY GLITTER !!!!

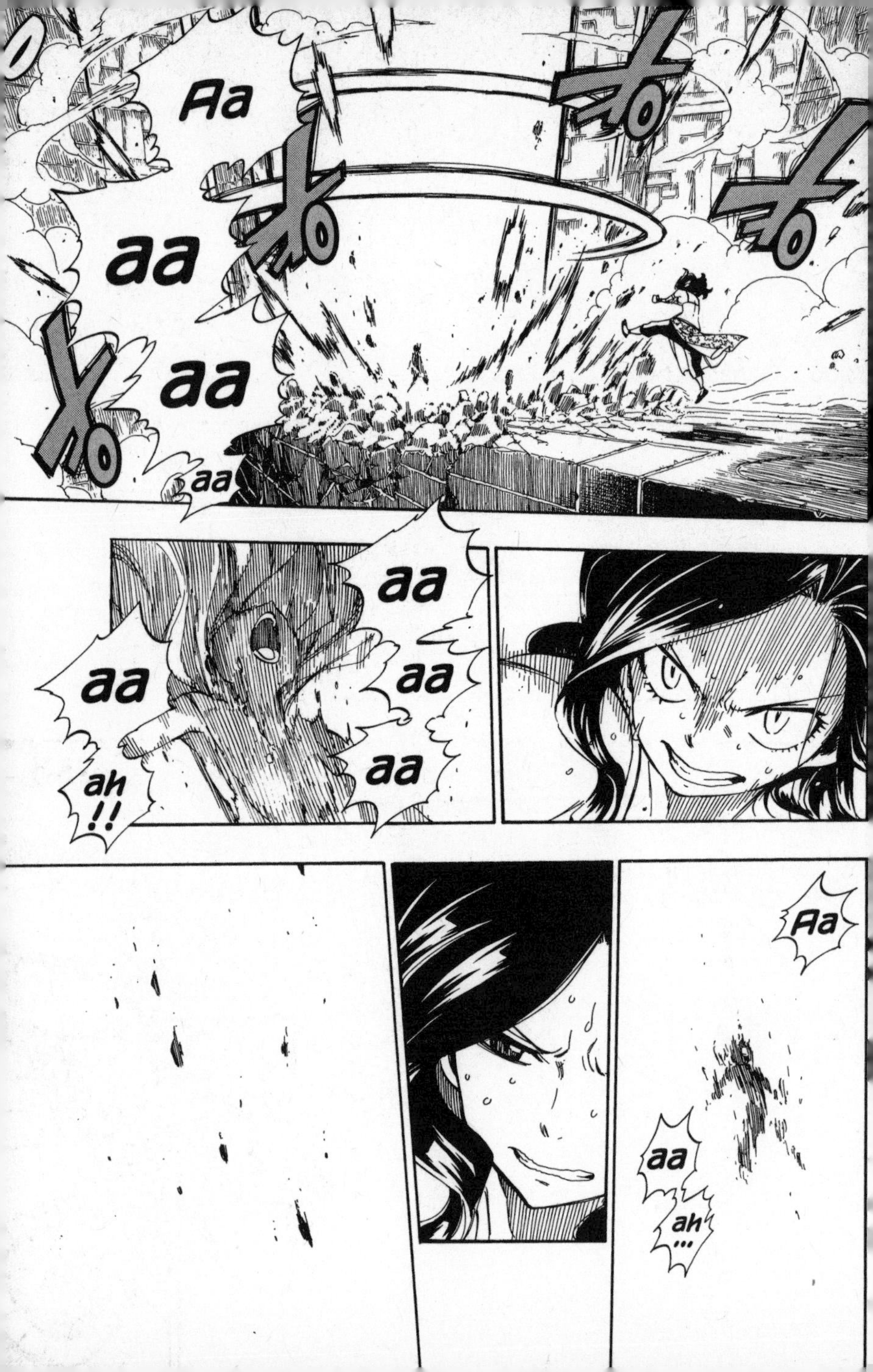
Aa
aa
aa
aa
aa
aa
aa
aa
ah!!
Aa
aa
ah...

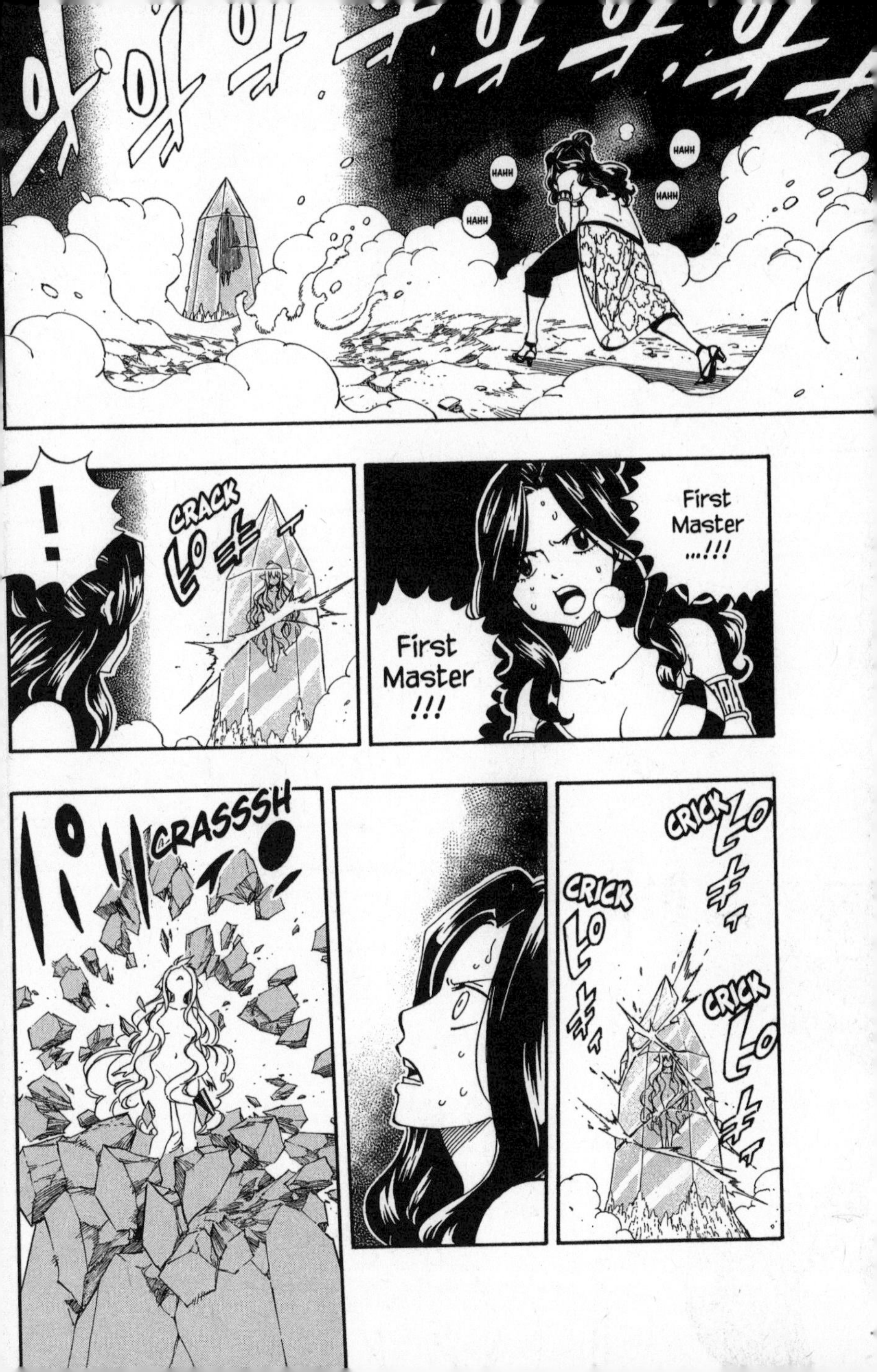
HAHH
HAHH
HAHH
HAHH
First Master ...!!!
First Master !!!
!
CRACK
CRICK
CRICK
CRICK
CRASSSH

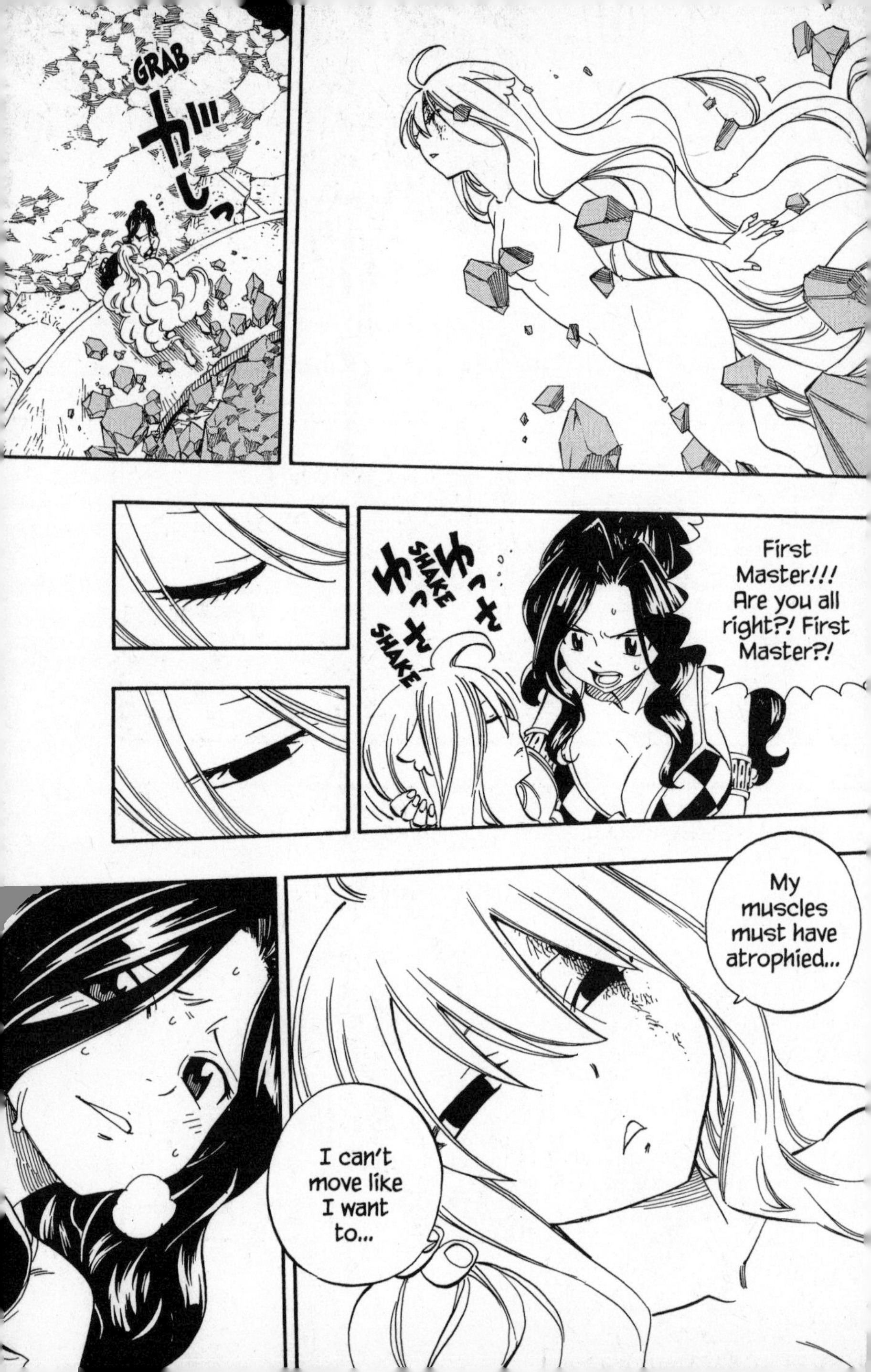
GRAB
ガしっ
ゆっさ
SHAKE
ゆっさ
SHAKE
First Master!!! Are you all right?! First Master?!
My muscles must have atrophied...
I can't move like I want to...

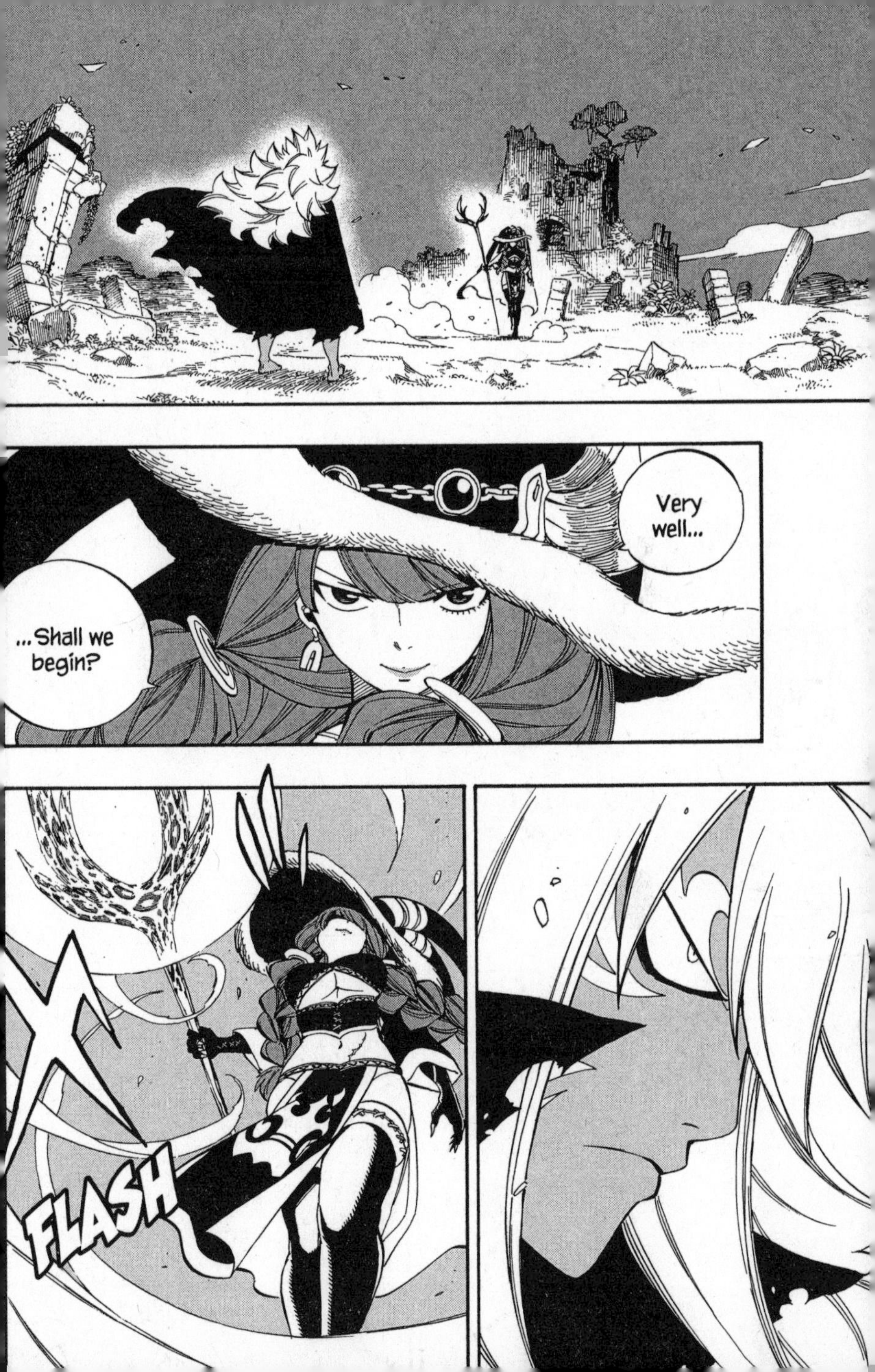
Very well...
...Shall we begin?
FLASH

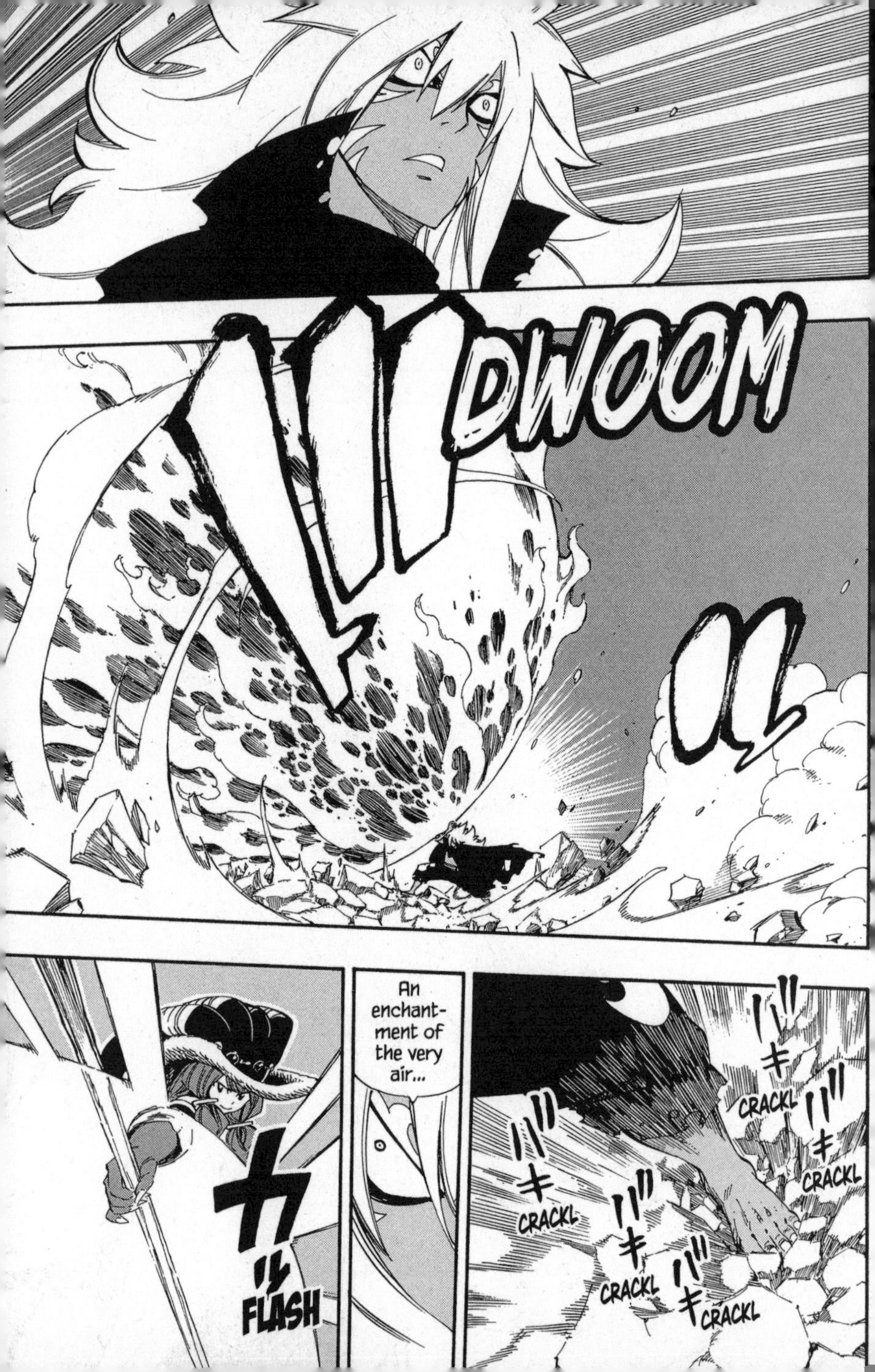
DWOOM
CRACKL
CRACKL
CRACKL
CRACKL
CRACKL
An enchant-ment of the very air...
FLASH

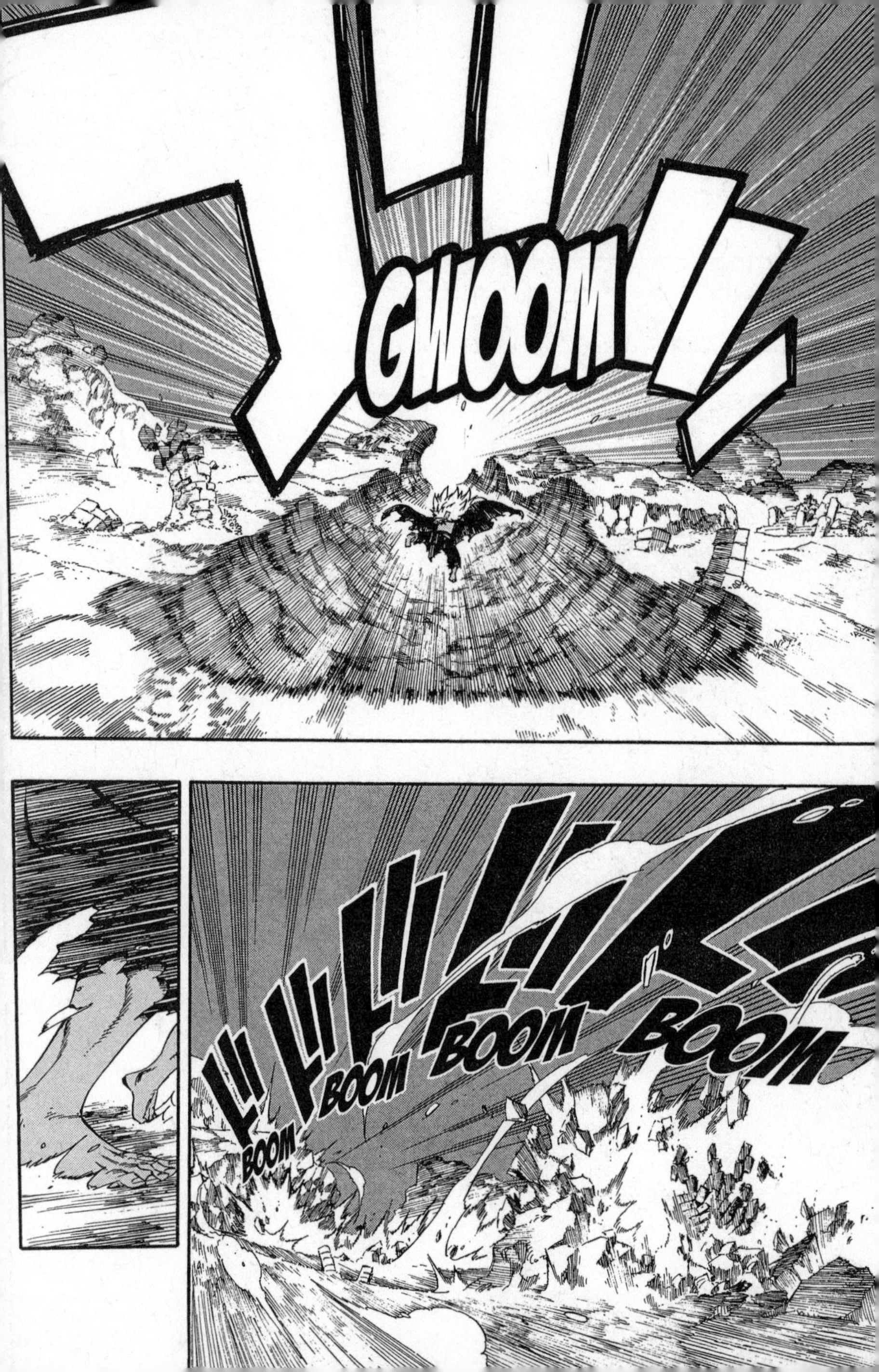
GWOOM
BOOM
BOOM
BOOM
BOOM

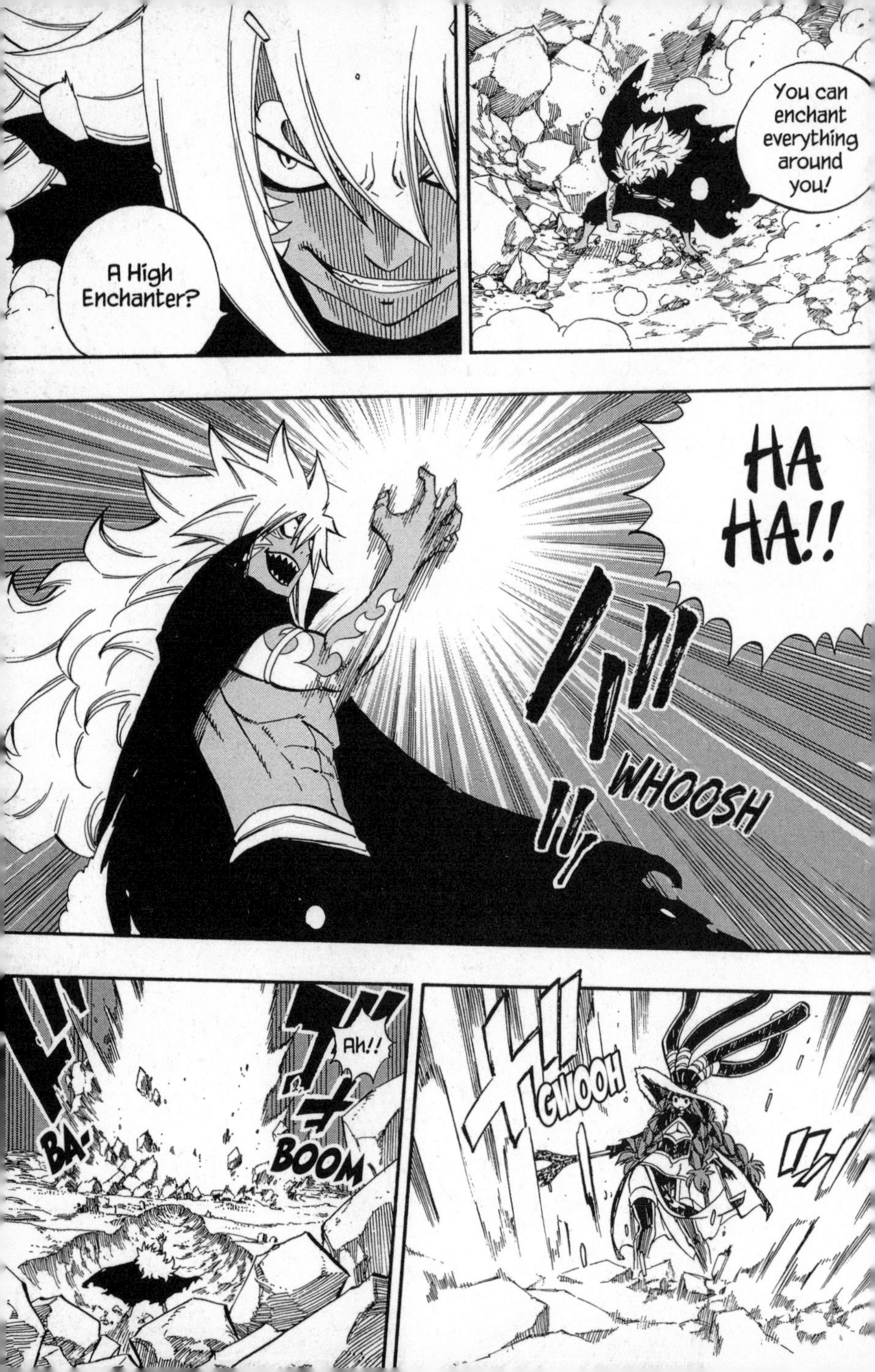
You can enchant everything around you!
A High Enchanter?
HA HA!!
WHOOSH
GWOOH
Ah!!
BA-
BOOM

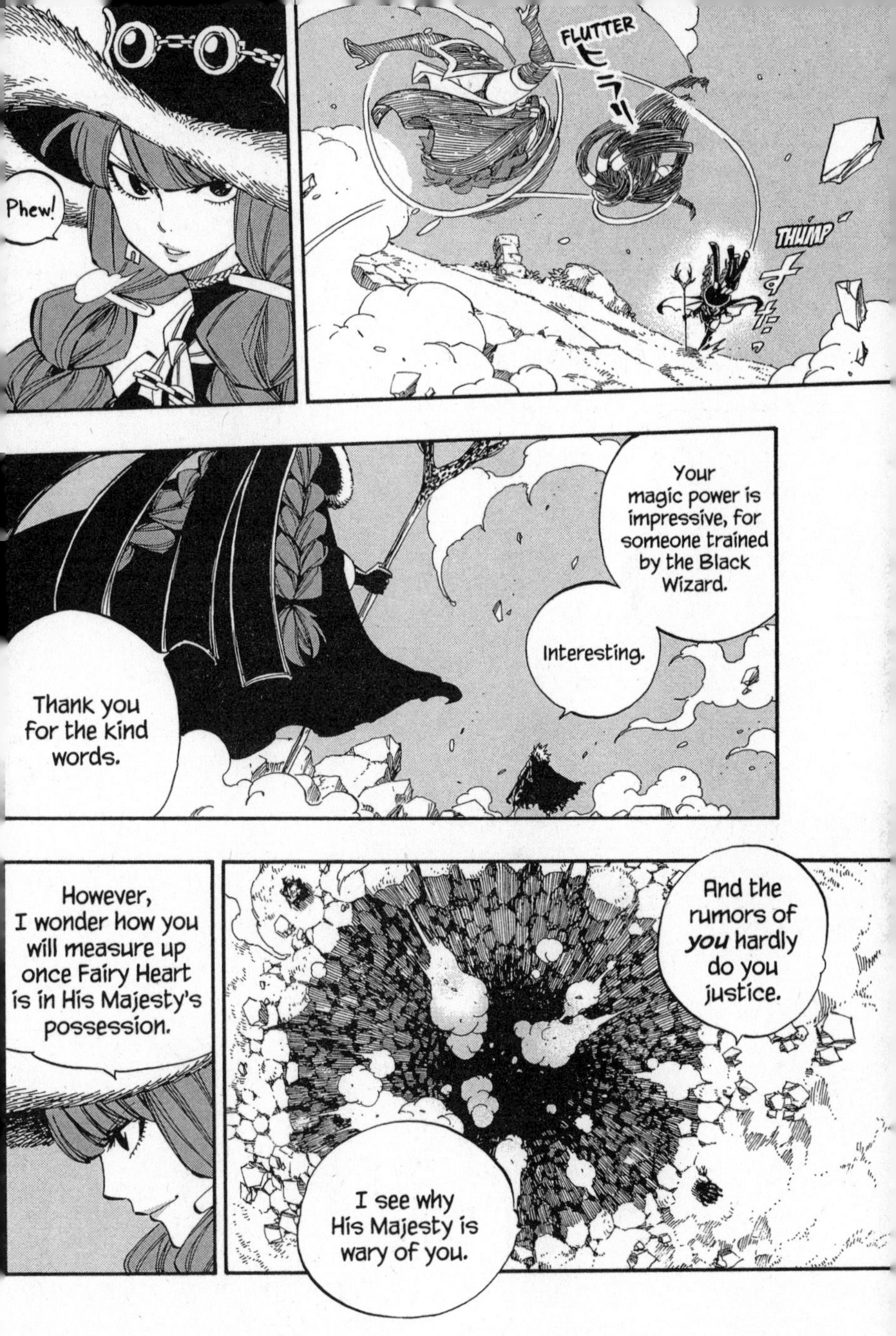
FLUTTER
THUMP
Phew!
Your magic power is impressive, for someone trained by the Black Wizard.
Interesting.
Thank you for the kind words.
And the rumors of *you* hardly do you justice.
I see why His Majesty is wary of you.
However, I wonder how you will measure up once Fairy Heart is in His Majesty's possession.

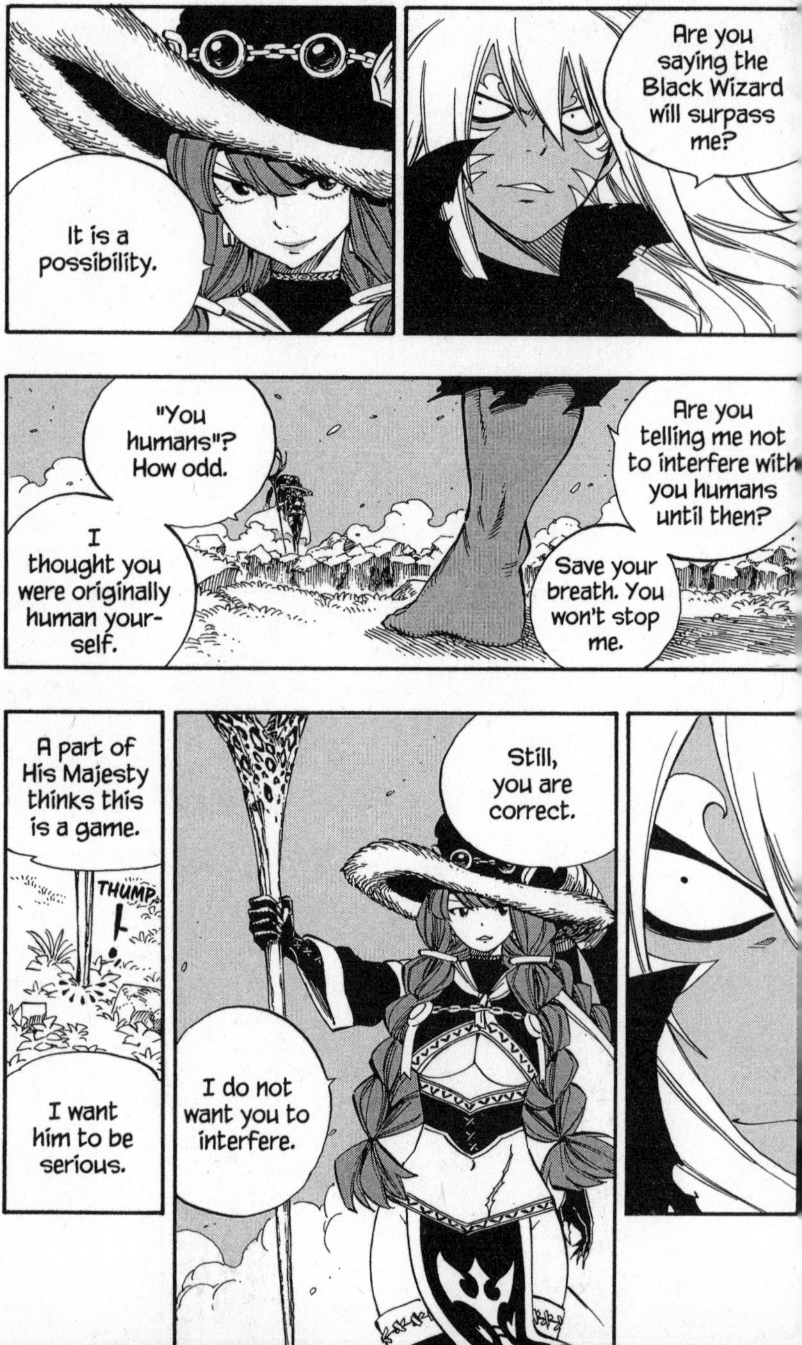
Are you saying the Black Wizard will surpass me?
It is a possibility.
Are you telling me not to interfere with you humans until then?
Save your breath. You won't stop me.
"You humans"? How odd.
I thought you were originally human yourself.
Still, you are correct.
I do not want you to interfere.
A part of His Majesty thinks this is a game.
THUMP
I want him to be serious.

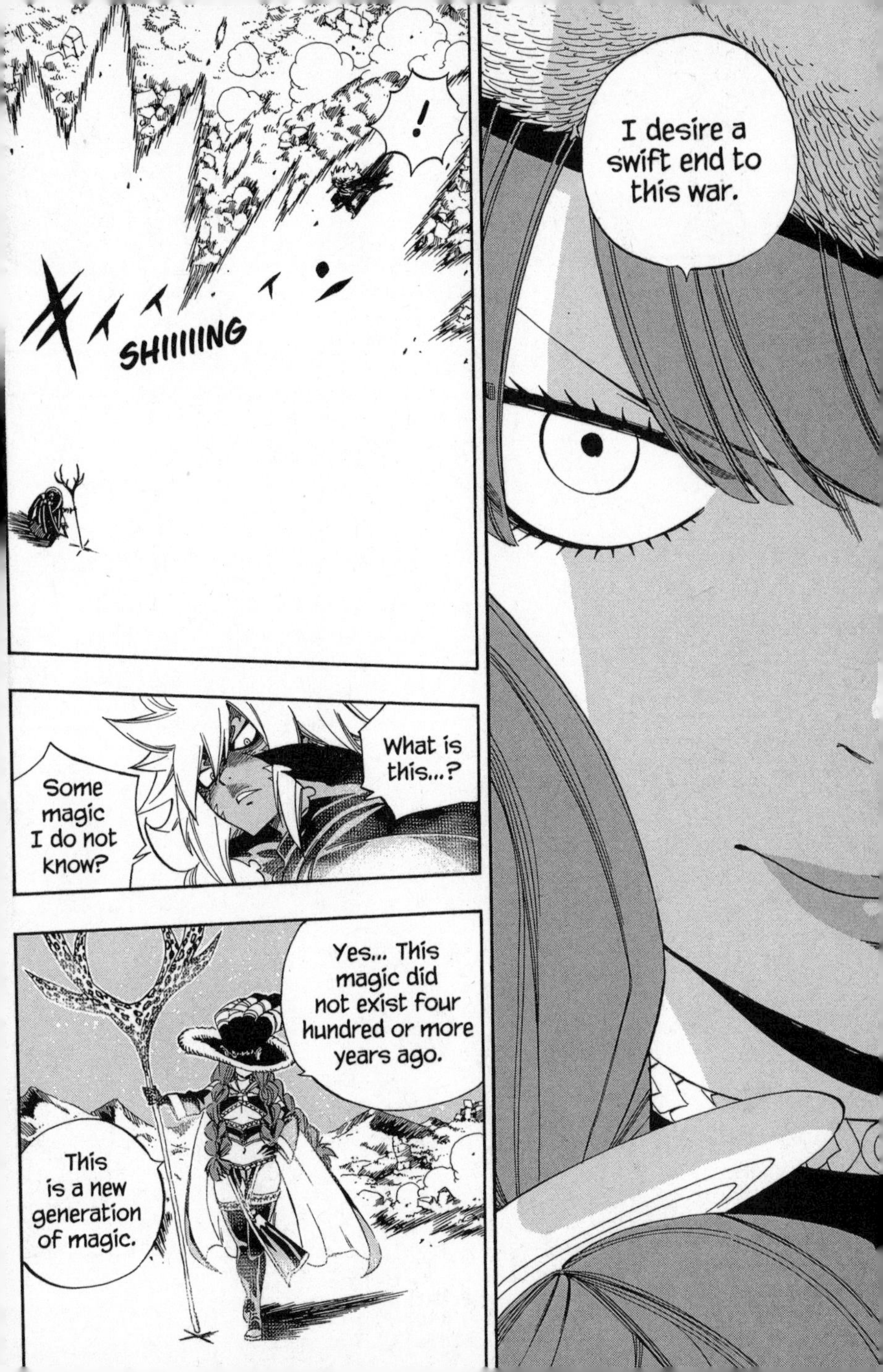
I desire a swift end to this war.
!
SHIIIIING
What is this...?
Some magic I do not know?
Yes... This magic did not exist four hundred or more years ago.
This is a new generation of magic.

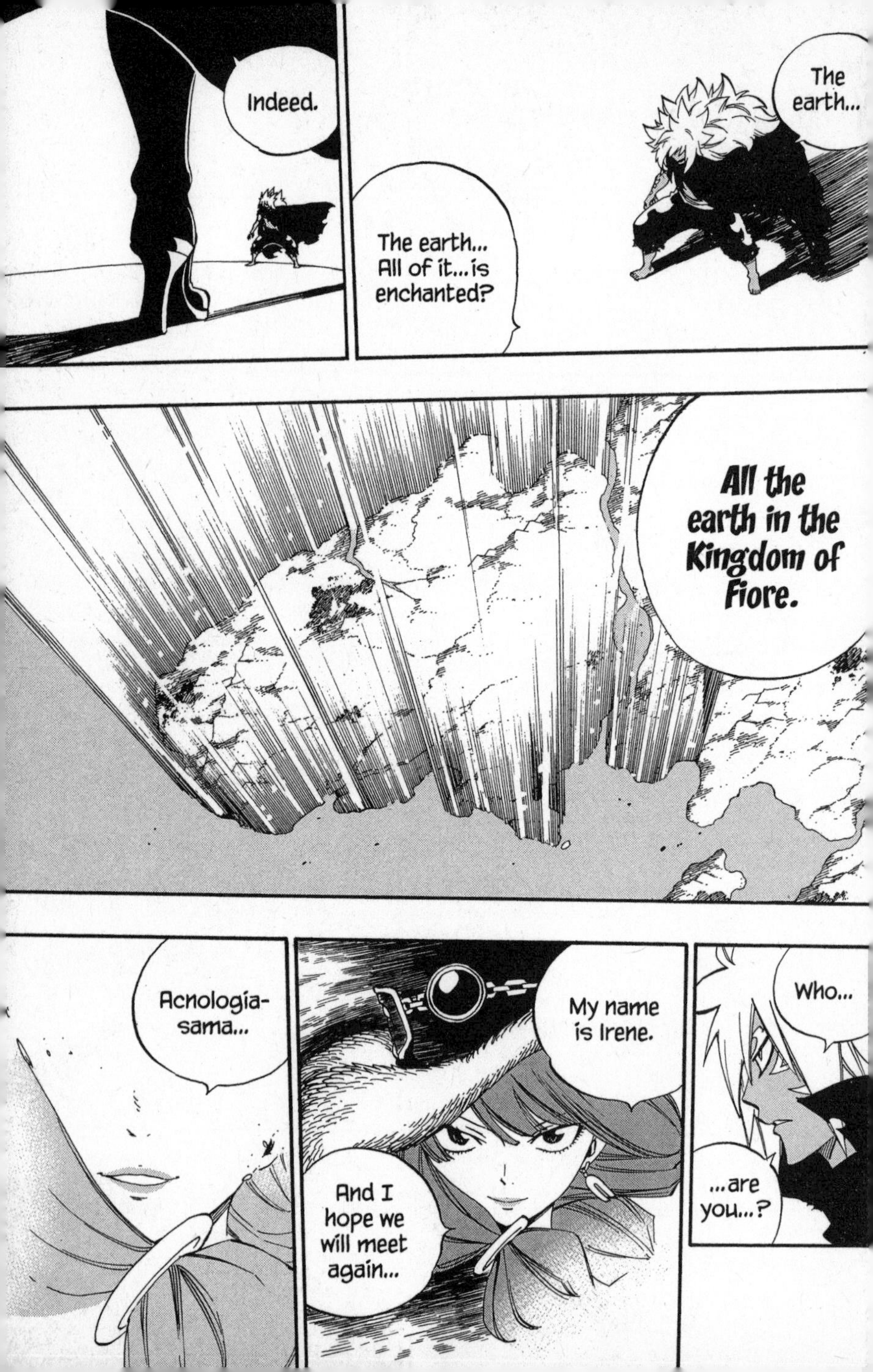
The earth...
The earth... All of it...is enchanted?
Indeed.
All the earth in the Kingdom of Fiore.
Who...
...are you...?
My name is Irene.
And I hope we will meet again...
Acnologia-sama...

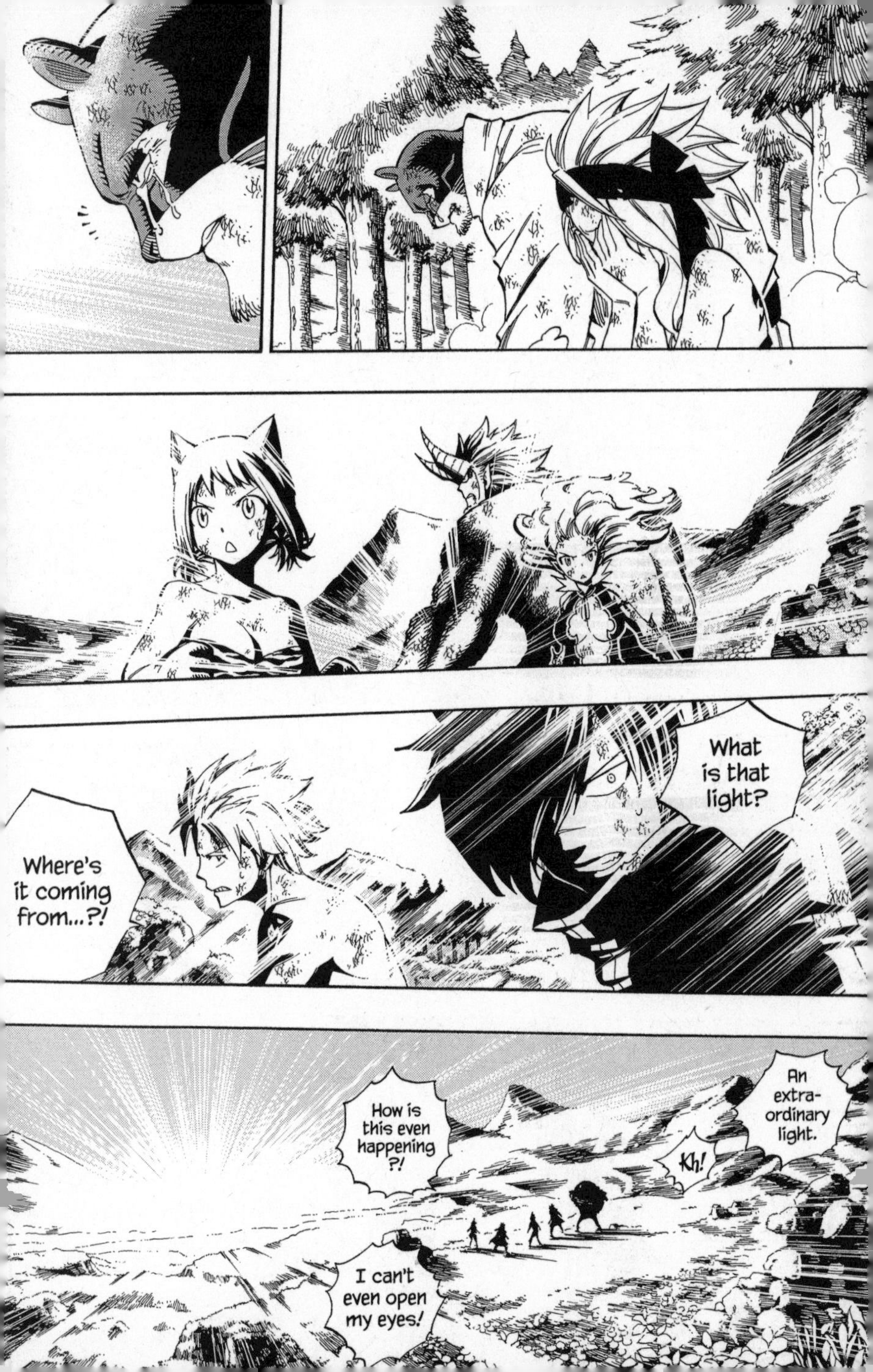
What is that light?
Where's it coming from...?!
An extra-ordinary light.
Kh!
How is this even happening?!
I can't even open my eyes!

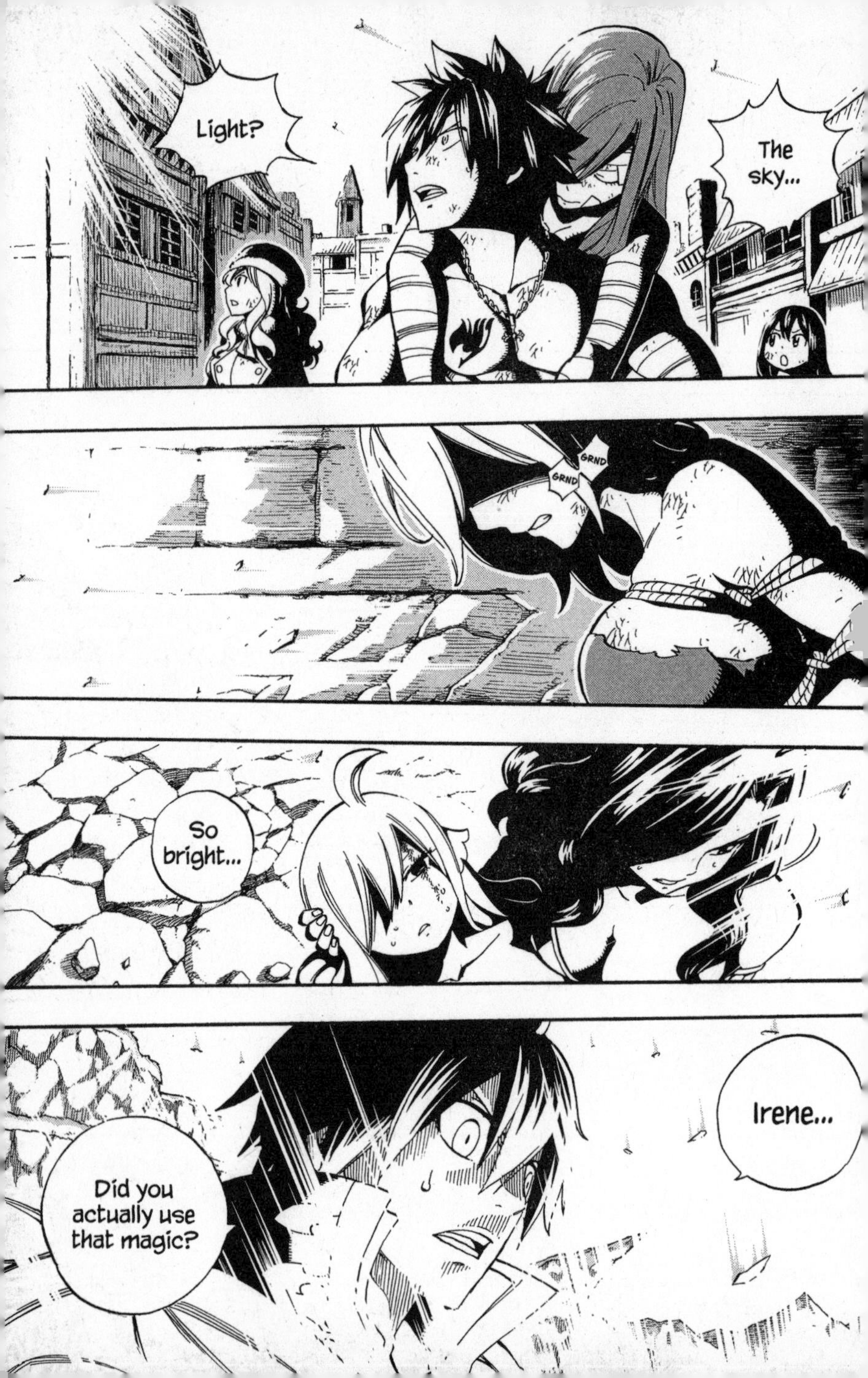
The sky...
Light?
GRND
GRND
So bright...
Irene...
Did you actually use that magic?

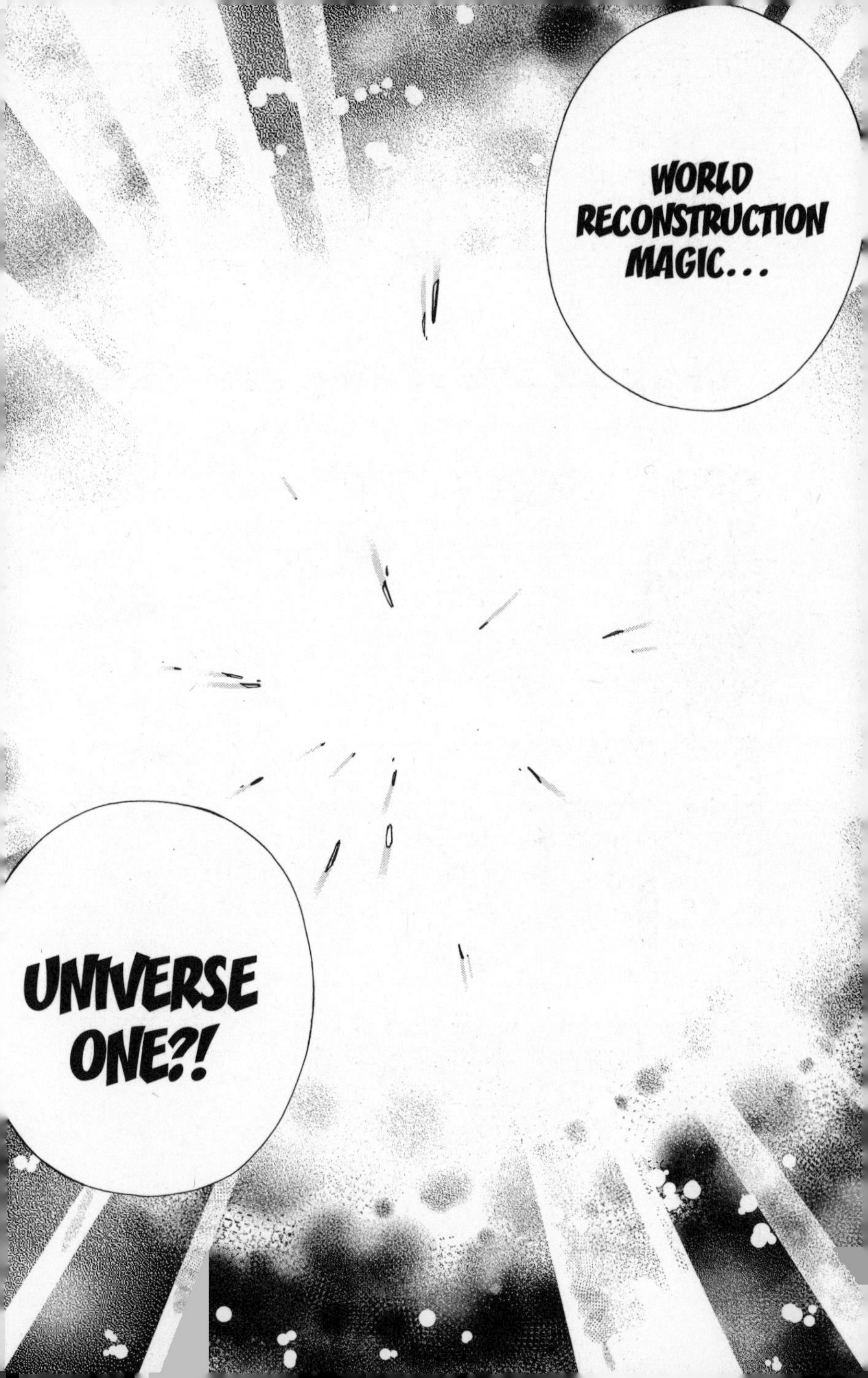
WORLD RECONSTRUCTION MAGIC...
UNIVERSE ONE?!

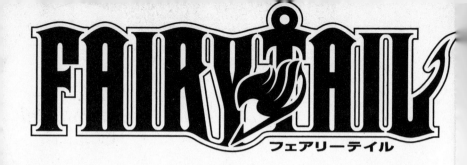

Chapter 490: Fairy Tail ZERØ

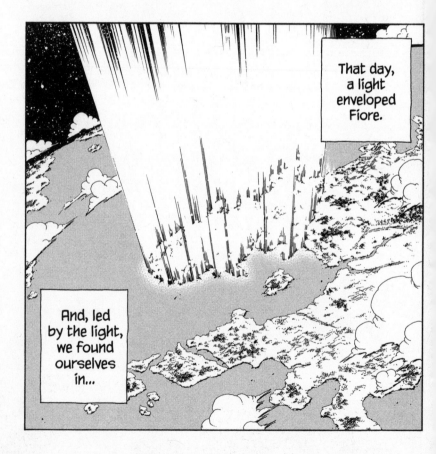

That day, a light enveloped Fiore.

And, led by the light, we found ourselves in...

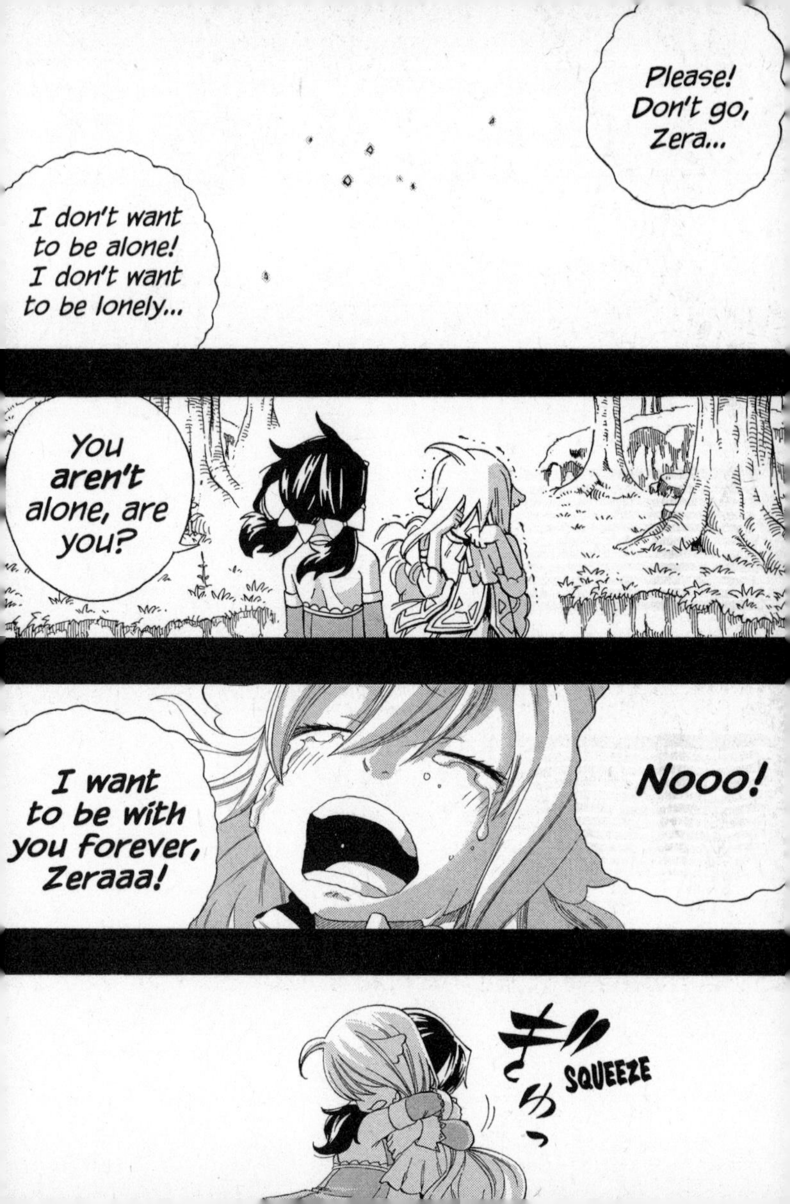
Please! Don't go, Zera...
I don't want to be alone! I don't want to be lonely...
You aren't alone, are you?
Nooo!
I want to be with you forever, Zeraaa!
ぎゅっ
SQUEEZE

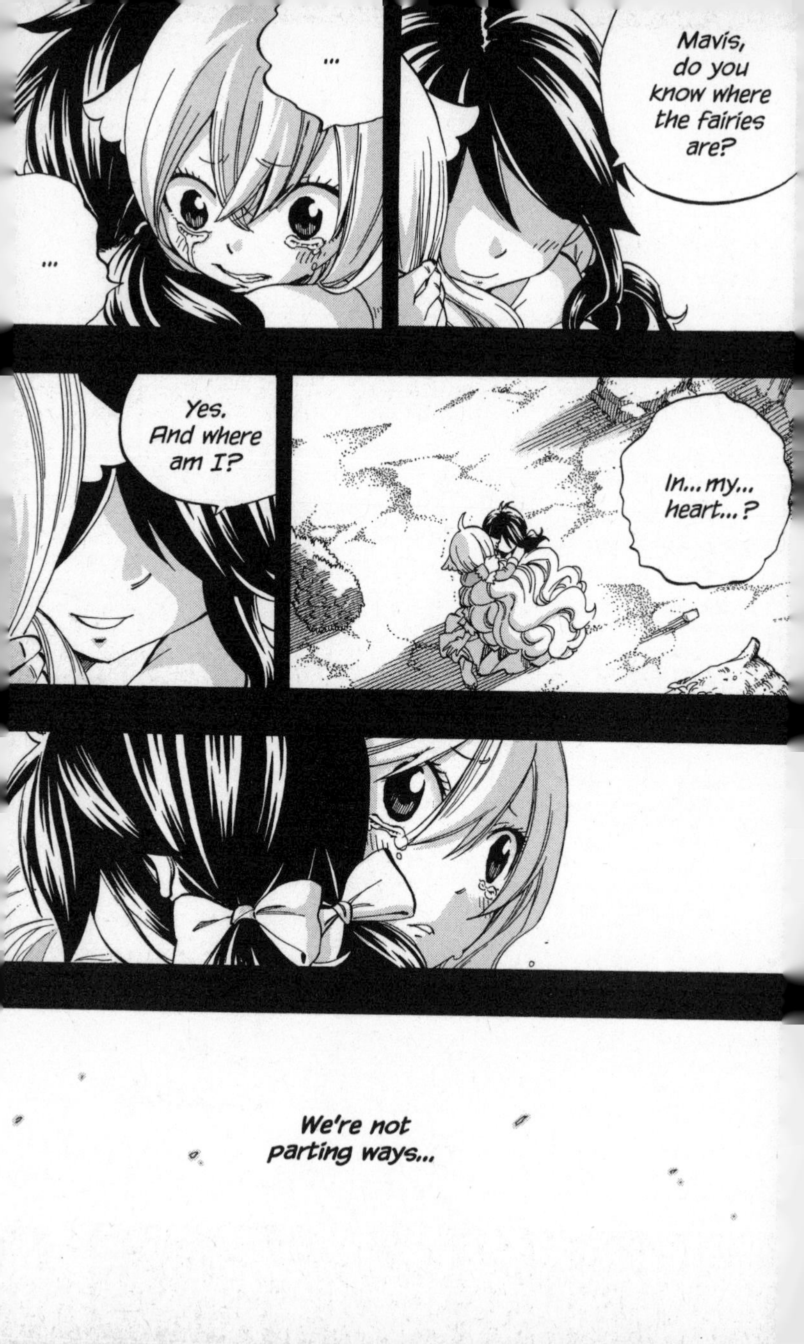
Mavis, do you know where the fairies are?
...
...
In...my... heart...?
Yes. And where am I?
We're not parting ways...

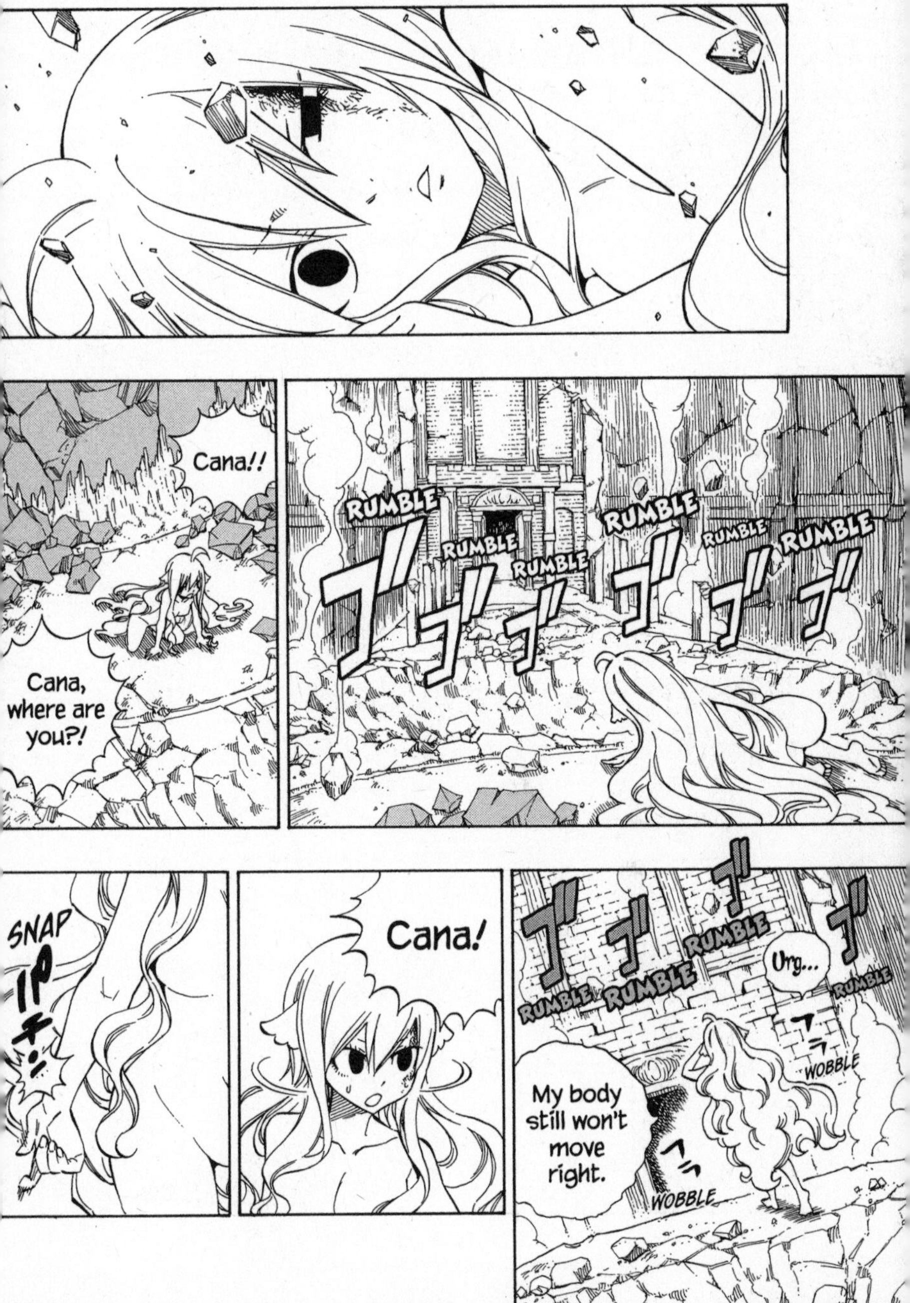
RUMBLE
RUMBLE
RUMBLE
RUMBLE
RUMBLE
RUMBLE
Cana!!
Cana, where are you?!
RUMBLE
RUMBLE
RUMBLE
RUMBLE
Urg...
WOBBLE
My body still won't move right.
WOBBLE
Cana!
SNAP

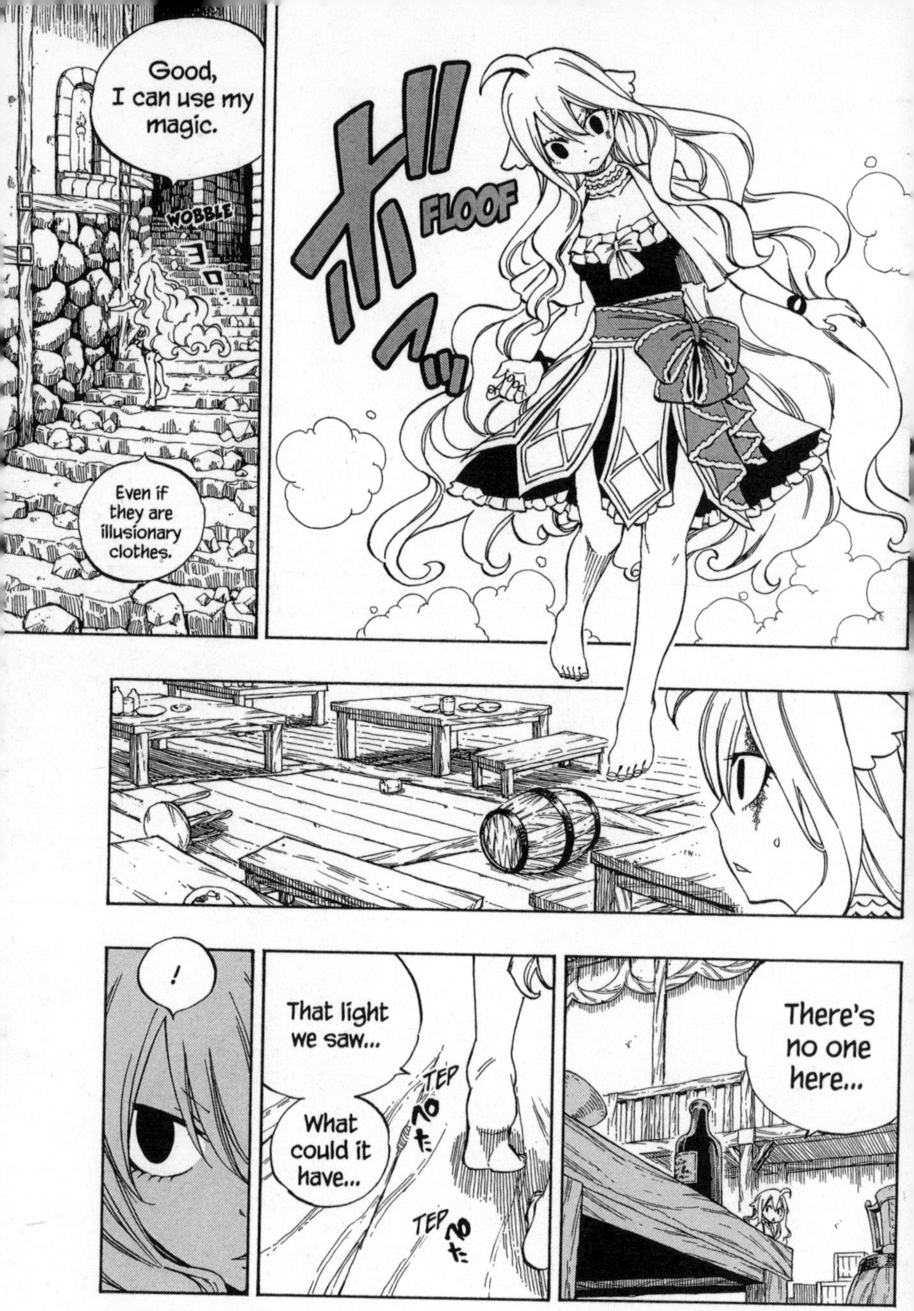
FLOOF
Good, I can use my magic.
WOBBLE
Even if they are illusionary clothes.
There's no one here...
That light we saw...
TEP
What could it have...
TEP
!

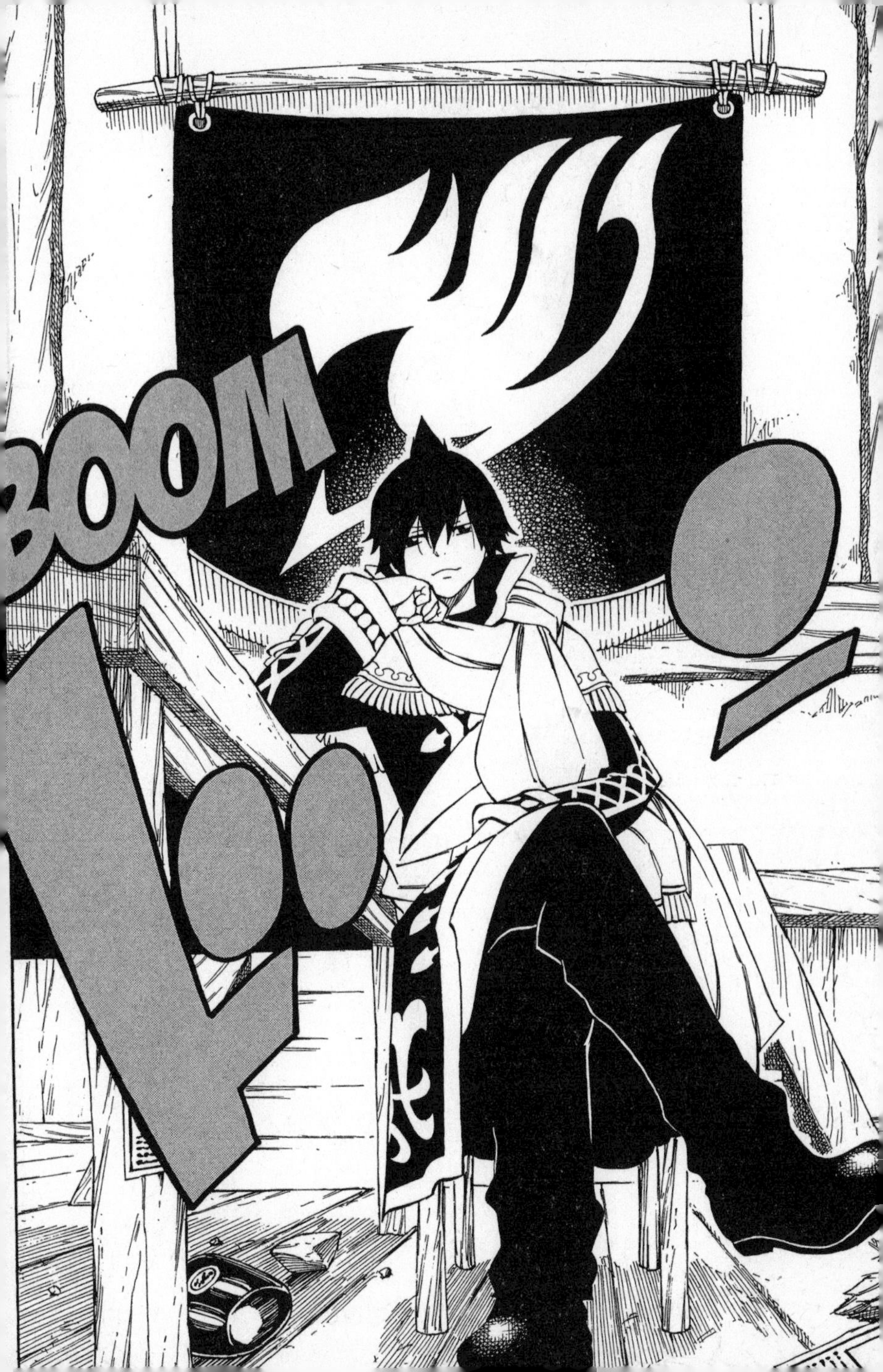
BOOM

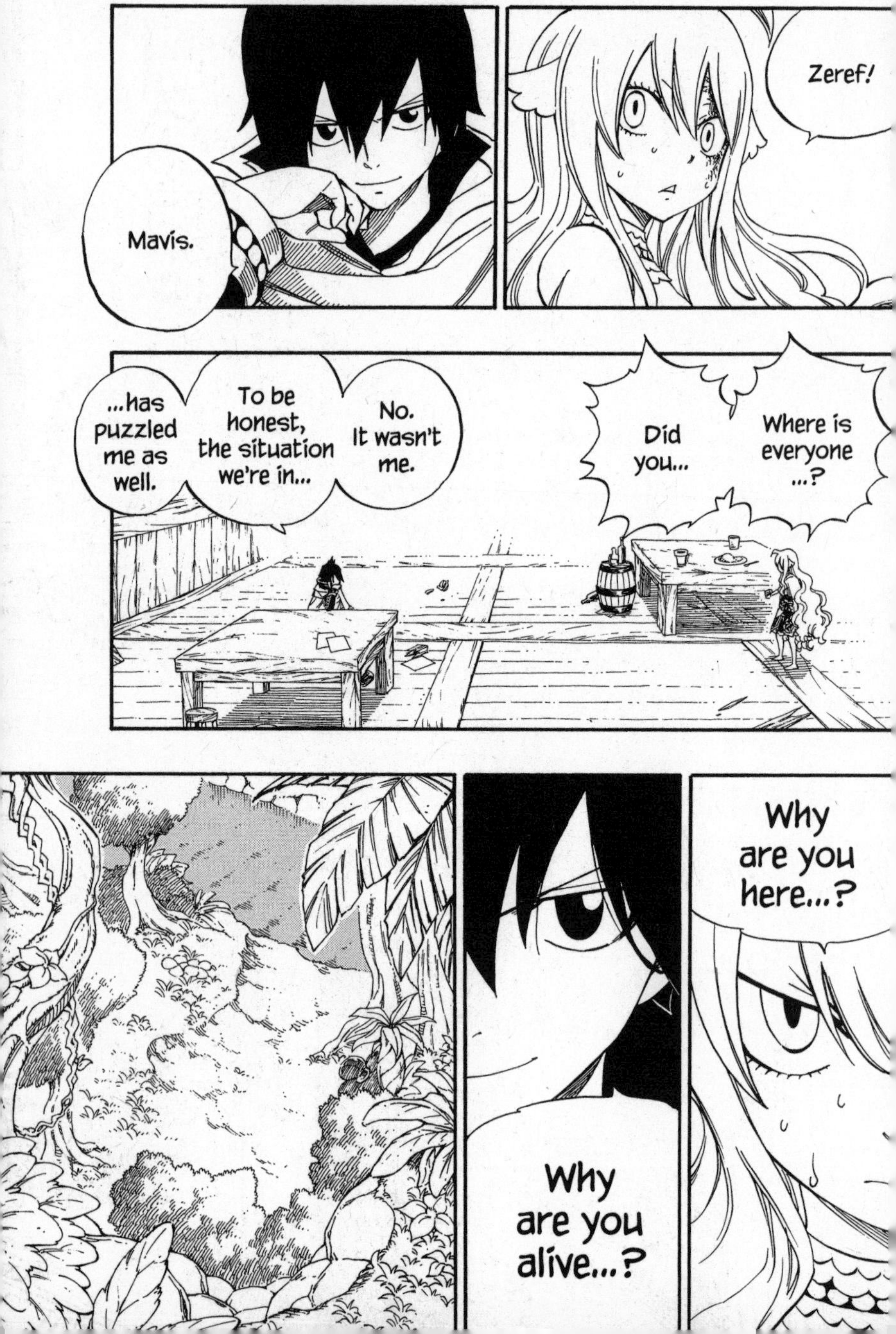
Zeref!
Mavis.
Where is everyone ...?
Did you...
No. It wasn't me.
To be honest, the situation we're in...
...has puzzled me as well.
Why are you here...?
Why are you alive...?

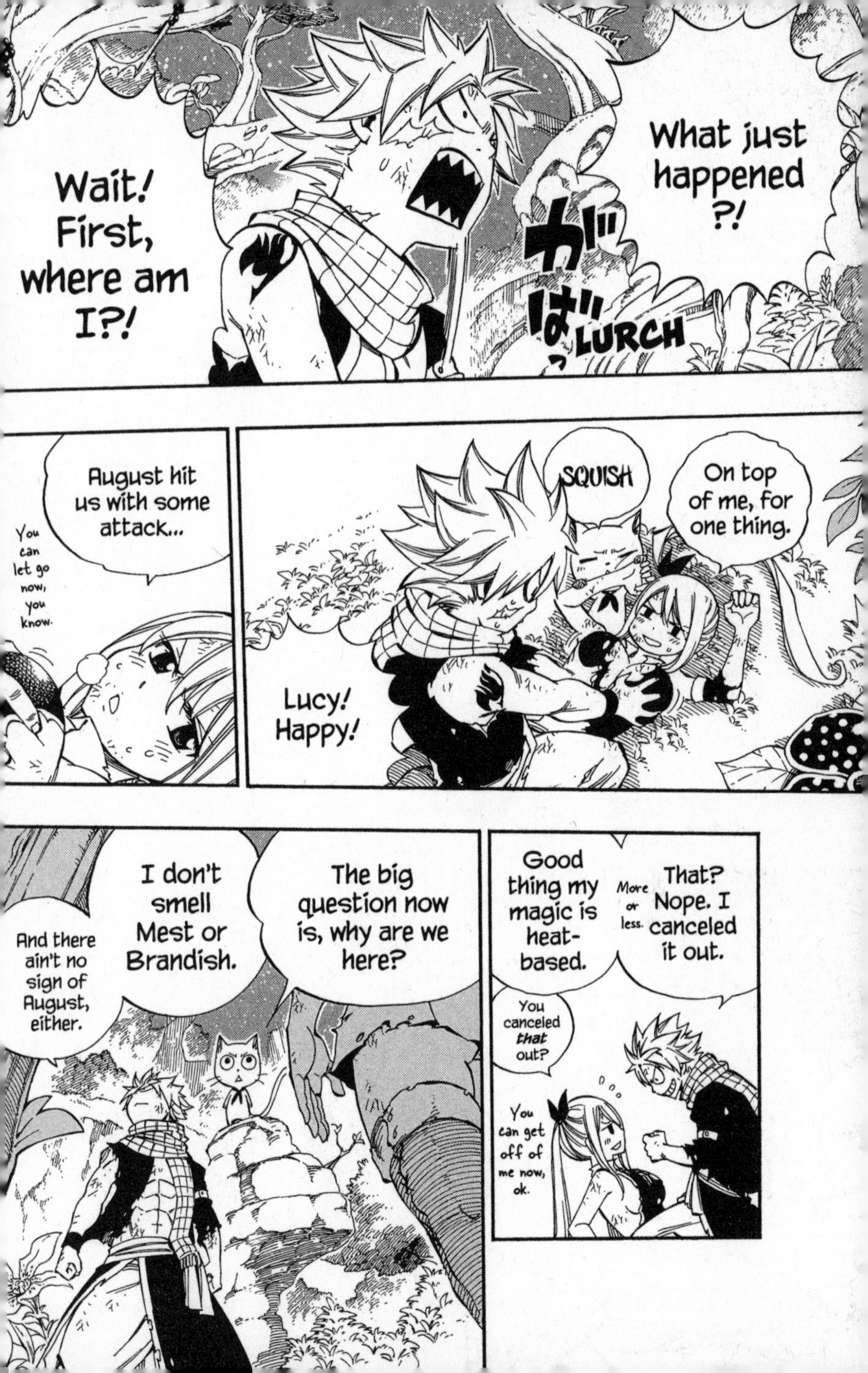
What just happened?!
ガばっ
LURCH
Wait! First, where am I?!
On top of me, for one thing.
SQUISH
Lucy! Happy!
August hit us with some attack...
You can let go now, you know.
That? Nope. I canceled it out.
More or less.
Good thing my magic is heat-based.
You canceled *that* out?
You can get off of me now, ok.
The big question now is, why are we here?
I don't smell Mest or Brandish.
And there ain't no sign of August, either.

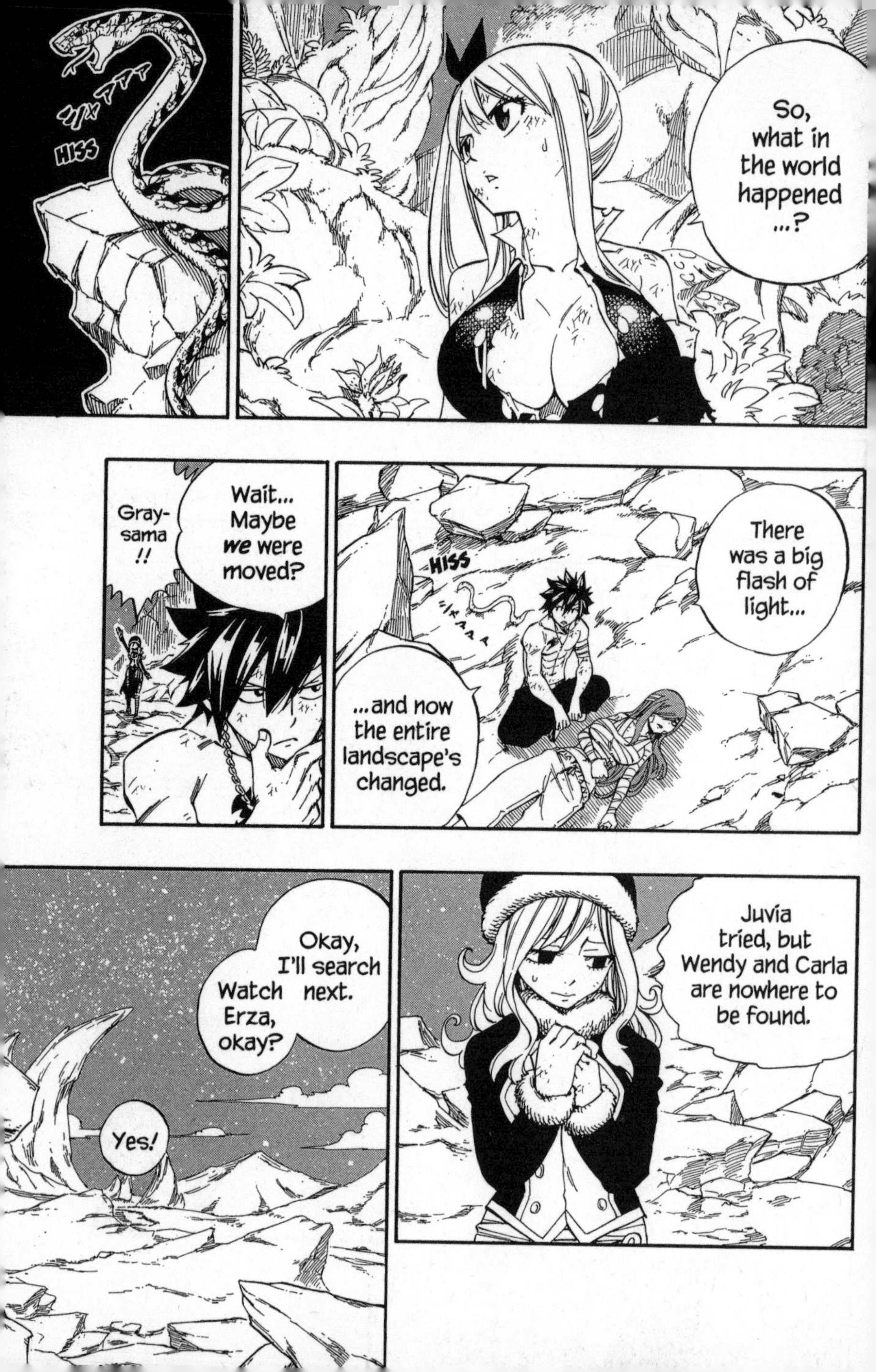
So, what in the world happened ...?
HISS
There was a big flash of light...
HISS
...and now the entire landscape's changed.
Wait... Maybe *we* were moved?
Gray-sama !!
Juvia tried, but Wendy and Carla are nowhere to be found.
Okay, I'll search next. Watch Erza, okay?
Yes!

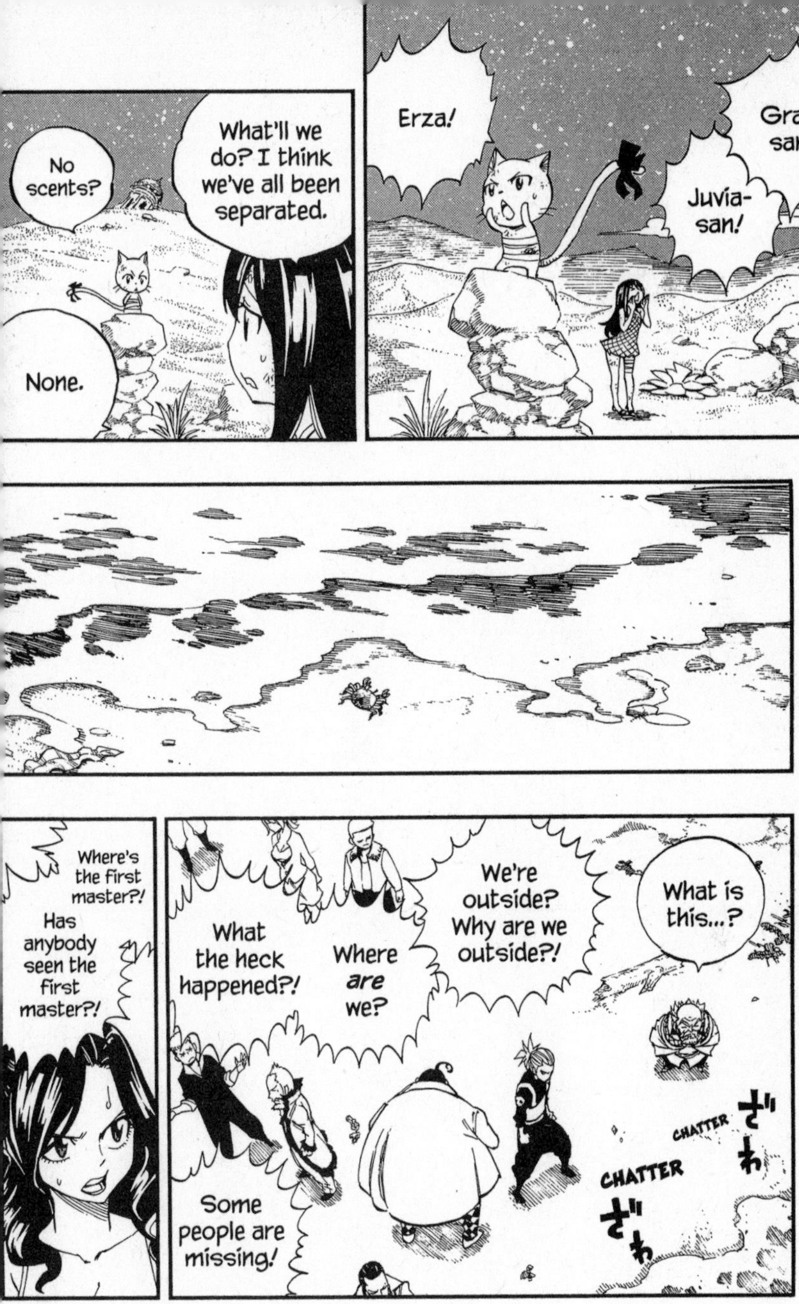
Gray-san!
Juvia-san!
Erza!
What'll we do? I think we've all been separated.
No scents?
None.
What is this...?
We're outside? Why are we outside?!
Where *are* we?
What the heck happened?!
Some people are missing!
CHATTER ざわ
CHATTER ざわ
Where's the first master?!
Has anybody seen the first master?!

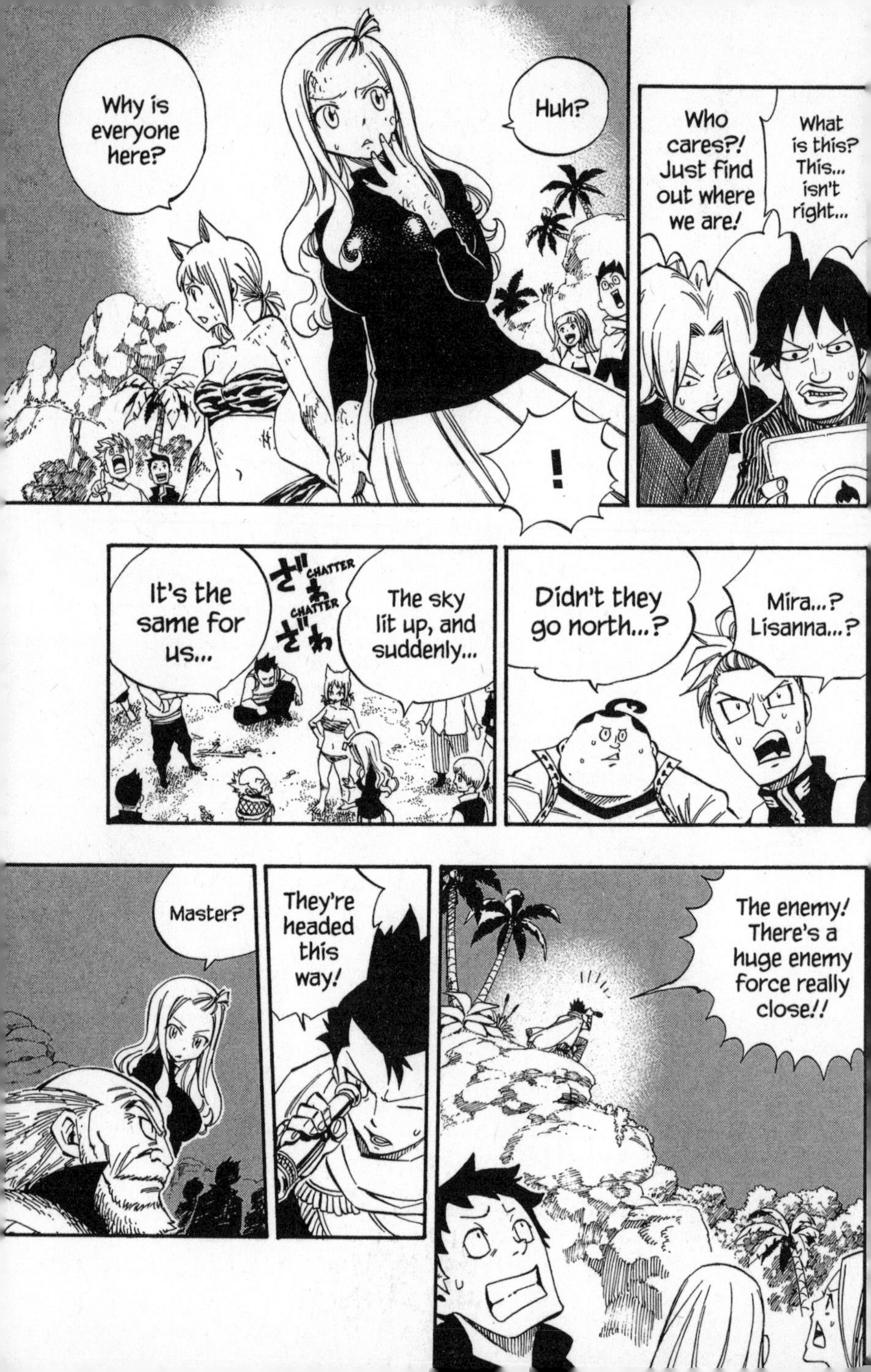
What is this? This... isn't right...
Who cares?! Just find out where we are!
Huh?
Why is everyone here?
!
Mira...? Lisanna...?
Didn't they go north...?
The sky lit up, and suddenly...
ざわ CHATTER
ざわ CHATTER
It's the same for us...
The enemy! There's a huge enemy force really close!!
They're headed this way!
Master?

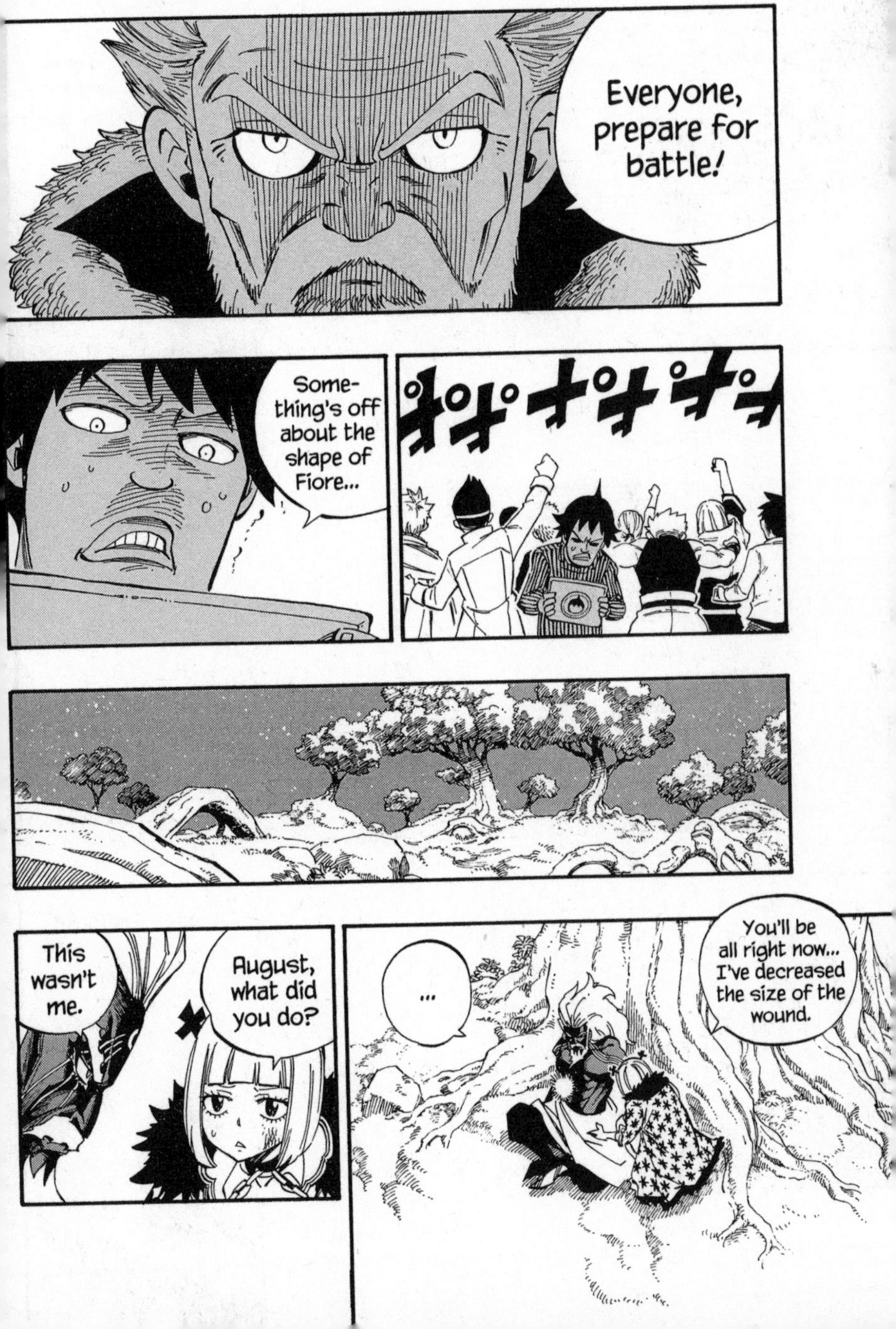
Everyone, prepare for battle!
Some-thing's off about the shape of Fiore...
You'll be all right now... I've decreased the size of the wound.
...
August, what did you do?
This wasn't me.

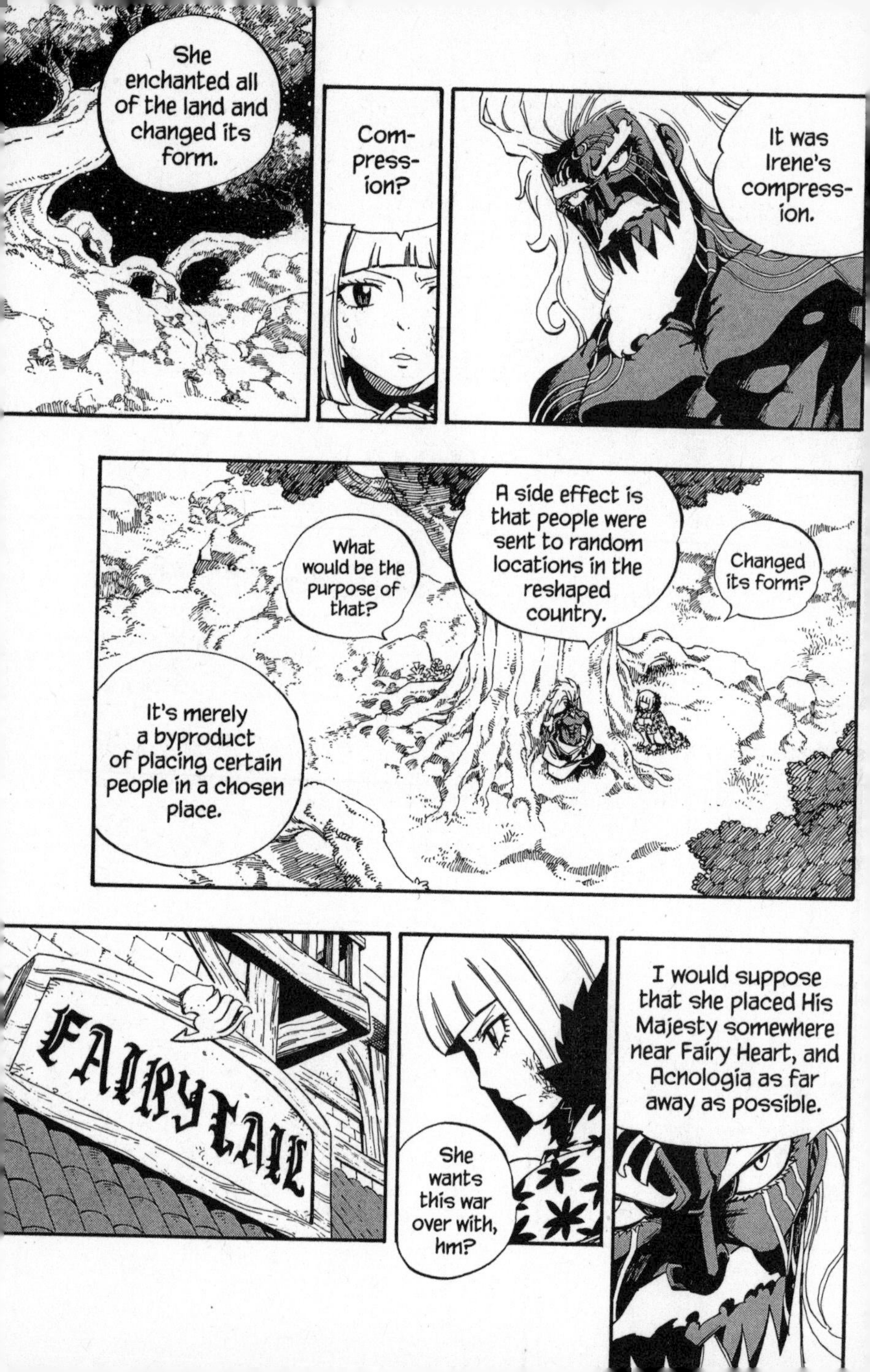
It was Irene's compress-ion.
Com-press-ion?
She enchanted all of the land and changed its form.
Changed its form?
A side effect is that people were sent to random locations in the reshaped country.
What would be the purpose of that?
It's merely a byproduct of placing certain people in a chosen place.
I would suppose that she placed His Majesty somewhere near Fairy Heart, and Acnologia as far away as possible.
She wants this war over with, hm?
FAIRY TAIL

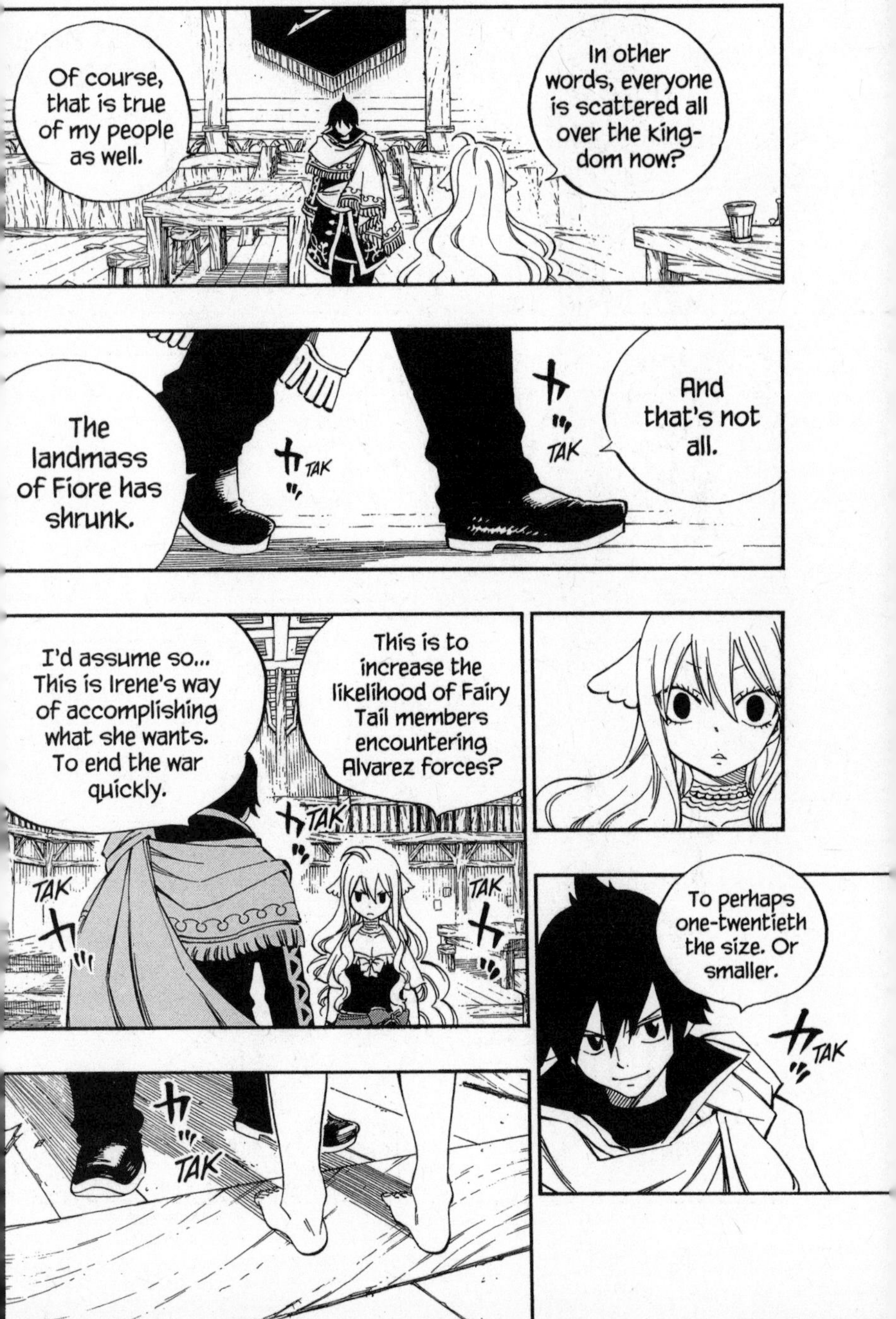

In other words, everyone is scattered all over the king-dom now?
Of course, that is true of my people as well.
TAK
And that's not all.
TAK
The landmass of Fiore has shrunk.
This is to increase the likelihood of Fairy Tail members encountering Alvarez forces?
I'd assume so... This is Irene's way of accomplishing what she wants. To end the war quickly.
TAK
TAK
TAK
To perhaps one-twentieth the size. Or smaller.
TAK
TAK

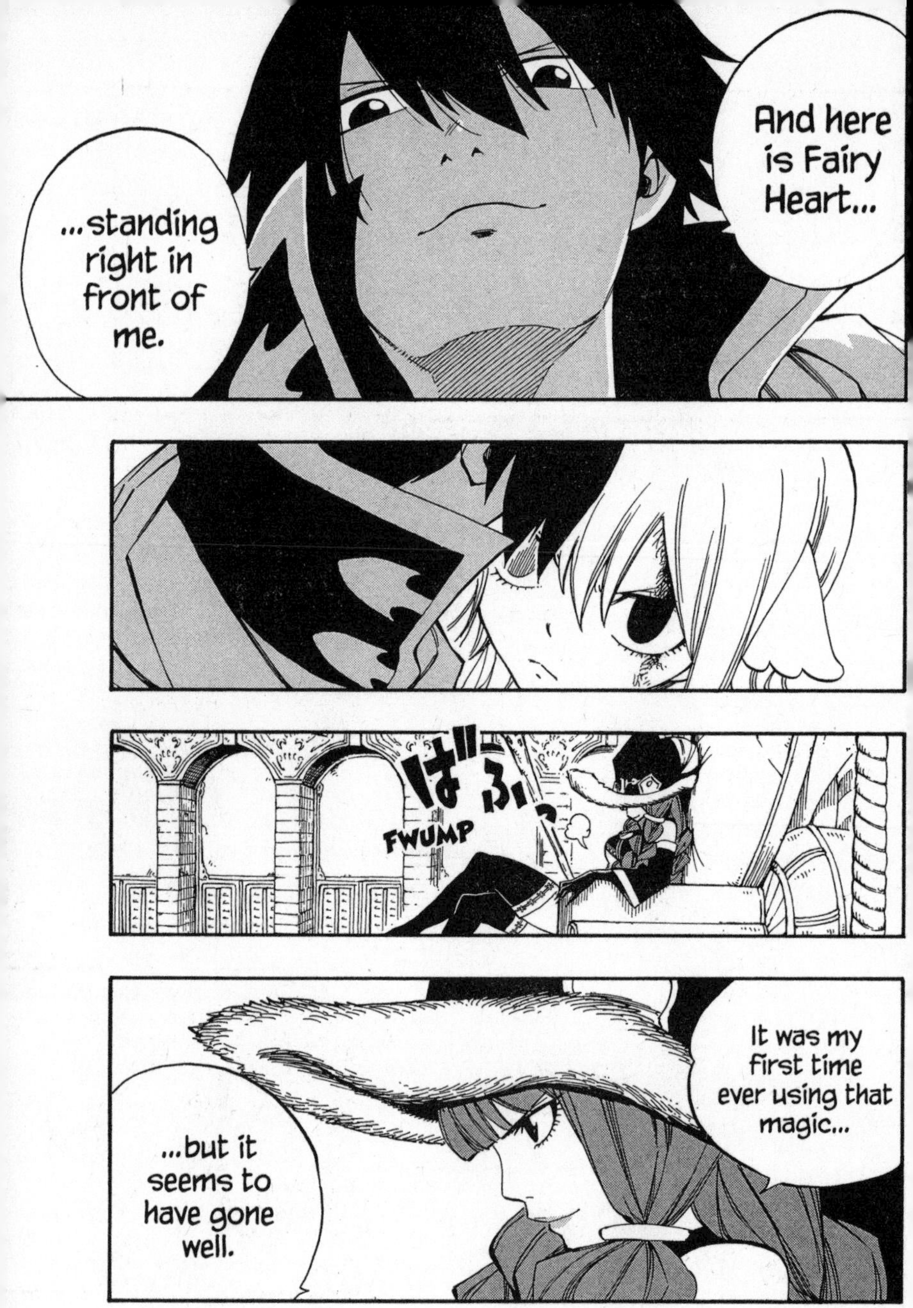
And here is Fairy Heart...
...standing right in front of me.
ばふっ
FWUMP
It was my first time ever using that magic...
...but it seems to have gone well.

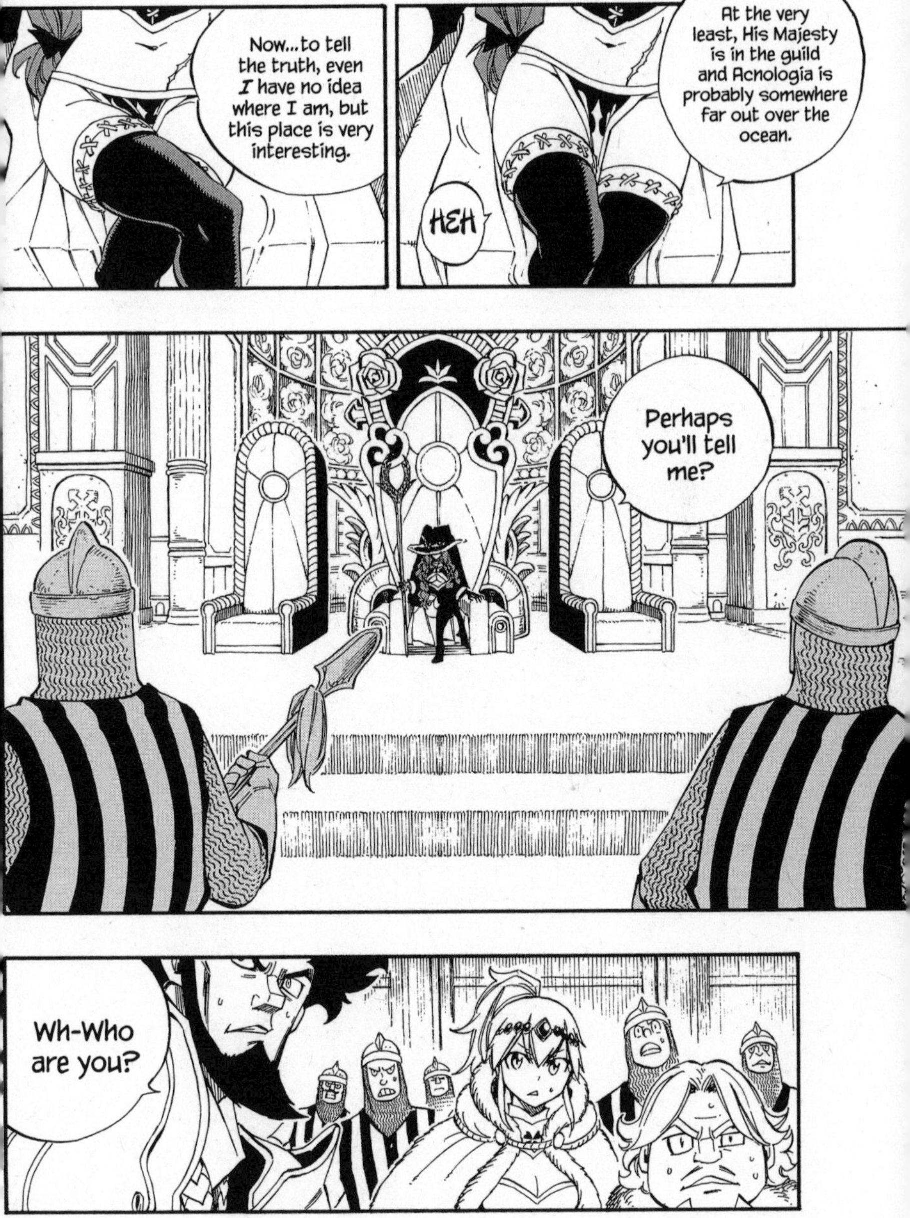
At the very least, His Majesty is in the guild and Acnologia is probably somewhere far out over the ocean.
HEH
Now...to tell the truth, even I have no idea where I am, but this place is very interesting.
Perhaps you'll tell me?
Wh-Who are you?

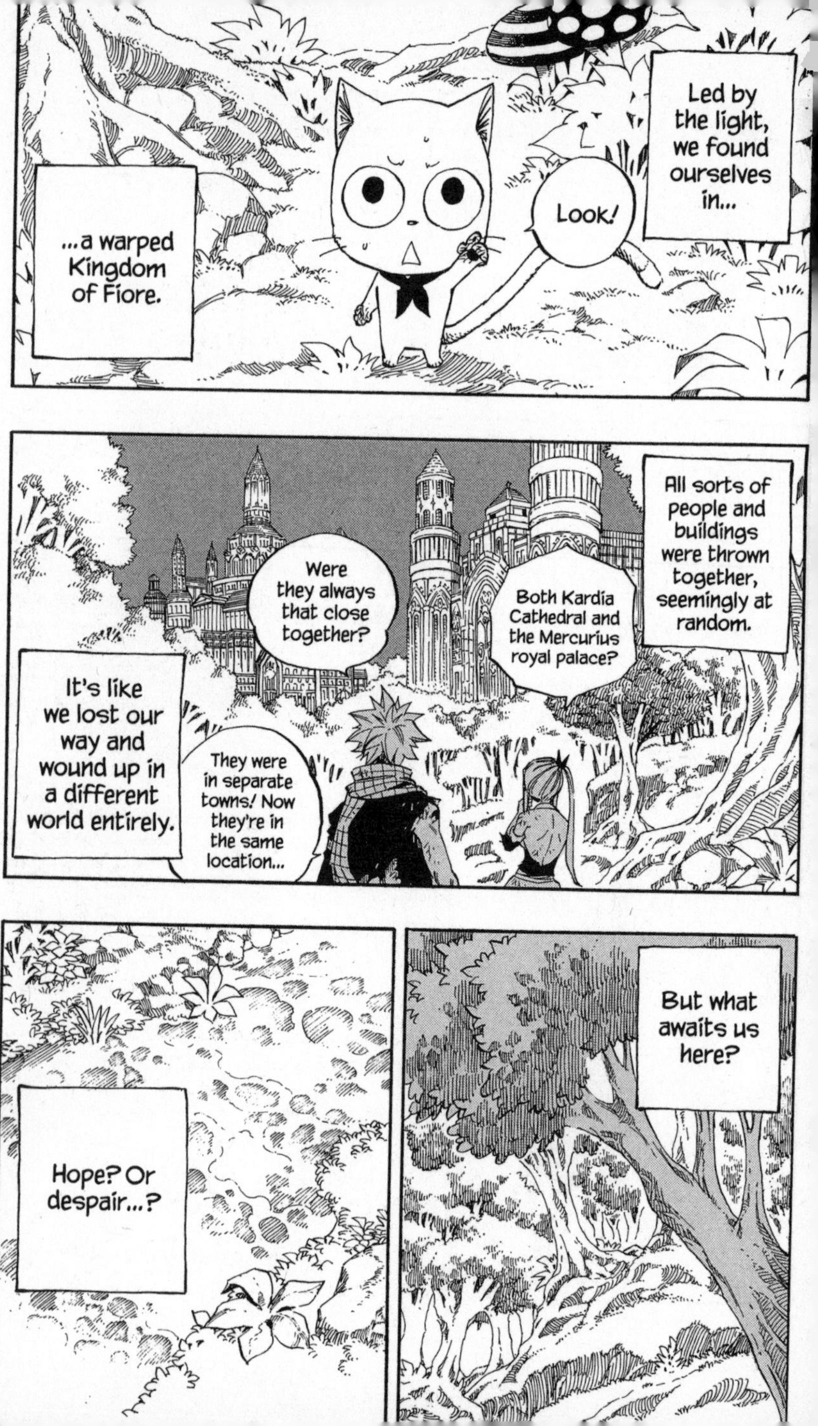

Led by the light, we found ourselves in...
Look!
...a warped Kingdom of Fiore.
All sorts of people and buildings were thrown together, seemingly at random.
Both Kardia Cathedral and the Mercurius royal palace?
Were they always that close together?
They were in separate towns! Now they're in the same location...
It's like we lost our way and wound up in a different world entirely.
But what awaits us here?
Hope? Or despair...?

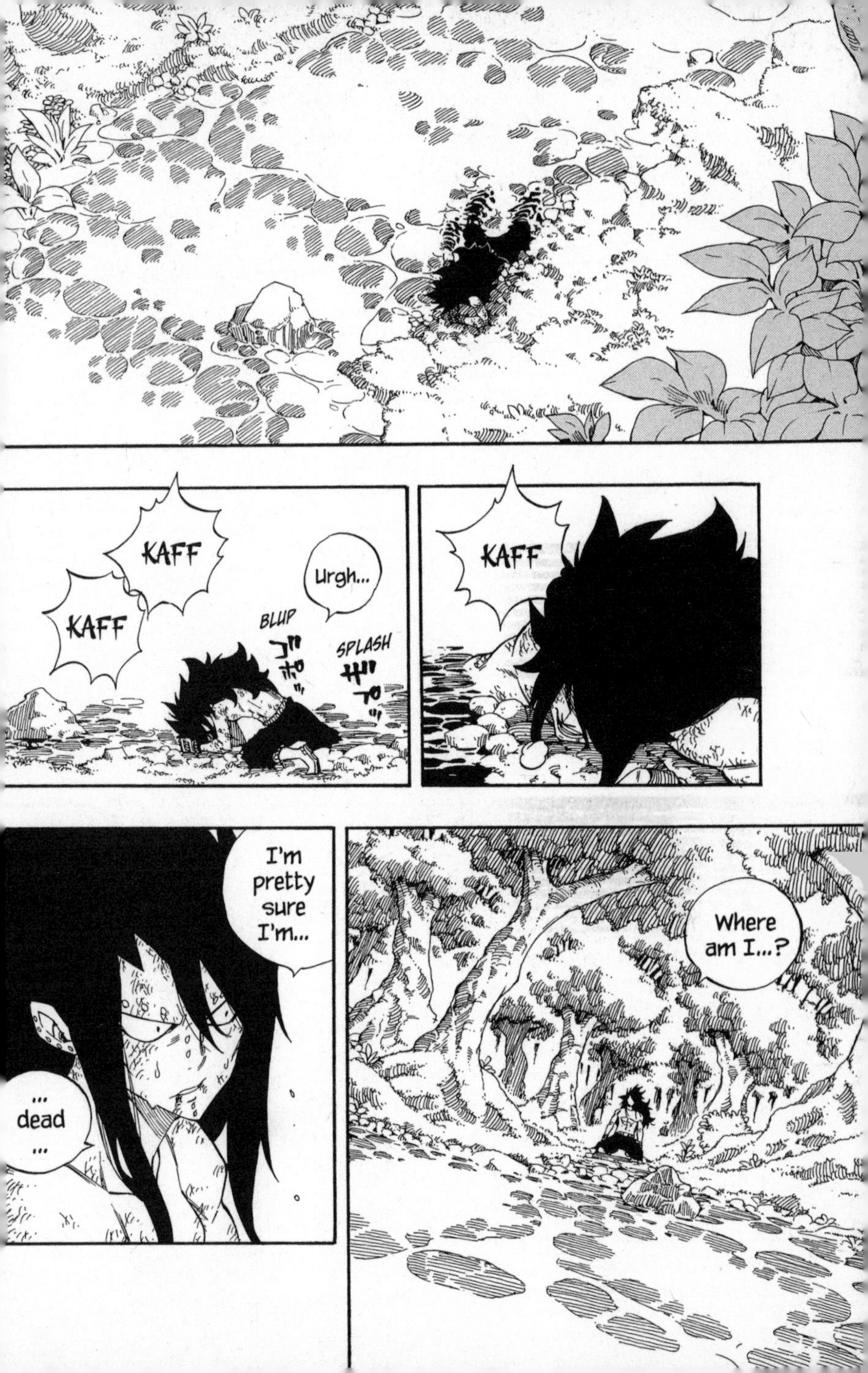
KAFF
Urgh...
KAFF
KAFF
BLUP
SPLASH
Where am I...?
I'm pretty sure I'm...
... dead ...

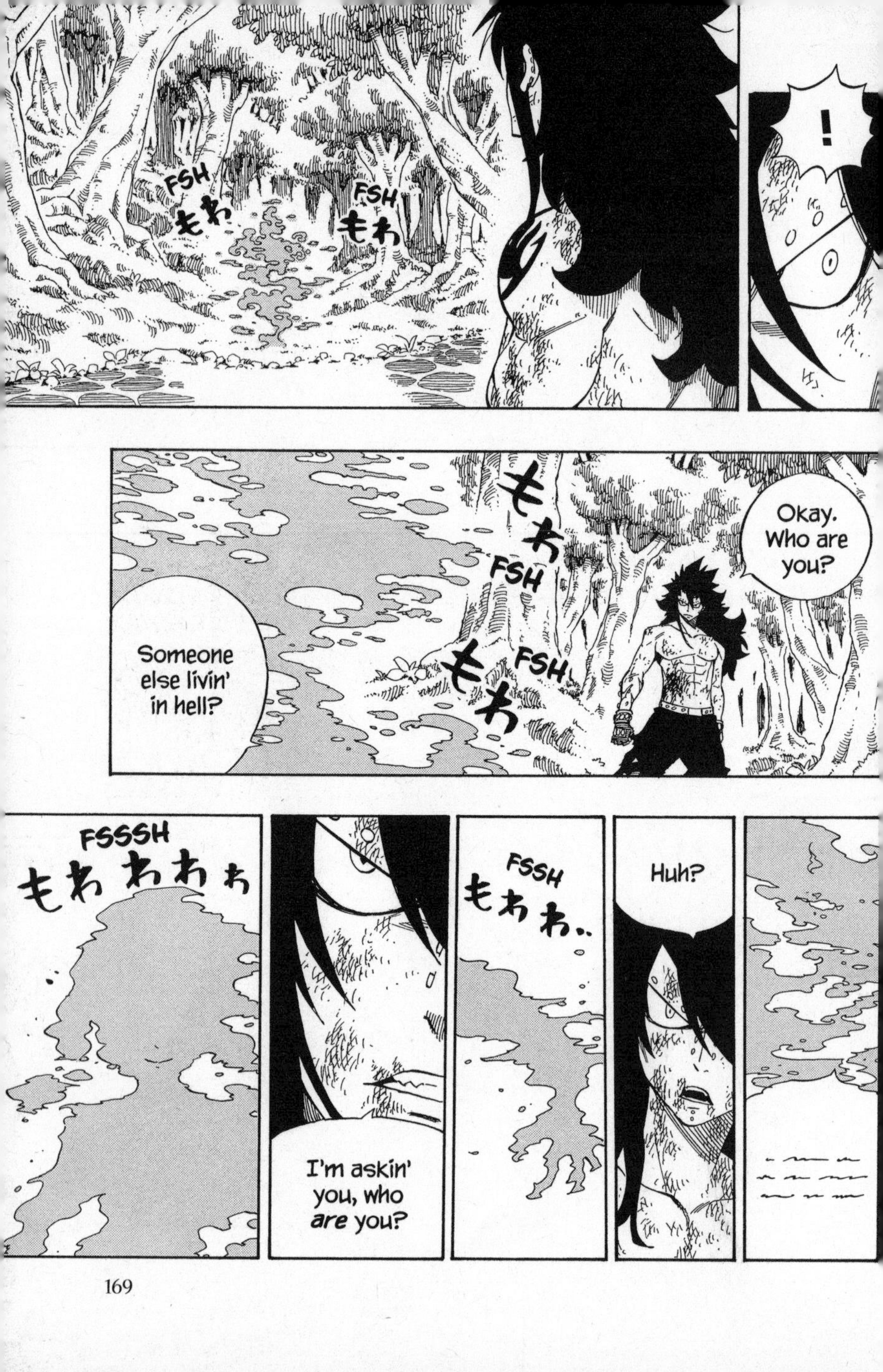
!
FSH
もわ
FSH
もわ
Okay. Who are you?
もわ
FSH
FSH
もわ
Someone else livin' in hell?
Huh?
FSSH
もわわ..
I'm askin' you, who *are* you?
FSSSH
もわわわぁ

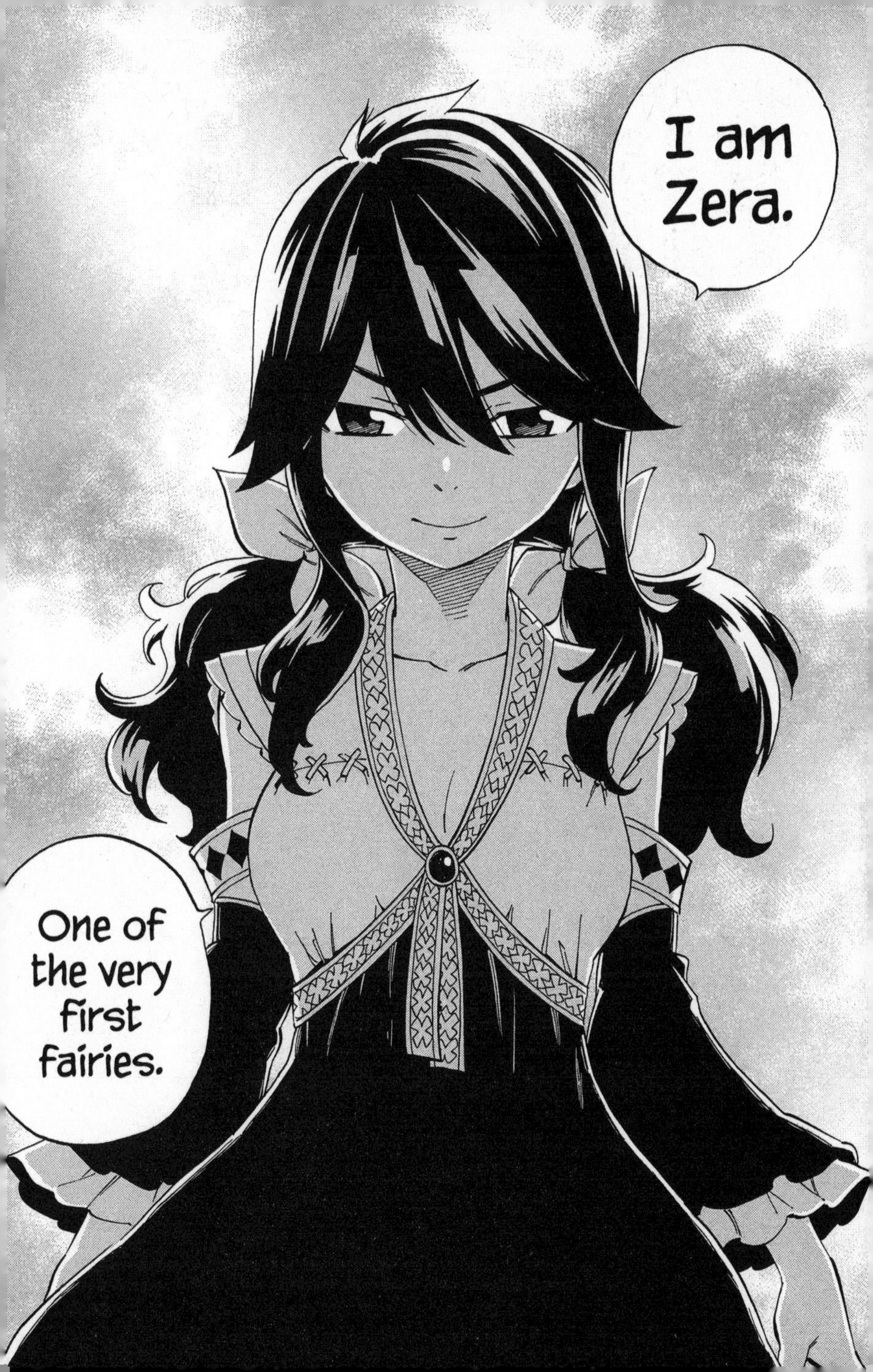
I am Zera.
One of the very first fairies.

FAIRY TAIL

フェアリーテイル

Chapter 491: Mother and Child

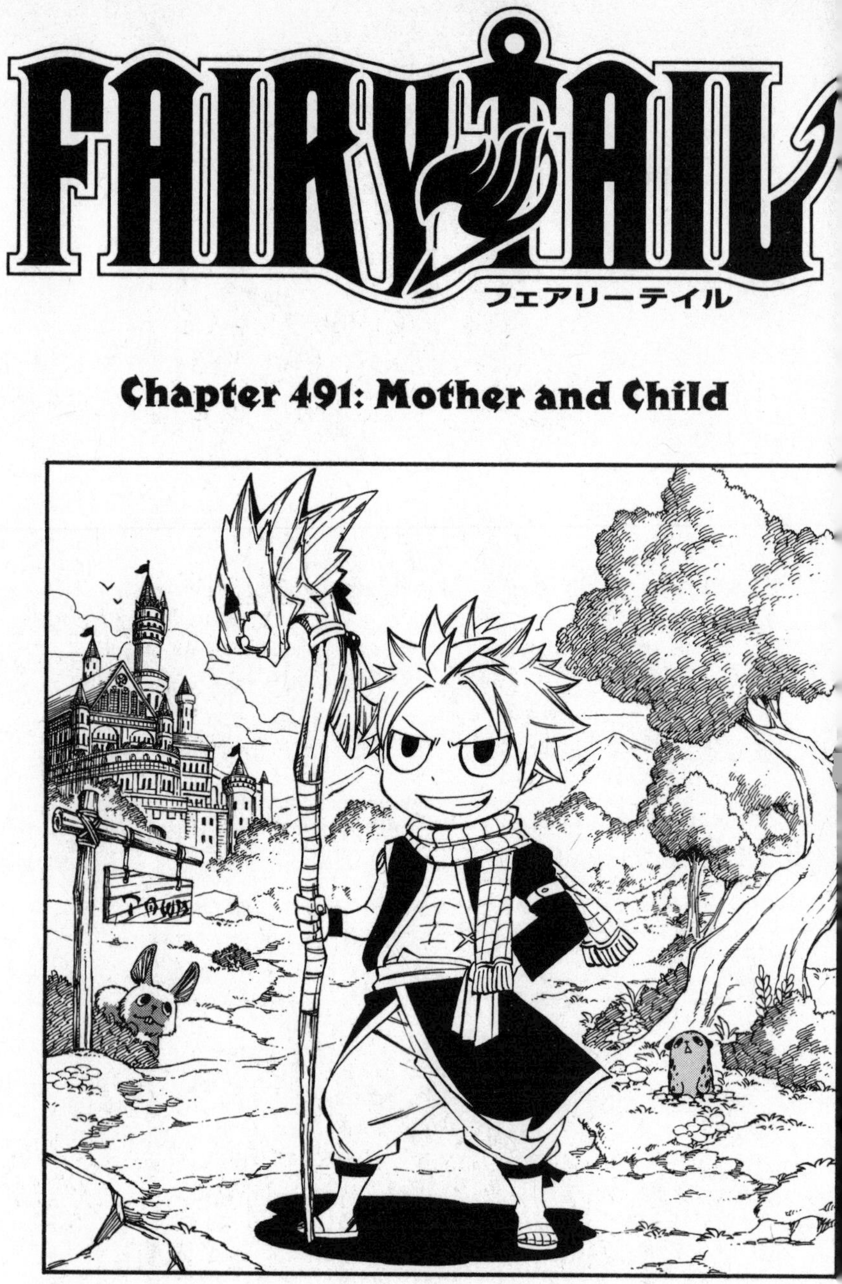

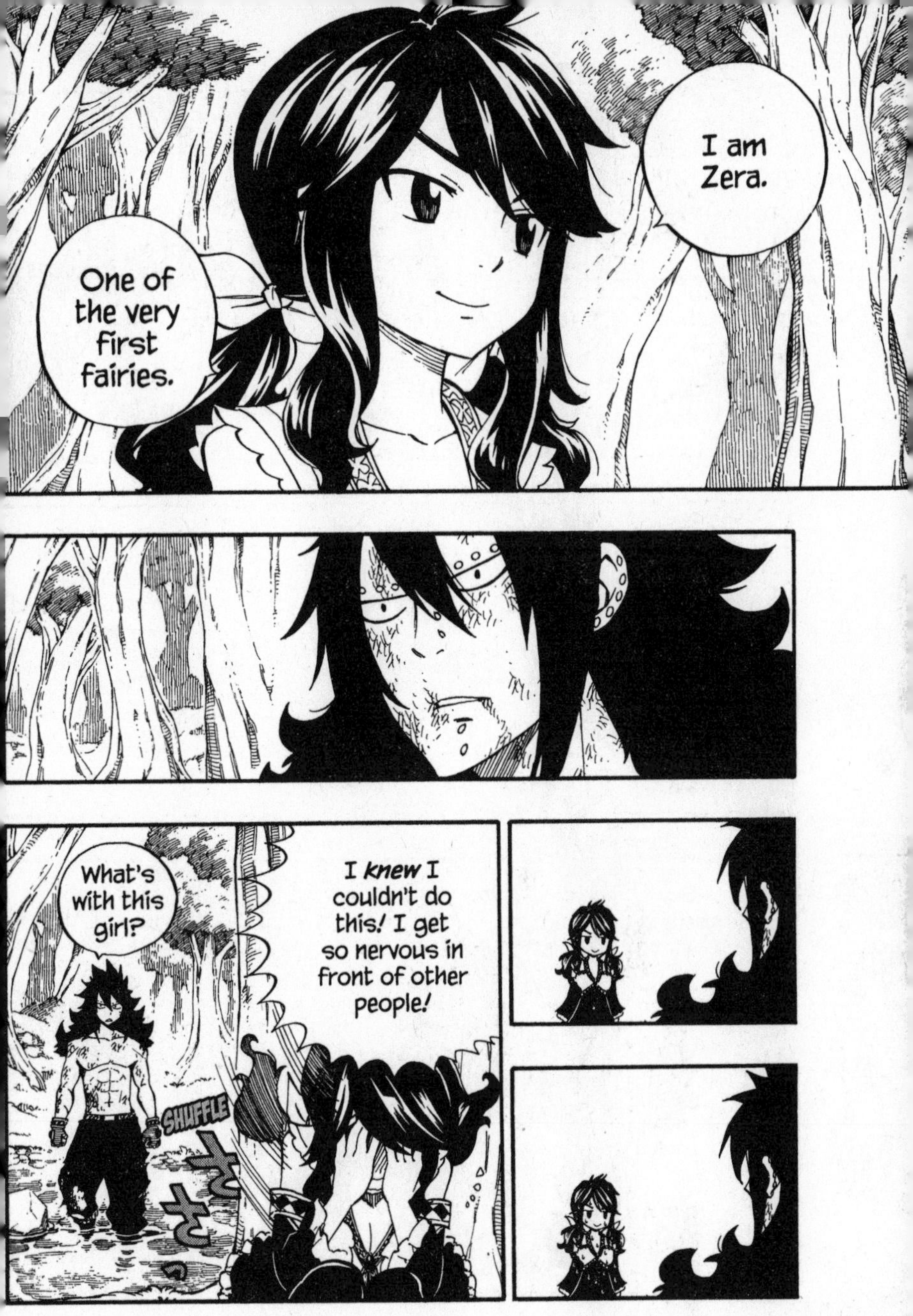
I am Zera.
One of the very first fairies.
I *knew* I couldn't do this! I get so nervous in front of other people!
What's with this girl?
SHUFFLE
ささっ

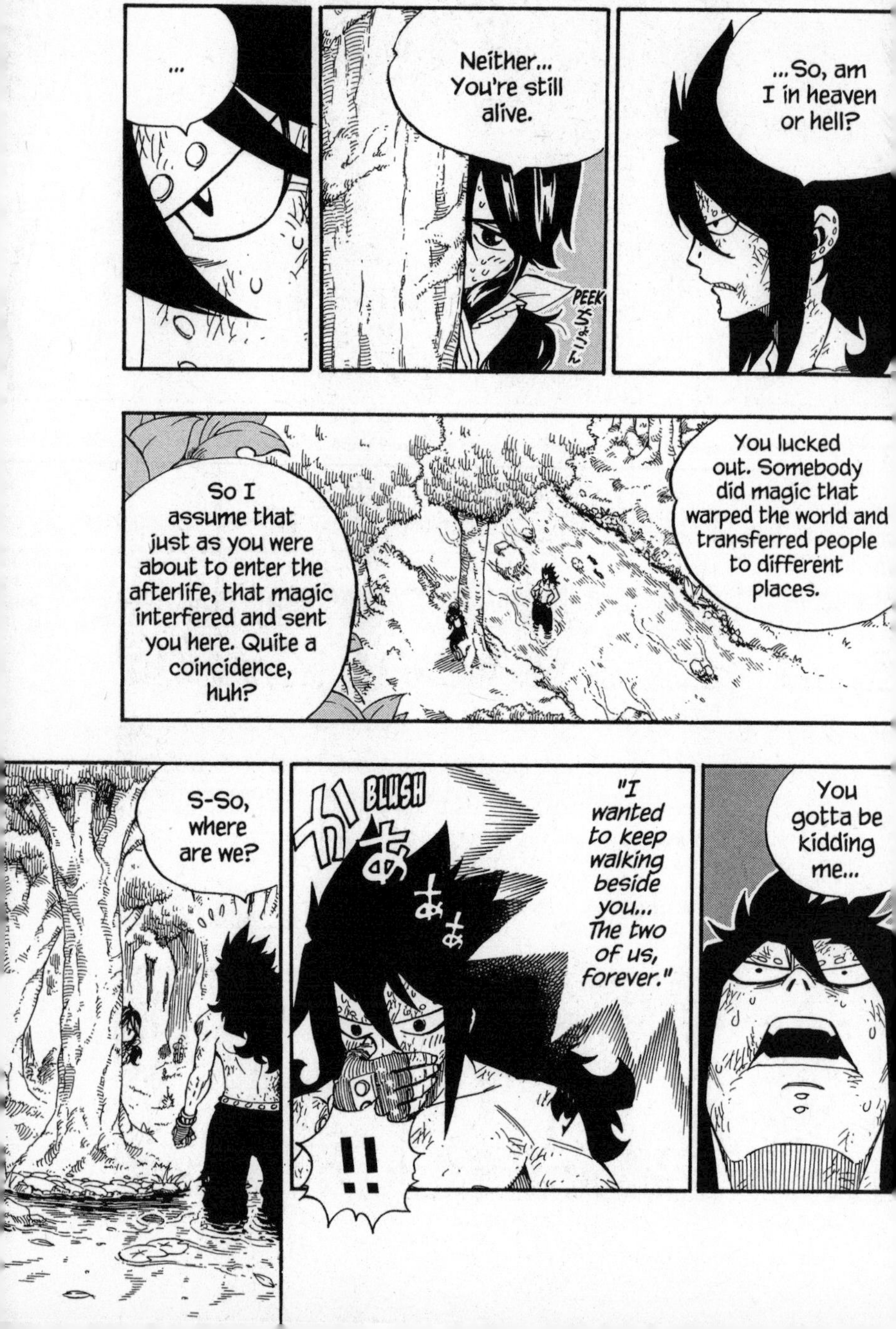
...So, am I in heaven or hell?
Neither... You're still alive.
PEEK
...
You lucked out. Somebody did magic that warped the world and transferred people to different places.
So I assume that just as you were about to enter the afterlife, that magic interfered and sent you here. Quite a coincidence, huh?
You gotta be kidding me...
"I wanted to keep walking beside you... The two of us, forever."
BLUSH
!!
S-So, where are we?

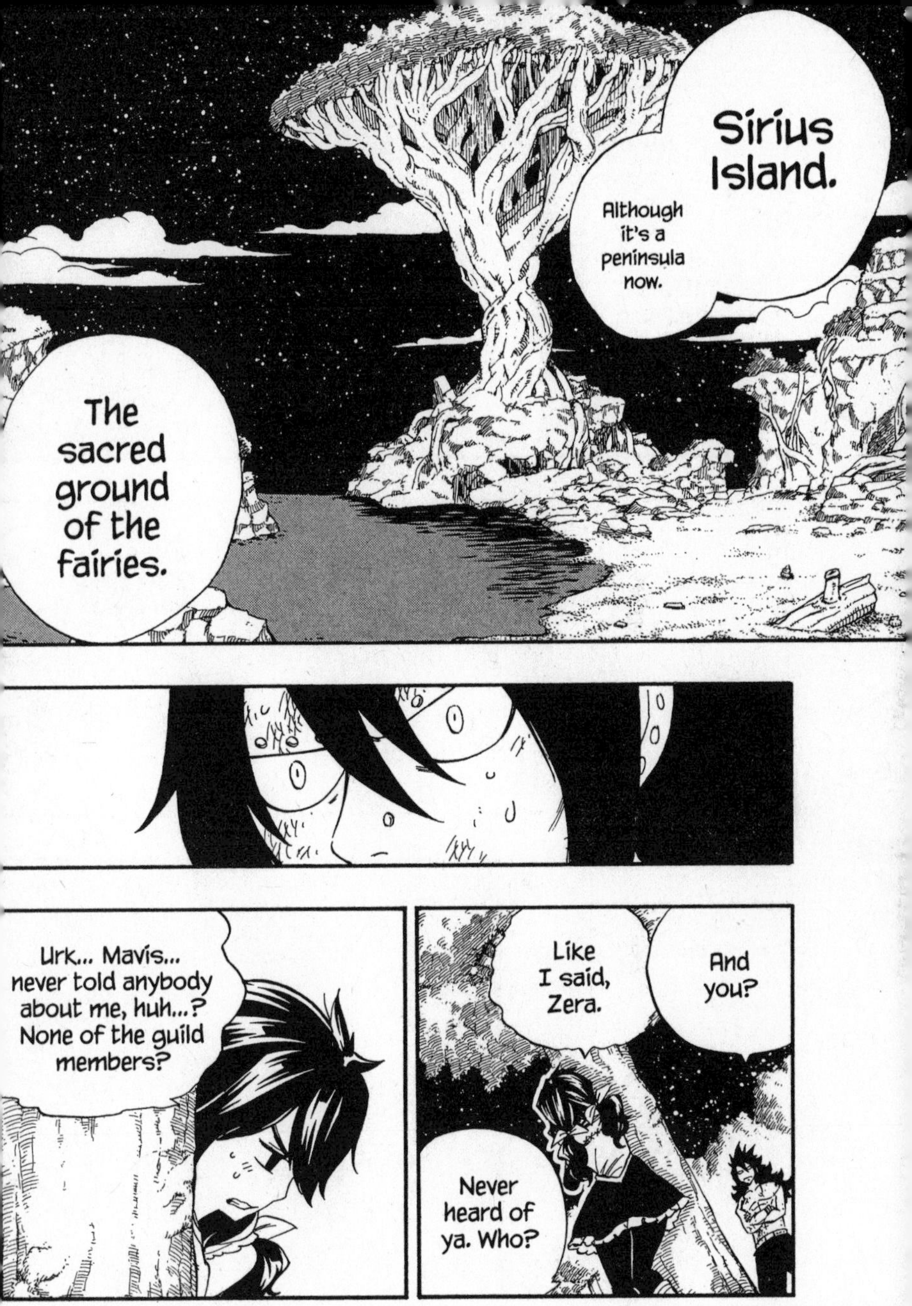
Sirius Island.
Although it's a peninsula now.
The sacred ground of the fairies.
And you?
Like I said, Zera.
Never heard of ya. Who?
Urk... Mavis... never told anybody about me, huh...? None of the guild members?

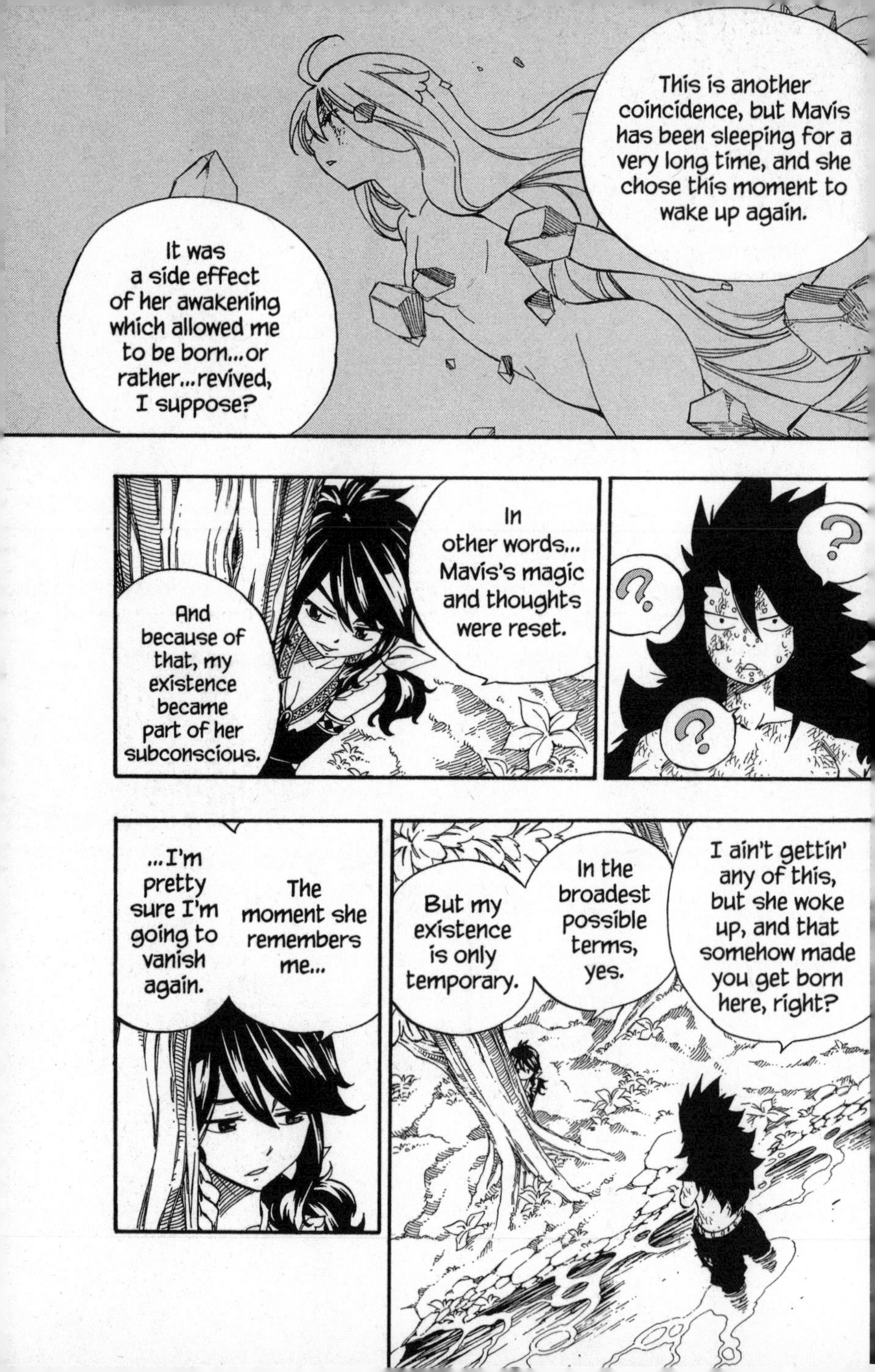
This is another coincidence, but Mavis has been sleeping for a very long time, and she chose this moment to wake up again.
It was a side effect of her awakening which allowed me to be born...or rather...revived, I suppose?
?
?
?
In other words... Mavis's magic and thoughts were reset.
And because of that, my existence became part of her subconscious.
I ain't gettin' any of this, but she woke up, and that somehow made you get born here, right?
In the broadest possible terms, yes.
But my existence is only temporary.
The moment she remembers me...
...I'm pretty sure I'm going to vanish again.

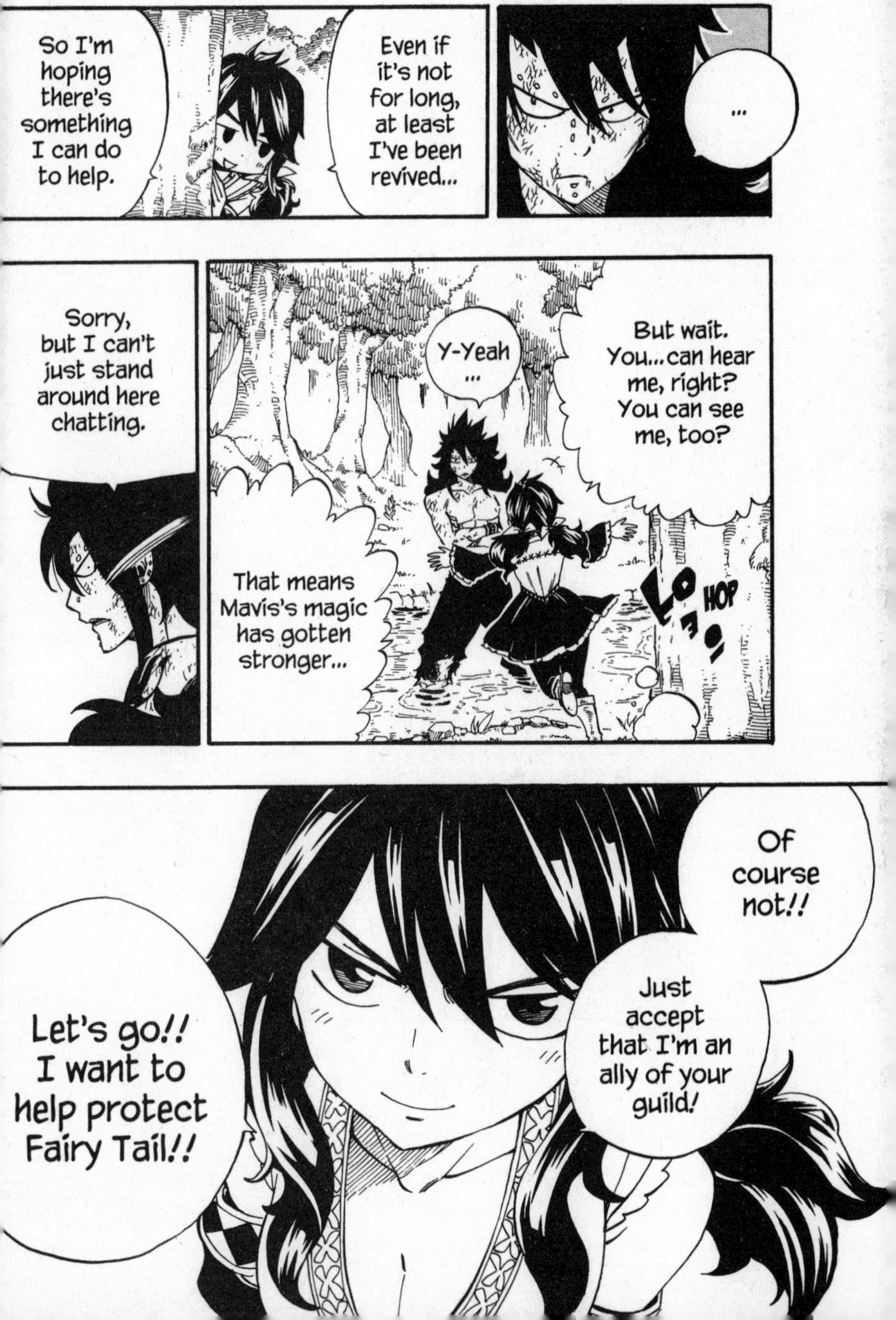
...
Even if it's not for long, at least I've been revived...
So I'm hoping there's something I can do to help.
But wait. You...can hear me, right? You can see me, too?
Y-Yeah ...
HOP
That means Mavis's magic has gotten stronger...
Sorry, but I can't just stand around here chatting.
Of course not!!
Just accept that I'm an ally of your guild!
Let's go!! I want to help protect Fairy Tail!!

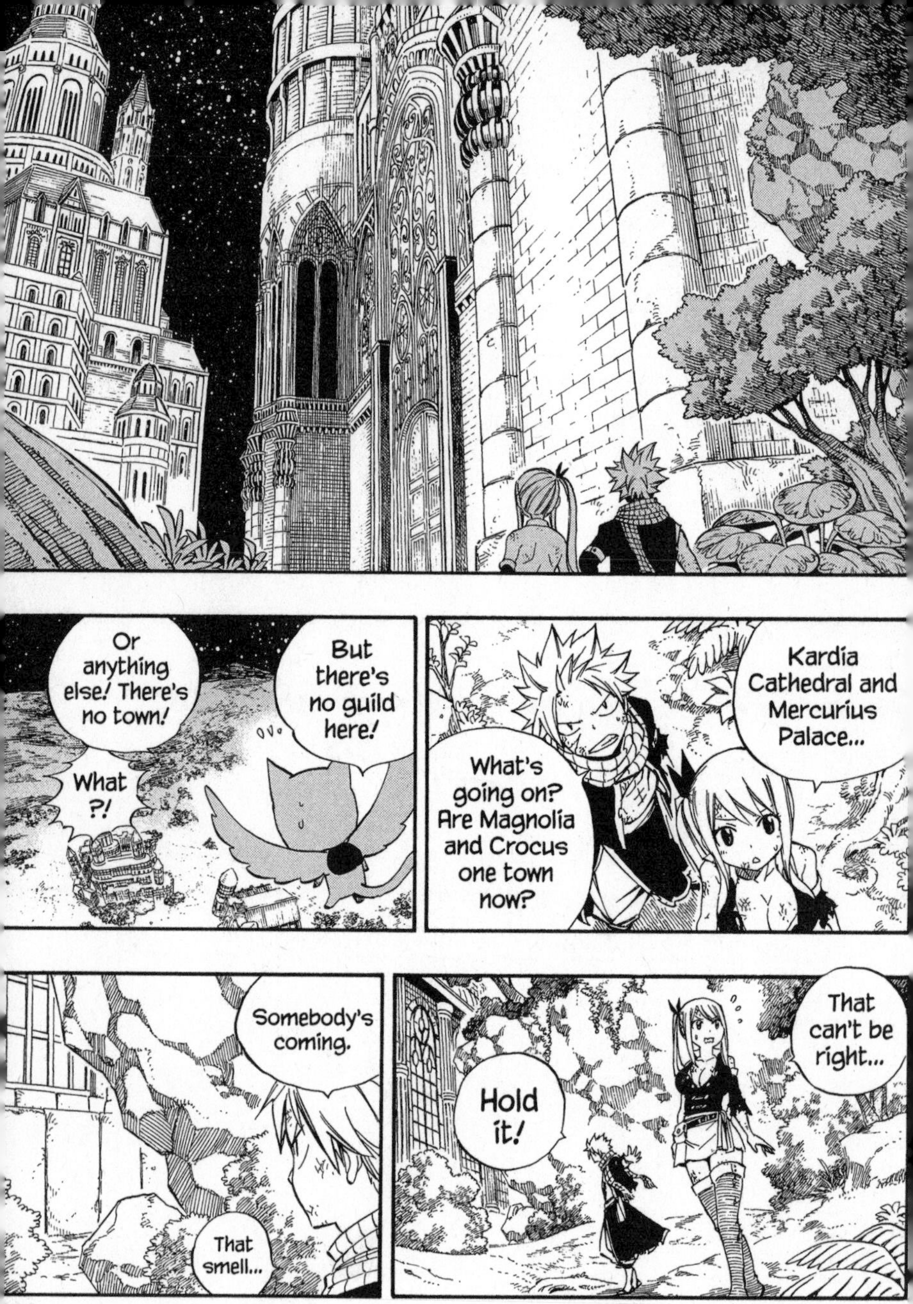
Kardia Cathedral and Mercurius Palace...
What's going on? Are Magnolia and Crocus one town now?
But there's no guild here!
Or anything else! There's no town!
What?!
That can't be right...
Hold it!
Somebody's coming.
That smell...

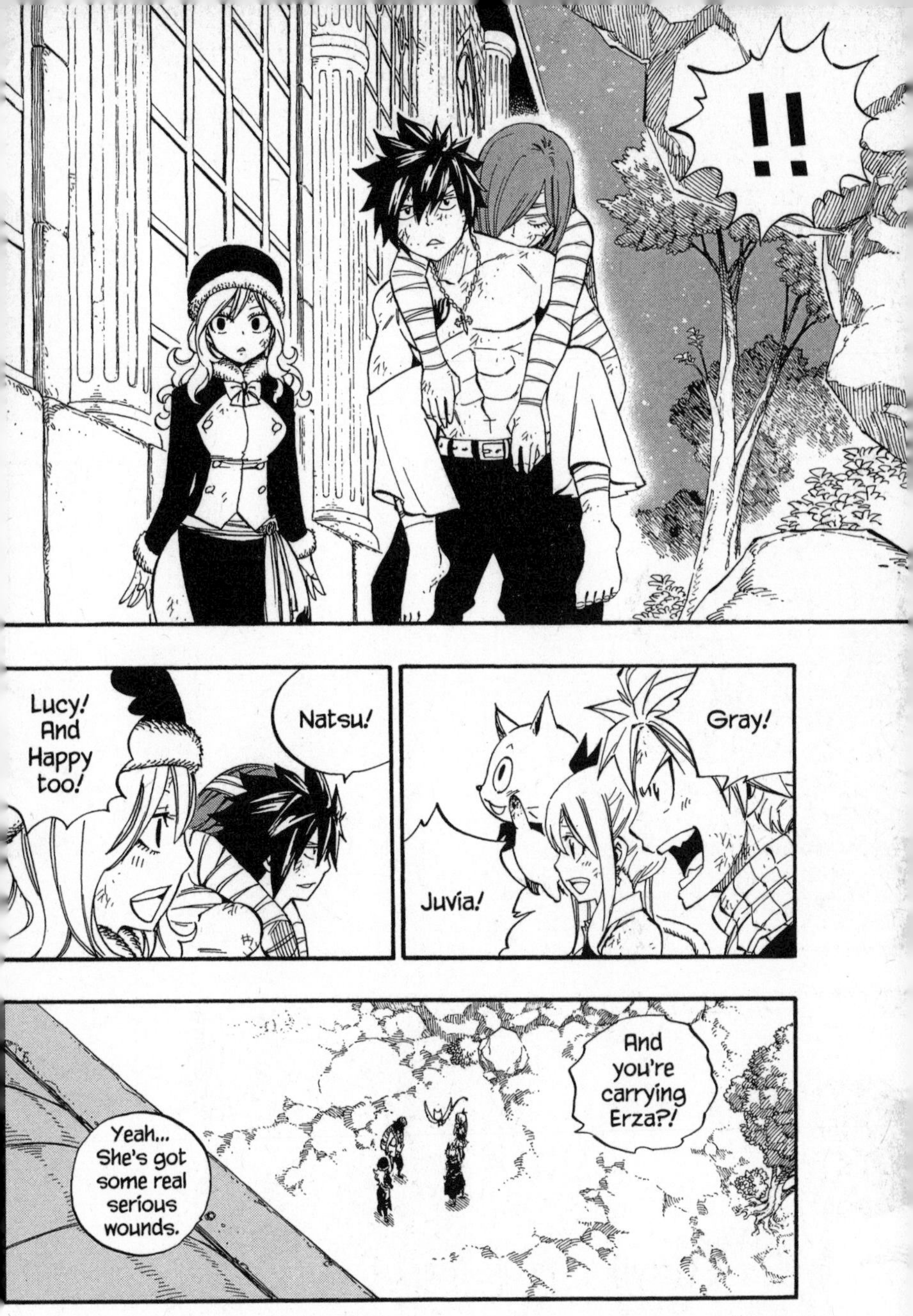
!!
Gray!
Juvia!
Natsu!
Lucy! And Happy too!
And you're carrying Erza?!
Yeah... She's got some real serious wounds.

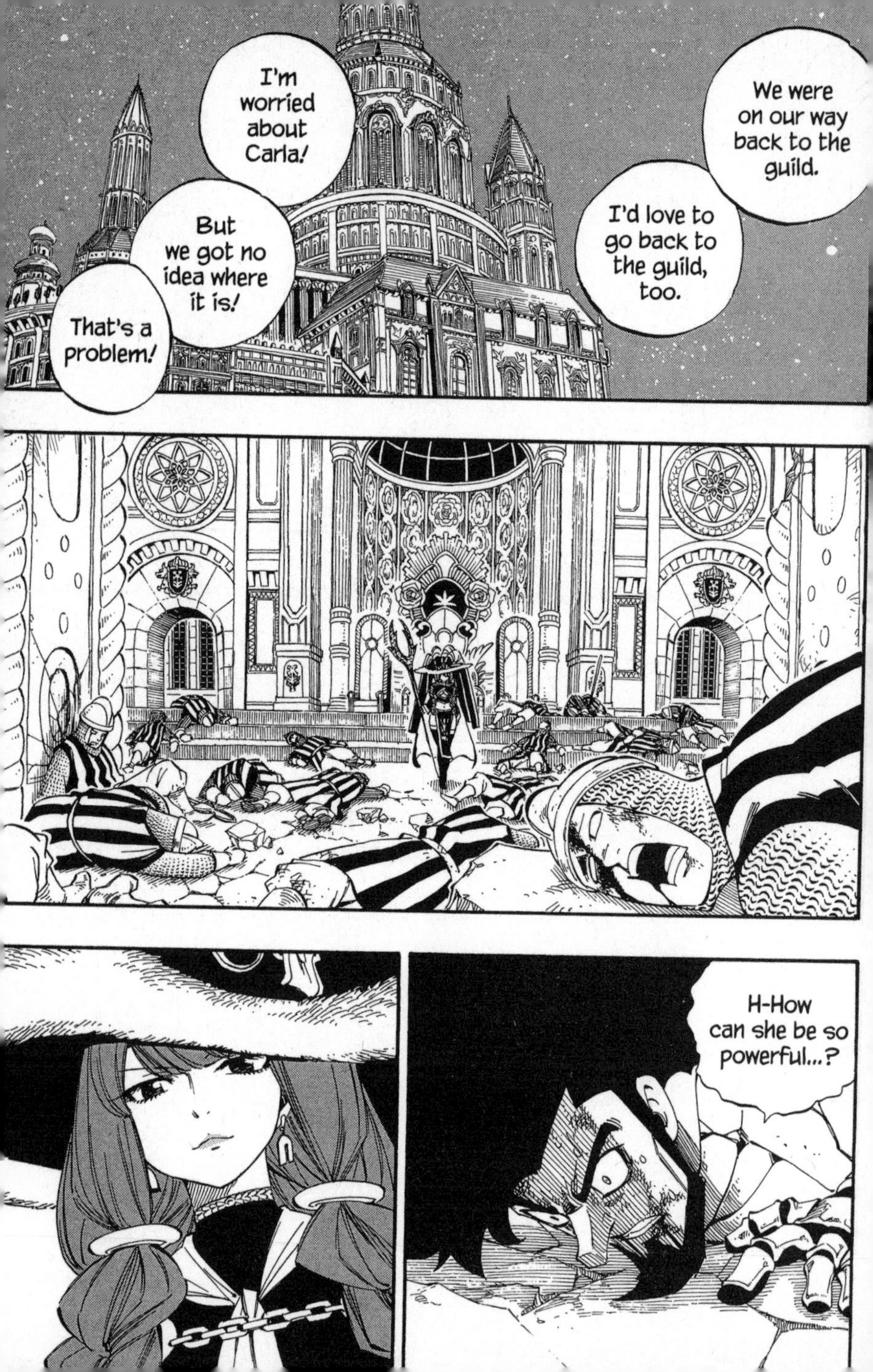
We were on our way back to the guild.
I'd love to go back to the guild, too.
I'm worried about Carla!
But we got no idea where it is!
That's a problem!
H-How can she be so powerful...?

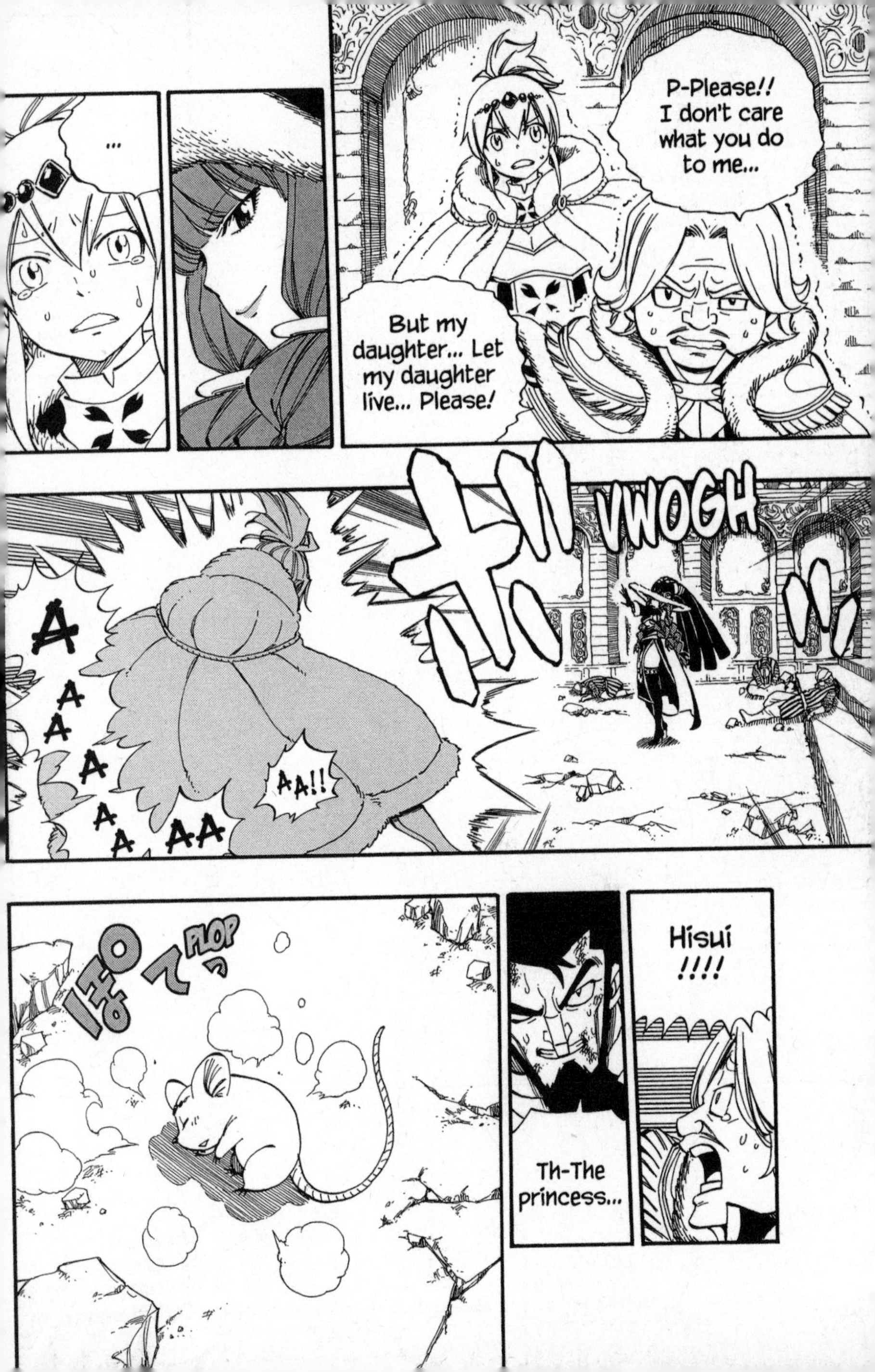
P-Please!! I don't care what you do to me...
But my daughter... Let my daughter live... Please!
...
VWOGH
AAAAAAA
AA
AA!!
Hisui !!!!
Th-The princess...
PLOP

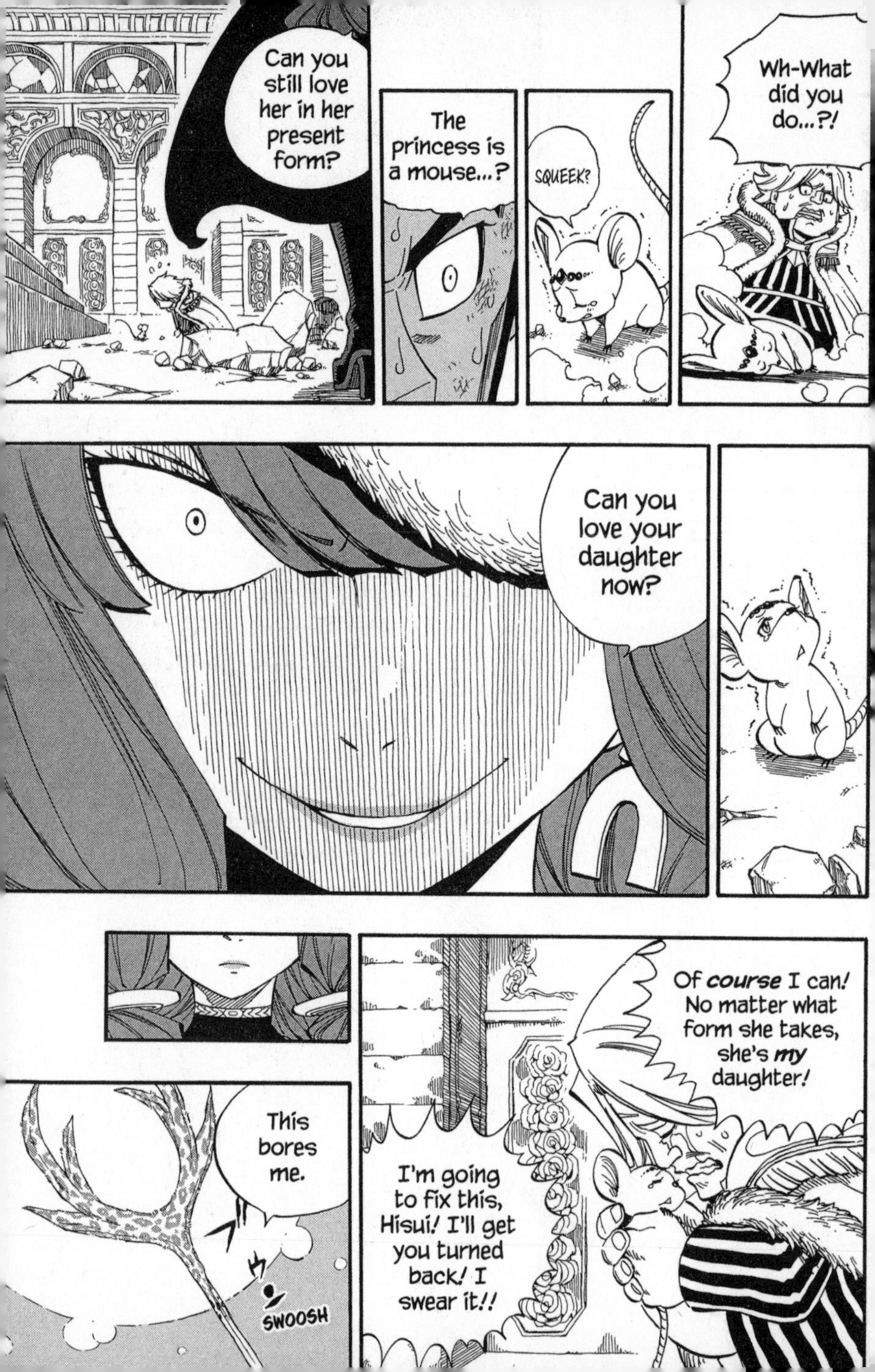
Wh-What did you do...?!
SQUEEK?
The princess is a mouse...?
Can you still love her in her present form?
Can you love your daughter now?
Of *course* I can! No matter what form she takes, she's *my* daughter!
I'm going to fix this, Hisui! I'll get you turned back! I swear it!!
This bores me.
SWOOSH

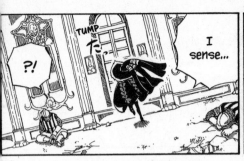

?!

TUMP

I sense...

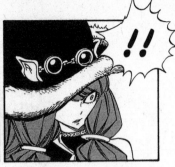

!!

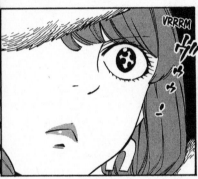

VRRRM

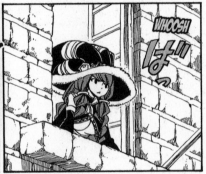

WHOOSH

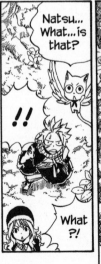

Natsu... What...is that?

!!

What ?!

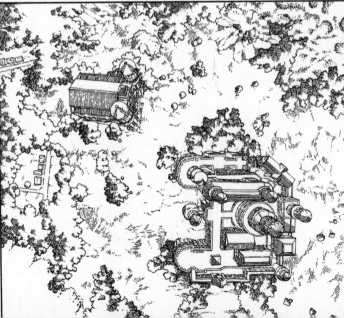

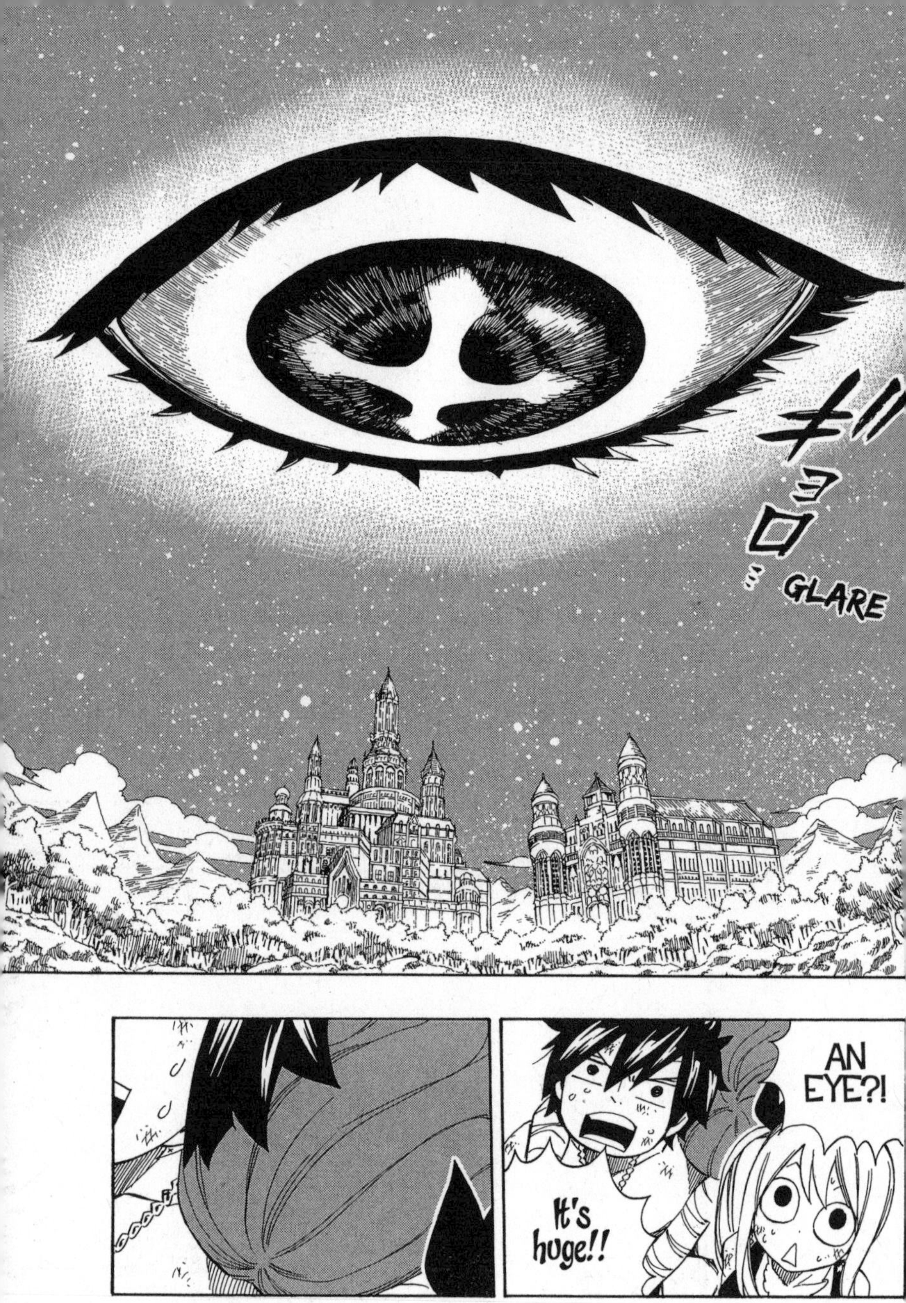
ギョロ
GLARE
AN EYE?!
It's huge!!

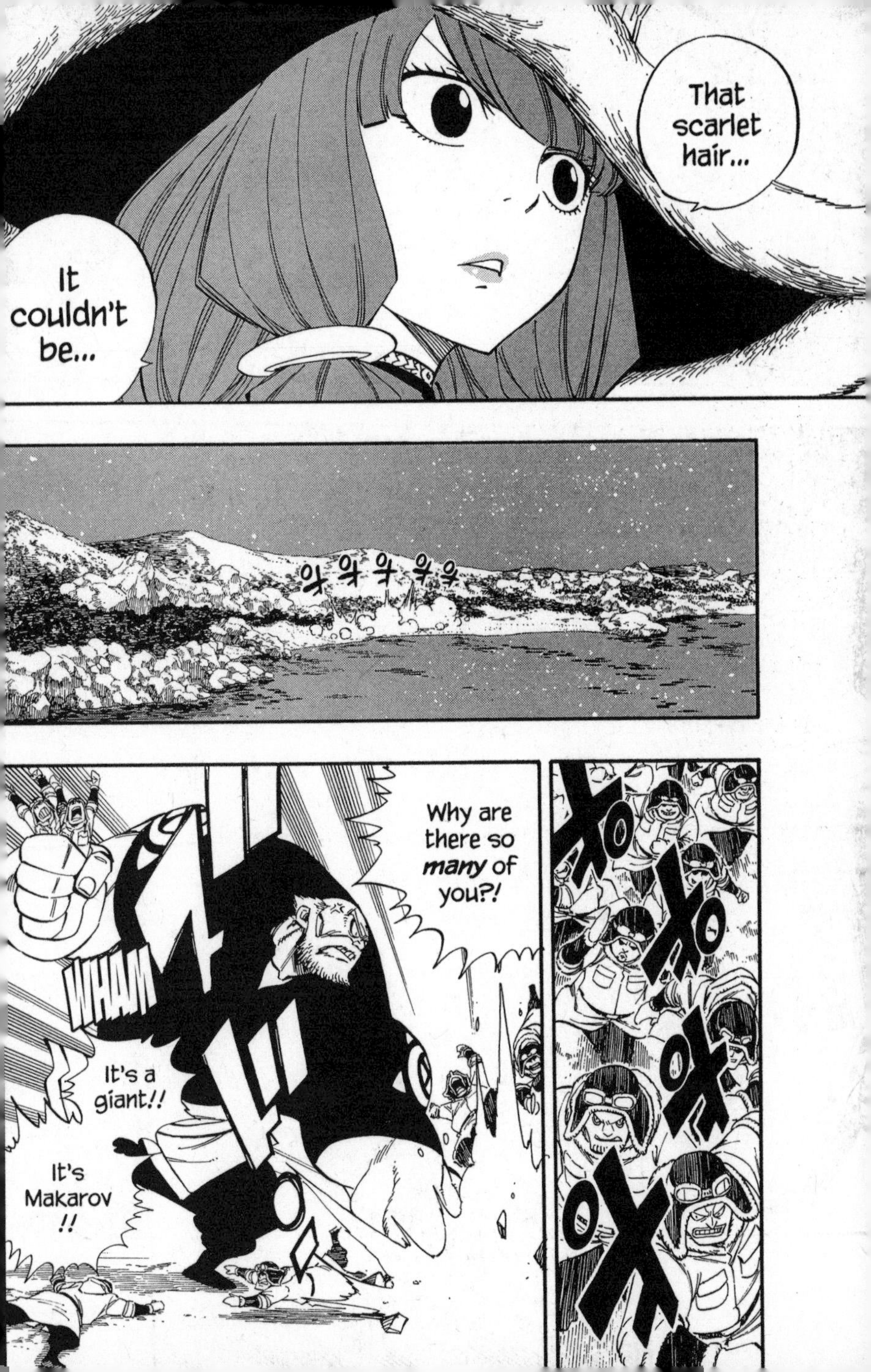
That scarlet hair...
It couldn't be...
Why are there so *many* of you?!
WHAM
It's a giant!!
It's Makarov !!

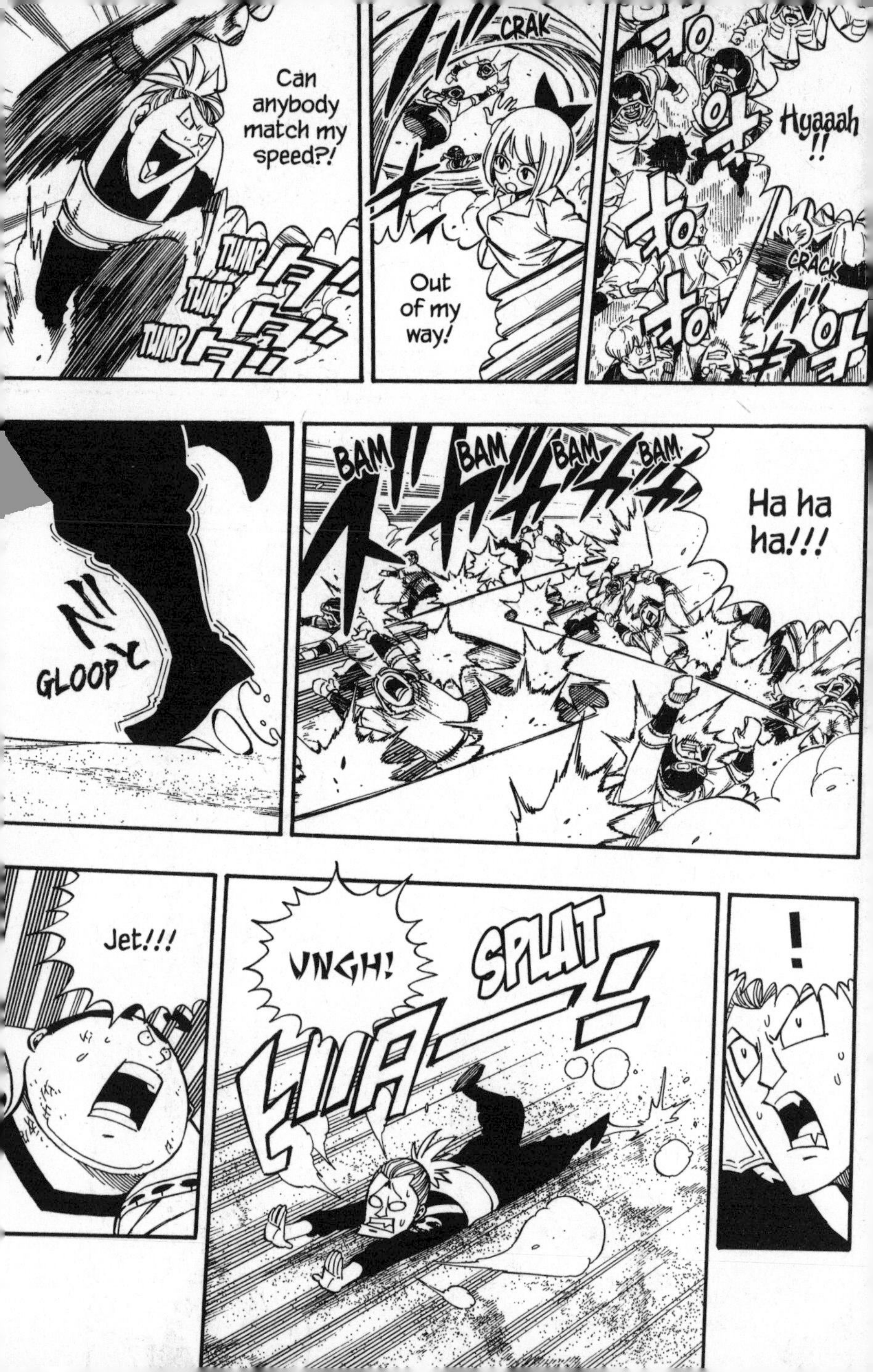
Hyaaah!!
CRACK
CRAK
Out of my way!
Can anybody match my speed?!
THMP
THMP
THMP
BAM
BAM
BAM
BAM
Ha ha ha!!!
GLOOP
!
UNGH!
SPLAT
Jet!!!

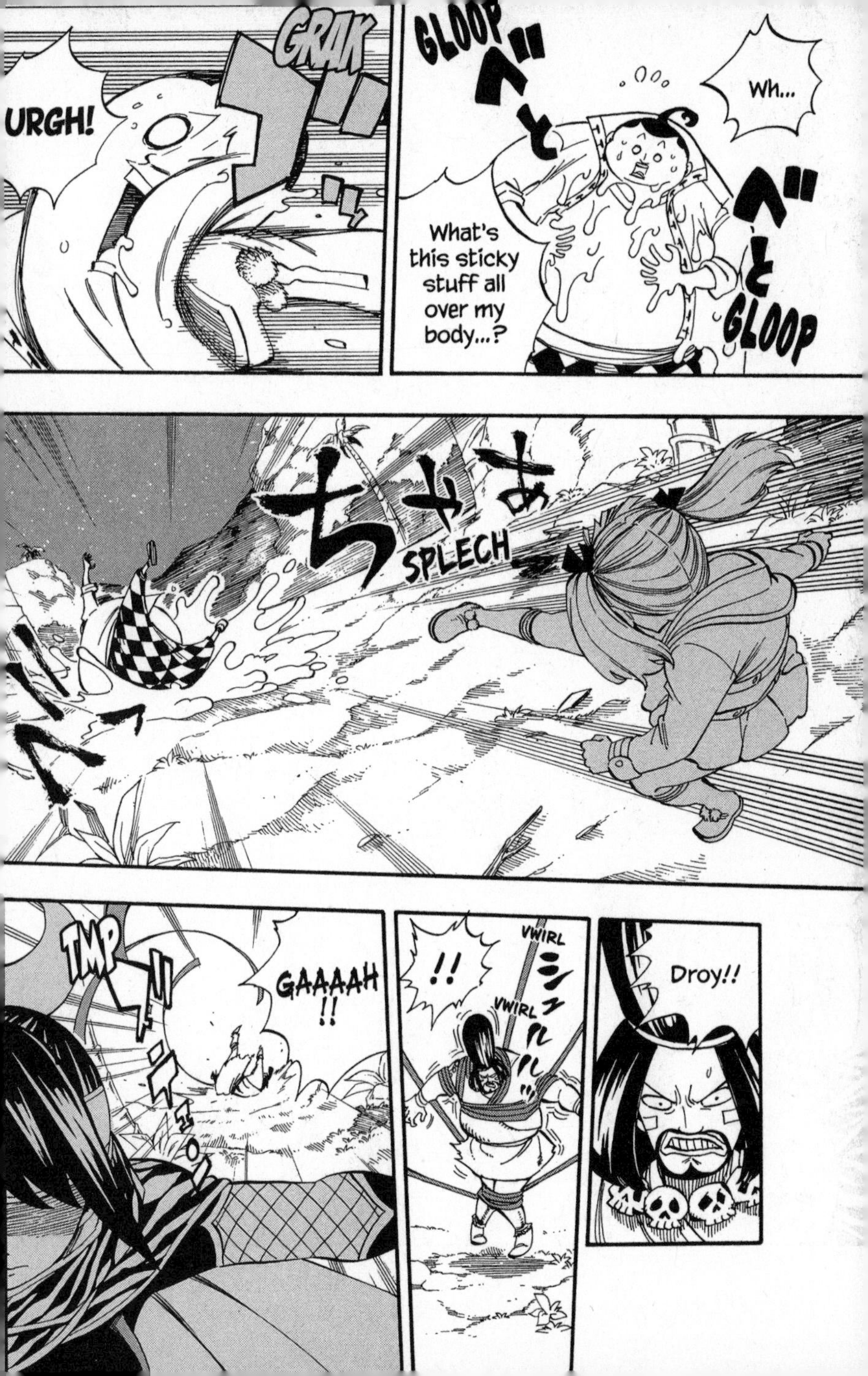
GLOOP
べと
Wh...
What's this sticky stuff all over my body...?
べと
GLOOP
GRAK
URGH!
SPLECH
Droy!!
!!
VWIRL
VWIRL
GAAAAH!!
TMP

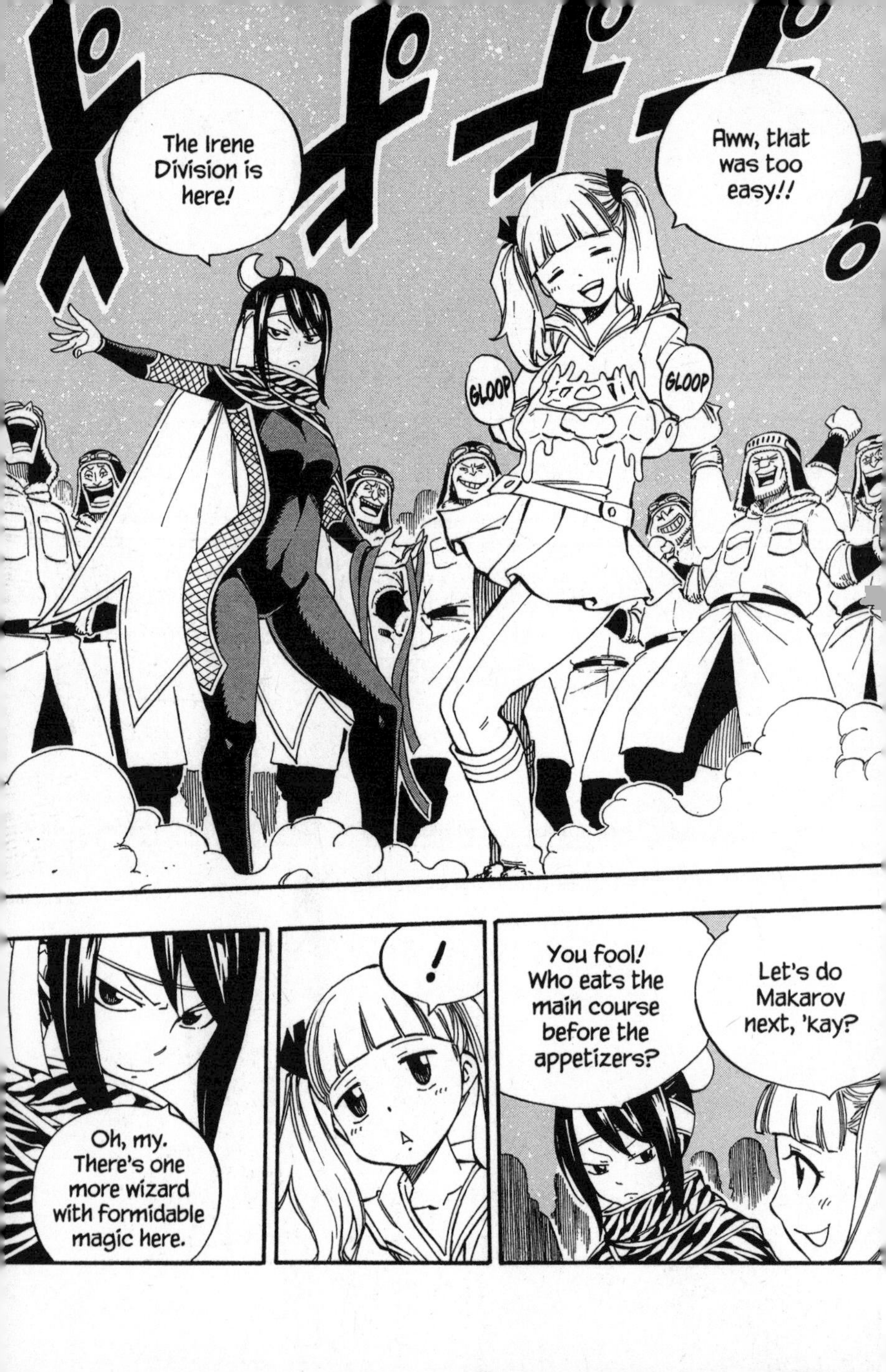
Aww, that was too easy!!
The Irene Division is here!
GLOOP
GLOOP
Let's do Makarov next, 'kay?
You fool! Who eats the main course before the appetizers?
!
Oh, my. There's one more wizard with formidable magic here.

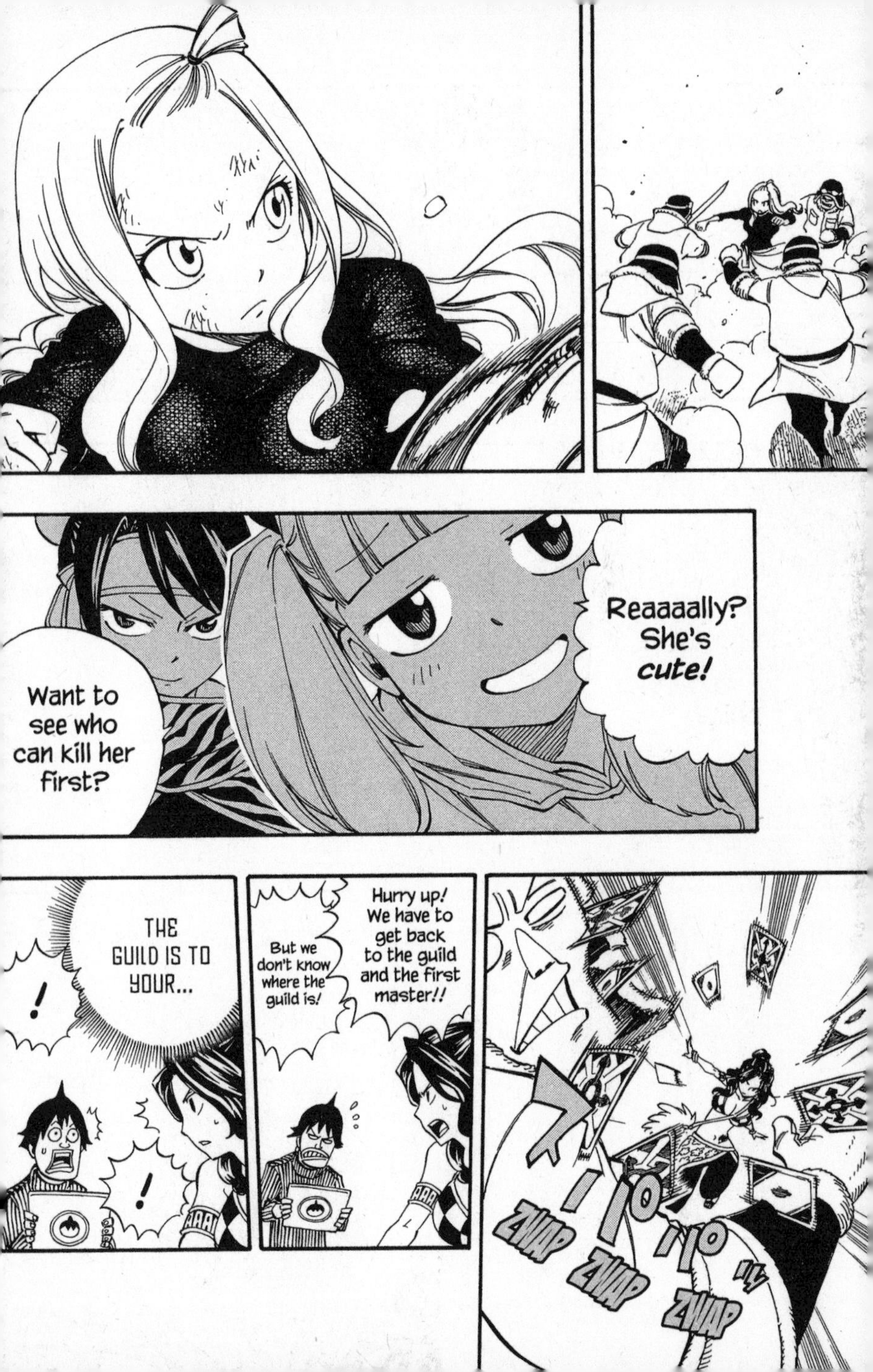
Reaaaally? She's cute!
Want to see who can kill her first?
ZWAP
ZWAP
ZWAP
Hurry up! We have to get back to the guild and the first master!!
But we don't know where the guild is!
THE GUILD IS TO YOUR...
!
!

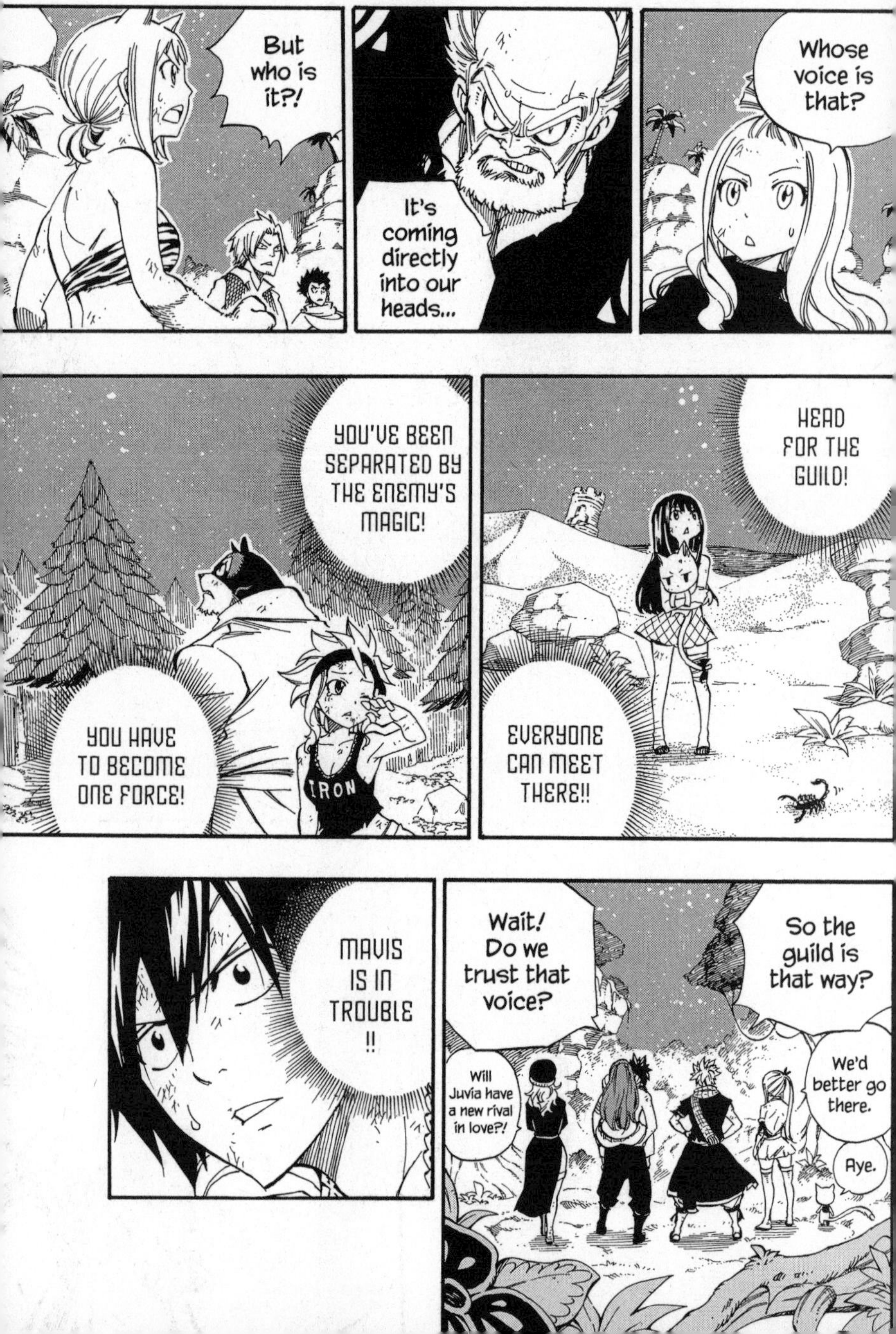
Whose voice is that?
It's coming directly into our heads...
But who is it?!
HEAD FOR THE GUILD!
EVERYONE CAN MEET THERE!!
YOU'VE BEEN SEPARATED BY THE ENEMY'S MAGIC!
YOU HAVE TO BECOME ONE FORCE!
So the guild is that way?
Wait! Do we trust that voice?
We'd better go there.
Aye.
Will Juvia have a new rival in love?!
MAVIS IS IN TROUBLE!!

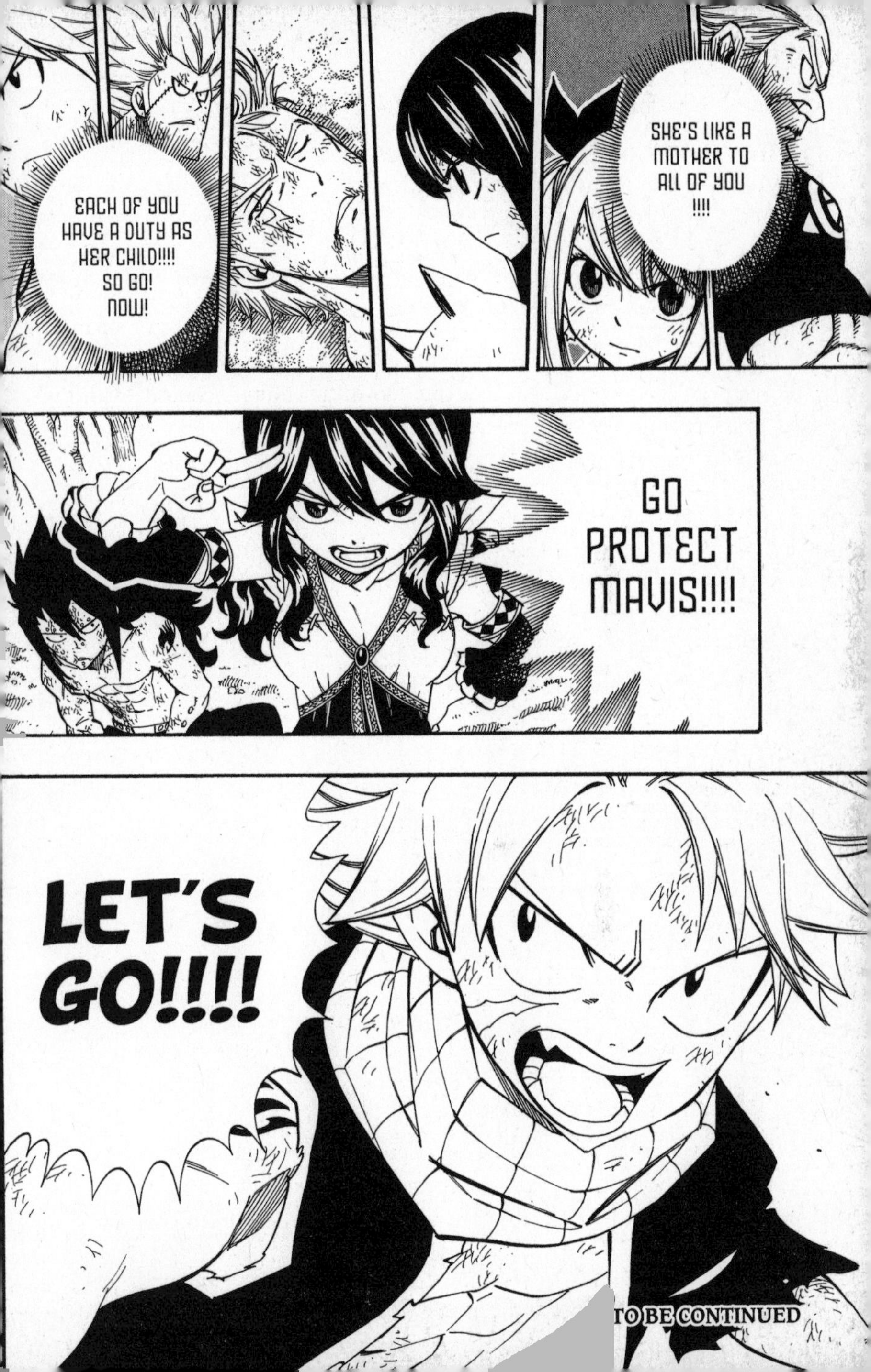
SHE'S LIKE A MOTHER TO ALL OF YOU !!!!
EACH OF YOU HAVE A DUTY AS HER CHILD!!!! SO GO! NOW!
GO PROTECT MAVIS!!!!
LET'S GO!!!!
TO BE CONTINUED

Afterword

I had a bit of fun with the eight chapter titles between chapters 483 and 490. I made sure that a number was in the title, and used it as a countdown. That actually works much better as a part of a weekly magazine, so you may not have noticed when reading the whole volume. It was all a countdown timed up to coincide with the appearance of a character from Fairy Tail ZERØ, Zera. People who haven't read Fairy Tail ZERØ will probably think, "Who's this Zera?" But don't worry, I've written it so that you can still enjoy the story even without having read the spin-off manga.

Now, I know I've been teasing people over and over again with people "dying," and this time when I got Gajeel caught up in it, apparently there were a lot of readers who were very sad at that. And after this, there will be more of this kind of thing, and I'm a little anxious that people will stop trusting me.

On a different subject, I attended the Japan Expo in France this past July. The purpose of this event is to give a taste of Japanese pop culture to Europeans, and they were selling things like Japanese manga, anime, games, and music, but they also sold traditional Japanese clothing, too. Some replicas of Japanese swords were very popular (there was also a replica of Erza's sword, "Beni-zakura" ("Red Cherry Blossom"), and for some reason, they were also selling Japanese pennants. The event was pretty chaotic and very fun.

I had a signing and a live-drawing panel, and I also had a great time interacting with the French fans. At the signing, there was an old man who was energetically waving a Fairy Tail flag, and when I looked closer, I could see he had on a Natsu T-shirt. I thought that maybe he was doing it in support of his grandchildren who are fans, but it turns out he's a fan himself whose favorite character is Midnight. He opened up about being pretty deep in the fandom so I was very happy!

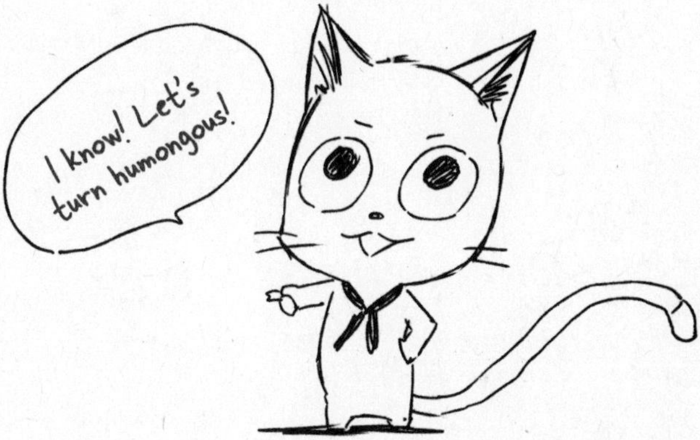
I know! Let's turn humongous!

FAIRY TAIL 57

フェアリーテイル

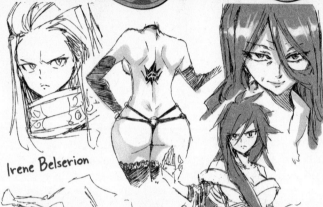

Irene Belserion

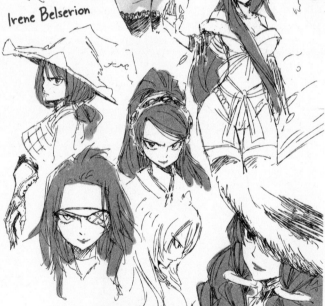

HIRO 真島ヒロ MASHIMA

FROM 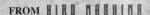 HIRO MASHIMA

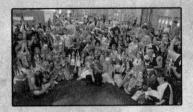

Every year in France, they hold an event called the Japan Expo. And it's been six years since I've been to one. This is a picture that was with all the Fairy Tail cosplayers in the hall.

Everyone was doing Fairy Tail calls in the middle of my signing and the event itself was overflowing with excitement!

Thank you! I'll come back again!

Original Jacket Design: Hisao Ogawa

Translation Notes:

Japanese is a difficult language for many readers, and translation is often more art than science. For your edification and reading pleasure, here are notes on some of the places where we could have gone in a different direction with our translation of the work, or where a Japanese cultural reference is used.

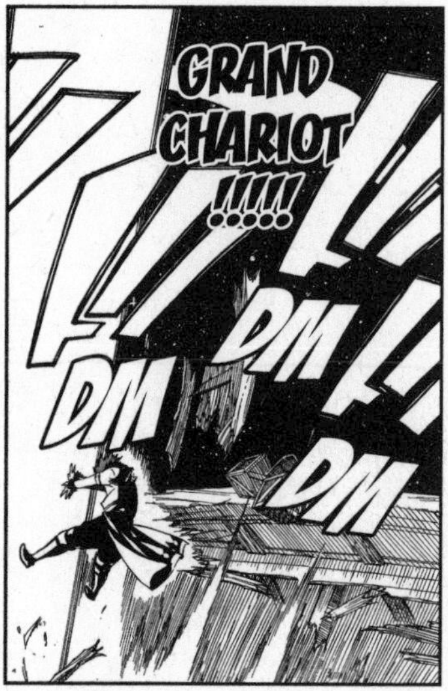
GRAND CHARIOT !!!!!
DM
DM
DM
DM

Page 18, Grand Chariot

As noted in Volume 12, the seven stars are a constellation of young stars that we English-speakers call the constellation, "The Pleiades." In French, it is called the Grand Chariot. The kanji used here can translate to, "the seven stars."

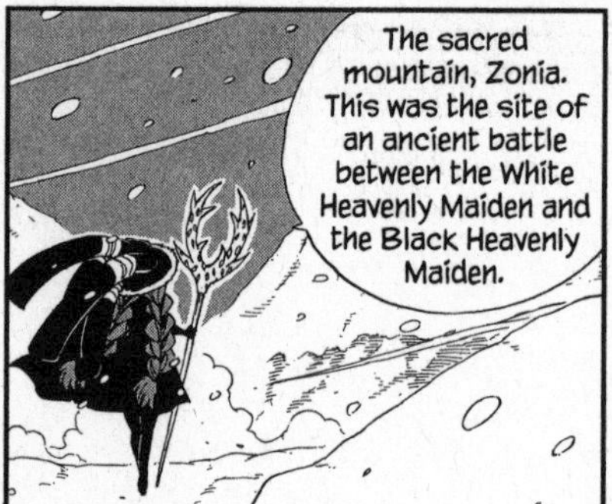
The sacred mountain, Zonia. This was the site of an ancient battle between the White Heavenly Maiden and the Black Heavenly Maiden.

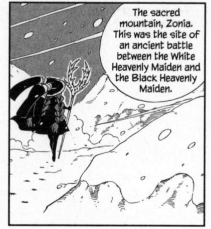

Page 39, Heavenly Maidens

Many of the Japanese myths and folktales concern the heavenly maidens, or *Tennyo*. They are considered to be beautiful women out of Japanese legends (reportedly brought to Japan from Chinese Buddhism). As messengers from Heaven, they can all use their feathered cloaks to fly, and some of them have great powers.

age 93-94,Tenga Goken & Onimaru

ıe Tenga Goken is a Japanese term first coined during the Muromachi era (1333 to 73 CE) that refers to five exceptional and legendary swords. Onimaru is one of the ve swords.

age 104, Kurogane

Japan, the local iron came out a dull black color, and for that reason it was called *rogane*, which literally translates to "black metal."

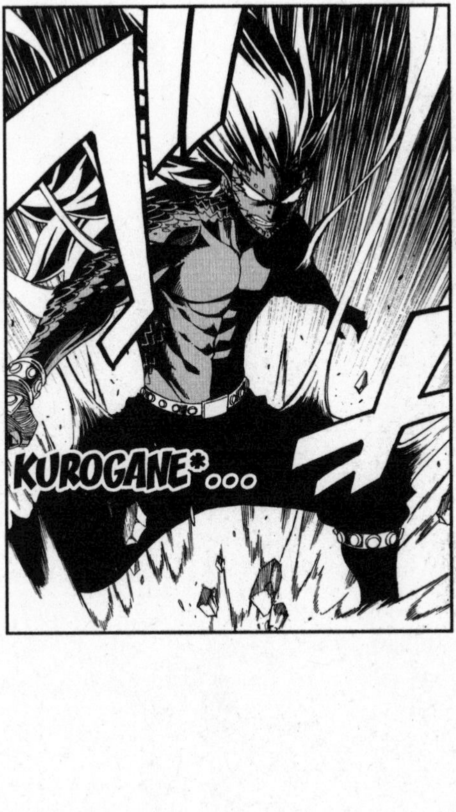
KUROGANE*...

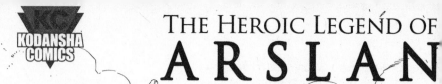

THE HEROIC LEGEND OF
ARSLAN

**READ THE NEW SERIES FROM THE CREATOR OF
FULLMETAL ALCHEMIST, HIROMU ARAKAWA!
NOW A HIT TV SERIES!**

ECBATANA IS BURNING!

Arslan is the young and curious prince of Pars who, despite his best efforts doesn't seem to have what it takes to be a proper king like his father. At the age of 14, Arslan goes to his first battle and loses everything as the blood-soaked mist of war gives way to scorching flames, bringing him to face the demise of his once glorious kingdom. However, it is Arslan's destiny to be a ruler, and despite the trials that face him, he must now embark on a journey to reclaim his fallen kingdom.

Available now in print and digitally!

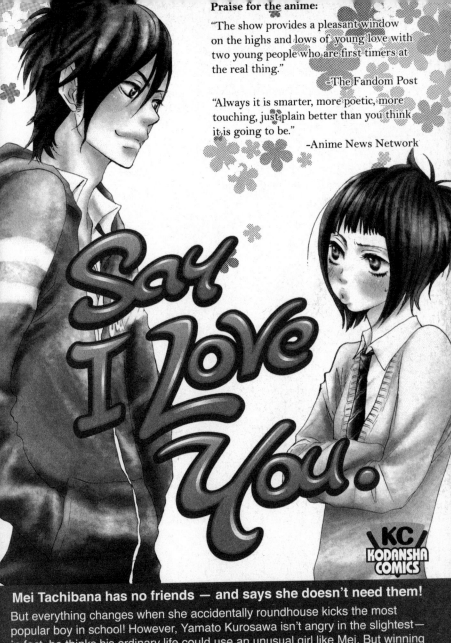

Mei Tachibana has no friends — and says she doesn't need them! But everything changes when she accidentally roundhouse kicks the most popular boy in school! However, Yamato Kurosawa isn't angry in the slightest— in fact, he thinks his ordinary life could use an unusual girl like Mei. But winning Mei's trust will be a tough task. How long will she refuse to say, "I love you"?

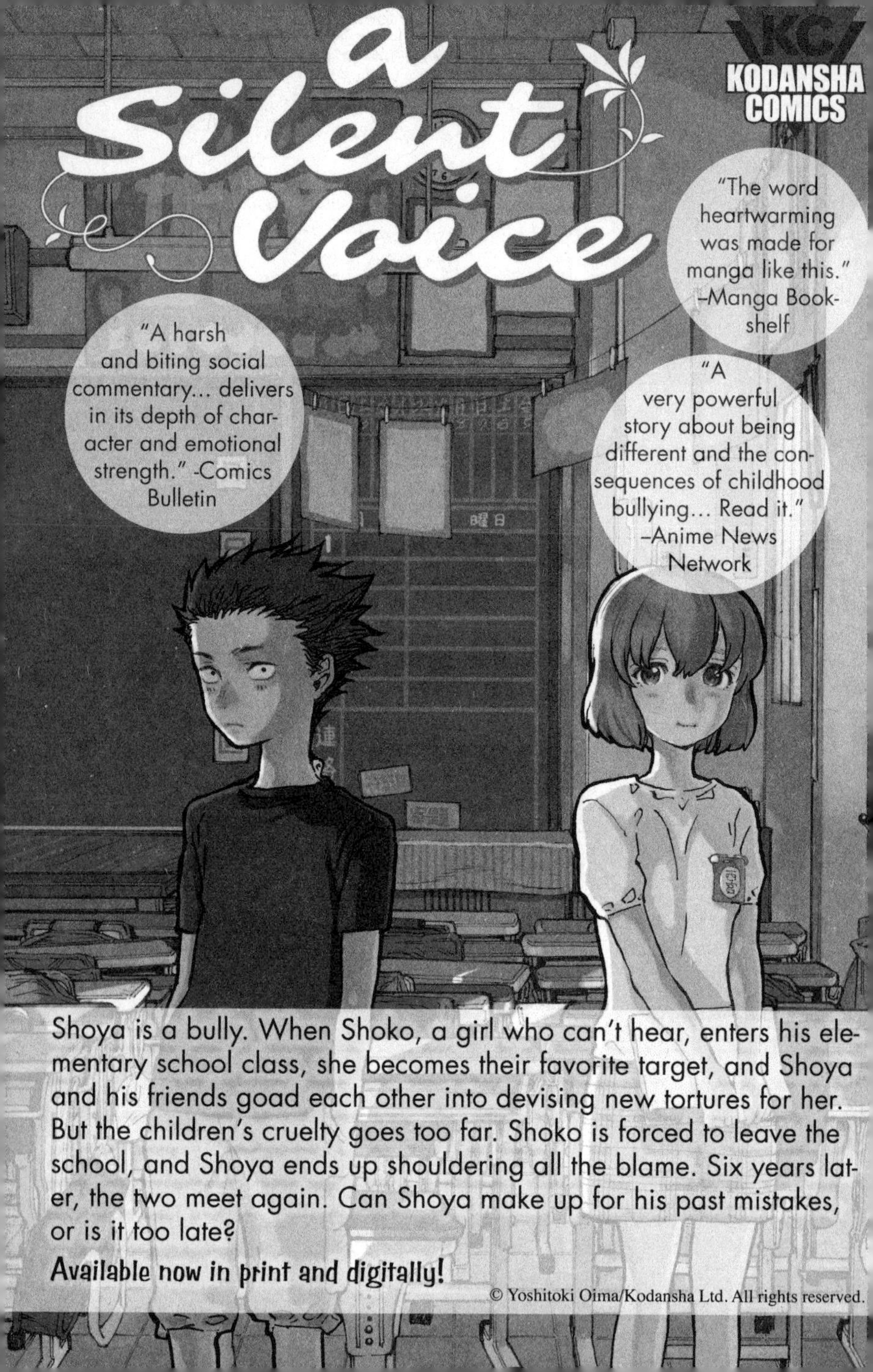
KC
KODANSHA COMICS
a Silent Voice
"The word heartwarming was made for manga like this." –Manga Bookshelf
"A harsh and biting social commentary... delivers in its depth of character and emotional strength." -Comics Bulletin
"A very powerful story about being different and the consequences of childhood bullying... Read it." –Anime News Network
Shoya is a bully. When Shoko, a girl who can't hear, enters his elementary school class, she becomes their favorite target, and Shoya and his friends goad each other into devising new tortures for her. But the children's cruelty goes too far. Shoko is forced to leave the school, and Shoya ends up shouldering all the blame. Six years later, the two meet again. Can Shoya make up for his past mistakes, or is it too late?
Available now in print and digitally!
© Yoshitoki Oima/Kodansha Ltd. All rights reserved.

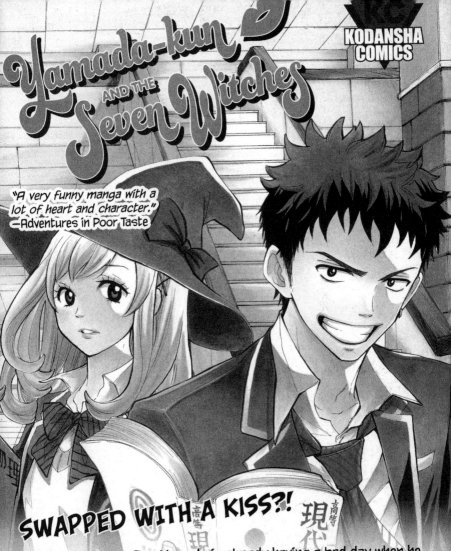

Yamada-kun AND THE Seven Witches

"A very funny manga with a lot of heart and character."
—Adventures in Poor Taste

SWAPPED WITH A KISS?!

Class troublemaker Ryu Yamada is already having a bad day when he stumbles down a staircase along with star student Urara Shiraishi. When he wakes up, he realizes they have switched bodies—and that Ryu has the power to trade places with anyone just by kissing them! Ryu and Urara take full advantage of the situation to improve their lives, but with such an oddly amazing power, just how long will they be able to keep their secret under wraps?

Available now in print and digitally!

INUYASHIKI

A superhero like none you've ever seen, from the creator of "Gantz"!

ICHIRO INUYASHIKI IS DOWN ON HIS LUCK. HE LOOKS MUCH OLDER THAN HIS 58 YEARS, HIS CHILDREN DESPISE HIM, AND HIS WIFE THINKS HE'S A USELESS COWARD. SO WHEN HE'S DIAGNOSED WITH STOMACH CANCER AND GIVEN THREE MONTHS TO LIVE, IT SEEMS THE ONLY ONE WHO'LL MISS HIM IS HIS DOG.

THEN A BLINDING LIGHT FILLS THE SKY, AND THE OLD MAN IS KILLED... ONLY TO WAKE UP LATER IN A BODY HE ALMOST RECOGNIZES AS HIS OWN. CAN IT BE THAT ICHIRO INUYASHIKI IS NO LONGER HUMAN?

COMES IN EXTRA-LARGE EDITIONS WITH COLOR PAGES!

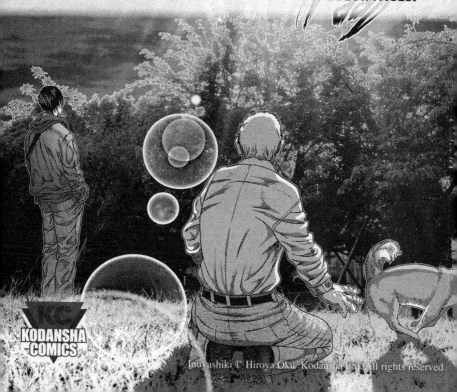

KC
KODANSHA
COMICS

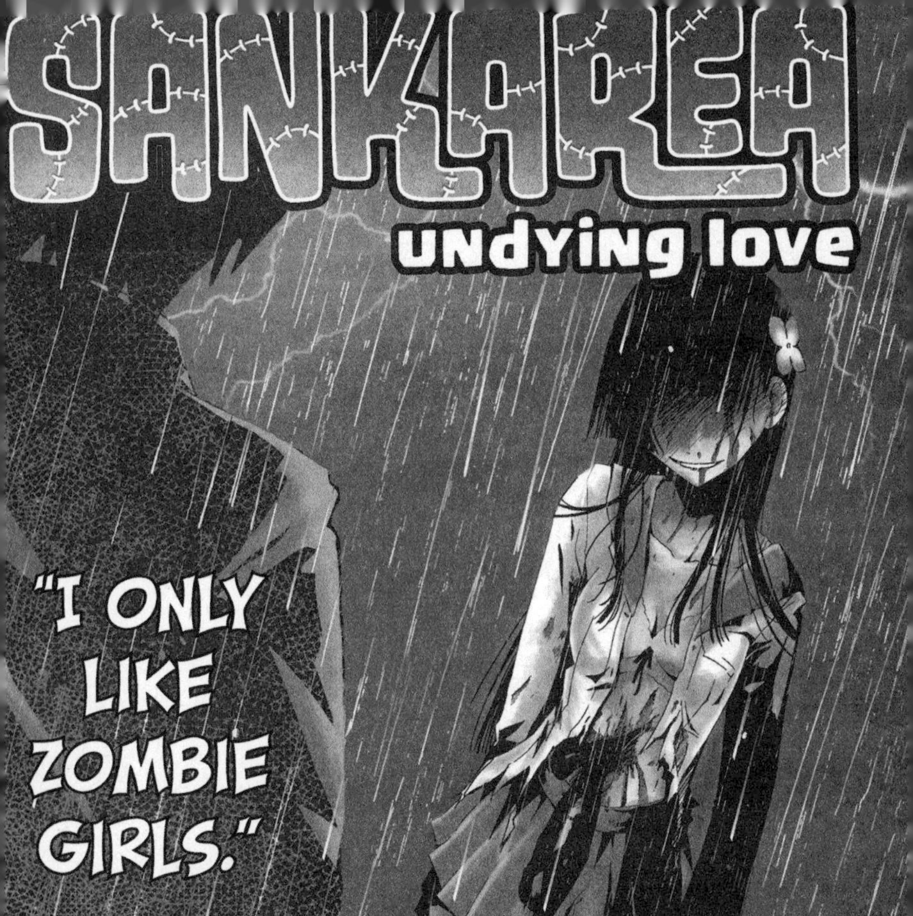

SANKAREA
undying love

"I ONLY
LIKE
ZOMBIE
GIRLS."

Chihiro has an unusual connection to zombie movies. He doesn't feel bad for
the survivors – he wants to comfort the undead girls they slaughter! When
his pet passes away, he brews a resurrection potion. He's discovered by
local heiress Sanka Rea, and she serves as his first test subject!

**KC
KODANSHA
COMICS**

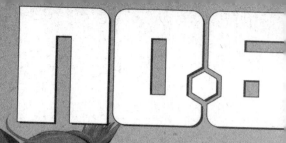

NO.6

A PERFECT LIFE
IN A PERFECT CITY

For Shion, an elite student in the technologically sophisticated city No. 6, life is carefully choreographed. One fateful day, he takes a misstep, sheltering a fugitive his age from a typhoon. Helping this boy throws Shion's life down a path to discovering the appalling secrets behind the "perfection" of No. 6.

KC
KODANSHA
COMICS

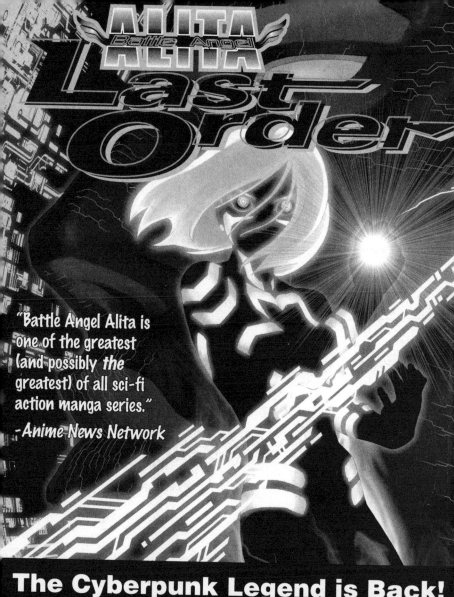

ALITA
Battle Angel
Last Order

"Battle Angel Alita is one of the greatest (and possibly *the* greatest) of all sci-fi action manga series."

— Anime News Network

The Cyberpunk Legend is Back!

In deluxe omnibus editions of 600+ pages, including ALL-NEW original stories by Alita creator Yukito Kishiro!

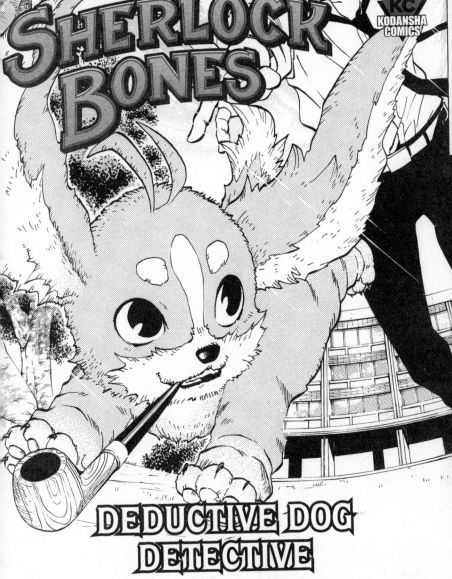

SHERLOCK BONES

DEDUCTIVE DOG DETECTIVE

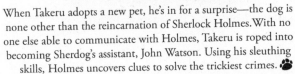

When Takeru adopts a new pet, he's in for a surprise—the dog is none other than the reincarnation of Sherlock Holmes. With no one else able to communicate with Holmes, Takeru is roped into becoming Sherdog's assistant, John Watson. Using his sleuthing skills, Holmes uncovers clues to solve the trickiest crimes.

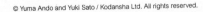

A Kodansha Comics Trade Paperback Original.

Fairy Tail volume 57 copyright © 2016 Hiro Mashima
English translation copyright © 2016 Hiro Mashima

Published in the United States by Kodansha Comics, an imprint of Kodansha USA Publishing, LLC, New York.

Publication rights for this English edition arranged through Kodansha Ltd., Tokyo.

First published in Japan in 2016 by Kodansha Ltd., Tokyo
ISBN 978-1-63236-291-9

Printed in the United States of America.

www.kodanshacomics.com

9 8 7 6 5 4 3 2 1

Translation: William Flanagan
Lettering: AndWorld Design
Editing: Molly Brenan and Haruko Hashimoto
Kodansha Comics edition cover design by Phil Balsman

TOMARE!

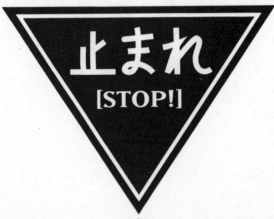

[STOP!]

You're going the wrong way!

Manga is a completely different type of reading experience.

To start at the beginning, go to the end!

hat's right! Authentic manga is read the traditional Japanese way— om right to left, exactly the opposite of how American books are ead. It's easy to follow: Just go to the other end of the book and read ch page—and each panel—from right side to left side, starting at e top right. Now you're experiencing manga as it was meant to be!